THE INDIAN BORDERLAND, 1880-1900

9 788121 201100

THE INDIAN BORDERLAND, 1880-1900

Sir, Thomas Hungerford Holdich

KALPAZ

THE INDIAN BORDERLAND, 1880-1900

Sir, Thomas Hungerford Holdich

ISBN : 9788121201100

First Published 1901, reprint 2017 in India by

Kalpaz Publications
C-30 Satyawati Nagar
Ashok Vihar, Phase-III
Delhi- 110052
Email:- kalpaz@hotmail.com

THE INDIAN BORDERLAND

HERAT CITADEL FROM THE CITY

PAGE 187

THE INDIAN BORDERLAND

1880–1900

BY

COLONEL SIR T. HUNGERFORD HOLDICH
K.C.I.E., C.B., F.S.A.
A VICE-PRESIDENT AND GOLD MEDALLIST OF THE
ROYAL GEOGRAPHICAL SOCIETY
AND LATE OF THE INDIAN SURVEY DEPARTMENT

WITH TWENTY-TWO ILLUSTRATIONS
AND A MAP

METHUEN AND CO.
36 ESSEX STREET, W.C.
LONDON
1901

PREFACE

DURING the last twenty-five years a great change has been effected in the measure of our information about the regions of farther India on the north-west. Twenty-five years ago all that we knew of frontier geography was narrowed to a few lines running westward from India and terminating in the cities of the Afghan and Baluch highlands. The hills which faced us on our own border, on to which we could step from the plains, were still shrouded in mystery, and our knowledge of the people was as shadowy as that of their land. Those who came to us we knew, but those who had no dealings with India formed for the most part but interesting ethnological problems.

It is with the object of illustrating some of the many steps in the process of this change, and with the hope of rescuing from oblivion a few minor frontier episodes, that I have written this book.

In it I have been careful (so far as is consistent with maintaining continuity of historical narrative) to write only of those things which my eyes have seen, or with which I have been personally concerned. I have not appealed to Blue Books or statistics that are within everybody's reach; but I have referred now and then to the pages of published narratives, and I am indebted to one or two authors (notably Bellew and

Thornton) for historical references. Much of the chapter on the Perso-Baluch boundary has appeared in the pages of the *Pioneer*.

If I have expressed any views as to past or future frontier polity they must be regarded as the views of an outsider—a looker-on at the game—and not as those of an official member of the Indian administration. Excepting only in the case of the Perso-Baluch boundary, where I held the chief political responsibility, I have been connected with these twenty years of frontier history in the capacity of a survey officer, not of a political adviser or of a military leader.

T. H. H.

CONTENTS

CONTENTS

LIST OF ILLUSTRATIONS

THE INDIAN BORDERLAND

CHAPTER I.

FIRST PHASE OF THE AFGHAN WAR OF 1879–80

First phase of the Afghan war of 1879–80—Our general ignorance of Afghanistan when the war broke out—The Southern Field Force—Quetta in 1878—Climatic conditions of Baluch highlands—Capture of Kandahar—General Biddulph's march to the frontiers of India—Surveying—Bolán floods—Peshin in spring—Juniper forests—Bori valley—Siasgai—No water—Panic in the ranks—The new frontier at Vitakri.

WHEN the Afghan war of 1878 broke out, after the refusal of Sher Ali to receive our representative at Kabul, or to accord to us the same courteous and honourable consideration that had lately been bestowed on the Russian envoy, we found that we possessed but little information as to the nature of the country which was to be the scene of military operations, or of the people with whom we had to deal.

That historic mountain-road which winds amongst the black-browed hills of the Peshawur border through the Khaibar pass to Jalalabad and Kabul was known well enough by repute, although the memory of the grim disasters which once befell a British brigade along that route were already faint; and there were certain internal roads connecting the great cities of the Afghan highlands which had been scientifically traversed and fairly well mapped. But of those more northerly tracks which connected Kabul with India, and which had been followed by invading hosts for many centuries before the Khaibar became the recognised trade route, we had lost all count; nor were there wanting high officials (nor even historians) who believed that the Kabul river traced its course to India by way of the Khaibar pass. In the southern districts of Afghanistan the Bolán was already a much-used—but still a very much unmapped—route, and Quetta was already the headquarters of a British resident; but the Afghan war of 1839-42, although it spread into nearly four years of occupation of the country, had not been productive of any great accession to our geographical knowledge of western Afghanistan. There was many an important route along which our soldiers and our guns had travelled which it was impossible to locate exactly on any map existing in 1878, and our knowledge of the topography of the country generally was limited to the immediate neighbourhood of such roads and lines of communication as had been properly traversed. All the more honour then to those energetic officers who kept clear records, and who dared much and did much to dispel the geographical mists which hung over the Afghan hills and valleys.

Chief amongst them were the young engineers Henry Durand and George Broadfoot, to whom we owe a very great deal of most excellent geographical information. Broadfoot's ventures in disguise through an unknown wilderness of frontier mountains and plains, which then included half the Punjab, resulted in a record which is an authority to this day. No one has followed in his footsteps from Ghazni to our present frontier since; and to Durand we chiefly owe the fact that amidst the wide blank spaces which adorned our maps, the positions of many of the principal towns and villages of Afghanistan were accurately laid down.

Many other distinguished travellers and observers, amongst whom were North, Leach, Lord, Burnes, Abbott, and Shakespear, contributed a great store of written information, which is no less interesting to read now that we know Afghanistan than it was when our knowledge was confined to but a few definite localities. But with all this wealth of previous literary information there was nothing in the shape of systematic mapping. There was, indeed, no assured basis for such mapping; there were none of the accurate and portable instruments which are in these days rendered so effective in the hands of the military surveyor; nor was there any school of instruction to teach men how such instruments should be used.

Moreover, the study of geography as a military study was distinctly at a discount. It had been found that the pursuit of geographical knowledge on our frontier was one which might lead to trouble and complications. Neither was it at all clear that any immediate benefit would accrue to military leaders from the study of geography. It was assumed that the demand for map-knowledge could be readily met as soon as the necessity for it arose, and that, until it did arise, it was well to let the frontier alone. It is not too much to say that this spirit of scepticism as to the military value of map-knowledge lasted till a very late period. It was certainly abroad at the commencement of the Afghan campaign of 1878–9–80.

If our knowledge of the farther wastes and wildernesses of Baluchistan and Afghanistan was nebulous, still more uncertain was our information about our own immediate frontier. Beyond the edges of the Peshawur plain fierce and unconquered tribes of Afghan origin held the mountains, and where the Indus issues from the dark gorges of the Himalaya there a barrier was set to further investigation. From Peshawur the triple peak of the Koh-i-Mor is visible above the intervening crags to the north, and the rugged outlines of Torsappa break the sky to the west, but none knew aught of Swat, or how the Kabul river washed the foot of Torsappa west of Sind, the straight, stiff back of Kirthar set a sharp limit to the eager quest of the explorer, and forbidding darkness covered the hills of Hazarajat. From every little group of two or three mud huts which formed a frontier outpost, the inspecting officer might, if he liked, look westward to a brown, rugged, tumbled mass of barren hills, streaked and seamed by water-courses, and scarred with fissures here and there denoting the passage of the more violent streams which break across the close-packed ridges of the outer hills; and he would have to admit to his inner consciousness that he knew absolutely nothing whatsoever of what lay behind those crumpled, brown folds. He knew that there certainly was a population from which sprang those bands of frontier robbers who were a daily terror to the Hindu bunniah of the villages in the plains, fragments of which bands might be found in the nearest station jail; but of the real nature of their inner existence; whether they scratched a scanty subsistence from the soil in the narrow, cultivated valleys intersecting the hills, or whether they lived entirely on the contributions of the border villages which they harried and worried periodically, he knew nothing from personal observation.

Neither could he say with any certainty which was the best route to follow should it be necessary to strike into the heart of those hills, and to reach the line of grey crests which were daily silhouetted against the evening sky far beyond them, and which he knew to define the eastern edge of the great Afghan and Baluch highlands. Less, perhaps, was known of the steps up to those highlands than of the highlands themselves. Of the border strip of mountain territory which stretched along the western limits of the "Sands of Sind," south of the Bolán; of the extension of that strip, northwards, under the eastern shadow of the Sulimani mountains; of Waziristan; of Tochi; nothing was known at all. We did know something of the Kuram route, and of the Khaibar; but of the intervening Afridi Tirah, and of all the border space north of the Khaibar—a space which included Mohmands and Mahmunds, Bajaoris and Swatis—we knew much less than did the officers of whatever department in Alexander's army answered to that of the modern Q.M.G. Nor was the spirit of adventure, which has always flourished healthily and strongly amongst the young soldiers of the frontier, and which would have led them frequently enough to find out things for themselves, specially encouraged by those in authority. The fact is that the sanctity of the white man's life had to be maintained on our frontier as a pre-eminent principle in all tribal dealings of Government. It was not merely a matter of a life for a life, vengeance for good blood spilled and valuable services lost. It was the maintenance of England's honour, and of respect for her strong right hand, which had to be inculcated at all hazards, and regardless of all expense, if we would face the fanatical spirit of Islam with an unanswerable argument against blood being shed on religious principles. The absolute certainty of retribution is still our only safeguard against the ghazi, and it is well that this should be understood.

Indeed, it is understood, nowadays, pretty well, and nothing can exceed the anxious care with which the life of a European is guarded when the exigencies of politics place him under the guardianship of a border chief. It follows, naturally, that the Government of India is slow to sanction the irresponsible efforts of frontier officers to gain information at first hand, which may lead them into positions of personal danger. What are officially called "complications" might easily arise, which would end in an expedition or a war. Thus it was that the blank veil of obscurity lay so long over a country and a people whom it so nearly concerned our interests to know all about. That veil has mostly been lifted now. There are a few dark corners yet; but they are comparatively remote, and there is nothing, at least of our own immediate border, which has not been thoroughly exploited, whilst much of it has been elaborately surveyed.

It is in this process of clearing up the mists that enveloped the geography of large and important transfrontier areas that I have had the good luck to assist during the last twenty years; and the process has been so interesting, and in some ways so instructive, that it is a real pleasure to cast back to old reminiscences and long-forgotten notes, and to reckon up those successive steps of it with which I was more immediately concerned.

India is not all frontier (a fact which sometimes seems to be overlooked), and the wild waste sands of that land of ancient histories, Rajputana, the broad plains and alternating forests and hills of Central India, and the interminable jungles of the Central Provinces have each of them attractions and charms of their own; attractions which owe something to the absorbing interest of historical association and antiquarian records; something to the vivid beauty of their own natural scenery; much to the variety and excellence of Indian sport, and to the quaintness of aboriginal manners and customs; but which taken separately, or all together, can never match the vivid, soul-absorbing interest that is awakened by the two words "active service." Thirteen years of the by-ways of the Indian backwoods (tempered by experiences on the Abyssinian highlands), however well sprinkled with big game and other attractions, were very thankfully exchanged for the chance of service on the frontier, which, commencing with the Afghan war of 1878, promised to continue indefinitely. It kept its promise. I never left the frontier again till I left India for good.

My experiences in the first phase of that memorable campaign were confined to the southern, or Kandahar, side of it, and included a struggle up the Bolán pass in those early times when its capacity for a railway route was as yet unmeasured. Bitter, agonising blasts of icy wind were the feature that has remained longest in my memory; nor have I altogether forgotten the view presented by the Dasht-i-bedaulat (the "plain of desolation") as I crawled out of my tent on the first morning after my arrival on its frozen edge. Carcases of bullocks, dogs, and camels were the decorative features of the landscape. The rest was a wild, weird waste of snow, with a black line of barren hills girdling the horizon on all sides.

Of the 40,000 camels which the early stages of that campaign are said to have cost India, a good many ended their career at this point. The long struggle up the slippery slopes which formed the final steps of the pass, followed by the intense cold and the insufficient food of the Dasht-i-bedaulat, was the end of them. We know more about camels now than we did then. Amongst other things, we have learnt that it is not good to ask the camel bred in the hot plains of Sind to climb the mountainous paths of Afghanistan, nor to expect the hill-bred camel of high Asia to prove a valuable transport animal in the lowlands.

A camel was a camel in those days, and was expected to do the work of one, wherever he might be found. Perhaps what cost the camel more suffering than anything else was the tradition that he could survive for long periods without water; that he carried, so to speak, his own private supply, on which he could draw at his own convenience. How every thoughtful camel (and all camels give me the impression of deep thoughtfulness) must have cursed that member of his race who first gave all his kindred away by proving that under certain favourable conditions this is a faculty which he actually possesses!

Further than Quetta I should probably never have gone with my hastily-constructed party of survey workmen (mostly recruited on the Karachi "bunder"), but for one of those artifices which are not unknown in times of stress, and for which I may perhaps now be forgiven. I was travelling with a subaltern whose duty carried him no further than Quetta. My camels just struggled to Quetta, and there two of them lay down and died. As my friend required no further transport, an exchange during the night of live stock for dead was secretly effected; and thus were my interests providentially safeguarded, and Government was not deprived of my services a day longer than was necessary.

Who could possibly imagine the Quetta of twenty-five years ago, who has but seen it lately! A few groups of aged and weather-beaten mulberry trees stood about in despondent attitudes, at intervals, in the swampy plain surrounding the ancient mud volcano which now forms the basis of the central fort; and round the fort clustered a mud-and-wattle collection of dome-crowned huts, which figured as the town. The residency was where the residency now is; but it was not the same residency. The early construction was of the same primitive materials as that of the bazaar. Some planting of poplars and planes had already begun. The genius of Sandeman for turning a wilderness into a garden had already borne a certain amount of fruit; and we must admit that he had most excellent material to work on. There is hardly a flower that blooms, or a fruit that ripens, which cannot be reared in the soil of Quetta. Nevertheless, the most sanguine enthusiast could never have constructed such a vision of luxuriant beauty as now greets the visitor, from the raw material offered by the Quetta landscape of 1878. Much of the open and unwholesome plain which is now covered with pretty villas and gardens was little better than a swamp then. My tent was pitched somewhere near the present site of the railway station, and it was only necessary to dig a stick some four or five inches into the soil to find water.

It goes without saying that Quetta was in those days poisonously unwholesome. There were indeed a whole series of inconvenient maladies which seemed peculiar to the soil and to the place, and which were mostly due to the effects of poisonous water. The fresh, bracing atmosphere of the Baluch highlands, which in winter is as the climate of an eastern Engadine, did much to restore the balance; but even the bright relief of clear blue skies and mountain breezes there hid a lurking danger; and it is that danger which to this day occasionally prevails against the efforts of a pure water supply and a sanitary system of existence. Owing to the absence of forest or other natural agencies in producing rainfall and tempering the direct action of the sun's rays, and the subsequent radiation of heat from the barren plains and rocks, the extremes of temperature are so great at certain seasons of the year that no precautions can secure immunity from chills. A range of 80° Fahrenheit is not uncommon within the twenty-four hours; nor is it unusual (especially about the highest part of the highlands near Kalát) for the sun to blister the skin by its intense and unmitigated glare by day, whilst ten or fifteen degrees of frost at night defy the thickest of blankets and rugs inside a tent.* No constitution (certainly none already sodden with malarial poison) can stand such extremes of heat and cold; and in the early autumn, when the nights grow long enough to admit of the dispersion by radiation of the heat acquired by day, there is always a risky time at Quetta. There is, however, such an abundant growth of vegetation now in existence that, within the limits of the cantonment, these extremes of temperature are much less marked than they used to be; but the necessity for irrigation in order to support the growth of trees also brings its own risks; and so the weary old tale of sickness has still to be told year after year.

The glory of Quetta are the mountains round about it. There are a series of great, gaunt peaks—Chahiltan, Murdar, and Takatu (the highest between the Himalaya and the volcanoes of the Persian border), which stand sentinel over the town, each owning its own legend of supernatural visitations, and each contributing its own quota of savage beauty to the landscape. Between the double-peaked Takatu and the great square head of Murdar the more distant line of the Kalifat cliffs fills up the horizon. These cliffs face westwards; they catch the latest rays of the setting sun, and light into a blaze of scarlet glory which is almost more brilliant than the burnishing of the west. Northward, to the left of

* The climate of Kalát, like that of the Nile valley and other desert spaces, "see-saws between a grill and an ice machine."

Takatu, across the width of the Peshin valley, the long level line of the Khojak is pencilled in dim grey against the sky, when that sky is clear enough to admit of any view at all. For many months in the year it does not admit of any view. It is subjected to a yellow obscurity introduced by clouds of wind-borne dust which pervades not only the atmosphere, but all the accessories of Quetta existence. The house is full of it; the furniture catches it in ridges and furrows; food is cooked in it; and men's lungs are packed with it. Too soon one realises that "khaki" is not adopted as the uniform colour of the British soldier from any mere scientific consideration of its suitability to its environment; it is a necessity induced by one of the main conditions of life in Baluchistan. The Baluch chief, if he is wealthy enough, sends his clothes to the wash before he appears at a Durbar or any public function demanding special attention to his appearance. Then, indeed, he is magnificently clothed in white array; but under ordinary circumstances the prevailing condition of the atmosphere fits him to his surroundings without effort on his part, and there is not a white rag about him. "Khaki" in summer is not only suitable—it is indispensable and unavoidable.

Beyond Quetta, Kalát, and the Peshin valley very little was known of Baluchistan in 1878. The Harnai route which now carries the railway, was unexplored then. The actual road to Kandahar was known by reputation, and had been mapped, but of all the vast expanse of plain and hill which stretched away to the Indian frontier on the east and north, or to the Persian borderland on the west, we were in the most profound ignorance. Only a thin line of information was marked on the maps linking up Jacobabad with Quetta and Kandahar; and yet in the earlier Afghan war at least one column, provided with guns, had marched from Ghazni straight away southward to the Arabian Sea, leaving Quetta to the east; but its records were so meagre and unsatisfactory that it was only when, in fulness of years, that country came to be systematically surveyed that we could fit the records to the actualities of the country. So there was quite enough prospect of occupation for the comparatively small staff of surveyors who were taken from the tail of the civil plough to fill up gaps and make good deficiencies in our military maps of Southern Afghanistan. Some of them worked a slow and painful course through the flat, salt desert that stretched from Jacobabad to the foot of the Bolán hills. They then climbed into the mountains till they reached the peaks that overlooked Quetta, and fastened the end of a "series" (of triangles) to the back of the Khojak. It was thus that they imported the Indian Survey into the Kandahar plains, and connected the hills about Kandahar with the Indian gháts.

To these gentlemen (amongst whom were Maxwell-Campbell, Heaviside, and Rogers) we owed it that wherever the brigades and columns of the Kandahar Field Force spread themselves, we others of the topographical staff could start with the satisfactory certainty of an assured position from whence to extend our mapping wherever the military or political powers might direct.

In the spring of 1879, when smiling peace seemed to have crept over the land (it was but a superficial creep), it was decided that a part of the Kandahar Field Force should return to India by a new and totally unknown route, which struck away about east from the Peshin valley and debouched into the plains of India opposite Dera Ghazi Khan. It is with a sense of the ridiculous now that one recalls how blankly ignorant we all were of that unopened and untraversed country. High-roads intersect it now. Rest houses and dák bungalows await the passing traveller at convenient intervals. A railway has been constructed through valleys beyond it which were then mentioned as unapproachable. It was indeed perhaps the most venturesome march that was undertaken by any force throughout the whole progress of the Afghan war; for the track which the force was to follow was untrodden by any European explorer. It was known to be difficult, and it was possibly dangerous, for we were as ignorant of the Pathan people (Kakars for the most part) who inhabited it, as we were of the nature of the country they lived in, and would probably fight for.

Kandahar had been taken without opposition by the Southern Afghanistan Field Force under Sir Donald Stewart on January 8th, 1879, on which date the first infantry brigades of two divisions marched through the Shikarpur gate of the city and found an apathetic population still engaged in their ordinary avocations, plying their trades and conducting their business much as usual. Only the Hindus of the city manifested any particular interest in the ceremonial proceedings of the march through the city. Passing out through the Kabul gate the force encamped on a plain near the Kabul road, and thenceforward was concerned far more in obtaining commissariat supplies, and in effecting extended reconnaissances into the country round Kandahar, than in maintaining their position by force of arms. Sir Donald Stewart, ever keen to know to the uttermost the nature of his surroundings, personally commanded the column which moved up to Kalát-i-Ghilzai on the Kabul road; and that redoubtable fortress surrendered to the summons of Colonel Browne, the political officer with the force, with an alacrity which must have been rather annoying to the leaders of a fighting contingent.

Meanwhile General Biddulph pushed a reconnaissance to the Helmund river, and employed his survey officers in clearing up some very vague geography in that direction. Never, since that reconnaissance, has any good explorer ever touched Girishk. The Southern Afghan campaigning was indeed productive of an immense amount of valuable mapping both then and subsequently, when the stern fighting days of Maiwand and the battle of Kandahar terminated our opportunities of making geography in that part of Afghanistan. Amongst the generals who throughout the course of that much-chequered campaign of two years' duration showed the keenest, most determined interest in clearing away geographical mists, in leaving no stone unturned that might add something to our knowledge of that strange combination of highland, plain, and rugged mountain, which has seen the passage of so many armies holding the destinies of India in their hands, General Biddulph ranked first. I have often thought, when watching his spare, light figure and extraordinary activity, his energy in supervision of the smallest detail of his military business, and noting his accuracy of eye and of judgment in seizing on each important feature of the country spread before him (a faculty which rendered his bold military sketches as instructive as any I have ever seen), that if General Biddulph had not been a great soldier he would have been an ideal explorer. It was consequently a happy omen for the success of the Thal-Chotiali Field Force, which was to find its way to India through an untraversed wilderness, that General Biddulph was placed in command of it.

The retirement of the Kalát-i-Ghilzai and Girishk columns upon Kandahar was part of the general scheme for reducing the Southern Afghanistan force before the hot weather set in. On March 1st General Biddulph reached Kandahar, and no time was lost in breaking up his division and in concentrating the columns which were to form the Thal-Chotiali Field Force at Khushdil Khan, in the Upper Peshin valley. Three columns quitted Khushdil Khan for the Indian frontier on March 11th, 21st, and 22nd, respectively. The first, under the command of Major Keen, of the 1st Punjab Infantry, included two squadrons of native cavalry, four guns, and the 1st P.I. regiment. With it was Major Sandeman, as political officer, whose name was already a power in Baluchistan.

The second column, commanded by Colonel Sale-Hill, consisted of the 15th Hussars, two guns, the 32nd Pioneers, and 1st Ghurkas. With this column was General Biddulph and the Headquarters' Staff.

The third column, under Brigadier-General Nuttall, comprised two squadrons of the 8th B.C., six companies of the 70th Foot, a wing of the 12th N.I., and a company of Sappers. A fourth column left the Indus at Dera Ghazi Khan (which was the point on the frontier on which the general advance was directed) to meet General Biddulph's force with supplies at the head of the passes leading to the plateau from the plains.

The excitement of clearing the ground of opposition naturally fell to the first column. Whilst making its way through the Smalan valley, about 100 miles from the point of departure, it was attacked by an armed rabble on March 22nd, who confined their attention chiefly to the rear-guard. This was but the preliminary to a much more determined stand which was made two days later at Bhagao. The whole country-side were in this second fight, although Major Keen's column appears to have been opposed by no regular troops. So effectually did the 1st Punjab Infantry work through that day's operations, that it is said that no less than 3,000 of the tribes-people were placed *hors de combat* when the day closed. After this there was no further attempt at obstruction, and General Biddulph's second and third columns were practically unhindered in their advance.

It was a glorious opportunity for making new geography. One could move about with comparative freedom, and dispense more or less with that most necessary, but at the same time most inconvenient, appendage to a military survey in an enemy's country—the military guard. An efficient protection for work of this nature has yet to be devised. The nearest to the ideal is perhaps an escort of Gurkha or Sikh scouts who possess the requisite training and mobility to keep pace with the lightly equipped survey staff over rough country. Cavalry are all very well where cavalry can move; but cavalry cannot climb mountains, and the first essential of modern field surveying is the faculty not only of climbing mountains, and of reaching the highest possible points thereof, but of climbing rapidly enough to include a fair attainment of commanding positions in a fair day's work. A small escort of picked men is generally possible; but where the escort is considerable it is obvious that the men cannot all be picked, and the pace of the party becomes the pace of the slowest. It is hardly necessary to say that the British soldier, who should be the backbone of our fighting strength in the flat field, is not an ideal mountaineer. Even the best of mountain-bred natives, when handicapped with rifles, ammunition, and kit, lose much of their elasticity over hills; neither is their home-bred activity increased by the comparatively inactive life of an Indian cantonment. So that the surveyor in the chequered field of a campaign has to measure possibilities with a critical eye, balancing the rough altitudes of the hills about him against the hours of daylight, and the capacity of his escort to fit the one into the other. This, however, is certain. The mountain-bred sepoy of Northern India, be he Gurkha or Afridi or Rajput of the hills, is as much superior to the European soldier in mobility amongst mountains as the Oorial (or mountain sheep) is to the Southdown; and consequently, feats of what may be called military mountaineering, with a native military guard, have been performed on our Indian borderland by Woodthorpe, McNair, Scott, and others (whom nature specially adapted for such performances), which are probably unsurpassed by any existing record elsewhere.

On this particular occasion the way was comparatively open, and nothing was to be guarded against except the casual risks due to those inevitable scattered bands of marauders to whom nothing is sacred—not even the sapper. Our escort could be small; the weather was gloriously clear; and nature had kindly disposed the lie of the hills in convenient form for attaining the widest possible view in the shortest possible space of time.

In March and April the high valleys around Quetta are probably at their best. There had been a sudden change; and one of those changes which mark the dividing line between winter and spring with a sharpness of definition which is not known in more northern latitudes. Early in March deep snow had been lying in the valley where now flourishes the little terminal railway station of New Chaman, where the ends of the Sind Peshin railway metals point the way to Kandahar. In 1879 the last of the winter blizzards struck the valley ere we left it, and life for two or three days became an unceasing effort to maintain the equilibrium of an 80-lb. tent, and to keep the breath of life in the tentless servants. Mine, I remember, lived under the heap of "bhusa" (or chopped straw) which was my horse's daily food.

Crossing the Khojak mountains was a horrible experience of bitter cold and painful difficulty. The road was blocked here and there with dead camels. Every suitable spot for pitching one's tent was then occupied with a frozen carcase; lurking behind every corner of the track was some hideous and evil-smelling object of decay, but fortunately the road was broad where the sappers had cut it out of the soft hillside, and there was room to shirk doubtful-looking crannies and projections.

At Kila Abdulla, where the Khojak pass drops on to the comparatively level plain of the Peshin, and where the railway station of the same name now stands, we had an experience of what happens when a local flood washes down the Baluchistan hillsides after heavy rain. The length of the flood-basin leading up to the pass is inconsiderable, and the width of water-way is in some places quite remarkable. It would indeed strike anyone unaccustomed to Baluchistan, as being wide absolutely out of all proportion to its length. But in Baluchistan the phenomenon of an irresistible flood let suddenly loose and carrying all before it, after a comparatively local rainfall, is not at all uncommon. It was such a flood that utterly destroyed the Bolán railway ere the Mashkaf alignment was adopted. When that railway was constructed the Baluch greyheads wagged their heads and said, "Wait till a flood comes; you haven't seen one yet." We waited a long time and then the flood did come, and it not only buried a large section of the line so deep that I doubt if the metals have ever yet been recovered, but it also washed away a ziarat (or shrine) or two belonging to these same Baluch advisers, a fact which seems to indicate that they had hardly appreciated the capacity of a Bolán flood themselves. On this particular occasion at Kila Abdulla the waters rushed with one rapid and comprehensive sweep straight down from the top of the Khojak (where we must presume that they originated) to the bottom, in the course of an hour. It was as if a reservoir had burst amongst the crests of the range and had emptied itself, as a bucket is emptied, on to the smooth unabsorbent slopes of the upper ridge, neither spreading wide nor losing force amongst the shaly gradients, but sliding in one unbroken mass of foaming, tearing, seething flood from the peaks to the plains. It was a flood of minutes rather than hours, and it took up the quarter-guard of the force in its embrace and whirled it away out into the open almost before the half-drowned sowars on guard could scramble up the low banks of the nullah. Some friends and brother officers, who were sleeping peacefully on an elevated patch of broken ground in the flood's course, were hopelessly cut off from the rest of the camp. They were, however, spared that anxiety for their own safety which was felt for them by those who watched the mad rush of the waters past their island. They continued to sleep peacefully till the flood subsided.

This was one of the last efforts of winter. A few more local showers, and spring burst on us with all the sweet freshness and beauty of that delightful interlude between the rigors of the cold, and the fierce grip of the hot, blasts of Baluchistan. Then was the time for flowers. The hills took on a green tint. Baluchistan hills are only green once a year, and then, in order to catch the effect of colour, it is necessary to look at them from a particular point of view; as, indeed, I have observed is the case with certain forms of silk. They become, as it were, shot with green; and tulips and daffodils, and a host of minor flowers of the field whose names I do not know, spangle the green with points of brightness.

It is also the time of tortoises in Baluchistan. From the long sleep of winter the tortoise awakes, and he first gives evidence of his existence by shoving his back upwards through the soft crust of the earth beneath which he has been embedded, for all the world like certain umbelliferous plants of the asafœtida species, which heave themselves upwards in the springtime of Turkestan. The tortoise may be found early in March in various stages of progression. First the earth cracks above his abode; then the shell protrudes, just as if the tortoise were swelling and found his quarters too tight; then the whole shell is above ground, lying close, like a flat-sided stone; finally the entire animal is outside, lean, active, and hungry. At this period he travels at a pace which would astonish a Baluchistan hare who ventured to make a match under the usual conditions of handicap. A very little provocation now will induce him to put his head out, and hiss, and show fight. It is this pugnacity which brings him to grief, for, owing to his armour, the only way to injure him fatally is to induce him to put out his head, and then with a sharp, swift stroke to cut it off. Rolling him down steep places is only an enjoyment to him; and, after all, trundling tortoises down a hillside is but a poor form of sport. The tortoise is not good to eat; at least the Baluchistan species was not a success in the kitchen.

Gradually the rain clouds of spring (the rainy season of Southern Baluchistan and Eastern Persia is in spring) cleared off, and the little force under General Biddulph's command made its way from camp to camp in the early freshness of those sweet March mornings with light hearts, and a cheery looking forward to the comforts of the cantonments ere the hot weather set in over the Indian plains. The light-heartedness was possibly not shared to any great extent by the general and his staff. It was impossible from day to day to tell what might lie at the end of the march. From first to last the route lay through a wilderness of hills, and it was often impossible to give a name to a halting-place or to indicate it otherwise than by its latitude and longitude as determined by the traverse, just as a ship might have her record kept at sea.

Nor was the chance of sudden attack amongst these hills to be lightly regarded. It required constant and extreme vigilance to keep the whole column prepared for such an eventuality. Although no serious opposition could be organised without our foreknowledge, a sudden and unexpected rush on the part of a few fanatical marauders was always a possibility.

From the Peshin valley we dropped into the long and rather narrow waterway of Yusuf Katz, which led us gradually upward amongst the highest peaks and mountains of Baluchistan to the water-divide between the Peshin drainage and that of the Anumbar, which is a part of the Indus basin. As we gradually emerged out of the Yusuf Katz valley on to the high ground, from which we could look eastward to the mountains which fringe the Indus frontier, we wandered into the juniper forest of Spiraragha. This is a curious feature which belongs especially to the hills about the modern station of Ziarat, the sanatorium of Quetta, which was, of course, in those days, undreamt of. At eight or nine thousand feet above sea-level this forest, which is, I believe, unique in this part of Asia, maintains a steady growth in a country which is otherwise singularly devoid of vegetation. Forests undoubtedly once existed in Baluchistan over large areas which are now absolutely denuded of trees, and with their disappearance (which in some parts is quite recent) there has been a reduction of rainfall, and a corresponding diminution of vegetable growth of all kinds. The soil of Baluchistan is not unfavourable to vegetable life—quite the contrary. Where there is water there also is the rankest profusion of grass and flowers. It is not at all unusual, in the region of the western flank of the Sulimani mountains (which dominate the Indian border from the Gomul to the latitude of Quetta), to find amidst the sterile limestone crags of the higher slopes, little rushing streamlets flowing in deep channels so covered in with masses of maidenhair fern and rank vegetation of low growth as to be almost hidden in the moist green clefts of the rocks. All around is black sterility. Only in the fissure which contains the stream is a clinging garden of green things—the strangest, suddenest contrast that it is possible to conceive. The forests of Baluchistan have been destroyed partly by fire, partly by wanton destruction in the search for wood; and the State Forest Department now finds much exercise for its patience in the process of preserving what little remains, and renewing what has failed.

A juniper forest is picturesque with a weird form of attractiveness. No ordinary forest tree could imitate the attitudes, or follow the fantasies, of the juniper. White skeleton arms, twisted and gnarled, riven and bent, with but a ragged covering of black foliage, lift themselves to the glowing sky, and cast inky shadows over the stunted yellow grass-growth below them. Each tree separates itself from the crowd, so that it is a dispersed and scattered forest, owning no friendly connection with trees of other sorts, but preserving a grim sort of isolation. Nevertheless, with a backing of snow peaks, and the light of spring sunshine upon it, the strange beauty of that juniper forest became crystallised in the memory, ranking, as a Baluch speciality, with the olive groves of the more eastern uplands, and the solitary group of magnificent myrtles which stand near Sinjao.

The descent from this forest-covered divide into the comparatively level flats watered by the Anumbar and its tributaries was rapid and easy. Between it and the Sulimani mountains, which always faced us clearly on the eastern horizon, was a series of more or less complicated passages through narrow valleys, intersecting a maze of clay-formed hills, rising here and there into isolated peaks, but generally low and accessible. Here and there the country opened out into wider spaces, and there were groups of villages, mud-walled and flat-roofed as to their houses, and well populated; with orchards and trees and such cultivation as could be secured by irrigation.

Such was the Bori valley, where now stands the unpopular little frontier station of Loralai. Where that name comes from I do not know. I did not find it when surveying the country, which, as far as I could see, had nothing of the mediæval romance about it which is suggested by that name. The station stands hard by a central village, which used to be called Bazaar, and the pretty name of Loralai is a late introduction. The Bori valley was attractive rather for the opportunity it gave of seeing a little further to the right and the left than was usually possible; also there was flat ground to ride over.

But ere we reached the level flats of Bori we encountered one of those fine natural strongholds, which through all time have been the favourite resorts of native ruffianism throughout the East. The fortress of Gwalior, the Droogs of the Dekkan, Kalát-i-Nadri on the Persian border, are all historic examples of the kindness with which Nature occasionally lends herself to the designs of those who live at the expense of others who cultivate the arts and graces of peace. Siasgai, near Chimjan, on the road which leads to Loralai from Quetta, is like any of these, only on a smaller scale. At first sight the solitary hill appears absolutely inaccessible. Up the steeply-shelving slopes which spring straight from the plain the way is clear, though not particularly easy, but above these shelving slopes is a straight, perpendicular scarp of some seventy feet, apparently unbroken, and continuous all round the hill. As, however, it was a well-known place of refuge for the local bandit it was clear that its unbroken character could be only apparent, and consequently up it General Biddulph determined to climb. I had arrived late in camp from a hot morning's work, when I was summoned to his tent and ordered to be ready to accompany him. We were soon picking our precarious way up the shelving slopes that formed the basement of the stronghold. There was, of course, a kind of track; and I may here declare that amongst all the many kinds of frontier hills that it has been my fate to climb I have never yet found one on which there is not some kind of track. It is all very well to call them goat-tracks, but as a matter of fact they are the byways of local humanity; and they exist wherever foothold is possible. Many a rough-sided and steeply-scarped pile of apparently impracticable rocks has been pronounced by our military experts to be an impassable barrier, and has been accepted as an integral part of some extensive scheme of defence, which has subsequently been found to be riddled with such tracks, and to be little more "inaccessible to infantry" than the plains on which it stands. Much depends, of course, on the character of the infantry, and still more on the character of the boots they wear; but it would not be difficult to point out many of our frontier defensive positions in which a great deal too much has been taken for granted in the matter of inaccessibility.

When it came to the final struggle up the face of the crowning scarp the inevitable cleft was discovered, which at once pointed the way to the summit. It was narrow and steep and difficult. The manner of ascending it was much the same as that which was once familiar to the chimney-sweep's apprentice, and which is now the daily exercise of many climbing enthusiasts in the English and Welsh mountains. I found it convenient to dispense with my thick sheepskin coat, and to take the ascent unencumbered; and of the small party who succeeded in reaching the top of that redoubtable hill I can distinctly recollect that General Biddulph was the only one who accomplished the feat clad in all the military paraphernalia of spurs and sword.

The small rock fortress of Siasgai is characteristic of many others which have played a more distinguished rôle in frontier history. It is comparatively level at the top, with a low wall of loose stones forming a sort of breastwork on the exposed flanks. A certain amount of rain water can be collected in the central depression, but otherwise there was no visible means of keeping the small garrison supplied. Its value lay in its comparative inaccessibility and its command of what must always have been a main road through the country. The descent was perhaps more awkward than the ascent, but here again the discovery of an opening which might be conveniently described as a "lubber's hole" through an outlying rib of rock, round which it was otherwise necessary to crawl, much modified the difficulties of the process. Only when the

SIASGAI

broad square shoulders of a distinguished member of General Biddulph's staff (Colonel Browne, whose name is now historical in this country and was even then invested with fantastic legends) blocked the way, and seriously threatened to become a permanent obstacle, were there any doubts as to the successful termination of the day's proceedings. All ended well, however, and Siasgai was soon blotted out in the blue of the distance behind us, never again to be seen by most of that band of military pioneers.

The march of the Thal-Chotiali Field Force was concluded without any serious misadventure. Scares occurred now and then, and rumours of opposition which was never effective. In the early days of April the broad flat plains of the Bori valley were subject to the same conditions of rarefied atmosphere which produces such weird results in desert spaces in the plains of India. The same thing had been observed in the plains about Kandahar. A flock of sheep became transformed into a numerous enemy on one occasion; and nothing could be more fantastic than the appearance of a column of British infantry on the march, viewed through the distorting haze. Their bodies were drawn out into long spiral phantom twists and their white helmets performed strange antics in the hazy atmosphere apart from the dancing wraiths beneath. One fine morning my survey colleague (Captain Heaviside) and I rode out to the foot of an attractive-looking hill which lay to the south of the line of route taken by the column. From the top of it we could look over the width of the valley and watch the troops snaking steadily forward with a long trail of baggage animals hidden in the dust behind, and make sure that no inconvenient demonstrations were taking place between us and them. Having finished the morning's observations, we betook ourselves and our guard to the foot of the hill again, and, knowing that nothing lay between us and the column, we cantered gently over the plain to the point where the long line of sun-tipped dust gave evidence of the existence of the moving force. As we neared the column we were astonished to find the rear of it halted, and dispositions made for repelling an attack which was evidently expected from the side on which we advanced. Explanations followed. It appeared that the vision of our two selves bearing down on the force had been magnified by the tricks of atmosphere into a wild array of Baluch horsemen, sweeping on to the baggage train and rear-guard. It was some little time before we could establish the fact that out of the southern plain there was absolutely nothing to be expected except ourselves, and behind us, at a considerable interval, our lagging escort. The column was set in motion again, and we were requested to play off no more deceptions of that sort on our confiding friends. It was a disappointment to them no doubt, but it wasn't our fault. A very much more serious scare (under the conditions which surrounded us) was caused by the report, on another occasion, that no water was obtainable at the forward camping-ground. As usual, we were out some little distance from the line of route, and had no idea of what was taking place with the moving column. It was a warm April morning, but by no means unduly or immoderately warm. Everyone had started as usual with the ordinary supply of water for the march. The march itself was not a long one, or one calling for unusual exertion. There was, in fact, no reason whatever for anticipating disaster, even if the water supply at the forward camp (to which sappers had already been sent to arrange the usual provision) did run a little short. But on rejoining the column (which we generally did about the time when we might expect the half-way halt to be called, and breakfast to be spread) we could see that something was very wrong indeed. In the first place there was no breakfast. This was always a bad sign, for its absence meant the absence of our chief, who never could find time for a square meal so long as there was any shadow of doubt about the proper conduct of the day's proceedings. When breakfast was late we knew that everything was not exactly as it should be; and the later it was the more serious was the situation. On this occasion there was no breakfast at all, and we knew thereby that things were going more than badly. The truth was that a report had been sent back to the column already on the move that no water had been found at the forward camping-ground, and the chief had at once ridden on to personally superintend the operation of sinking wells. A very little digging was sufficient. The water was all there, but a little further down than usual; and by the time we were in camp the difficulty had vanished. But, somehow or other, that report had become inflated like a balloon, in passing backward, and in ten minutes a scare was started, the like of which, I trust, I may never see again. No one had apparently dreamt of being especially thirsty before the report arrived. The instant it was known that our water supply might be short, the fiend of an imaginary thirst seized on British and native alike. The soldier, *more suo*, immediately drank up all that was left in his water-tin. The hospital doolie-bearer dropped his doolie anywhere, and commenced to gasp in agony. Camp followers broke loose and scattered over the face of the country, seeking water in dry nullahs and finding none; and had we been caught at that juncture by anything like an organised attacking force we should have fared very badly indeed. I found one of my most trusted adherents frantically digging holes in a nullah-bed with the legs of my best theodolite. He never forgot those efforts—neither did I. In short, the whole force went to pieces for about an hour or so. Then another report floated down the wind that water was to be had as usual, so the doolie wala pushed up his doolie, the trooper and the sepoy fell into the ranks, and all seemed equally prepared to forget that they had ever been thirsty. It was a weird experience.

In the quiet plain of Barkhan the force broke up, part of it remaining to establish a new frontier fort at Vitakri, and part returning to India.

In the gradual development of our geographical knowledge of the frontier much had been achieved—so much that it is doubtful whether any subsequent operation was more productive. After leaving the long open Bori valley (the valley that is marked now by the well-known frontier station of Loralai), General Biddulph's column struck eastward for a couple of marches from the Anumbar river, which drains that valley, and then traverses the tangled mass of low hills which fill up the space between the great central valley of Zhob and the Sulimani mountains of our frontier. This entailed a great deal of severe labour in the narrow defiles which here, as everywhere on the frontier, mark the passage of the main streams across the general strike of the close-packed ridges. Consequently he left the nominal objective of the expedition, the plain in which the two prominent towns of Thal and Chotiali are situated, far to the south of his route; this part of new Baluchistan being traversed by the column under Major Keen. A good comprehensive grasp was thus effected of many thousands of square miles of perhaps the most unattractive country in the world. The barren dust-ridden desolation of much of this part of Baluchistan must be seen to be appreciated. There are green spots here and there; there are narrow valleys and fern-bordered streams to be found if one looks for them; and above and about all is the clear invigorating air which, were it not for poisonous malarial influences, should make these uplands an Engadine for Western India. They are not an Engadine, and the little post of Vitakri, which was then established for strategic purposes in the Barkhan valley, has long ceased to exist. The tribes hereabouts have ceased from troubling, as our frontier stations are now far beyond them in the valley of the Zhob river, which was, in 1878, a valley as unknown as that of any river in darkest Africa.

At the end of that memorable expedition followed a period of rest on the summits of the Sulimani hills overlooking the plains of India. We halted at the immature little station of Fort Monro, a station which in spite of its remoteness from all centres of frontier interest, perched up on the crags which overlook the Sakki Sarwar (a pass which leads into Baluchistan from the plains at Dera Ghazi), has been the saving of many a good life soaked with heat and rotted with malaria in the sun-cracked plains. At Fort Monro it was possible to study the peculiar adaptability of the soil derived from the (geologically) recent deposits of the frontier to the growth of all kinds of vegetation, so long as water can be brought to it. There was a new little garden started down the hillside on the way to Rakni (which is on the far side of the Sulimanis from India), and in this little garden roses had been planted. All the frontier is celebrated for roses—indeed, all Afghanistan is a rose garden (such as Persia is supposed to be, and is not), and the beauty of these developing trees and flowers was a joy that has lasted me for twenty years, and will probably last much longer. There were not many of them, but their sweetness and colour were of the essence of rose perfection. I should doubt if Persia were the aboriginal home of the rose. I am not a botanist, and do not know whether the many-hued tangle of wild magnificence that decorates the Kashmir hillsides in June is all composed of true roses. In Afghanistan, too, the deep yellow variety which grows as a bush, and the sweet upturned creeping sort—yellow with maroon centre—which spangles the plains about Herat, may not be the true rose; but if it be so, then Kashmir and Afghanistan may at least claim the honour, equally with Persia, of originating the best and sweetest flower of the modern English garden, the typical flower of English chivalry.

CHAPTER II.

THE SECOND PHASE OF THE AFGHAN WAR OF 1879-80

Northern surveys—Cavagnari's mission and recommencement of war with Afghanistan—General Roberts' advance—Sherpur and Kabul in autumn—Expedition to Hindu Kush—Life in a Mahomedan household—The word and faith of an Afghan—Gathering of the clans—Defence of Sherpur—Expedition to Kohistan—Expedition to Laghmán—Expedition to Logar—Some of the Afghan peoples—News of Maiwand—Effect at Kabul—Return to India—Summary of results.

THE pioneers of geography in Southern Afghanistan had every reason to be satisfied with the results of that part of the campaign which is usually called the "first phase" of it. An enormous area of new military mapping was secured, and a good sound triangulation had been carried from the Indus to the Khojak, and there extended in less exact and accurate forms to Kandahar and the Helmund river. A great deal more was done in the south than was effected in the north, where the comparatively restricted operations which ended with the Peiwar and Shutargardan on one line, and at Gandamak, beyond Jalalabad, on the other, offered no such field as the adventurous march of Biddulph's column from Kandahar to India.

But what might be wanting in quantity was distinctly made up in the quality of those northern performances. Tanner, Charles Strahan, Edward Leach, Samuells, and Scott had all been busy along the Khaibar line, and Woodthorpe, with Martin, had made his name great in Kuram. When the roll was called at the conclusion of this first part of the campaign; when the "Peace of Gandamak" was signed, and Jennings had made his record ride to Peshawur; when that terrible march was concluded in which the gallant 10th Hussars showed all the world how cholera can be faced, even on the pent-up straits of a narrow valley, flooded with the fierce heat of June—then the list of those who had been on survey duty was reckoned up. Samuells was dead of typhoid; Strahan was, soon after, brought as near the brink of the grave as a man can go and yet live; Tanner had been carried back from a gallant attempt to carry his survey into Kafirstan, much more dead than alive; Edward Leach was in hospital with a V.C., a brevet, and a stiff arm; Scott was still to the front—he had found out what became of the Kabul river, and had greatly distinguished himself in fighting his way back from the Mohmand hills to the Khaibar; and Woodthorpe, though wounded, had survived quite a long chapter of experiences. Fortunately for him Afghans were badly armed in those days. Never again probably will any man jump during an action into an Afghan "sungur," by mistake, and live to tell the tale However, triangulation had been carried up the Kuram and up the Khaibar, as far as the military forces penetrated. It was centred on the great snow peak of Sikarám, the giant of the Safed-Koh range, whose 16,000 foot sides had been surmounted both by Scott from the Khaibar, and by Woodthorpe from the Kuram.

Thus ended the first chapter of the Afghan war of 1879-80; with the death of Sher Ali, the installation of his son Yakub Khan on the Kabul throne, and the despatch of the long-delayed mission under Louis Cavagnari to Kabul. The treaty of Gandamak, signed on 26th May, 1879, decided certain points on the frontier line only. The head of the Kuram valley, the pass of Lundi Kotal (in the Khaibar), and the foot of the northern slopes of the Khojak mountains were points in the boundary line which was henceforth to separate the interests of India from those of Afghanistan. At these points consequently the territories of British India and of Afghanistan touched each other. At these points they still touch each other, and only at these points. Peshin and Sibi were at the same time assigned to British jurisdiction.

The fate of Cavagnari's mission, which is one of the blackest records in the history of our relations with Afghanistan, started the campaign on a new phase. Early in September, 1879, a force of about 6,500 men in three brigades, under Sir F. Roberts, was once more mobilised in the Kuram valley for an advance on Kabul. A force of similar strength, under General Bright, acted on the Khaibar line, and a division of 9,000 men, under Sir Donald Stewart, was concentrated in Southern Afghanistan for the occupation of Kalát-i-Ghilzai and for movement, if need be, on Ghazni. By the 24th September the Kuram column was ready to advance; and then commenced what must ever be regarded as the most brilliant episode of this long campaign, *i.e.* General Roberts' swoop on to Kabul in spite of insufficient transport and supplies, and the capture of that city after the determined stand made by the flower of the Afghan army at Charasia. No subsequent march equalled that in the skill, the determination, and energy of its leading; and no subsequent fight was more brilliantly successful.

It was my good fortune to be attached as survey officer to General Bright's column in the Khaibar, and to take up the thread of the work dropped by the surveyors of the early period of the campaign, who were all, or nearly all, *hors de combat.* Captain Woodthorpe was at his old place in the Kuram.

On the 1st November a brigade, under General Macpherson, left Kabul with the object of opening up communications with General Bright's force in the Khaibar, and the junction was effected on the 6th at a place called Kata Sang, near Jagdalak. The two brigades did not actually touch, but they were close enough to admit of intercommunication, and I lost no time in passing across the intervening space to join Macpherson's brigade, and push on survey operations to Kabul. In this manner I was, I believe, one of the first officers to traverse the whole length of the Khaibar, from Peshawur to Kabul, since the Afghan war of 1843. The route of Cavagnari's mission had been by the Kuram. On the rough battlemented summit of the hill overlooking the Bala Hissar, Woodthorpe and I ran our work to a junction. Our small parties of topographers had covered the ground nobly, and from that day our fears as to the successful issue of the methods we had adopted for carrying out a connected and consistent scheme of triangulation from beginning to end were dissipated, and we betook ourselves to the dust-ridden camp in Sherpur in the certain hope that our respective computations would land us in a position of pleasing agreement.

THE OLD BALA HISSAR, EASTERN WALLS

There was a short period of dusty activity which set in between the voluntary occupation of Sherpur (which, as most people will remember, was a defensive cantonment on the opposite side of the city to the Bala Hissar, situated about half a mile from the city gates) and that more compulsory occupation which was the result of the tribal risings of December, when Sherpur was besieged. Then was the Bala Hissar and the old palace of the Amir despoiled of such treasures as it possessed, and the energies of all who could spare time from more serious duties were directed to the collecting and storage of wood for the long winter which was just setting in. To none was a period of exemption from field work more acceptable than to surveyors, who could now bring their computations up to date, and piece together all the miscellaneous patchwork that the mapping of a campaign piled into their hands. Nevertheless, opportunities for reaching conspicuous positions in the country surrounding Kabul so as to extend observations over as wide an area as possible, were by no means to be neglected; and I consequently hailed a chance of reaching the summit of a main branch of the Hindu Kush which blocked the western horizon beyond the Chardeh plain, with much satisfaction.

It was hardly the weather for mountaineering. The first gusty, dusty, cold winds of winter were settling steadily down to the process of snipping off the last remnants of vegetation from earth and trees; the scarlet and gold of autumn had given place to the grim nakedness of Afghan winter; but no snow had fallen. As I rode out westward over the main road leading to Maidán, crossing here and there one of the irrigation channels drawn from the Kabul river which turn the natural barrenness of Chardeh into a vision of fields and orchards such as may be seen again in Lombardy but not in many other countries, I found ice thick enough to bear the weight of myself and my horse already formed. The little artificial waterfalls had adopted fantastic shapes with long icicles and twisted spirals of crystal interlaced; the last yellow leaves of the mulberry were fluttering to the ground; and orange pumpkins and red millet were spread out on the roofs of the flat housetops.

Chardeh was well sprinkled with orchards even in those days.

Mulberries, walnuts, and apricots were abundant; but there was not the extraordinary wealth of poplars and willows which I found on my return to Kabul in 1886. These latter were the result of the present Amir's fancy for planting, and he must daily congratulate himself, as he looks out from his summer palace on the western slopes of the hill of Babar's tomb over the broad fields of Chardeh, on his skill as a landscape maker. A good deal of the western road, which runs to Maidán and Bamián and Turkestan, was sound and well laid out, running between mud walls, and it was readily recognisable. At certain points, such as nullah crossings, etc., it was difficult to detect that there was a road at all. It was at an unrecognisable point such as this, that, a little later in the year (on the 11th December), a small force of cavalry and artillery, under General Massy, which had worked its way across country from a more northerly route, was nearly overwhelmed by the rush of a mass of tribespeople who were collecting for the attack of Kabul. Whether the guns were outflanked and forced off the road by a determined rush, or whether the road itself was unrecognised, I cannot say; but instead of retiring on Sherpur by this most convenient line of retreat, they were withdrawn again much on the line by which they had arrived, and were speedily and hopelessly entangled in the network of irrigation channels which intersect the cultivated plain. There, for a brief space, they fell into the hands of the enemy, and nothing but the arrival of Macpherson's force on the scene, and the speedy recovery of the guns saved this reverse from ranking as a serious disaster.

My guide and protector on this excursion to the Hindu Kush was an ex-officer of Hodgson's Horse (the present 9th Bengal Lancers), who was lord paramount of certain estates at the foot of the Paghmán mountains, which are, as I have said, an important offshoot of the Hindu Kush. The Hindu Kush is here rapidly tailing off to its southern extremity in the neighbourhood of Bamián, where it may be considered as lost in another mountain system which parts the basin of the Oxus from that of the Helmund. My host's mind and memory were still full of Hodgson and the Mutiny, and he beguiled the ride with stirring tales of Mutiny days, whilst he fished out of his capacious pockets every now and then specimens of the orchard produce of the Paghmán slopes—magnificent golden pippins, which remain in my recollection as the best apples I have ever seen in the East.

His home in Paghmán was of the usual Afghan pattern, an open and defensible courtyard surrounded by buildings; his own residence facing the gateway, with open rooms and balconies in front. There were no glass windows, but at night wooden shutters pretty effectually closed up the front of the dwelling-rooms, although they left opportunity for biting draughts through the cracks which separated the ill-fitting boards. Probably all the furniture in the establishment was introduced into the room set apart for me. It consisted of a chair and a charpoy. What was lacking in furniture was, however, made up in carpets. Turkestan and Afghanistan rank little behind Persia in wealth of carpet production. The bazaars of Kabul city are full of the carpets of Turkestan and Herat, thick felt numnahs from Central Asia, "soznis" or embroidered cloths from Bokhara, and all the many varieties of woven productions for fighting that natural enemy of Afghan humanity—bitter cold. The central reception-room was provided with a square recess in the floor, which was the hearth or fireplace of the establishment. Therein a huge wood fire was lighted, the smoke whereof was left to find its own way into the outer air. As the fire gradually reduced itself to a condition of red-hot embers, a four-legged wooden contrivance shaped much like the native bed, or charpoy, was placed over it, and on this again a wide numnah, or felt cloth, was spread, which could be conveniently pulled over the knees of anyone sitting on the edge of the recess. This, indeed, was the right position for the guests of the house to assume. I was treated on strictly military principles as a brother officer, and shared this most consoling position (after a long, cold ride) with a cheery party of Afghan gentlemen, some of whom were of our escort, and others were householders in the scattered village of which my host was the "squire."

The village or township of Paghman extends well up the slopes of the mountains, which are terraced and revetted so as to gain level space enough for cultivation. The winding, irregular streets lead through all sorts of picturesque effects of mountain-side and gully, where the rushing mountain-stream, sweeping down like a highland burn, is overhung by the white-sided, mud-built houses of the well-to-do inhabitants. Like Istalif and Charikar and all the pretty climbing towns of the Koh Daman and Kohistán, it is embosomed in fruit trees. Fruit is the great product of the Kohistán plains, and the glory of the Kabul market. There may be found shops literally piled to the roof with melons, grapes, apples, walnuts, and apricots, all in their due season; and it is not a fictitious pile like the sloping array of a London shop backed by an artful banking of boards, but an honest collection of wholesome fruit, which arrives daily on the backs of donkeys, packed in baskets or panniers, and fresh from the picking. This is, of course, during the time of fruit. In November there was nothing outside the shops but naked trees, interlacing their shadows on the dark brown earth.

It was good to see the patriarchal character of the local "squirearchy." Here there was no municipal board, no vestry, but there was a parish church, or what answered to one, open on three sides to the winds of heaven; and the mullah was distinctly a person of secondary consequence. It was my friend the Khan who represented local authority and the court of final appeal in this hill-bred community—he who had gazed on the face of the Amir and was not affrighted (poor fellow! he had good reason to be affrighted all the same; his friendliness with the alien was his own undoing, and he rests now with his fathers), and had tales to tell of the wonderful city of Kabul, which truly was within a long day's ride, but to which these mountaineers but seldom trusted themselves.

It was nice to see the little rosy-cheeked Afghan children come to him for a kind word and the blessing which is ever ready to Mahomedan lips, but not so often heard in Christian language, and the reverent affection with which all the villagers greeted him. I have seen something of the same thing in other lands—in England, for instance—but the bond of sympathy always appeared more artificial and more perfunctory. The Afghan certainly clings to home and kindred with an affectionate regard which is lacking in the plains-bred native of India generally. Let us say what good we can of him, for his evil practices are many.

So long as I was the guest of Mahomed Khan of Paghmán I was treated with a frank soldierly courtesy such as would be expected from an officer who is likewise a gentleman, all the world over. There was no affectation of display, no attempt to make either more or less of the ordinary surroundings of an Afghan home than was their due. I was at perfect liberty, and, at the same time, I was well looked after; and I enjoyed my country visit immensely.

But there was the business of ascending the Paghmán mountains to be accomplished, a business which could not be completed in one day, and which demanded careful preparation. On a fine, clear morning in late November we made the first day's excursion into the hills, following a route which was evidently trodden pretty frequently, and camped at an altitude which would render the rest of the ascent to the summit possible within a few hours. It was a bitterly, intensely cold and windy night. My ink froze hard, I recollect, and I was thankful when daybreak put an end to a most chequered night's rest. Had there been time to spare I should have deferred that climb to another day, for there were ominous signs of the coming of one of those north-westerly blizzards which render travelling impossible and life an uncertain burden in districts more to the north, and which are occasionally severe even about Kabul. However there was no time to spare, and in the early hours of the grey morning we struggled, weighted with sheepskin poshteens and all the other necessaries of survey existence, up the narrow goat track which streaked the craggy mountain-side. It was still early when we reached the summit (about 15,000 feet) and looked cautiously over the edge as we emerged from the shelter of the eastern slopes.

It was necessary to be cautious. The wind was raging in curling sweeps and eddies across the narrow ridge which divided us from the black depths of the valley beyond. Small, hard pellets of frozen snow were driven with the force of shot across that interval, and were caught and twisted into white bands of smoke, and sent swirling high into the air as if from the depths of a wind volcano. To stand up against it was impossible. The sturdy little Gurkhas of my escort sat down behind boulders, or lay flat. I attempted to get a look out to the north-west at the hitherto unseen peaks of the Koh-i-Baba, and across to the main range of the Hindu Kush, but could distinguish nothing but grey swirling masses of snow-smoke rising from the depths of a hidden valley. It was disappointing, but there was nothing for it but to come down, leaving the crowning effort to establish a survey station on those rugged heights to a subsequent occasion—and to Woodthorpe.

Already my Àfghan friend had whispered words of kindly warning into my ear, and already I detected a note of anxiety in his voice, and signs of special caution on the part of the havildar of my escort, whose business it was to preserve the integrity of my skin till I got back again to Kabul. From north and south and west the tribes of Afghanistan were collecting. Was not this the winter season, when crops were gathered in, and the field was open to all good fighting men who could leave their bread-winning pursuits till the spring came round, and join in a jehad against the "feringhi," and a possible loot of the Kabul bazaar? It is true that the old high priest Mushki Alam had been preaching jehad ever since the half-hearted troops of the Amir had curled up before the fighting chief of the little force that had come over the Peiwar and Shutargardan from India. But he might have preached till his throat cracked had this been harvesting time, or the time of sowing. Now it was different. The winter time was the time for jehad. A well-known chief had arisen in the person of Mahomed Jan, and there was time to meet in "jirgahs" and hammer out some principle of combined action, so that Afghan and Ghilzai, Tajak and border Pathan (of whatever doubtful nationality), might assemble together in their thousands, and simply eat up the little foreign army that sat about the gates of Kabul.

So the head of the Afghan family took down his long-barrelled jezail, or, if he were the lucky possessor of a feringhi rifle, he handed the jezail over to his eldest son, and they both stuffed their pockets full of dried mulberries, and slung bags of the thick Pathan "roti" on their backs, and slouched off to the sacred war.

For my own part I made a long day's ride of it into Kabul

THE CITY OF KABUL FROM THE BALA HISSAR

when I heard that they were coming, where I arrived just a day earlier than our winter visitors. And I must here acknowledge, not only the care with which an old soldier like Mahomed Khan carried out his engagements with regard to my safety, but the equally punctilious regard to the claims of hospitality which was shown by those who were *not* old soldiers, and had no previous ties of military brotherhood to bind them. There were two very eminent Ghilzai bandits, named Sádu and Dádu, who kept watch and ward over the passes towards Jugdalak and the Khurd Kabul. These gentlemen had no fixed principles, but they preferred if possible to be on the winning side; and they regarded a combined rising of the whole of Afghanistan as good security for backing the final annihilation of the British. They had a sort of precedent to guide them in the disaster of 1843; and perhaps they forgot the subsequent retribution. Anyhow, they were keen to take the field against our line of communications. Nevertheless did one of that fraternity see to it that my assistant, whom they were safeguarding for a consideration, and who was busy mapping their own country, should be returned safe and sound within the gates of Kabul before they themselves hurried matters to the fighting stage. Here again you may observe a trait in Afghan character which deserves an entry on the credit side of his account by the recording angel. He is true to his engagements as a host, even to his own disadvantage.

The story of the siege of Sherpur wants no telling in this book. It was a time when survey operations were suspended, and survey officers were turned into field engineers. It was a relief when the end came—when the tottering old saint Mushki Alam was carried up the snow-bound peak of the Takht-i-Shah, and with his own trembling hand lighted the beacon fire that was to be the signal for the attack in the early morning of December 23rd. But we knew all about it beforehand, and each man tumbled into his appointed place when the warning bugle called, with a sleepy certainty that before evening we should see the outside of those walls with the inside of which we had become so sickeningly familiar.

When I reached my post that morning I was just in time to find Sir H. Gough, the commanding officer of my section of the defences, propped up against a "chabutra" with a bullet-hole through the breast of his poshteen that had every appearance of being conclusive, so far as his further participation in the proceedings was concerned. But it was fortunately a bullet that had spent its last momentum on making the hole, and it resulted in no serious mischief. The enemy's fire was incessant and close at that far corner of the Bemaru ridge, and a few creeping tribesmen probably got closer to the line of defence there than they had got anywhere else. When they were finally driven back, and the appearance of our cavalry in the open plain beyond the walls had quickened their perceptions, it was surprising to see the number that emerged from the apparently inadequate shelter which they had secured below the ridge. Some of them indeed refused to go. A few steady shots took refuge in a tower of the mud-built village of Bemaru, and defied all the efforts of the mountain artillery at short ranges to turn them out. The shells of Morgan's battery went through and through the soft mud walls, but they failed to disturb the plucky little garrison, which held its own until the shades of night gave them the chance of retreat.

The release of the Sherpur garrison was the signal for a renewal of survey operations, and a movement of Baker's brigade into the Kohistan country gave us the first welcome opportunity of looking over the historic plains which lead to Charikar. It was intensely cold when that movement was made—so cold that it was impossible to ride at a foot's pace without being frozen in one's saddle, and impossible to clear off the hard snow from the ground whereon we pitched our tents. At night the baggage mules in their desperate efforts to get shelter from the biting wind forced their way inside the tents, much to the inconvenience of the occupants. But it was a successful expedition, and thenceforward we knew what lay beyond Kabul to the northward up to the edge of the hills, the true Kohistan.

Spring and the approaching summer gave us yet furth opportunities, as from time to time foraging parties ar brigades scoured the country in all directions. General Brigh reconnaissance (January 27th) into Laghman was geographical most instructive. Here we had the opportunity of tracing out at last the route of those prisoners who were carried by the orders of Akbar Khan from the deadly Khurd Kabul during the disastrous retreat of the previous Afghan war, and shut up at Badiabad. They were taken in a north-easterly direction over the low water-divide of Adrak Badrak, between the Jagdalak drainage and the Kabul river, and convoyed along that river through the Laghman valley to a remote village on the Alishang river, which is a river of Kafirstan, starting from the great snow peaks which dominate the Laghman landscape. Very few relics of that unhappy little party were found; indeed, throughout the whole campaign I can only recollect the discovery of one letter, written by Captain Soutar of the 44th, whilst a prisoner in the hands of the tribesmen near Gandamak. The letter, needless to say, had never been delivered, and the avaricious old village chief into whose hands it had fallen thought to earn an honest rupee or two after preserving it for so long, by bringing it to a British market for sale. In the course of the rolling years the market had come back to him, and here was his opportunity. A good many "chits" or letters of recommendation for service performed were produced at Kabul by the older inhabitants who remembered the previous occupation, and who must have wondered silently at the change which had come over the spirit of the British army. Where were now the family tents and the buggies, the elephants and retinues of servants, the "memsahibs" and the fair-haired children of the former generations of English invaders? One bent and withered old Kabul gatekeeper was quite anxious in his inquiries after Jánie (Johnny) Baba and Willee Baba—the unforgotten children of the Trevor family; and pleased with a pleasure that certainly was genuine to hear of the fortunes of these two gallant officers, once his little English protégés. The absence of non-fighting material of this description, and the general business aptitude of the whole force was reassuring to them to a certain extent. If they perceived that they had a harder and much more difficult nut to crack this time, they were sharp enough also to see that no one had come to Kabul to stay.

Laghman was interesting from many points of view. It is

the actual valley of the Kabul river, which river is usually left at Jalalabad for the straight route through Nangrahar to Jagdalak. Although we made no use of the Laghman route between Kabul and India, it is nevertheless the best known route of ancient times. Through that valley (and through Nangrahar also) Alexander's force made its way to India. By that route Babar's conquering host of Turks reached the Peshawur plains, not touching the Khaibar (except perhaps as a subsidiary track), but driving straight across the Kunar valley into Swat and Bajaor, and disposing of the fighting clans of the hills about Kafirstan before entering the plains at all. The Kabul river route is the route of the ancients.

North of Laghman are the Kafirstan mountains, and from them two noble torrents descend, the Alingar and the Alishang, draining straight away from the snows of the Hindu Kush, and leading, as we still suppose, to the very heart of the most provokingly inaccessible tangle of mountain glens and glaciers in Asia; for the Kafir still holds his own throughout the greater part of what we call Kafirstan, and still defies the Amir, who claims the right of his reclamation and the honour of his introduction into the ranks of Islam.

All that could be surveyed of this most interesting corner of Afghanistan was brought into our maps. Here I had the assistance of the gallant McNair, who probably acquired the fancy then for exploring the Kafir strongholds, which subsequently led to important results. From Laghman I hurried back to Kabul to join fresh expeditions, the most important of which, from the geographical point of view, was the reconnaissance of General Roberts into the district south of Kabul known as Logar, where the Ghazni Field Force, which had arrived from Kandahar, was already in position.

The Kabul river, above Kabul, is quite an insignificant stream, rising in the eastern slopes of an extension of the Paghmán range, which separates its sources from those of the Helmund. The river in irrigation seasons is literally run dry, all the water being diverted from it into the fields which border it. The Logar river, which joins a little below Kabul, is really a bigger stream than the Kabul, and plays an important par in the agricultural economy of a very large district to th south; and it is a district which rivals any in Afghanistan for natural beauty of scenery and richness of cultivation. Certainly a casual observer in Afghanistan, no matter whether in the north or south (but perhaps especially in the north), would carry away with him an idea of wealth and prosperity which is not warranted by an inspection of the actual area of possible cultivation shown in the map.

We were in Logar in late spring-time, and the fruit blossoms were blowing across the fields in pink and white showers. The hedgerows were full of wild roses and clematis, the borders of every little irrigation channel were deep in grass and lilies; the smell of the sweet-scented willow was all through the air; beds of lucerne and pulse were thick with the knee-deep pile of summer carpeting. The warm, moist scented breath of the slow breeze was enervating, and one looked lazily across the wide, shimmering fields of growing wheat to the white piles of country villages flecked with sharp little blue shadows, and backed by a more distant line of red-brown hills, with faint reminiscences of Egyptian delta scenery. The hills looked far off and sleepy, with hazy outlines, whilst at one's feet and beyond, almost as far as the eye could reach, was nothing but a vista of peaceful loveliness. Not till the exigencies of survey duty compelled a weary climb up the hillsides (which if beautified by new-found grass and flower were still steep, and afforded but a rugged morning's walk), and stood on the commanding points of them, did one realise how large were the waste places, and how small the area of production. They were but narrow ribbons of green after all, these sweet Afghan valleys, intersecting a wilderness of mountain and unprofitable hill. I have known a general officer to object seriously to a map which showed Afghanistan to be all hills intersected by a network of valleys. He maintained that, on the contrary, it was valley and plain tempered by bordering hills—and so it is for the practical purposes of military manœuvring; but so it is not, when regarded from the economic point of view, which balances its productive possibilities with its area of waste—magnificent waste perhaps—but none the less adding nothing to the productive capacity of the country in vegetable wealth, and very little in minerals.

And it is probably a mistake to suppose that under a more enlightened and civilised government there would be much reclamation of unproductive land and development of cultivation. The Afghan landowner has nothing to learn from us in the matter of irrigation. There are experts in the science of bringing water to dry places amongst certain clans of the Ghilzais who could possibly give points to European engineers. It is nothing to them to sink a shaft at the base of a hill till water is reached, and then to bring that water by underground channels within reach of the surface. But the science of irrigation must at any rate stop short with the exhaustion of the water supply. This point the Afghan engineer reaches all over Afghanistan, from Herat to Kabul and from Kabul to Kandahar. No source is neglected and no water is lost.

One is so tempted to linger over descriptions of the richness and beauty of the valleys of Afghanistan that there is imminent risk of producing a false impression about the country. Probably not one-tenth part of the total area of the country either is, or could be, brought under cultivation. However, so far as the valleys of Logar and Wardak are concerned, the memory of their seductive beauty is with me still; and with me still are recollections of the stiff climb up many a hill, wherein I found myself no match for such mountaineers as Woodthorpe and McNair.

At this time we made acquaintance with a good many of the Logar villagers, who acted as guides, and were in no ways reticent about their views of Afghan policy and the future relations between the English and the Afghan people; which acquaintance afterwards proved exceedingly useful. In many a remote corner subsequently between Herat and Kafirstan I have met old Afghan friends from Logar, who have been prompt to give me cordial and kindly greeting.

No more successful reconnaissance was made than this one to the plains of Baraki Rogan, in the spring of 1880. Here, at Baraki, Bellew thinks that one may look for a survival of one of the old Barkai settlements that followed the establishment of Kyrenean colonies in Northern Afghanistan in the days of Darius Hydaspes. Whether this is so or not, there is distinctly to be traced a kindlier note in the recognition of Europeans amongst the Afghans of Logar than is usually apparent elsewhere. The Logaris make excellent soldiers, and one of the Amir's most trusted regiments is recruited from this district. When a guard is required for the protection of European guests I observe that it is the Logar regiment that usually has the honour of furnishing it.

There followed on this reconnaissance a period of military inactivity during which native explorers were sent abroad seeking fresh geographical fields which lay beyond the reach of any possible military action. Now that triangulation had been successfully imported into Northern Afghanistan, and the far-away peaks of the Hindu Kush and Koh-i-Baba were all well-established points for reference, there was a basis for this sort of work such as had never existed before. None of these explorers ever came to grief, but one of them at that time commenced a remarkable career which had a tragic ending, as I shall relate further on.

Sir Donald Stewart's march from Kandahar to Kabul had taken place in April, and Sir Donald himself had assumed chief military and political command at Kabul before Sir F. Roberts started on his Logar expedition. The march gave opportunity to Captain Gore for a comprehensive survey of the country contiguous to the route which had been traversed before by British troops, but never surveyed. It is a grand high-road, that which links up Kandahar, Kalát-i-Ghilzai, and Ghazni with Kabul, with but one tight place (the Sher Dahán pass, about eight miles on the Kabul side of Ghazni) in the whole length of it. To the west, about Ghazni, are the great mountain peaks (running to 15,000 feet) which hide the upper sources of the Helmund, and overlook the great unknown highlands where the Hazaras live. To the east is a wide, open stretch of plain country (for the most part), where a great salt lake, the Ab-i-stada, receives the waters of several big rivers from the north-east, and occasionally spreads out into a vast lagoon, covering hundreds of square miles of plain. This is the Ghilzai country.

The Ghilzais differ from other inhabitants of Afghanistan in that they are of Turkish origin, and possess a reputable history. Their great clans—the Suliman Khel, the Nasirs, Kharotis, and others—are better known in India than most Afghan peoples, for they furnish the great trading community. The travelling Afghan merchants, or Povindahs, who make their way about India with strings of camels, carrying dried fruit and cloth goods of Afghan or Bokharan manufacture, are mostly Ghilzais. They form a very powerful factor in the Afghan state, and it is only by virtue of the possession of better arms and a regular army that the Amir can retain his hold on these independent warriors and traders. All Ghilzais are Sunnis by faith, Pathans by speech, warriors by right of their courage and physique, and robbers by nature.

On the other side of the Kabul-Kandahar road are the Hazara Monguls, who occupy a wild, mountainous country of which no European has seen much more than the outside edge. It is a high, bleak, and intensely inhospitable country, where the snow lies for most months of the year, where little or no fuel is to be found, and cultivation is confined to the narrow banks of the Helmund and its affluents. But, in truth, we know very little about the Hazara country. These people have, likewise, a credible history. They are comparatively recent importations into Afghanistan, Mongolians by origin, not unlike Gurkhas in physical appearance, only larger and more powerfully built; Shiahs by faith, and working, rather than fighting, men by nature. They are not Pathans, but Parsiwáns—*i.e.* they do not speak the Pathan language, but a dialect of Persian. The Hazaras were of great value to us during the Afghan war as diggers and delvers. The Amir finds them of great value still. His corps of sappers is composed of Hazaras, and they are excellent workmen, as I have had reason to know. They are always well inclined towards the British, being quite free from any foolish fanaticism, and always ready to meet us on business terms. But for the fact that they live in such a remote wilderness, and would have to cross the whole breadth of Afghanistan to get to India, a splendid corps might be raised for Indian service out of the Hazaras. There are a few of them in some of the local border regiments already.

It is not a bad illustration of the patchwork nature of nationalities which goes to make up Afghanistan as a whole, that when Sir Donald Stewart's force was attacked at Ahmad Khel, near Ghazni, on its march to Kabul, and when such a savage rush was made on the extended line that nothing but the determined front shown by the 3rd Gurkhas, 19th Punjab Infantry, and 2nd Sikhs saved the situation, neither Ghilzais on the one side, nor Hazaras on the other, had very much to say to it, although the position of the fight was on the dividing line between them. I have been told by a man who was in the action (on the Ghazi side, not on the British), that the nucleus of the Afghan force was composed of a rabble who followed the British troops all the way from Kandahar; and who originally hailed from that nest of fanaticism to the north of Kandahar, known as Zamindáwar. This is the real home of Ghazidom, the headquarters of some of the most rampant Islamites of the Durani clans, the true Afghans, who, whether they be Israelites or not, still fight with all the ferocity of the destroyers of the ancient civilization of Canaan. Zamindáwar is a beautiful country, stretching up in picturesque valleys and sweeping hills from the Helmund, filled in with a swarming population of well-to-do cultivators. But we never got near it during the Afghan war. It was under other circumstances that Zamindáwar came to be mapped and explored.

For a short space at any rate, after Sir Donald assumed the chief command, there was comparative peace. It was getting on for harvest-time, and as the Afghan fighting man is also a working man and a tiller of the fields, he is always busy about the summer months. Nor does he want to run any risk of having his crops spoiled. Reprisals are inconvenient when the wheat is up far enough to show a yellowing end to it. When it is quite small, just showing above ground, it is almost impossible to destroy it. Nothing short of re-ploughing the ground would make much difference, and even that, if followed by rain, would not be completely destructive. But when it has reached the stage of juicy fulness and the ears are formed, when it is known as "kasil," and as excellent forage for four-footed beasts of all sorts, then it is well for the owners not to attract any hostile attention to it.

So the hot, glaring months of June and most of July passed pretty quietly, except for the necessity of constant activity on the Khaibar line of communications, and it was not until the end of July that anything occurred to disturb the even tenor of Kabul existence. Sir F. Roberts had left Kabul for Peshawur, and many thought that his connection with the Afghan campaign had come to an end. Never, perhaps, were the chances that attend a military career so strongly exemplified as in the events which followed.

It was a hot still morning at the end of July, when the white mud walls of Sherpur were shimmering in the sun, and the cool shade of the poplar avenue leading away towards the city looked specially inviting, that I strolled out with Woodthorpe to make sketches of Kabul city life. The fruit season had set in, and the shops about the entrance of the main street, before reaching the shade of the covered bazaar, were piled with fruit to their very roofs. Lazy indifference to the world in general was the prevailing tone of the good people of Kabul that summer morning. They sat in their shops in easy Afghan attitudes (much more European than are the attitudes of the natives of India), occasionally disputing possession of some succulent piece of sweetmeat with the flies, and looking as if the advent of a customer would be a most unmitigated bore, and the necessity for running a bargain an evil to be discouraged.

Woodthorpe's art proclivities tended towards the sketching of humanity rather than of landscape. A dirty Kabul boy, with rosy cheeks, and one shadowy garment as his only protection against wind and weather, impelling a lazy donkey which staggered under two gigantic panniers full of apples, was exactly the particular feature of humanity that suited his fancy that day. So the boy was seized and put into an attitude, and the donkey was only too ready to assist the boy in standing still, and the sketch began. The boy and the donkey were in the street. We were sitting on the boards of a fruit shop, with the grey-headed old proprietor behind us, when he suddenly woke up and entered into conversation. "Have you heard the news from Kandahar?" he said. No, we had heard no news at all. "Well, you British have been well beaten down there: a whole regiment has been cut up, and Ayub Khan is now besieging Kandahar." We told him frankly that we didn't believe him, and that he oughtn't to circulate such untruths, because it might have a disturbing effect in Kabul. But a sudden thought flashed through my mind—that the old gentleman was speaking of times and seasons that we knew not of. For some totally inexplicable reason the post, which had hitherto been so regular, had failed for the last day or two, and neither letters nor papers nor telegrams had been delivered to us. *Could* it be that this old man knew more than we knew, and that we were purposely being kept in ignorance for deep political reasons? However, the old shopkeeper was in no way disturbed by our incredulity. In fact, he didn't believe in it. "You may *say* you don't believe, but I fancy you know all about it. Anyhow, you will find it is true, and as for raising a disturbance in Kabul, that is just exactly what won't happen. Ayub Khan has been foolish enough to run his head against Kandahar. Now your General Roberts will go down and smash him up, and he has no further chance of reaching Kabul. We shall have to accept that——Abdurrahman."

We will hope that by this time the old man has been gathered to his fathers, or has changed his political creed.

Ayub Khan was ever the popular hero of Afghanistan, the "Prince Charlie" of the frontier, the favourite of the people, and Ayub Khan made the worst mistake of his life (and is ready to admit it) when he obtained his success against Burrows' brigade at Maiwand. Whether he ever expected to pass Kandahar without a collision with the British troops I do not know, but I do know that had he been able to do so he would have raised the whole of Northern Afghanistan in his favour, and we should have had a difficult time in supporting our own nominee. By one of those curious phases of fortune in war, the results of which it is impossible to forecast, the Maiwand disaster, by detaining Ayub and exciting his half-disciplined army with the hopes of the loot of Kandahar, tended more to the settlement of affairs at the capital than anything else that could have happened. Till then Abdurrahman had given but a very half-hearted response to our invitation to accept the thorny crown of Afghanistan. But the news of Maiwand decided him. His view of the matter was the view of the old apple-seller. He burnt his ships and handed over much of his transport to assist the force which was immediately organised to march on Kandahar, and forthwith he "came in." On the 7th August the Kandahar Field Force left Kabul by way of Logar for Ghazni, and on the 11th Abdurrahman, the present Amir, held a durbar just outside the gates of Sherpur, which all officers attended. As we marched out from Sherpur, his troops marched in, and Sir Donald Stewart at once commenced the withdrawal of the northern forces to India.

The force which Sir F. Roberts took with him to Kandahar numbered about 10,000 of the best troops now massed at Sherpur. Sir Donald Stewart, after seeing the Amir duly installed, retired on the Khaibar line with the remainder of the army of Northern Afghanistan, about 7,000 strong, leaving the Kuram route open to tribal occupation on his flank, and feeling by no means certain that the retirement would be unmolested. The best guarantee for its success (it was carried out without a shot being fired so far as I remember) was the rapidity with which it was conducted. There was no time for mobile organisation amongst tribespeople who were now widely scattered in the pursuit of their ordinary autumn field avocations. On the line which Sir F. Roberts was to take to Kandahar, Major Gore had left (unhappily) no further room for the extension of surveys. Our knowledge of it was fairly complete. So Majors Woodthorpe and Gore retired with Sir Donald Stewart's force to India.

Then ensued one of those weary experiences which chequer the career of the campaigner. A daily struggle through thick clouds of dust, under a blistering sun and over a hard-baked road from camp to camp; the daily pitching of the inadequate "Kabul" tent (inadequate, that is, to keep out either heat or the yet more insufferable nuisance of flies); the weary attempt to get through the hottest portion of the day by sleeping an uneasy sleep under some sort of muslin protection that would prevent the fly swarms, hot from an investigation of the nearest dead camel, from investigating oneself; till the comparative cool of the evening justified a long, trickling drink, and an attempt at dinner. Sweetest episode of all those weary days of sub-tropical and sticky existence was the early morning rise, and the application of a lighted candle to the black mass of torpid flies that hung in swarms of blissful sleep to everything that afforded them a night's foothold. They died in their thousands. It was better even than the effect of blank charges of gunpowder expended over the crawling battalions of Red Sea flies, attracted to thin lines of sugar artfully laid out at that memorable camp where the Abyssinian expedition started its long route to Magdala.

But the march came to an end with commendable rapidity, and with it terminated (but for some additional work subsequently effected by Longe and Talbot about Kandahar) our first systematic attempt at reducing the geography of Afghanistan to a scientifically constructed map.

We had no reason to be dissatisfied with the results. Many thousands of square miles of previously unmapped country were now sufficiently well surveyed for all practical purposes, regarding the country as a possible theatre for future military operations; and technical maps and plans innumerable had been added to the general store of information. If the work of the Survey Staff was not recognised in the final despatches of the Commander-in-Chief in Afghanistan, it was not for want of appreciation of these results. It was simply due to the fact that the military officers engaged on this undeniably military duty drew their pay from civil sources, and, when in India, belonged to a civil department. So their work could not be officially recognised by the military authorities. They were in the field by invitation only, and formed no integral part of the army staff. Even now military officers engaged in making military surveys, if they belong to the one department in India which makes a speciality of these things, have an indefinite position, which does not entitle them to military recognition, though they frequently get it. It is one of the minor anomalies of Indian service.

Our position on the north-west frontier of India at the close of the Afghan war may be shortly summarised.

We had gained absolute command of the three most important lines of access to the Afghan highlands, having placed ourselves outside two of them on the dominating passes, and occupied the third from end to end. The two northern passes, the Khaibar and the Kuram, were occupied only as far as the Lundi Kotal and the Peiwar Kotal respectively, and at these points they touched Afghanistan. The tribes whose lands bordered these routes beyond the old unscientific (but most practical) boundary which we inherited from the Sikhs, were left in their primeval state of independence. All we claimed from the Afridis who occupied the Khaibar was the fulfilment of certain obligations for safeguarding the pass in consideration of regular pay for services rendered to the Indian Government. Levies were raised under native officers, and these levies for twenty years held to their engagements, and were true to their salt. They were still true when the irruption of 1897 took place, and, shifty and untrustworthy as the Afridi is held to be by certain authorities, we certainly had no cause to complain of him in any matter pertaining to the defence or abandonment of the Khaibar at that critical juncture. The Kuram, although by no means so important a gateway to Afghanistan as the Khaibar, presented no great difficulties to occupation. The Turi tribes of the valley are Shiah Mahomedans. The Shiah sect always seems to compare favourably with the Sunni, as regards fanatical instincts, when the two are together. The Shiah of Afghanistan and the north-west frontier is almost invariably friendly to British interests, and disposed to assist the British officer. Hence our occupation of Kuram has led to but few disagreeable complications, and it may be regarded as a complete success. It was in the south, in the direction of Quetta, however, that the most important alterations in the political *status quo ante* were expected. Here the cession of a nebulous corner of Afghanistan, which included Peshin, Thal Chotiali, and Sibi (districts over which the Amir had long ceased to wield any active authority), by the treaty of Gandamak, in 1879, was an important corollary to the treaty of 1876 which was effected with Baluchistan by Sandeman. By that later treaty, which recognised as still effective the offensive and defensive alliance formed in 1854, and which, in 1876, included the Sirdars of Baluchistan as an active factor in the administration of the country, Quetta was leased to the Indian Government, together with its immediate surroundings and the line of approach from India. Telegraphs and railways were commenced, and an annual subsidy of 100,000 rupees per annum was granted to the Khan of Kalát. Soon afterwards (in 1882) the annual quit-rent of Quetta was fixed at 25,000 rupees, and the Khan received a further 30,000 rupees in lieu of transit duties in the Bolán. This quit-rent has quite lately been again increased, so as to bring Nushki (which place commands the new trade route to Sistan) within the boundaries of British Baluchistan. But it was the treaty of Gandamak which practically founded British Baluchistan, by adding to the Quetta leasehold the assigned districts of Peshin, Thal Chotiali, and Sibi. By a resolution of November 1st, 1887, British Baluchistan became incorporated with British India, and its staff of political administrators became Deputy Commissioners and Assistants, similar to the staff of any Indian regulation province. Hence you will see on the map a political island in the midst of Baluchistan, which is connected by the Bolán with British India, and is called "British Baluchistan." The rest of that country is presumably "independent" Baluchistan; but the independence of it is not that of Afghanistan, which is nearly absolute; hardly even that of an independent native state of Central India. It is a chastened independence, admitting of close political control where British interests are involved, and leaving very wide tracts of the country unvisited and untouched by political authority.

The importance of Quetta as the outpost to Western India can hardly be overestimated. Quetta occupies a position of extraordinary natural strength as well as one of great strategical importance. Knowing well the nature of the country which intervenes between Quetta and Herat to the north-west, between Quetta and Sistan to the west, or between Quetta and the Arabian Sea coasts on the south-west, I find it impossible to indicate any possible line of advance on the Sind, or southern, section of the north-west frontier of India that would not be dominated by the Quetta position. There is nothing obligatory about Herat as a base for attack on India; but should Herat ever be selected as the point of departure for such a venture, it would be found that all roads south of Herat lead to Quetta. Kandahar might be avoided by way of Sistan, but the end would be—Quetta. Even the historical route of Arab invasion through Makrán from the Persian border, which passes by Las Bela to Karachi, is no exception. A force at Quetta could not be ignored even were a line of advance within easy reach of the sea-coast a practicable line to adopt. But it would obviously be just as possible to invade India by sea at once as to make use of such a route, for it involves command of the ocean.

At Quetta lies one of the keys to the front doors of India. At Kabul lies the other; and if these two doors are locked there is nothing in this year of grace 1900 that need cause us any apprehension for the future safety of the country. Nor need there ever be reason, provided roads are never made where roads do not at present exist. It is only an accurate knowledge of the geography of the whole width of surrounding country that can justify these convictions. Advancing armies must conform to certain strategical rules which are themselves governed by geographical conditions, and these conditions in our western transfrontier have hitherto been only partially understood. Armies, practically unopposed, have reached India from the west by routes intermediate to those of the Bolán and the Khaibar, but such routes have not been beyond striking distance from Quetta or Kabul, and, moreover, the military equation between offensive and defensive strength has so changed with modern weapons that none of them could now be considered possible in face of determined resistance.

It is then a matter of great significance that the natural surroundings of Quetta lend themselves to strong defensive tactics. Quetta can only be approached from the north or from the south. On the north, at Baléli, in the narrow exit from the Quetta plain into Peshin, between the steep, scarped walls of Takatu and the rugged foothills of Mashélak, are defensive lines of about four miles in length, which cannot be turned, and which, by the light of recent experiences in South Africa, may justly be called impregnable. An advance from the south assumes an open road from Sistan to Nushki, and unopposed progress through the narrow valleys and intricate hills that lie between Nushki and Quetta, where strong defensive positions may be found at every few miles of the route. It is true that the Quetta position does not actually cover the Harnai branch of the Sind-Peshin Railway, but a divergence through the Peshin valley into the Harnai only leads to an encounter with other strong positions, based on Quetta by interior lines, and dominated by permanent works as impregnable as those of Baléli. The Quetta position is, indeed, not only one of remarkable natural strength, increased by scientific development, but it is one of infinite further possibilities; a position which, whether we reoccupy Kandahar, or whether we do not, must ever be our defensive mainstay —the real citadel of our southern frontier system of defence; and the assignment of those districts which contain the Harnai branch and the Khojak extension of the Sind-Peshin Railway must be regarded as the most valuable assets of the Afghan campaign of 1878–80.

CHAPTER III.

WAZIRISTAN

Waziristan—Our position on the frontier at the close of the Afghan war—Consolidation of the Amir's Government—Geography of the frontier—The Waziri expedition of 1881—Advance into Waziristan—Ascent of Shuidar—Turning ambuscade—Surveying results—March down the Shakdu defile—A hot day to finish with—Frontier explorations subsequently.

THE position of frontier political affairs when Abdurrahman ascended the throne of Kabul was as follows. The Russians were then north of the Kopet Dagh (the line of mountains which now defines Persia's northern frontier), exceedingly busy in reducing the Tekke Turkmans, a movement which was finally effected by the brilliant victory of Scobeloff at Denghi Tepe, when some 14,000 nomads of all sizes and both sexes were destroyed; and by the subsequent occupation of Askabad. This, however, did not take place till January 24th, 1881. Although Merve was distinctly threatened, they were still at a considerable distance from that place, separated therefrom by a wide space of desert country. But by September the Trans-Caspian Railway had reached Askabad, and then commenced that series of remarkable journeys of exploration by a young engineer named Lessar towards Herat, which, with the Russians, seems to be the usual precursor of territorial expansion. The successful issue of the Afghan campaign, undertaken because a Russian mission had been received at Kabul whilst our own mission had been denied entrance, had settled the question of Russian predominance in the Court of Kabul, and the result was immediate activity on the Herat border.

Meanwhile Abdurrahman had his own kingdom to consolidate, and it may be well doubted if any Afghan sirdar of his time could have consolidated it so well and so quickly. Elsewhere I have pointed out that Afghanistan can hardly be said to possess a distinct nationality of its own. The Barakzai clan of the Duranis (true Afghans) are in the ascendant; but the Turkish Ghilzai tribes, and even the ancient Tajak or Persian population, who speak Persian dialects and claim no affinity with more modern interlopers, are strong, self-contained, fighting factors in the kingdom, and it would be hard to say that either of them would not eventually establish a representative on the Kabul throne were they as strong in arms as they are in fighting capacity. Abdurrahman's methods were undoubtedly severe; they were the methods of the king who levelled the poppy heads, and they ultimately produced the usual crop of rebellions (of which those of the Ghilzais and Hazaras were especially difficult to subdue), and nearly led to final disaster on the field of Tashkurghan, where he met his cousin Issak Khan in Afghan Turkestan.

Nevertheless, he has survived to take his place in history as a strong and, in many respects, a wise ruler. It is not for us, sitting at home at ease, to question his methods. It is true that many Afghan notabilities have disappeared just as Mahomed Jan, the leader of the attack on Sherpur, has disappeared, and amongst them some who were friendly to the British; but we must remember that the Amir has been able to encourage and protect many European professional men (and women) at his capital, although he will not admit of a British resident; and that he has proved absolutely true to his engagements whenever those engagements involved the safety and honour of a British commission. But whilst, in the early days of his sovereignty, he was occupied in strengthening his own position, that process did not involve any interference with the Pathan tribes who occupied his frontier Indiawards.

That long strip of rugged mountain country which runs practically the whole length of Eastern Afghanistan, and which extends northwards through the Kuram and the Khaibar, up the borders of the Swat river till it merges in the general Hindu Kush system, was no integral part of his sovereignty. Through this band of unutterably rugged and unattractive hills all the passes of the frontier run. It forms no great water-divide, for all the big rivers which pass through its limestone gates, cutting across the main strike of the hills, come from the highlands of Afghanistan. It is a wide strip of mountain wilderness (which used to be considered inaccessible, but which has not altogether proved so), called by the ancients Roh, and from time immemorial this has been the home of the original Pathan, the speaker of the Pushtu tongue. His first arrival here belongs to prehistoric days. He was here when Skylax undertook his adventurous reconnaissance of the Indus. It was a little earlier than the time of Skylax that the Israelitish tribes were scattered abroad, and (according to Afghan traditions) some of them came to Afghanistan. This, at least, is what they say of themselves. They point to their family names—Abraham, Isaac, and Jacob—and to their traditional ceremonials, and to the evidences of former influence of Mosaic institutions which is contained in their unwritten code of civil procedure, and they proudly claim to be the true Ben-i-Israel, hating the Yahudi (Jew) with all the fervour of their ancestry. But they have lost the Chaldaic form of speech, and now talk the Pushtu tongue, which is but an archaic dialect of Persian. The Pathan tribes of the frontier (Kakurs, Waziris, Afridis, etc.) are probably partly of Indian origin, dating their occupation of these highlands (about which they have shifted and changed their location indefinitely) from the days celebrated by the Mahabharata, when the great struggle between the races of the Sun and the Moon sent a good many of the former into exile from the plains to the hills.

With these people no Amir of Afghanistan has ever greatly interfered. There was no object in interfering so long as they refrained from interference themselves. Their country is, as a rule, so wild and so difficult that, if occupied by any people who could fight with modern weapons, they would be practically unassailable. The collection of revenue would be a work of difficulty and patience, and the process of enforcing submission would cost a good deal more than the value of the revenue.

Dost Mahomed the Great wisely left these troublesome folk alone, and Abdurrahman at first followed his example. It was the proud boast of these mountaineers that they were independent and unconquered, and, as a matter of fact, I think the boast has been justified by history. Yet these tribes of the frontier have always owned affinity with the Afghan peoples in community of language and religion. If the king of Afghanistan has not been their king, he has been their religious chief, their prophet, and their political referee. With few exceptions (such as the Turis of Kuram and another clan on the Kohat borders) they are all Sunnis by faith, and we must not regard too lightly the bonds of religious conviction. Moreover, temptation with these border people lies all on the side of India. Their own lands are barren and rough, and cultivation is confined to the narrowest strips of alluvial soil which may be found alongside their mountain streams. Yet they have good store of cattle and sheep and goats, and some of them breed an admirable race of donkeys and horses. Their houses are substantially built, and they live in fair comfort, paying no taxes. But they are born with the instincts of the old Scottish border robber in them, and the fat plains of the Punjab are their traditional hunting-grounds. And so things will remain until a new generation arises that sees more clearly the financial advantages of law and order.

Of all these people none have given more trouble than the Wazirs or Waziris. They are divided into two great clans, the Mahsuds and the Darwesh Khel, and they occupy a little Switzerland of their own, dovetailed in between the Gomul and Tochi rivers. It is sufficiently far north to partake rather of the characteristics of the mountains of the Kuram and Safed-Koh than of the Sulimani hills to the south. There are pine trees and grand deodars on the far slopes of Waziristan to the west; there are magnificent ilex (oak) trees which throw broad, square spaces of solid shade. The young ilex sprouts all over the lower slopes of the hills, imitating holly in its early stages. The spreading poplar is the glory of many a village, and the ubiquitous "bher," or jujube, is in every low-lying nullah. And Waziristan possesses a glorious group of mountains, culminating in two giant peaks—Shuidar to the north, Pirghal to the south—each of them rising 11,000 feet above the plains of the Indus, and standing like twin sentinels, guardians of the western passes of the country. From Shuidar, looking northward, one may see the flat, white back of the Safed-Koh, which divides the Khaibar from the Kuram, culminating in Sikaram (16,000 feet), and from Pirghal, the craggy outline of Kaisarghar, the highest peak of the mountain called the Takht-i-Suliman, bars further view to the south. From both peaks westward there stretches a boundless vista of ridge and hazy plain, a diapason of tender distances fainting to lighter tints of blue, till it is only against the yellowing evening sky that the pale silhouette of the hills that stand about Ghazni can be detected.

So it may easily be understood that the soul of a surveyor would be possessed with a longing to stand on Shuidar and Pirghal, and definitely and for ever fix therefrom a large array of landscape points such as would enable his explorers, groping their artful way about the borders of Afghanistan, to tie up their work with satisfactory exactness. Besides, all Waziristan to the east could be overlooked from them.

The opportunity came in the spring of 1881. The Waziris had previously been on the warpath, and had raided Tank, a town not far from Dera Ismail Khan, which lies conveniently handy to the hills, and which is periodically burnt to the ground—much to its advantage, probably. I know some other frontier towns that would be the wholesomer for the process. But such a deliberate insult could not pass unavenged, and as the political process of blockading (*i.e.* stopping all trade and traffic with the country) proved unavailing, a force was organised to hunt the recalcitrant chiefs and compel them to "come in."

The Waziri Field Force was divided into two columns, a northern and a southern. It was the southern force, under General Kennedy, which was expected to meet with most resistance, and to bring to book the arch-offender Mushaki, who was supposed to be responsible for the mischief done. Now Mushaki dwelt in caves; or at any rate he was in the habit, under stress of adverse circumstances, to take refuge in a cave, which he considered a more secure position than his village home. The frontier Pathan very frequently lives in caves, and always, if he can, keeps up a connection with cave-residences in the hills, where his wife and family may be stowed away when he takes the field for a doubtful campaign. A well-drained and sufficiently well-lighted cave, with room for the smoke to get out without inconvenience, is not a bad substitute for a four-walled house, and is infinitely to be preferred to a tent in winter, so that cave-dwellings are not necessarily mere refuges for the destitute on the frontier; they frequently occupy the position of a country-house.

Mushaki's country-house was in a well-selected position in one of the southern valleys of Waziristan, leading directly from Tank to Kaniguram, which is the capital of the country. It was on that line, therefore, that most resistance was to be expected, and on which the invading columns were chiefly concentrated. But it was not my luck to be able to join that column. Whilst arranging for a signalling station on the flat roof of a bungalow at Bannu I had a fall from a ladder, or rather *with* the ladder (which slipped up at the foot when I was at the top), and the result was that I could not get away in time to start with the first advance, which entered Waziristan from Dera Ismail Khan and Tank.

With some regret (a regret which I afterwards considered as superfluous) I sent my energetic assistant, Captain Gerald Martin, with the southern column, and waited a few days longer for the movement of the northern force, which was to advance by the Khaisor valley and make Rasmak (one of the chief northern villages in the country of the Mahsud Waziris) its objective. I had no reason to regret the delay, for I fell under the direct command of General John Gordon, and that meant a good deal to me. I knew that everything that could be done to gain geographical information and to support the surveyors would be done; even to the extent of running a little risk for the sake of it.

The march up the valley was uneventful. There was no opposition. Day by day we lifted ourselves a little higher out of the heat and dust of the plains, and arrived amongst cooler breezes and under clearer skies. The barrenness of the outside ridges of the frontier hills, running to sharp edges on the stony dasht which shelves in long slopes down to the cultivable acres of the Indus valley, gave place to higher hills on either hand, terminating in precipitous cliffs, where the water-ways forced an opening. Here the higher slopes were dotted over with the smooth round bushes of the young ilex. The valley was literally the water-way of the Khaisor stream. It was the nullah bed, now dry except for a trickling stream here and there which wandered in crooked ways about the shelving heaps of sand and boulders piled in its breadth of bed from bank to bank. It was a typical frontier river approach to the highlands, broad and easy to pass along in its lower reaches, narrowing and much more inconvenient as to the nature of its boulders higher up, where the periodical torrent runs fierce and strong; but inasmuch as its sources were in the hills for which we were making, and not beyond them, it was free from any of those gigantic gorges, those veritable "gates in the hills," where the way between the limestone cliffs on either side could be absolutely and completely barred, as a tunnel or a bridge is barred. We worked our way gradually upward, a stiff climb now and then, to the most commanding points near the line of route. This was generally sufficient to open up a view of survey points fixed by previous triangulation, and enough to support the mapping.

The most important incident of that frontier expedition to me was the ascent of the great peak Shuidar (or Sheikh Haidar), which towered up to 11,500 feet above the sea-level, and which we knew must overlook a vast area of hitherto unseen country. So important a feature as the snow-capped Shuidar had of course been seized upon and "fixed" by the Indus valley surveyors in the course of their triangulation. It had its place, not only in line with Sikarám and Pirghal and Kaisarghar, and a hundred other hoary-headed frontier sentinels as a border landmark, but it had also, in common with those others, its own fixed place in scientific geography, which was reckoned out to the last foot. And this made Shuidar all the more valuable as a point to be gained in the course of our surveying. It is the first and greatest of all desiderata for a surveyor to know exactly where he is, and if all this has been comfortably and accurately determined for him beforehand an immense deal of anxiety is spared.

So for Shuidar we started one fine morning with a sufficient escort (drawn mostly from the 5th Punjab Infantry), commanded by that well-known and well-loved soldier, Colonel Sam Hall. With me was one of the best of all assistants,

Captain the Hon. Milo Talbot, R.E. The Egyptian Intelligence Department is at present responsible for his career, and if he enjoys life more in the Egyptian Intelligence Department than he did over the frontier hills he is exceptionally lucky! It was a fine morning, as I have said. There are many fine mornings in India, but the expression as applied to the frontier means that there was a blazing sun in a sky which was too hot to be blue, but little wind, and no haze to speak of. Haze is the constant bugbear of the frontier, nor is it easy to say how it arises. The strong north-west winds, which sweep down Western Afghanistan and raise the periodic "shumal" in the Persian Gulf, including most of Persia in their icy embrace, undoubtedly touch the frontier; and it is due to them, and to the sudden fall in temperature which they produce, that clouds of fine dust become suspended in the atmosphere, and occasionally assume almost the consistency of a fog. When a dust haze occurs it usually puts an end to all opportunity for such observing as is necessary in triangulation for days together. There was no haze when we started for Shuidar, and all promised well. We wended our slow way up a comparatively easy valley; the hills, rising in steep slopes broken by out-cropping rocks, and filled in with the miscellaneous green of frontier bush, narrowed our way to just the near bank of the stream. There was a little cultivation here and there, but not much. Ahead stalked our guide, tall, angular, and grim, with an anxious expression in his eye. He had accepted his responsibilities with diffidence, not to say with reluctance, and nothing but the promise of a very substantial valuation of his services had induced him to start. Now he was uneasy, but he still stalked on ahead, saying nothing. And then, when we had well entered the narrowing part of the valley, there occurred a strange episode. There was nothing to be seen around us but rocks and bush; the outline of the hills cut the clear air without a sign of any living creature along them; not a sound was to be heard but the trickling of the stream and the calling of a few partridges; the peacefulness of a hot spring afternoon was brooding over the valley. But the guide stopped suddenly, and then in clear-pitched tones (such as those use who live in mountains and are accustomed to talk across the breadth of valleys) he commenced an address to the rocks and the bushes and the hills, turning himself about so that no stone should be left out of his appeal.

He said that we were peaceful folk, though we might look otherwise. We were on a quest for information, which would take us up that valley to the very head of it, and that if no one injured us we should certainly injure no one; but that we meant to go to the head of that valley anyhow, therefore it was wise that we should travel unmolested. This was his speech in effect, though I do not pretend that I understood much of it. I had never seen a man address the "country-side" in this fashion before, and the effect of it was almost uncanny.

Not a voice was heard in reply—only the echo caught faintly the conclusion of his speech, and dropped it quietly back again to where we stood. There was a dramatic weirdness about the whole proceeding that seemed to touch even the sepoy. No one laughed. On the contrary, a look of relief came over the faces of some, as much as to say that it was well for us that this explicit statement of our intentions was made to the seemingly empty rocks.

We pushed on till evening, and then occupied a position for our camp which had been selected by the guide. It had been well selected, for on three sides of it were precipices which might have defied even an Afridi or a Kafir, and the fourth side was but a narrow neck, along which we approached. It was a glorious night, and the moon lit up the open spaces, and put in black shadows under the cliffs with a vividness of contrast such as one never notices except amongst the monochromes of night. But over against our position, across the valley up which we had ascended, which, some mile or so below our camp, had narrowed to a gorge set deep down between scarped cliffs, we observed the twinkling lights of a few camp fires. There were not many of them when we sat down to our cheery camp dinner under the open sky, and we did not think much about them; but in the early morning I had the curiosity to look again at those fires, and the four or five had increased to about a hundred—a number that betokened a pretty considerable collection of tribespeople.

Next morning we were off betimes, and we made straight for the topmost peak of the mountain. It was not excessively steep nor difficult; the air was keen and cool, and vegetation grew almost rank as we moved upwards, till near the summit we found ourselves skirting the fringe of an oak forest. Talbot, with the guide, went first and picked the way. I was behind him with a few sepoys who formed the advance guard of the companies which followed. Nearing the summit, when almost within sight of the cairn of stones which forms the ziarat of the immortal Sheikh, we suddenly met two or three men coming over the crest from the valleys on the opposite side. As they were armed the guide promptly intervened his person between Talbot and these new-comers, and entered into explanations. These were apparently satisfactory, and as they had evidently expected to be shot at sight, and were obviously relieved to find that we meant no mischief to them, they were allowed to proceed. This was unwise. They promptly got off the line on which we were advancing, and as soon as the small advanced party with me were level with the point where the guide had stood, they fired straight into the thick of us. One sepoy just behind me was killed, and, needless to say, not a sight was ever again obtained of these two wayfarers whom we let off so easily. Such are Waziri methods.

Once on the top of the hill, where we stood (as indeed we have stood on many hills) with the serene consciousness that no European had ever stood there before (nor since, probably), we had all before us that the most enthusiastic surveyor could desire—a vast expanse of broken country, more highland than plateau, stretching away westward beyond the valleys of Shawál and Birmal, which lay at our feet on the western slopes of Shuidar, filled in with most delightful "points," all asking in that clear summer morning to have their portraits taken at the end of the theodolite wires. It was such a scene as is only to be obtained in such a conformation of hill and valley, and in such an atmosphere. We lost no time in getting into action, and, knowing that we had to be back in the main camp that night, observations were taken and recorded with a rapidity that only stress of circumstances can justify. Nor were they uninterrupted, for in the middle of a round Hall gently touched me on the shoulder, and asked me to direct my observations back for an instant to the way we had come.

Nothing much was observable to the naked eye, but a little searching with the telescope detected swarming numbers of evil-looking bandits making their way through bush and dell to the cliffs that overhung that narrow part of the valley to which I have referred. Clearly they were laying a very neat ambush for our return in a very well-selected position. But one of the great advantages of such a command as the Shuidar peak gave was that of a comprehensive view of the whole position below. As in a map, we could not only see how the people collected at the fires of last night had worked their way to the gorge, but how it might be possible for us to work our own way to yet another position behind and above that gorge, which might make an effective repartee to their proposed ambush.

It was, in fact, a game that both could play, and we accordingly set to work to play our share of it. A keen and most energetic young subaltern of the 5th P.I. was at once despatched with a picked company of "jawans" to outmanœuvre the ambuscade, and we finished our observations in peace. Then we packed up the instruments and descended the hill, past our night's camp, with just enough celerity to keep pace with the probable progress of our flanking party.

Meanwhile the brilliant morning had clouded up into a threatening day. Deep, heavy thunderclouds were overhead, and there was an ominous muttering of thunder in the air. At the foot of the steep declivity of the hill we mounted our horses, and, making the party as compact as possible, with a strong rear-guard, we trekked straight down the nullah for the gorge. Not a soul was to be seen, nor was a sound heard, until we were well in the middle of it, and then—shall I ever forget the awful din that arose? The thunderstorm burst just as the ambuscade began to play on to us, and the re-echoing rattle of musketry jerked back and forward from cliff to cliff, with the condensed din of thunderclaps immediately overhead, was as if a special compartment of "jehannum" had been opened up for the benefit of those unbelievers who had disturbed the sanctity of Sheikh Haidar's mountain rest. I was badly mounted. My horse was flighty and frightened (never, my young friends on the frontier, commit yourselves to this silliest of all silly positions—a seat on an unsteady horse in action), and it was difficult to take notes; but as far as I can remember the military combination arranged by Hall and carried out by his subaltern came off almost to a second.

It isn't often that such combinations are such a complete success. Added to the din of thunder and of rifle there soon arose the war cry of the Sikhs as they descended on the unhappy Waziri from behind. It was soon over. No frontier tribespeople can stand being taken in the rear. Like hares they bolted, and like hares they were hunted through the jungle till they had lost about thirty of their number. Such was the end of that little fight, and although the rear-guard all the way back had a difficult time, until they again resorted to the artifice of an ambuscade to catch the enemy pressing up too closely on the column, no casualties occurred, and we returned with the honours of war and a fair bag of miscellaneous weapons of ancient make, as well as a good survey record.

I may here add that had the Waziris of 1881 been armed as the Afridis of 1898 were armed, neither advance up that valley nor retirement down it would have been possible. Times have changed, and it is no longer of any use to refer back to the records or experiences of twenty years ago in support of a well-worn system of frontier administration, which was based on the comparative facility with which raids and risings could be repressed by military demonstrations on a small scale. When the Waziris meet us with our own weapons they will be adversaries quite as awkward to deal with as the Afridis. But in those days it was not in their power to make much impression on such a well-organised force as invaded their country. The southern advance towards Kaniguram did indeed experience some desultory hill fighting, which always terminated in the scattering of the tribespeople, but they were able to effect little in the shape of a wholesome military thrashing. Villages (which can be rebuilt in a week) were destroyed in a few hours. Towers were blown up here and there, and the cave strongholds were purified and disinfected with gunpowder. Obviously *they* could not be blown up, but the contents were blown out of them, including such a myriad host of fleas that their awful slaughter found a place in despatches! But Mushaki still wandered over the hills, and failed to come in till the campaign had done its work.

The south, like the north, was a fine field for the surveyor, and Gerald Martin was busy with theodolite and plane table. The sacred head of Pirghal was gently scratched by the British surveyor, even as was the ziarat of Sheikh Haidar. Between the two the foundation was laid of a most useful network of triangulation spreading over Eastern Afghanistan, which served the purposes of those nameless native explorers who, under one pretext or another, find a useful vocation in unmapped countries for years afterwards.

Turning to the northern column again, the retirement from Rasmak was made the opportunity for a reconnaissance down a brand new route that nobody had as yet ever looked into. Enough was known to justify the venture, but no European had seen a yard of it. This was the Shakdu passage out of the country, following a nullah of that name which rapidly broadened into a respectable valley. It was more than respectable, it was a lovely valley, hedged in by steep rolling downs, scarped here and there into cliffs, and rent and twisted by rain-cut nullahs which seamed their ruddy spurs. There were rows of well-grown, rounded ilex trees and feathery willows, clean, clear, inviting pools in the busy stream, and the usual impediment of aggravating boulders, amongst which the choice lay between breaking your own legs or your horse's. The beauty of the scenery was tempered by the exceeding roughness of the route, and consequently the day's march was usually short as to distance, and long as to reckoning. It is extraordinary how even the best-regulated mind will succumb to the temptation of misreckoning the distance when the road is bad and the day is hot, and breakfast is at the end of the day's march. If it hadn't been for the inexorable plane tabler, who admitted of no contradiction, we should have had an estimate of the length of that succession of marches down the Shakdu, based on the conclusions of officers of the staff (both those who could write P.S.C. after their name and those who could not) which would have carried us far out into the open plains of India instead of to the edge of the eternal hills. And the last march out of those hills was the worst.

The hot weather was well advanced ere we emerged from the Shakdu and made for the frontier station of Bannu. It was deemed advisable that part of the force should push on by a double march to a little frontier post on the high-road to Bannu which would hardly accommodate the entire brigade. So that smartest of smart Bengal Cavalry regiments, the 18th Lancers, was sent ahead; and I rode with it. We reached the usual halting-place which terminated the first half of the double march whilst there was still some pretence, not exactly of coolness, but of the modified heat of night in the air. Under a stony bank a patch of shade about as big as a large tablecloth was still lingering. There was water trickling somewhere around the base of the sun-baked boulders of the stream bed; and it could be scooped out sufficiently to give the horses a drink; but the white-hot sky had not the vestige of a cloud in it, and it reflected back the glare from the white-hot plains of sand and "put" which stretched away to Janimela with malignant intensity. So we sat down and enjoyed that refreshing meal called "chotahazri." It will be an English institution some day, and it will take the place of the heavy meal which renders the morning hours of office life a burden. I have found that it takes a large measure of hard experience to teach one the tricks of a campaign; but I *had* learnt that it is most unwise to drink freely in the early hours of a hot day, with the day's work as yet incomplete. This is a matter of which the native of India takes but little heed. As soon as ever he is thirsty he will (as the British soldier also will), if unrestrained, fill himself up with any drink that is handy. Not being constructed with that apparatus which the camel is generally supposed to possess, whereby superfluous liquid can be stowed away for a convenient season, the water swallowed by the man very soon disappears through the pores of his skin, and the process of becoming thirsty again seems to become intensified with the process of perspiration. And it is a curious fact that this sort of thirst seems even more fatal than that gradual drying-up process which has not the chance of being arrested at its commencement. At any rate, it is a fact that if you do not drink early in the day more than enough to moisten your lips and tongue you will not feel the craving of thirst until the slanting rays of the declining sun warn you that you may safely indulge in a "long" drink.

Never have I seen this so forcibly illustrated as during that May morning's march from the mouth of the Shakdu pass to the station of Janimela. We rode slowly in the scorching sun over the glaring sand and "put." "Put" is an alluvial formation of fine clay, occasionally mixed with sand, which spreads in wide areas over the Punjab and Baluch flats, hard and firm and level and undecorated with vegetation, and infinitely uninteresting so long as the sun shines and its smooth shiny surface is dry. But when the rain descends and washes the top layer for an inch deep or so into a greasy, clinging form of mud, then the interest of it lies in its exceeding slipperiness. No camel can move with its soft padded feet over wet "put." The construction of the camel is not adapted to a slimy surface. He is often ruptured if his foothold fails him. Having been originally built for sand navigation, the ship of the desert easily founders on slippery clay.

But it is easy and pleasant enough to ride over "put" when the sun bakes it to the consistency of a smooth brick floor, and the passing winds strew a few sand-drifts over the surface. The road from the Shakdu defile to the frontier outpost was delightfully easy after the weary struggle amongst stones and boulders. But soon a fine pungent dust arose from under the horses' hoofs, and the sun and the glare were the summer sunshine and glare of the frontier; and I know none like it. In an hour or so thirst began to tell on the sepoy who had not taken the precaution to start "dry," and as the day wore on, and hour after hour was spent on that seemingly interminable road, with nothing but a far-off vision of a white-walled station shining like a spark of light in the distance, one after another began to fall out parched and shrivelled with a thirst that was intolerable; but which was, after all, only the thirst of a few hours. When the march came to an end, mules with "pukkals," or leather bags of water, were sent back along the road quickly for the relief of the thirst victims, and most of them were brought in. Nevertheless lives were lost that day; and I began to understand the weird frontier tales that I had heard about men being literally shrivelled up in detachments on the march between points on the frontier, at any of which water was to be had in plenty. I only really found out how thirsty I was by the measure of tepid salt water which I drank after reaching Janimela, and the sensations experienced in the effort to relieve that thirst were most disappointing. Once on the drink, there seemed to be no resting and no stay to it. One drank till one had to sit down, and then drank till it was necessary to stand up again—and all to no purpose. The thirst remained.

The Waziri expedition of 1881 was a satisfactory little campaign, judged by the standard of its results. The surveyors were jubilant; and the Waziris gave no trouble for years afterwards. It was not until a boundary was assigned between themselves and Afghanistan that they rose again; and this next rising was signalised by an attack so desperate, and so well planned, as very nearly to sweep a British brigade off its camping ground. But this is another story, and belongs to a later date. In 1881 they made their show of resistance, but it was a faint-hearted show. Still, they did fight, and casualties occurred, and the hardships of the campaign told so severely on the British troops engaged that it hardly deserved to sink into the complete official oblivion which has shrouded it.

To surveyors it was a godsend. Thenceforward well-trained native workmen were pushed out beyond the Waziri hills (across which no road leads to the Afghan plateau) armed with such data as we had culled from the heights of Shuidar and Pirghal; and with this in their hands, travelling as physicians, or pundits, or itinerant merchants, they went in quest of further information, and usually obtained what they sought.

The wide cultivated camp formed by the valley of the Tochi to the north of Waziristan, as well as the more restricted valley of the Gomul to the south, are both of them high-roads to Ghazni. They figure in history, although no modern force has ever made use of either. Tradition, which seems to be supported by material evidence in the shape of ancient roadways and camps, points to the former as the route sometimes selected by that arch-raider of the Indian frontier, Mahmud of Ghazni, early in the eleventh century, who is said to have swept down with hordes of irregular cavalry through the band of hills which heads the Tochi valley with a rapidity that seems almost incredible in these days, and to have laid waste the Indus valley from Bannu to Multan. Between Multan and Gujrat he made use of desert routes which no modern general would dream of adopting, and he paid heavily for his rashness. So that Mahmud of Ghazni, successful as he was, must not be quoted as a model military pioneer for frontier expeditions.

The Gomul route is to this day the great trade route along which the picturesque Povindah khafila makes its crooked way from Ghazni to India. The Povindahs are a Ghilzai people who are terribly blackmailed by the Waziris, along the edge of whose territory they trail their strings of camels in the autumn, bringing down their store of fruit and skins and Bokhara cloths for disposal either in the frontier markets or in the plains of India. They travel far, leaving their wives and children camped on the border, after they have brought them down the pass perched in picturesque disorder upon the top of their gigantic camels; and with them they also leave their weapons in the hands of the first civil authority whom they encounter within British limits. Having disposed of wives and weapons, they lay themselves out for a pleasant winter tour in the plains, not unfrequently reaching Madras in the course of their wanderings; and not unfrequently terrorising the peaceful inhabitants of remoter villages into making a deal by means which are not recognised as lawful in the civil courts. They are, in fact, in many districts a most profound nuisance. Yet they are built of splendid material, and I should doubt whether in any city of Europe such magnificent specimens of humanity are to be found as you may jostle against any winter day in the bazaar at Dera Ismail Khan.

With the end of the Waziri campaign of 1881 came the first good chance of exploiting certain unknown byways into the heart of Afghanistan; and many and exciting were the adventures that befell the plucky native explorers who made their way about them. One explorer disguised himself so excellently well, that on arriving at an unexpected point of the frontier, our own local police positively declined to recognise him as anything but the foreigner he had pretended to be. His indignation with the police led to a scrimmage, and landed him in a frontier jail, from whence he was extracted with the loss of some important records.

Not least amongst those adventurous surveyors who, having made themselves intimately acquainted with the manners and methods of the border people and established a personal friendship with some of the local khans, could safely venture across the border line, was one of my European assistants, Mr. W. McNair. McNair possessed the rare faculty of commanding the confidence of natives. He was not a specially good linguist, but he understood local idiosyncrasies. He could make three or four rupees as useful as three or four hundred would be in the hands of a more clumsy negotiator. He would set up an old slipper with a four anna bit balanced on the toe as a handsome prize for the best spear at the game of "neza bazi," or tent pegging; and it was a sight to see some of the wild border horsemen, with an eighteen-foot spear and the swoop of an eagle, speed down the course for the four anna reward. There was no mistake about style. The spear which was flashing in the sun six feet above the head when the first shout to Allah went up was as level as a streak of sunlit water twenty yards before it dropped to the strike; and the pace was all that the long-limbed Waziri steed could make it.

A great friendship existed between McNair and one Mani Khan, a well-known Darwesh Khel chief of gigantic stature, every square foot of whose body was scarred with a wound; and who was, I believe, regarded with much suspicion by the local political officials. But Mani Khan stood true to his engagements to McNair, and safeguarded him through many a day's ride over the border. Strict orders had been issued that on no account was any European officer or assistant to sleep on the wrong side of the frontier line. This restriction involved rising early and late taking rest, and many a long hard ride over rough country to reach a commanding peak for the plane table, whence it might be possible to see into the valleys that lay hidden behind the outer ridges and minor spurs of the Sulimani hills; but in this way enormous areas of frontier geography were reduced to mapping, and hardly a footpath or goat-track was left unrecorded.

It may seem a little surprising that a chief of undoubted authority amongst his own people should so readily give his country away as a prey to the surveyor with his compass and plane table; but so far as my experience goes, the fierce objection which is supposed to exist in the minds of frontier tribespeople to the lifting of their "purdah," or veil, is one which is very readily overcome with a little judicious management. Only the best educated amongst our frontier friends (such as the Afghan sirdars for instance) know what a map really means. The ordinary folk are, as a rule, not only quite ready to part with their information, but very often keenly anxious to give it. Many a time have I been astonished at the accuracy with which a local herdsman or shepherd, taken from his ordinary day's work to show the way to the top of a high mountain, and, when there, asked to point out positions and places of importance round the horizon, will tell all he knows. He will frequently invent a name if he doesn't know one; and he will enlarge on the importance of his own village and clan in a way which tends to fill our gazetteers with most erroneous figures; but for all that, there is a good balance of sound information at the end of the day's reckoning; and very much more of it than would be obtainable from the mouth of the ordinary English village clodhopper.

As for objecting to any process of survey, he naturally leaves that to his betters, being infinitely more concerned in getting his rupee safely stowed away in the end of his kamarband than in lifting any "purdah" whatsoever. With regard to offers of assistance and promises of safeguard there was no difficulty whatever in obtaining them, provided the explorer (European or native) were known to the people concerned. Shy of a stranger, the frontier tribesman is generally ready to fraternise on terms of good fellowship with anyone who will associate with him. Another assistant of mine disguised himself as a shikari, or native hunter, and accompanied other shikaris right into the heart of that most difficult country which overlooks the Afridi Ṭirah, some years before any campaigning in that country was dreamt of. His experiences were most amusing, but he was never inclined to repeat them. He lived in dens and caves for the most part, and the caves possessed more than human occupants. He could not undress, and he could not wash. He lived with the people, and as one of them. He took his plane table and surveyed boldly till he was shot at by an alien clan. Then he returned, with a most useful contribution to our frontier geography. This stood us in good stead afterwards when we visited the Afridi country under other auspices.

That is the way in which most of the rough places on the frontier were made plain (in maps), and those years of searching for the byways of the frontier, whilst, under more systematic and regular forms of procedure, the district of Kohat was being mapped, were amongst the most entertaining of my life. Some of the remoter corners of the Kohat district were none so peacefully settled in those days that the survey of them could be carried out without an occasional *mauvais quart d'heure* of anxiety; but on the whole it was, and is, astonishing how these Pathan districts of the plains (for there are many millions of Pathans who are subjects of the Queen) are under the grip of the political authorities who administer them—how well ordered, how well governed, and how generally contented they are.

CHAPTER IV.

THE TAKHT-I-SULIMAN

The first ascent of the Takht-i-Suliman—The Sulimani mountains—Kaisargarh peak—Arrangements for expedition—Advance up the passes—Difficulties of route—Pazai—Unpromising situation—Crawling up the mountain by night—Defeat of the Kidarzai clan—Surveying on the top of the mountain—Return—Present state of Sherani frontier.

WAZIRISTAN, the land of the Waziris or Wazirs, constitutes a little independent mountain state, geographically apart from the larger mountain systems to the north and south. No roads through Waziristan lead to Afghanistan—at least no roads that are better than mere mountain footpaths. Of these there is no lack at any part of the frontier. North of Waziristan the Tochi valley affords a through route about which we know little; and south of it the Gomul valley leads to Ghazni; but at the back of Waziristan, between it and the plateau or highland of Afghanistan, there is a band of rough hills packed in more or less parallel lines across the path from India, which shuts off the head of the Tochi from the Ghazni plains, and forms the barrier through which the Gomul breaks ere it reaches the open stony plain of Wana. Wana lies to the south-west of Waziristan. From the Gomul river southward commences the true Sulimani mountain system, presenting a band of rugged, serrated ridges facing the Indus, and preserving the attitude of an impenetrable barrier (an attitude which is, after all, only a magnificent assumption) between the plains of the Indus and Afghanistan. The Sulimani mountains merge finally into the grand rough and tumble of those hills which are sacred to the Baluch tribes of Mari and Bugti, overlooking to the south the great sand bay of Kach Gandava, which is traversed by the railway between the Indus and the Bolán. The Sulimani hills

THE ROAD TO THE TAKHT-I-SULIMAN

are rugged, barren, and unprofitable as to their outer or Indus ridges (which run north and south parallel to the Indus, and throw out no important spurs), where the sun-cracked walls of conglomerate and hard-baked mud or clay are objectionable to climb over, and unattractive in appearance. It takes distance to veil them with enchantment, and a good deal of distance is necessary. In amongst them are narrow little valleys, where an occasional trickle of briny fluid, meandering between white, saline-edged banks fringed with tamarisk (also permeated with a white powder of salty dust) constitutes the local water supply. At intervals, however, the mighty rush of the combined streams which drain the uplands beyond, and west of, the Sulimani crests breaks clean through the rocky walls, and swirls into the plains, making gates for itself through ridges which it does not take the trouble to turn.

It is along the banks of these rivers, wide and overfull of boulders near the plains, but narrowing into gorges of inconceivable tightness where the main ridges are intersected, that access to the highlands lies. There are many of these staircases, and they occur at fairly regular intervals all down the line of the frontier between the Gomul and the Peshin railway. Taking them "by and large" they are hopelessly impracticable as military lines of communication between the plateau and the plains; and even where they may be made to afford a temporary right of way to a small force in dry weather, it is only at the expense of large outlay on road making, and by grace of the goodwill of those people who inhabit the hills wherein they run their crooked course, that they can be so utilised.

Mightiest of all the Sulimani mountains is the one which is called Solomon's Throne. It may be seen on the western horizon from Dera Ismail Khan against the evening sky, a grey, flat-looking rampart rising from the lower line of mountains north and south of it, slightly depressed or saddle-backed in the middle, but culminating in a very well-defined peak at its northern extremity. Such is the appearance of the Takht-i-Suliman from afar. The actual "takht," or throne, from whence Solomon is supposed to have cast a last look over India as he conveyed a dusky Indian bride away to Jerusalem (I suppose it was Jerusalem, but tradition does not say), is not on the top of the mountain at all. It is a ziarat, or shrine, situated on a ledge some distance below the crest on the southernmost bluff of the mountain. It is difficult to approach by reason of the steepness of the cliffs and scarps which surround it. It is, nevertheless, annually visited by thousands of pilgrims, both Hindu and Mahomedan, who thus acquire a sort of sanctity; though what the nature of the saving grace may be which is thus appropriated by both it is hard to understand.

The highest peak of the mountain overlooks its northern precipices, and is known as Kaisargarh. This magnificent peak is 11,300 feet above sea, a height which places it in a position of predominance over all other frontier peaks between Sakarám, on the Safed-Koh, which is 16,000, and Zerghun (near Quetta), which is 11,750. The frontier people generally know the whole mountain as Kaisargarh; Europeans still call it Takht-i-Suliman.

Up to the year of grace 1883 no European had ever been seen on the giant Takht. Naturally it was an object of great speculative interest to those who abhor a map-vacuum. But the way to it was as much a matter of speculation as were its possibilities when one got there. It was certain that no one could possibly ascend that mountain without the goodwill of the particular clan of frontier robbers who held it; and it was equally certain that there was no goodwill to draw upon.

But in 1881 one of those frontier junctures occurred which opened up an unexpected way, and for the first time in history did there appear to be a prospect of reaching that mountain. All this part of the frontier belongs to the Sheranis, a truculent tribe of several clans which never fails to give trouble when a reasonable opportunity presents itself. They had been giving trouble for a long time; indeed, the trouble had grown chronic, and the measure termed "blockading" by frontier officials had been put in force against them. Blockading is a species of boycotting, and as none of these frontier people can possibly live without communication with the plains, it is usually effective. In this particular case it was only effective as regards certain of the Sherani clans; and these, naturally, were the clans nearest the border. Those more remote still swaggered in confidence about their native hills and declined to "come in"—even partially, as it were. So there was nothing for it but to go to them, and argue the question out with the usual logic of force. The Kidarzais were, on this occasion, the particular clan that declined all overtures which might lead to promises of amendment.

Thus in November, 1883, was set on foot the whole paraphernalia of a frontier expedition on a small scale. It was to be a survey excursion supported by an escort; and it was to be made dependent on the assent of the friendly Sheranis. No European troops took part in it, the escort consisting of three native regiments and two guns. Then, with much difficulty and adroit management on the part of the Deputy-Commissioner of Dera Ismail Khan (Mr. Thorburn) was the serious business of collecting transport accomplished. The Nasirs (a tribe of Ghilzais who take great share in the Povindah traffic between Afghanistan and India) were finally persuaded to hire out certain of their camels. They were she camels not at that season engaged in the ordinary khafila traffic of the border. They were at any rate hill-bred camels, and so far were better than camels bred in the plains, and they were more to be relied on than the bullock transport of the Sheranis, which might have failed under critical circumstances. There were drawbacks, however, to this class of transport, as we shall see later on.

It may seem a curious fact to the uninitiated that the great bugbear of all frontier expeditions should be dried straw. Huge bales of dried and chopped straw have (or had in those days) to be conveyed with any frontier force in sufficient quantity to provide fodder for all the four-legged contingent belonging to it. This dried straw is called "bhusa," and it is very frequently, in times of drought when grass fails, all the fodder available. It may be doubted, in some cases, whether preliminary training would not enable animals who are accustomed to eat many pounds of this daily to do with very much less on service. The Baluch raider manages to dispense with it altogether; that is to say, he did without it in the days when he raided. I have been told by many a Baluch horseman that grain is the best food for a horse in hard work; and I have never borrowed a Baluch mount for a hard day's ride without the stipulation that I was to give the horse nothing whatever to eat till the day's work was done, and never let him drink without giving him a gallop afterwards. Times have changed since the survey party visited the Takht-i-Suliman, and bhusa now is specially packed, and takes not one quarter of the room it used to take. Patent substitutes will probably soon rout it altogether. In 1883, however, stacks of bhusa had to be carried, and a small brigade of camels was required to carry it. Grass we might find in the higher valleys on the northern slopes of the Takht; but times had been bad, and there had been long drought, so that it was impossible to depend upon it. After an amount of tribal negotiation which would have justified an extensive campaign, the military caravan was set in motion; and it crooked its way along through the tamarisk-covered flats that intervened between Dera Ismail Khan and the frontier hills in the early days of November. The expedition was under the command of General Kennedy, C.B., and we had with us many distinguished frontier officers, all anxious to scale the Takht.

By degrees we worked our way off the alluvial formations of the Indus, and leaving behind the scanty wheat and pulse crops which made a green patch around the mud-coloured villages, we stepped on to the stony "dasht" which ramps to the foot-hills of the frontier. I say "by degrees" because it took some time for the caravan to move over the edge; but the edge itself was definite enough. It is one of the most curious features of the frontier, this sudden exchange from soft silted flats intersected by deep irrigation cuts and channels, to the first gentle stone-strewn slopes of the hills, spreading like a glacier from the rocks to the plains. This dividing line is the old Sikh frontier of the Punjab, and it is also (generally) our frontier to this day—not the frontier of Afghanistan, but the frontier of those independent tribes who lie between us and Afghanistan. The Sikhs knew what they were about when they chose it. It may be unscientific, but it is at least practical. All the cultivation was theirs. All the rocks and the stones and the crooked hills were Pathan or Afghan—the property of anyone who cared to claim them. All over this stone-covered glacis, or "dasht," there is a scanty vegetable growth which takes the shape of thin tufts of grass, and of many-tinted flowers in spring—tulips, irises, and the like; and

THE DABARRAH ROCK

on the Afghan highlands these "dashts," which spread in fans of talus from the adjoining hills, are covered with wormwood scrub. At a distance all this looks very pretty, and gives a delusive effect of green abundance.

Slowly into the depths of the hills we crawled, and were soon surrounded by conglomerate cliffs in which masses of boulders were distributed as in a gigantic mud pie, and which, from its excessive hardness, always proves to be most fatally obstructive to the engineer. As we moved further into the hills these recent "Siwalik" beds gave way to older formations; and the bed of the nullah which we followed narrowed up towards the gates in the central range through which we were to follow it. One or two marches are usually necessary to reach the craggy gorges of this central chain, where limestone becomes predominant, and where one passes betwixt such walls of solid shining rock as to cause a lasting wonderment as to how they possibly came to be so fashioned. Huge, white-sided, slippery boulders bestrewed the narrow waterway. In and out amongst them, occasionally dropping or rising a few feet where artificial ramps were introduced, the military khafila struggled along. Up above, for one thousand feet on either hand, were the creased and cracked sides of the limestone gates of these extraordinary hills, narrowing in perspective at top to a three-cornered patch of blue sky.

Two days' marching up the nullah bed had brought us to the neck of the Zao pass, and here at its upper end we found ourselves face to face with the far-famed Dabarrah rock. It was far-famed because, some seventy or eighty years before, this Zao pass was reckoned one of the safest routes between India and High Asia; but a vast square mass of limestone, from forty to fifty feet thick, had fallen from the cliffs above, and had jammed itself into the narrow way, setting a permanent bar to Povindah enterprise in this direction (as it seemed) for ever. We knew about it beforehand, because the pass, so far, had been reconnoitred by a couple of venturesome officers a year or so previously. In High Asia, as far, likely enough, as Bokhara, they also knew all about it, because it was a solid and permanent hindrance to trade; so that if we could only remove it, our "izzat" would be great, and the fame of it would spread over very far regions. But could we do it? Our political guide and counsellor sat on the top and reckoned up the situation, and the Chief of the Staff sat with him. We had no dynamite, no gun-cotton, no sappers, no pioneers (except the stray colonel of a pioneer regiment, who would not be denied a share in the excursion), and there were the camels (eleven hundred of them, five hundred carrying "bhusa") coming on, not exactly apace, but crawling up and down steep places and progressing by a few yards at a time; as is the manner of Povindah camels, who recognise difficulties in the road, never shirk them, but just take their time over them. We had a limited amount of gunpowder, however, and with this a few of the most awkward corners of the rock were finally dispersed. Then an incipient hollowing of the hillside opposite the rock was further developed, and the road ramped, and finally a narrow passage about four and a half feet wide was fashioned out—a veritable needle's-eye through which the camels had *got* to go; and they did it. Some hundreds of them were passed through at night by moonlight, Nasir drivers and sepoys alike working like slaves at loading, unloading, and heaving camels up the ramp. It took twenty-six hours of hard labour to get the whole khafila to the upper side of that ugly defile; and then, when Nasir drivers and sepoys were equally busy, the disadvantages of the Povindah camel methods became apparent. The ordinary plains camel of India is accustomed to move in single file. He is hooked by the nose to the tail of his predecessor, and one man is sufficient to conduct twenty camels in this fashion without fear of any breaking away. But the Nasir and the Suliman Khel, and other Povindah traders, drive their camels instead of leading them. Everyone knows that the average intelligence of the camel is not of a high order, and it is certainly a marvel if, when left to himself, he does not do the wrong thing. The object, no doubt, of letting camels go free is that each individual may be unhampered in a tight place; but the result is that, collectively, they pack themselves into a hopeless mass in narrow roads, which it takes hours to unravel and pull out into a string again. After clearing the gorge they had thus packed themselves with their usual pertinacity on this occasion, and it was not until five days of our precious fifteen days' rations had been consumed, whilst we still had all our work before us, that we cleared that infernal rock, and stepped into high altitudes. Then we turned the northern flank of the Takht-i-Suliman, and crept along southward in the shadow of its mighty cliffs and buttresses. That awful defile had now cut us clean away from British territory, and there was nothing for it but to face our work, and face it quickly. Ten days might bring rain, and the effect of a torrent down that pass was one of those things that we did not care to discuss.

We were making for a spring called Pazai. No one had seen it, but reliable information had been furnished that somewhere under the northern spurs of the mountain a fresh-water spring was to be found that would keep one half of the force alive whilst the other went up the hill. I fancy there must have been something more than a *mauvais quart d'heure* for the adventurous political officer who guided us from the next night's camp. That camp was in a deep basin of the hills immediately below the northern peak of the Takht (the Kaisargarh), which pierced the thin air 6,000 feet above us like "the point of a rusty lance," and there was water enough and to spare in the rushing, swirling stream of the Draband, which here dashed headlong through a mighty rift in the mountain, and washed down a crooked course to the plains of India. But next day we left the Draband and started on a quest for Pazai (or the "Woman's Nose") with some misgivings as to the value of the information we had received about its locality.

We pushed along parallel to the main ridge, following the dry course of an upper Draband affluent towards its head, and then wound and twisted into a torrent bed which led straight towards the unscaleable cliffs. We were now somewhere opposite the point which report denoted to be the high-road up the mountain. On all sides of us, except to the west, were the giant buttresses of the great limestone mass, reaching out to us here and there in rugged spurs, but offering about as much chance of ascent as might have served the purpose of a squirrel.

And where was the water? A sowar had been sent to look

for it and had not returned, so we had to look for him. We soon came across his dead body, hacked out of all possibility of recognition. This was a gentle indication of the sort of reception that awaited us. Into a narrow cleft of the hills we slowly worked our trailing column, gradually gaining altitude as we went, until at last our guide's heart was gladdened with the sound of a small trickling rill, which betokened running water. Here the tight little valley opened out a bit, and into the small amphitheatre we crammed the entire caravan, fitting ourselves into vacant spaces like the bits of a child's puzzle, and satisfied that the water was enough for us all.

This, then, was Pazai. So far so good; but how about the road up the mountain? The summit, which showed a scarred line of cliffs without a break as far as one could see, might have been about two miles from us, and up a narrow knife-backed ridge, rising to 4,000 feet above the camp in that distance, was a crazy little track which the aborigines called a footpath.

Up to the foot of the precipitous cliff-wall it was known to be practicable, but the wall itself was only to be negotiated by means of a narrow cleft, into which (as we found afterwards) only one man might squeeze at a time, and only then with difficulty. And we knew very well what that single file of mountaineers might expect at the top. Six determined men, with a few big stones and the most elementary of firearms, could keep a whole army out of such a mountain staircase as that. I have seen many tight places (including Dargai), and they were all royal high-roads compared to the last steps up the Takht-i-Suliman.

Nor did our Kidarzai friends leave us long in doubt about their intentions. They shrieked their defiance down the wind, and sent a few boulders whizzing over the edge, which crashed like thunder as they sped their way through 4,500 feet of mountain descent. Our foes could not contain their delight! They whirled about in a wild Pathan ecstasy, glinting their swords and their long knives in the afternoon sun with such an abandonment of defiance that their mountain ballet came to be their own undoing. As for our few border retainers, the casual guides and the Nasir camel drivers, they didn't care to conceal their opinion that we were in a very tight place indeed. We had said we would go up the Takht, and up we had to go. And if we failed, and had also to retire down that unnatural and singularly nasty Dabarrah staircase, it was tolerably clear that there would not be many of us left to tell the tale of how we did it. So they sat about in truculent attitudes, and gave short answers to anxious questioners. They talked aloud and laughed, and generally aired those very objectionable manners which every native knows how to assume when he thinks the sahib is just a little bit off his "izzat"; but they did not actively commit themselves to any imprudence.

At night the long line of the mountain crest (so I was told) was lit up with log fires from end to end. I did not see them, as I was otherwise occupied, and perhaps it was as well that I did not. During that day I had been busy with the plane table as usual, and in the course of working out the topography of the lower hills I had marked, and fairly well fixed, a long irregular line of nullah or watercourse which drained away from the northern extremity of the mountain, where a tumbled mass of ancient landslip appeared in the distance to take off from its very crest, and to afford a rough sort of ramp right up to the flat line of summit. This nullah ran a general course parallel to the great mountain wall for four or five miles, catching here and there the drainage which swept in broad, scarred lines down the northern sides and slopes, and finally joined into the general entanglement of nullah beds and steep-sided ravines which lay in a network close to our camp below it. If one could make use of this line of ascent there was just a possibility of reaching the crest without passing through any such rat-trap as had been laid for us about the Pazai, and, once on the summit, the dancing line of figures which showed the glint of light on their weapons all along that distance, proved conclusively that there must be a tolerably direct line of communication skirting the edge to the gorge above us.

There is no way of disturbing Asiatics so effectually, when planted in a strong position, as appearing on their flank and threatening their rear. They cannot stand the prospect of being cut off from a safe line of retreat. A very small force moving round their flank is enough. They do not wait to count heads, and as at the Peiwar (and many another frontier fight), all advantages of position and defence are at once thrown away, and a fight, till then successfully carried on, is at once abandoned in a headlong rush to get away before the back door is closed. A turning movement is thus generally recognised as an integral part of any attack. Where it is omitted the results are often disastrous.

The nullah which I have described seemed to offer the chance of such a flank approach. At any rate our chief decided to accept it, and that night under a windy, half-starlit sky a little force of about four hundred men from the 1st Sikhs and 4th Punjab Infantry were silently gathered together in the deep nullah bed, prepared to make the attempt. It was a cheerless sort of night. Light gusts of wind passed overhead, and it was not always possible to see for more than a yard or two at a time. No guides were to be taken; no Sherani could be trusted, and there were no others who knew that country. The camp was asleep when about 2 a.m. we moved out with as little noise as possible, and stole into the mouth of that well-marked nullah. There was no great difficulty at first. The rush of many torrents had swept a broad, smooth way of sufficient width to allow of fairly comfortable movement, and the white floor of sand and clay, chequered with boulders, was unmistakable even in the gloom of a moonless night. But we could hardly hope for much of that sort of thing. A mile or so was all we expected, and all we got, and then we came to our first difficulty. We were now deep in a gorge from which a narrow line of sky alone was visible. Black crags and jagged rocks encompassed us, and we could see but a short way to where the black shadows closed in. Yet even then it was not pitch dark. It never is so on a starlit night, and the sky remained partially clear—clear enough to show that there was a parting of the ways. There were two nullahs instead of one, and there was nothing to choose between them for size. We sat down, and the gallant officers who commanded that party discussed the position.

The big mountain loomed up on our left at a little distance, and to our left also there branched off a wide, smooth-looking line of nullah, which invited our attention and our footsteps.

I consulted a volunteer guide, who had come from the ranks to assist me (an Afridi, if I remember rightly), and I asked him what he thought of it. "Sahib," said he, "I don't know the way a bit better than you do. You have got it laid down on your 'takhta.' But I do know this. The longest nullah must be the right-hand one, although it doesn't look it; and it is the longest nullah that we have to follow. The left-hand nullah can only spring from the walls of the mountain." Then it occurred to me that I had observed certain trees (junipers) near the slopes of that rock avalanche which headed the nullah, and that if we pushed on for half a mile or so more we should either see them above us against the sky-line or we should be on the wrong track. So we blindly pushed our weary way along the right-hand nullah, and we stumbled over big boulders and shinned ourselves against fallen timber, crawling here and gaining a few steps of comparative smoothness there, till above us on the sky-line I saw those blessed trees, black and weird against the sky, but none the less welcome for their ghostly appearance. After that it was but a weary drag for hours over stones and shelving banks, and the collected rubbish of a hill torrent near its beginnings, and right glad was I when the wan white light of dawn crossed the eastern sky, and the hills came out of the night, and the shiver of the early breeze put morning's life into the air again. I looked around then, and I found that the party had scattered; we were out of the head of the nullah, crawling up the last of the slopes to the crest of the mountain. There was a pale green vegetation on the broken slopes, and the smell of pines was about, and the dampness of a dew which spoke of altitude. We were, in fact, high enough to look over the grey flats of Afghanistan to the west. Low-lying mists hid the level spaces, and the sharp corners of successive lines of distant hills stood up above the misty floor—silhouetted in pale and yet paler grey as distance toned them down against the white light which tinged the western sky at dawn. Some of the Sikhs were crawling up in little groups above me, and my place as guide had been taken.

I shall never forget the satisfaction which warmed my heart as I pulled my poshteen close around me when I found that we were really on the crest, and must be close on to the farthest Sherani picket whose position I had identified the day before.

Then were the smiling and grimy Sikhs and Pathans pulled together for the capture of the post, and military dispositions were made. One track was found which led along the very edge of the mountain crest, northwards to the position above our camp. Another, and apparently a better one, was below us on our right as we faced northwards, and evidently led from the central fastnesses of the mountain down to the plains somewhere (we couldn't tell where) southward. The Sherani position was carefully stalked; every possible effort was to be made to suppress firing, and as we silently closed in upon the picket fires we became aware that they had been abandoned during the night. This was a great find. It seemed more than probable that the whole line of them would be found abandoned. The war-dance of the day before had, likely enough, been well rounded off with a dinner at the main position, and the dinner concluded with a good comfortable sleep at headquarters, instead of on the gusty, wind-swept heights of the western ridge of the mountain. So the force was divided, half taking the line of the crest and half following the better-defined track below, both moving silently on to the main position above that awful approach which was to be forced this day, at 10 a.m., from below. We now moved pretty rapidly—picket after picket was found deserted, just the warm embers of a fire telling the tale of its occupation the evening before—and soon we, who were making our way along the western crest, lost sight of the party that was moving parallel to us on our right down in the central depths of the mountain.

We now found that the mountain had no flat top, but consisted of two parallel ridges running north and south, joined somewhere near the middle, but split apart by terrific gorges at the northern end. Nothing stopped our way—not a shot was fired—hardly a man spoke, when suddenly we lit on a curious scene. There was a break in the continuity of the ridge along which we had made our way so far. A declivity of some 300 or 400 feet yawned below us. It was precipitous, as if the ridge had been cleft in two; and it was wide. Five or six hundred yards away the ridge continued at the same elevation, but to reach the other side of that cleft involved some painful climbing. And deep down in the fork of this cleft was a busy crowd of Sherani folk, planting an abattis and raising earthworks, collecting stones and boulders, and making convenient little positions from which to plant their bullets with effect. They were all looking downward, craning their necks to see the first advance of those idiotic sahibs who thought they could walk up to the top of the Takht by the Pazai staircase; a crowd as of busy ants, if ants could be filled with an inflated pride at their own vast ingenuity, and with a whole gamut of Mussulman invective besides.

The sahibs were just beginning to walk up. Even as we got our first hurried glance at the position, the first shell came curving up into the mountain air, and burst above our heads in a pretty but ineffective shower. It was answered by a yell of derision from the Sheranis, and by yet another fiercer, louder yell from the Sikhs above them. They could be held no longer. It was impossible to get down to the enemy without tumbling on to his head, so it was best to let him take what he might get from where we stood on the heights above. One fierce volley right into the midst of them—one wild shriek of delight from the sepoys, and then ensued such a getting away from out of that cleft as I have never seen before, and never shall see again. It was as if hot water had been poured into the ants' nest. There was no waiting to see where the volley came from. The Kidarzai section of the Sheranis will remember that day. They are not a large clan, and they were all there. A few of the best and the bravest (including their chief Jumal) remained stretched on the ground where they had stood; and the rest in a scattered crowd rushed straight down the track beneath us to our right; where they suddenly became aware that a second detachment of our little force was making its way to meet them. The surprise was mutual. So completely did the rugged line of the western crest of the mountain intervene between us and that detachment that not a sound of our firing had reached them, and they were quite unaware that they were close on the head of the Pazai defile when the flying crowd bore down on them. Before they could come into effective action the crowd was scattered down the hillsides—anywhere and anyhow—like a herd of ibex they disappeared into the rifts and clefts of the hills. Yet there were some (as there always are a few on such occasions) who turned and found a way back again by a route that we knew not, and with their knives in their teeth, and their fingers clutching the projecting crags of the precipices above the Pazai, they climbed on to the heights where we had stood for that volley, and made for the small party that had been left on guard ere we descended to the Kidarzai position. But Bunny of the 1st Sikhs (who died in the Tochi valley not so long ago, with Fred Browne and other brave men, who were trapped in a manner which will be an eternal disgrace to the Mahomedan tribes of that borderland) easily held his own, and we were masters of the mountain ere half an hour had passed from the first shot fired. Very soon the head of the little column that was to carry out the direct attack showed itself over the edge of the staircase. Among the first to arrive was Mr. Thorburn, our political adviser and commissioner, who had so earnestly endeavoured to persuade the Kidarzais to "come in" with the rest of the Sherani tribe; and amongst the first of the slain whom he recognised was the chief Jumal, who had told him with grim significance at the frontier outpost that they should meet on the mountain, and nowhere else. It was thus that he kept his promise; and it was thus that his people learnt their lesson.

It was a hard lesson, we must all admit. About thirty brave men laid down their lives in learning it, and that is a large sum for a small clan to pay for the teaching. Like rats the rest of the Sheranis rounded on the beaten clan. They were always pests and robbers, they said. They never could be induced to listen to reason, and it was a most happy and blessed thing that they had been so severely punished, that they would not hold up their heads again for many a year to come. Nothing could exceed the delightful energy of our border friends in assisting us to find wood and water, and the wherewithal for camping. The Nasirs were as charmingly polite and attentive as a tailor whose bill has just been settled. Yet they are a brave race too, and a manly one, and their servility was but the outcome of a phase of human nature which is not always quite so naïvely expressed.

But this was but the preliminary for the work for which we had come. We had got our footing on the mountain without the loss of a man. There had been some few narrow shaves, as there always are. Daniel, bravest of all company leaders (who lost his life subsequently from being too brave at Chilas), had the sole of his boot shot off as he sat at breakfast, and a few other stray bullets nearly found billets which would have reduced our party, but no one was actually the worse for them. It now remained to reach the great peak—the Kaisargarh—the Pisgah of the frontier, from which all the land, parched, brown, and grey, was to be viewed afar off.

But the great peak was still many miles off, and a way to it had to be found. The rest of the day was spent in reconnoitring, and in collecting water and supplies for the trip. We now discovered what a strange wild mountain tract we had surmounted. So far from the top of the Takht being level and traversable there was hardly a practicable footpath about it. Two ten-mile-long, tumbled, limestone ridges lay parallel to each other at about one mile distance apart. Between them was a connecting link, where the interior slopes of the two ridges swept down to a depression about midway, whilst north and south of this central "Maidán" deep chasms rent the ridges apart, and split the mountain into sections. The flat part of the Maidán should have held rain water, but the exceptionally dry season had burnt it to the consistency of brick, and there was not, so far as we could discover, a drop of water to be obtained anywhere on the whole mountain, except by melting snow.

The masses of tumbled, nummulitic limestone blocks, which piled themselves into irregular confusion all over the summit, were interspersed here and there with soil sufficient to maintain a fairly vigorous forest growth. The chilghosa (or edible) pine spread its weird white branches abroad wherever it could gain foothold, and such economic value as the Takht possesses is derived from the collection of the nuts of this pine, which are gathered in autumn and taken to the markets of the plains. But there were many varieties of pines and (if I remember right) a few firs also to be seen in the clefts of the hillsides, and the general impression left was that of a yellow-green forest, encircling and binding together masses of grey-green rocks. The ziarat, which, with a few sticks and fluttering rags, represented the actual resting-place of the King of Israel, was on the eastern of the two ridges overlooking the plains of India; but as it was the plains of Afghanistan that we had come to see, and not the plains of India, we decided on fixing our trigonometrical stations on the western ridge, and went straight for the highest peak of the mountain — the Kaisargarh. That is to say, we went as straight as circumstances would admit, for the extraordinary mixture of deep waterways and fissures, combined with piles of broken and many-cornered rocks, rendered progress difficult for men on foot, and absolutely impossible for mules. At 1 p.m. next day we started with 250 armed and 250 unarmed sepoys as escort. The unarmed men carried water and provisions. Tents, clothes, even blankets and greatcoats had to be left behind. Five hours of painful climbing brought us to the Maidán, at the foot of the Kaisargarh peak. Here we made shift to spend the night in a wooden shanty, which had been left for our benefit by thè chilghosa gatherers. It was cold and cheerless work, in spite of the gigantic log fire which was kept up all night. Sleep inside was impossible for the smoke. Outside it was but a chequered process, divided between grilling and freezing. One member of the little party set himself alight, as in a fitful slumber he rolled himself gradually into the fire.

The ascent to the summit of the peak next day was not difficult, but it was long. It ended in a race for the top between the gallant Highlander (Colonel Maclean), who commanded the party, and a Punjab cavalry officer (Captain O'Mealy), whose long legs carried him up the rugged staircase with quite surprising facility. I forget who won it. I know I was a bad third, and I know that I was right glad when the round of observations was finished on that bleak and windy peak. All Afghanistan lay athwart us. It was such an opportunity as might never occur again, and the oppressive weight of that reflection chained me to the theodolite in spite of chattering teeth and numbed fingers. Forty thousand square miles of new country lay below within view, and hundreds of grey and crumpled hills appealed to one's sense of duty

VIEW FROM THE TAKHT-I-SULIMAN

and the instinct of the surveyor. I cannot say that the great rolling plains, intersected by interminable rows of jagged mountain, were attractive. There is always a fascination in looking down from great heights over new ground hitherto unseen and unmapped; but the monochrome of frontier landscape in winter, and the pale grey reflections in the windy sky answering back to the neutral tint of dusty plains, calls up no feeling of enchantment, especially when one is hungry, thirsty, and intensely cold. However, it was over at last, and the results of that morning's work lasted us for years until later frontier developments carried us farther afield, and added thousands of square miles west of the Takht-i-Suliman to the sphere of British influence in Baluchistan.

Not that we have ever reduced the Takht to a British mountain. It is just as we left it. No European, so far as I know, has ever since ascended the Kaisargarh peak, and the unkempt chilghosa gatherer may sit aloft there in the proud security of absolute independence. But we have gone beyond the Takht, and even on the very next hill westward (*i.e.* Afghanward) there is now established a little military station which overlooks the Pazai spring, and keeps watch on the Sherani back doors.

We came down from that peak conscious, at least, that the success of the expedition was assured. We had enjoyed that inestimable boon, clear weather, and we had seen all we went to see. So far it was good. Then followed another night in the woods with the pine smoke blackening us, and the snow melting down to nothing at all in the kettle. Remember that it takes thirteen inches of snow to make one inch of water. There was no water to wash, and next morning when we started back for Pazai the only trace of original colour of the man was in the furrows on our faces, washed out by the tears bred of the pungent pine-wood smoke. It was necessary to get back quickly, for yet another station had to be fixed and further observations taken therefrom in order to secure the triangulation. One station will not make a triangulation any more than two swallows will make a summer. And there were warning clouds coming up—clouds which left white patches on high places, and which gave us the strongest possible hint to be off. So we hustled back to the ridge above Pazai, and there, overlooking the camp below, another position was taken up, and another very satisfactory "shoot" was obtained to all that had been observed before. Other observations from elsewhere subsequently completed that network of fixings over the face of Eastern Afghanistan, which served as the basis for map-making. Map-making had, as a matter of fact, been going on all through the expedition. All that we could see from high places from day to day had been reduced to mapping by the native surveyors with the party.

Chief amongst them was the old warrior known as the Bozdar. He belonged to the Bozdar tribe, and years of survey training had hardly modified certain grim characteristics which envelope the Baluch character. He was a good surveyor and a better explorer. His nervous fingers, which could trace out the light lines of a topographical drawing with rapidity and clearness, could also, when occasion demanded, grip a stone and fling it with such unerring force and precision that, on one occasion, he saved the life of his chief by this truly Baluch method of counter attack. On the other hand, he could balance a small round shield with sufficient dexterity to allow of anyone else pelting him with stones at any range they pleased without any serious inconvenience to himself. I never was quite certain to what use he might not apply his plane table if occasion arose. On the way to the peak he had looked around with practised eye to see what might lie on the mountain tops or under the forest; and he had observed the curling smoke of a fire. This he pointed out at once as indication of Kidarzai occupation. His remarks on the subject were not well received; they were mistaken for nervousness on his part by the leader of the party, and he was warned that any further suggestions about a hidden enemy would lead to his being sent back again. His indignation at being mistaken was too deep for words. Had he not alone and single-handed made his way right through this Sherani country before—even to the very shores of the Afghan lake Abistada? Did he not reckon the Kidarzais as little better than kites and jackals? Was he to be told that he was afraid? He couldn't get over it, and thenceforward for days

I couldn't get a word out of him. But he did his work all the same, and he did it fairly well, only there was the grim ferocity of the half-tamed Baluch underlying it, and his topography, though correct, was savagely inartistic.

The descent from the peak was rapid enough. We were all glad enough when we had worked our way down into the Pazai camp, where we realised, if we had never done so before, what a luxury is cleanliness! No one, I fancy, was more relieved than our genial chief. We had been heavily handicapped at starting. The time was short, the weather was uncertain, the route was unknown, or rather known to be exceptionally difficult. We had no scientific road-makers with us (as we should have had), and we were dependent on the goodwill of a clan of drivers for our transport, who are about the most independent of all hill clansmen. How we were to face any position taken up by a determined foe was a problem that had to take care of itself. In short, it was quite a typical little frontier expedition, carried out on lines which suited the past well enough, but will never suit a future of accurate long-range rifles in the hands of expert tribespeople. It was thoroughly successful, and we loaded up for the return journey with light hearts.

The bhusa was mostly eaten up, and our impedimenta was no longer a difficulty. Provided we could get down the Zao defiles without rain there was nothing more to fear. And the fates were kind. It did not rain. A weather-worn and rather ragged little force marched out of the pass on to the flats of the Indus valley plains on December 5th, very well content with their experiences.

About the end of January the Lieut.-Governor of the Punjab held a Durbar at Dera Ismail Khan, at which all the sectional heads of the Sherani tribe were present. Metaphorically, the axe was buried, and the pipe went round. Abdullah Khan, the Nasir chief who brought his people and his camels to our aid, received a robe of honour—and he received a yet higher and more valued recognition, a recognition that at once lifted him above the level of the local khans and placed him on that official eminence which had long been the desire of his heart—he was allowed to sit in a chair.

Thus ended an expedition which is worth a passing record, as typical of scores of other frontier expeditions of the days that are passing. It soon lapsed into the historical obscurity which usually envelopes such episodes on our Indian frontier. I doubt if it ever ranked as military service. Being successful, it was unnoted in military annals, and so clean forgotten in the course of a few years that when the eastern ridge of the Takht-i-Suliman mountain was ascended some years afterwards by that gallant mountaineer Sir George White, most people thought it was the first time that the summit of the mountain had ever been trodden by a European. The Sheranis will trouble us no more, not because we then lifted the veil from their hills and villages, but because in the gradual development of our influence in Baluchistan the valley that lies beyond them, between them and Afghanistan—the valley of the Zhob—has been occupied by military posts, and their back doors are at our command.

Since the Takht expedition a road has been driven right through their country, connecting the Indus plains with the highlands beyond. It is not the road we followed then. It is one which even in those days was known to be a traversable road in exceptionally favourable seasons, and it had already been traversed, as a matter of fact, by that native surveyor, the Bozdar, whom I have mentioned as having pushed his exploration right across Afghanistan.

The Sheranis have ever been politically unimportant. The value of the excursion of 1881 lay in the insight which it afforded us of the districts lying beyond to the westward, then totally unknown, and the basis which it gave us for extending our surveys into Afghanistan. The moral effect of such expeditions is also to be reckoned. It is the same effect that a whipping has on a naughty child. The child will remain good until the whipping is forgotten (quite a long while sometimes), and this is the system of parental correction which has kept our borders for us since the days when we first acquired borders from the Sikhs.

I have often been asked why, if this excellent system of retributive blockades and expeditions answered so well during the last fifty years, we should not be content to apply it now?

So far as Sheranis are concerned, or any tribes south of the Sheranis who occupy our border, it probably might still answer for years to come were it necessary to apply it. Year by year these independent Pathan tribes south of the Gomul, and the Baluch people south of the Pathans, fall more and more under the political influence which governs Baluchistan. The occupation of the Zhob is checkmate to any comprehensive scheme of opposition to British supremacy on their part, and even the introduction of modern firearms of precision, whilst it would make the advance of a small force up such a villainous compound of defiles and stone walls as the Zao pass impracticable, would not save the tribespeople from a blockade which could now be applied on both sides of them, and which would soon starve them into submission. But *north* of the Gomul river we have to deal with very different conditions—conditions which demand careful consideration subsequently.

CHAPTER V.

THE RUSSO-AFGHAN BOUNDARY COMMISSION

What led to it—Our ignorance of the country—Constitution of Commission—Equipment—Route—Quetta in 1884—Nushki—The Helmund desert—The Helmund valley—Sistan—Western Afghanistan—Railway possibilities—Russian position on arrival near Herat—Surveying—Badghis—Persian transport—Mules and camels—Marmots, rats, and pigs—Turkman carpets and kibitkas—Panjdeh to Bala Murghab—Winter quarters.

THE next opportunity which presented itself of spreading abroad in order to compass the development of Asiatic geography was so far-reaching, and led to such unexpected results, that a few words are necessary by way of introduction.

About the end of February, 1884, when England was in difficulties in the Sudan, and her military resources much taxed, the Russian general, Komaroff, formally annexed Merve in the name of the Czar, after announcing to all whom it might concern that this movement was in accordance with the wishes of the people, and that the Merve chiefs had asked for annexation. This step greatly affected the strategical position of Russia in relation to India. The armies of Trans-Caspia and Turkestan were brought into direct touch with each other, and the way was at once prepared for the construction of that railway which, connecting Askabad, Merve, and Charjui, completed the power of rapid concentration on the Afghan frontier, and secured the commerce of Bokhara and Ferghana to Russia.

The movement southward of Russian troops in the direction of Herat impressed on the Government of England the necessity for demarcating a boundary on the north-west of Afghanistan which should definitely check any further advance; and negotiations were set on foot to reduce to practical reality that theoretical boundary which had been accepted by treaty between Lord Granville and the Russian Government in 1873 as the limit of the Amir's dominions in Turkestan between the Oxus and the Hari-Rud.

But the total absence of anything like exact geographical information about the regions in question rendered the definitions of that treaty nebulous and uncertain. It was, however, acknowledged by the Russian Ambassador, M. de Giers, in February, 1882, and again in April, 1883, to be a line connecting Khoje Sale (Khwaja Sala) with the Persian frontier at Sarrakhs. Khoje Sale had been mentioned in the treaty of 1873, and was therein defined as a "post" on the Oxus. Sarrakhs was a tolerably well-known Persian term on the frontiers of the Mashad district. The latter could be identified, but the meagre information which existed about the former could only have been derived from the records of Alexander Burnes in the early half of the century. It certainly appeared, however, as a fixed position in the map known as "Walker's Turkestan," which was the best map authority then existing. The original proposal for the delimitation of this line emanated from Russia. This proposal was now formally accepted by the British Government, and October 13th, 1884, was the date fixed for the meeting of the Boundary Commissioners at Sarrakhs.

On this understanding, Sir Peter Lumsden, as Chief Commissioner, with a staff of political officers, left England to make his way by Tehrán and Mashad to the frontiers of Afghan Turkestan, where he expected to meet an escort despatched from India with another political detachment, which was to join him there. It was clear, however, that it would be impossible for the Indian section of the Commission to reach the rendezvous before November, so the date of the general meeting between the English and Russian Commissions was fixed for November 7th.

It was under these conditions that I found myself attached to the Indian section of the Russo-Afghan Boundary Commission as chief survey officer; having been recalled from an expedition to the Zhob valley (the first expedition that reached Zhob) which was organised during that same autumn. The story of that boundary episode—an episode which nearly involved us in a war with Russia, and which opened up to us a vast field for geographical exploration—has never been fully told. It certainly cannot be fully told in one or two chapters of this book, wherein nothing more will be attempted than the narration of a few incidents sufficient to illustrate the nature of the work that was then accomplished, and what we found concerning the strategical relations existing between Herat and India.

It is worth while to consider what lay before us when we took the first plunge into the "dashts" and deserts that lie between Quetta and the Helmund river. We had to find our way across 400 miles of untraversed wilderness, commencing with the arid flats of Baluchistan lying south of the Helmund (much of which is absolute desert), concluding with the wide rolling scrub-covered "dashts," which stretch all the way from the Helmund river to Herat along the Perso-Afghan border, till we reached the Hari-Rud river and Herat. Here we should join hands with Sir Peter Lumsden. We then had to cross what we believed to be a high, broken, and difficult range of hills (the same hills which we call Paropamisus) till we struck into the Turkman country, watered by the Hari-Rud, the Murghab, and other rivers; where we trusted that the Russian contingent would be ready to meet us and conjointly take up the work of demarcation.

There was only one certainty about all this, and that was our ignorance of the country we had to pass through, and the whereabouts of the boundary we had to lay down. A mutual understanding about that boundary, its position in detail from end to end, could readily be arrived at by the high contracting parties in England and Russia, if maps in detail, attested by both sides, could be produced as a basis for an agreement. But there were no such maps. Of the nature of the approaches to Herat from the north, or the route connections between Herat and India, we had but the most shadowy conception. Russia was ahead of us in this respect. Already her pioneers had been over much of the country which lay between her advanced posts and the valley of the Hari-Rud, and she had all the advantage of entering on the discussion with a certain amount of useful geographical information up her sleeve. But Russia's

THE HARI RUD RIVER

thirst for geographical knowledge, and the processes by which that knowledge were attained, were ever supported by the gradual pushing forward of small military contingents. Each step in advance that was thus taken remained a step in advance, so that by the time that Sir Peter Lumsden reached Sarrakhs he not only found Russians in possession of that town, but forty miles south of it, at Pul-i-Katun on the Hari-Rud, well beyond those limits which had been agreed upon as the future boundary between Russia and Afghanistan.

On our own side nothing had been done to shed light on the dark places of that far-off frontier. The Indian Government does not encourage geographical explorations in far countries if there is a possibility of complications arising therefrom; and since the days of Pottinger's historic defence of Herat no Englishman had set his foot in that city, neither had it been possible to push native explorations forward into the well-guarded province; so that we had everything before us. Not only the prospect of an open field extending almost from Quetta to the Herat valley, within which not a single point existed that would help us to the attainment of sound topographical mapping, but all Western Afghanistan, Eastern Persia, and Afghan Turkestan lay before us for our survey marks. It was quite impossible to limit our work to a mere local illustration of the actual boundary. That was our ostensible *raison d'être* as surveyors, but the greater, and the better, part consisted in carrying up link by link a connecting chain of measurements all the way from India to the Oxus so as to place every square mile of those regions in its right position on the map of the world; and on the basis of those measurements to extend our mapping so as to leave nothing obscure regarding our own strategical position on the Indian frontier in relation to Russia's position on the far north-west.

It was, therefore, with mixed feelings that I reckoned up the means at my disposal for dealing with so large a problem. In Captains St. G. Gore and the Hon. Milo Talbot I had the two ablest assistants that the Survey Department could possibly have found; but the rest of my staff was, to say the least of it, a trifle uneven. It included three native assistants, not one of whom had any really sound experience in the class of surveying which was wanted. It speaks volumes for the adaptability of native character that they all distinguished themselves on lines that were practically new to them. A square-built Gurkha, Hira Sing, whose powers of balancing accounts to the very uttermost farthing had often given me the uneasiness which is born of a too rigid appearance of accuracy, very soon found himself making a neck-and-neck race of it with Russian topographers of an advanced school, and usually winning (as they themselves expressed it) by the length of his snub nose. He was a Cossack when with Cossacks; a Mahomedan dignitary when sufficiently isolated from headquarters not to be found out, and a bad Hindu at any time. He was all things to all men, and a most excellent servant to Government, except, perhaps, when there was the chance of a fight. Then all else was forgotten in the grim delight which every Gurkha seems to feel in the prospect of blows—and loot.

A gentle and gentlemanly Moslem, Imám Sharif, was the next in order. He commenced a career then which has taken him to many strange places since. He has been with Sawyer in Western Persia, in Southern Arabia with Theodore Bent, and in Eastern Africa with our British Boundary Commissioners; and he is now a sort of Surveyor-General to the Sultan of Zanzibar, a member of the Order of the Brilliant Star, and altogether a shining light in what is probably an enlightened place. I do not know Zanzibar.

Lastly, there was the Yusufzai, Ata Mahomed, best of good fellows, keen and intelligent, but with very little experience as a topographer, and not too much as an explorer. As for the rank and file, the less said about them the better. They had been recruited from many sources, and on these occasions one does not expect a State Department to contribute its best and most useful members in the subordinate staff to swell the ranks of an experimental contingent. And that was all. Three officers, three native assistants, and a half-trained following to deal with a hundred thousand square miles of High Asia.

But what might be wanting in strength in the geographical section of that Commission was made up in weight of political counsel. When we were all united, ten officers and nine native attachés represented this branch of the Commission alone. The length of boundary to be demarcated between the Hari-Rud and the Oxus was less than four hundred miles, so that our resources in political strength to deal with such local questions as might arise in the course of its construction were ample. As matters turned out, all, or very nearly all such questions were referred to the high authorities at home. Nothing of importance was settled without reference to the Governments concerned.

With the military escort, which included both cavalry and infantry, and numbered about five hundred men with its full complement of officers and followers; also a few scientific experts and correspondents with *their* followers, and an enormous baggage train, the total strength of the Commission mounted up to a figure which certainly seemed disproportionate to the object in view, and which might naturally have caused some misapprehension in the minds of our Russian colleagues. Sixteen hundred men and sixteen hundred baggage animals left the Helmund for the Hari-Rud, and there they encountered a second British party numbering several hundreds more, which had traversed Persia to reach the rendezvous.

During the winter of 1884–85 there must have been between two and three thousand members of the British Commission in Turkestan, without reckoning the small army of local employés who served as couriers and agents in their own country.

It is no doubt easy to be wise after the event. Looking back to that remarkable mission, it certainly seems as if a small and compact working party of surveyors, with one or two political officers and an Afghan escort, might have secured all the information necessary to enable English and Russian diplomats to define the boundary in detail with perfect precision without the risk of a local conflict, and with infinitely less expense. The outfit of the Commission was on a scale of liberality which left nothing to be desired. Tents such as had never before been seen in Turkestan, mess equipment and mess attendants, stores of wine and delicacies such as might serve the purpose of a series of royal banquets in the Turkestan wilderness, were all provided. As quasi-president of the mess in its early days, ere the tide of field work set in, I had every reason to know all about it, for I spent many a weary hour hunting through the piles of wooden boxes, seeking to find some sort of connection between an elaborate invoice and their contents; wanting jam, perhaps, and finding pickles, or wondering what the inward construction of the Russian officer could be if he delighted in such potent drinks as those provided for his entertainment.

We found a little later that the Russian officer did not delight in them at all. With his own Caucasian wines and inimitable vodka he was very well set up for himself; and as for our dry champagne and fiery chartreuse, he frankly disavowed all fancy for it. A Russian does not mind mixing his drinks. An alternation between his own intensely sweet champagne and British stout, for instance, is not at all distasteful to him; but his tastes are decided, and much that we drink is not included in his *carte*. Ginger wine *is* admitted; and there I think he shows great discrimination, for a subtle admixture of ginger wine and whisky is as good a restorative in the biting cold of his wintry solitudes as anything I know, better even than his vodka.

It was evidently intended that the English Commission should carry with it the prestige of India's wealth and luxury. The dwellers in Turkestan were to be impressed with the greatness of it, and I think they were impressed—finally. But the cost of the impression was considerable, and the trouble of conveying the means of making it, from Quetta to the Hari-Rud river (the river of Herat) was even more considerable. All the most bulky commissariat supplies—"bhusa," flour, etc.—were found *en route* as we moved from point to point along the Afghan border, and thus our carriage was enormously reduced; but even so we wanted 1,600 camels to convey us from the Helmund and place us on the banks of the Hari-Rud, and for each one of these camels something like a rupee per diem was demanded and paid.

Being delayed by the start that I had made for the Zhob expedition and the necessity for retracing my steps, I did not join my survey camp till we reached the Helmund; and there I found that my energetic assistants had carried the necessary triangulation and mapping right across the desert already in advance of the main column, and had laid out the base for a fresh start from the point on the river where the various sections of the Commission closed in. It was necessary to cross that almost waterless stretch of Baluchistan between Quetta and the Helmund river in sections. Up to a certain point advanced parties had been able to develop the local supply of tanks and wells sufficiently to meet the wants of the whole caravan, provided it did not draw on these supplies *en masse*, but left intervals for the collection of water between the arrival of different detachments. Beyond this point for nearly sixty miles there was an absolutely waterless space where no well-sinking had been profitable, and across which water had to be conveyed in skins. It was a rather hazardous experiment to march so large a force across such a tract of absolutely waste country, and in feebler hands than Colonel Ridgeway's there might easily have been grief. Under his direction, and with the invaluable assistance of Mr. Barnes, who was then a member of the political staff at Quetta (where he has since risen to be chief administrator), it was safely accomplished; but the incidents of that march were picturesque enough to deserve a record; and a much better record than it is in my power to give them.

It is always interesting to note the process of evolution of a frontier town. Cities do not spring up in the East like mushrooms. The process is slow, for nothing but the necessities of government leads to development. There is little, if any, private enterprise concerned, especially on the part of Europeans, who are nowadays more than ever loth to sink any portion of their capital in the land of strangers, so that house property all through India is rapidly passing into the hands of natives. Yet the Quetta of 1884 was a very different Quetta to that of 1878. It was more than half-way to the Quetta of 1898. The basis of its construction was (and is) mud. The residency of 1884 was but a superior sort of bungalow, built of materials which largely suggested mud. The walls of its compound were (as were the walls of the infant station everywhere) uncompromising mud. Such houses as then existed possessed roofs which, like the roofs of most of the larger homes in Western Afghan villages, centred in a dome, and the dome was built of sun-dried mud bricks. This construction saves the use of timber in a country where timber is scarce.

Some of the poplars, which are now such a feature in the Quetta landscape, were already well grown; but all upper Quetta, where now stands Yorktown and the infantry lines, was as bare as any other plain around Peshin; and a few clumps of crabbed-looking mulberry trees, with a sprinkling of apricots, denoted the position where once stood the aboriginal villages of the district. I believe that the Quetta club existed in 1884 much as in its present form. There are certainly indications that it might have existed then, but, like the residency, the comforts and luxuries of its interior were enfolded in an envelope which was but a superior form of mud casket. The crown of Quetta was the Miri. The Miri has been the fortress of Quetta from time immemorial, and the basis of the fortress is what was probably a mud volcano in days that are prehistoric. It is now a strong position looking towards the lines of Quetta's defences to the west; where no such lines existed in the days of which I am writing.

Mud is a most useful auxiliary in Baluchistan constructions so long as the climate is dry. All the buildings—living or dead and decayed—that we came across in our journey between Quetta and Herat were more or less composed of sun-dried mud bricks. Kiln-burnt bricks were not entirely absent. They were to be found here and there in the construction of important positions, such as the citadels of fortresses and the like; but the mainstay of the old Khorasan builders in Sistan and Baluchistan, whether Arab or Kaiáni, was sun-dried bricks. In Quetta this material for construction lasted well until a season of exceptional rain occurred. I remember the spring when it did occur, and it was my privilege to look on Quetta towards the end of it. The mud had largely melted; walls had sunk down; domes had collapsed; and the spirit of ruin which hovered over Quetta then would have graced (or disgraced) a successful bombardment. It took years to repair the devastation of it, and then neat iron roofs and smart iron railings appeared, and Quetta assumed much of her present aspect.

Between Quetta and Nushki, which lies seventy miles to the south-west as the crow flies, we wandered amongst the mountains. There is nothing approaching desert in this part of Kalát. The hills tower in rough and fantastic forms on either side of the narrow valleys along which the route to Nushki runs, and in crossing from valley to valley new vistas of Baluch mountain scenery open out in monotonous succession. All this country is about 6,000 feet above sea-level, and there is a dry bracing atmosphere which possesses, however, the faculty of rapid alternation between furnace heat and intense biting cold. Within twenty-four hours you may suffer from either extreme, and be lucky if you can so adjust your wardrobe as to be equal to either emergency. The valleys are sometimes quite pretty. The grass is coarse and grows in tufts, but it grows freely. The tamarisk trees are graceful, though never remarkable for intensity of colour save in the short season when they blossom into tufted heads of russet and purple-red. Even then it takes the level rays of a dropping sun to warm them from their æsthetic tendency to undecided tones into the bright vividness of wholesome vegetation. There is water in these valleys, but it is frequently salt water, and it leaves a leprous white edge to its trickles in spite of its delusive clearness.

Arrived at Nushki, which is just on the edge of the desert stretching away westwards and northwards to the Helmund river, it was difficult to realise that we had arrived anywhere in particular. There is this prevailing characteristic about many of the halting-places in Baluchistan, *i.e.* a featureless blank space in the general wilderness, which might be any other houseless, treeless space but for the presence somewhere or other of a trickle of water. At Nushki this trickle had really been turned to good effect. There was a small irrigation channel, which no doubt in the proper season did something towards developing a few immature crops; and there was, I think, a mulberry tree. The mulberry tree was a record in itself, albeit an unreadable one. It attested to better things in other days, when Nushki (which is a place of some importance to the Baluch borderer) may perhaps have boasted a bazaar. If so, balanced as it was between the happy hunting-grounds of Registan on the north, and the deserts owned by that prince of Baluch freebooters, Azad Khan of Kharán, on the south, it must have had a precarious existence, and it had probably come to the conclusion that life was not worth living in such a position.

It was from Nushki that the real business of tackling the desert commenced. Not that the physical obstacles to be overcome were of any great account. Nowhere in that desert does there exist an uninterrupted sea of deep sand for any great space. The sandhills form themselves on underlying alluvial "put," or on gravel beds which the wind often leaves bare, and there is often excellent ground for marching over so long as this bareness lasts. In many parts of the desert the sandhills run to a considerable height, and their conformation is not only regular, but to a certain extent, permanent. Deep-rooted vegetation, occasional tamarisk, and sometimes tufted grass, binds them into consolidated shape, and the track which winds among them is easily followed even at night. This is the formation near the hills. But there are very wide spaces where the dunes are but shifting, restless heaps of sand, deep and yielding, changing with every strong wind, impossible to surmount on horseback. Here the track runs in and out, now showing clearly for a few yards, then lost in a sand wave; and the process of following it by the uncertain light of a starlit sky is one which inevitably ends in discomfort, if not in disaster. We were obliged to travel by night owing to the fierce sun-glare by day, and there was the ever-present danger of losing one's way, if by any chance one was separated from the rest of the party.

For a hundred and fifty miles or so we struck almost due west, skirting the northern slopes of the rough Naro hills, which now form the boundary between Afghanistan and Baluchistan. So long as the hills were within sight, bearings were easily obtainable, but when night dropped a veil over the distance we were all of us in much the same position as a ship on the wide ocean, so far as the navigation of that wilderness was concerned. Fires had to be lit at intervals, and we made our way from fire to fire. Here and there in the open spaces lines were marked by the trail of a plough run lightly over the surface, forming a most excellent indication of the route.

Night travelling under clear skies in a desert has attractions of its own which go far to balance its inconveniences. The pure, fresh, invigorating air—air that may be eaten, as the natives say—produces sensations almost akin to those of intoxication, a light-hearted gladness which is never born of a thicker atmosphere. The mere physical sensation of pleasure in living is a delight in itself. Then there is the purple starlit sky, alight with familiar constellations that come back like old friends at the appointed time; and the soft talk of the desert wind, which breaks rippling over the tops of the sand waves with a sound like the sound of a far-away sea. The glint of the guiding fire ahead, flashing into sight or dropping back to darkness, is an object of intense interest, especially when it has disappeared for any length of time. It seems so close, whatever the distance may really be; and only the weird look of figures around it, as they grow from little black sand sprites into full-grown human shadows, measures the intervening space. I possessed that inestimable treasure, a horse that could really walk. Over the flats, where sand was not, he walked at night, when alone, with a swing such as he never seemed to possess by daylight. Far away behind me would I sometimes hear the click, click of another horse's hoofs, and the clang of scabbard against spur as another rider came on to the course. It was a sort of challenge. There was but one horse in the whole caravan that could outwalk mine, and the sound of his pacing grew quite familiar. It took him hours to make up a few hundred yards, but he generally did it at last. As the click got stronger, and that other black fiend gradually drew level with mine, my horse would begin fretting and fuming till at last there was nothing for it but to "break." There were times when my treasure was not so inestimable. His deadly intoleration of anything ahead of him was occasionally a serious annoyance.

Thus we journeyed on, our nightly caravan of camels jolting and swinging itself along the route, till we reached the last stage of the desert journey which intervened between the foot of the Naro hills (where water was to be had at intervals) and the Helmund. Here were nigh upon sixty miles of sheer desert to be crossed without a drop of water; and this was practically the only serious difficulty of that route. We took it in detachments, water for each detachment being sent half-way in skins, on camels. This was just enough for a drink, but no more. Across that last glaring, sun-baked, cracked, and shrivelled sixty miles of desert we encountered no great obstacle of sand. It was not difficult, even if it was thirsty, travelling. Somewhere about the middle of it, at an indefinite spot in the infinity of indefiniteness that extended around, was an empty space called Garmushki. At Garmushki a few small tents were pitched, and a few mussaks of tepid water were collected for our refreshment. The halt there was not prolonged. There was nothing to tempt anyone to prolong it, but the break of four or five hours just gave our animals a rest, and that was all. A mile or two short of the Helmund we dropped down from gravel-strewn flats into a gully which led to the refreshment of green pastures by the river-brink. Here in a narrow little space of a mile or so in width we found the great river shut in, with a green abundance which was infinitely refreshing and delightful; and here I found my two assistants, Gore and Talbot, with a clean record of triangulation carried across the desert, and all mapping so far completed. Not only so, but a fair amount of fixings in advance promised a successful continuation of survey which had its roots in India, and had stretched out thus far without a missing link.

We did not rest here long. The gradual combination of all detachments into a concrete whole, and the re-sorting and readjustment of transport were soon accomplished by our indefatigable chief, Colonel Ridgeway (who never succeeded better in his busy life than he did in the management of that command), and barring a free and very cheery fight between our retainers and certain Afghans (in which our chief camel contractor, Abdulla Khan, lost all his front teeth) there was no incident that was worth recording. Then followed a disappointment. For days afterwards, whilst we were trekking at our best pace down the narrow but fertile Helmund valley, a thick veil of haze, caused by dust suspended in the atmosphere, blocked out our view of the surrounding country, and confined our work to a local survey of that curious green ribbon of Helmund cultivation which divides the great untraversed

A DEAD CITY OF THE HELMAND VALLEY

wastes of the Dasht-i-Margo from the somewhat less formidable sand deserts of the south.

As we progressed we encountered strange sights, the sights of the cities of the dead spreading out like gigantic cemeteries for miles on either side the river, gaunt relics of palaces and mosques and houses, upright and bleached, scattered over acres of débris, masses of broken pottery, mounds of mud ruins.

So little rain falls in this region that a century and a half have made no final impression on these relics of the barbarism of Nadir Shah's conquests in Sistan. Here are all that remains of the Kaiáni cities which flourished under the rule of those Maliks some of whom lie buried in quaint tile-bedecked tombs further south, on the northern borders of Makran. Nadir Shah, and his misbegotten horde of bandits, were fit inheritors of the savage barbarism of the Mogul and Tartar. What they could not carry away with them they destroyed, like a troop of baboons in a South African vineyard. The extent of these Kaiáni ruins would be incomprehensible were it not for the extent of the indications of that canal system which was developed from the Helmund to assist in supporting the crowd of humanity which must have dwelt in the Helmund valley.

When we reached the great bend of the Helmund northward (marked by Chaharburjak) the atmosphere of brown opaqueness had given place to grey translucency. Through it we were once more, by the grace of Providence, enabled to discern afar off one single peak which had been brought into the Indian Survey branch of the Baluchistan family. This was great luck, as it set our traverses straight, and sent us on our way rejoicing, knowing now that we should lose our place no more. From here to the Herat valley we wandered through open spaces of sandy dasht sprinkled with wormwood scrub, alternating with gravel-covered plains, and ribbed with jagged black-browed lines of hills, which appeared as if set athwart our path on purpose to obstruct the way. They were, however, surprisingly easy to make a passage through, and for some three hundred miles—first skirting the banks of the Helmund to its terminus in the great swamps which lie to the north of Sistan; then following northward with Persia on our left, leaving the great cities of Western Afghanistan, Farah and Sabzawar, on our right—we encountered nothing but occasional waterless intervals to hamper rapid movement.

This is a district which will one day be important, if it is not so already. That part of Afghan Sistan which lies to the east of the Helmund is but a narrow province, although full of cultivation and well populated. Still, it is not to be compared to the Sistan which lies to the west of the Helmund, either for the possible extent of its cultivated area, or the extraordinary amount of ruins which attest to its high development in the mediæval days of Arab occupation. Unfortunately for Western Sistan a slanting line from north-east to south-west cuts it in half, giving Persia the western, and Afghanistan the eastern, half. No division of property that could have been made could so certainly have relegated this ancient Drangia (once called the "granary of Asia") to a future of comparative desolation. The splendid system of canal irrigation, which once turned the vast dry alluvial plains into a sea of wheat, had its head in the Helmund, and was entirely dependent on the Helmund for its supply of water. The Afghans hold the Helmund and the canal heads, and have reasons of their own for not permitting a revival of a system which would benefit Persian territory quite as much as, if not more than, their own. Here we have an object-lesson on the lasting disadvantages of a boundary which cuts an irrigation system in two.

North of Sistan is that extraordinary depression which contains the vast lagoons or swamps, into which not only the Helmund, but all the rivers of Western Afghanistan empty themselves. It is a curious feature in the physical conformation of Northern and Western Afghanistan that none of the rivers flow to the sea. These lagoons, which spread over hundreds or thousands of square miles (according to the season and the extent of the rains), stretched away to the horizon in a shivering sheet of reeds, when we passed them. They are, in fact, a vast reed jungle, in which water-fowl of many kinds breed and abound, and which has developed a special population—amphibious dwellers in reed-built huts; snarers of the birds on which they feed. Neither the Durani Afghan nor the more ancient Tajak or Persian stock of the Afghan population acknowledge them as a civilised people; and I doubt whether any European save Colonel C. Yate has ever penetrated their strongholds. But the important feature of this inland sea is its curious enlargement in seasons of flood. It then encircles all Sistan, flowing southwards, and bending back on the curve of the Helmund in a line very nearly parallel to that river—a counter march of the river, as it were, which leaves Sistan as a dry promontory in the long narrow loop thus formed. This extension ends in another gigantic (and usually, salt) swamp called the Gaod-i-Zirreh, which becomes another huge inland sea, the northern extremity of which is only divided from the Helmund by a narrow neck, or isthmus, not ten miles wide. Were a connection between the river and the Gaod-i-Zirreh to be made across this isthmus Sistan would become an island. This is the one prominent geographical feature of the position which those have to consider who talk about a railway to Sistan. The isthmus is now Afghan territory.

North of the Hamun, or swamps, as far as the Herat valley, it was once the fashion to talk of the western edge of Afghanistan as a desert. It is nothing of the sort. Water is scarce, no doubt, but there are many places at the foot of the scattered chains of hills, or in the depressions of the vast rolling downs, where water could be found if wanted. Jawain, Kin, Kang, Zakin, and many others are large and comparatively important provincial towns, suffering in those days from the lawlessness of the border bandit, but nevertheless exhibiting an amount of vitality and thriving industry which redeems the country effectually from being classed as unprofitable. Western Afghanistan is a redeveloping country. It has doubtless been a rich country, and it may even be so again. To speak of it as profitless, or to talk of a railway project in that part of Asia as commercially destined to failure, can only result from a misapprehension of the geographical conditions of it and the value of its products. It is at least quite as promising as Sind could ever have been.

The military objection to a railway between Herat and Quetta is another matter. We have helped to make the road to India easy in other directions. Whether we should do so here until we are obliged, is a question which we will not now discuss; but that this connection between Europe and India must be made, in spite of military objections, is an eventuality that future generations will certainly have to contemplate. It is marked out by Nature in lines that are unmistakable to any-one who knows what lies south of it, and what lies to the north-east between Kabul and the Oxus; and it is difficult to conceive that military objections will finally stand in the way of the world's convenience here, any more than they have on the frontiers of France and Germany, or in any European borderland.

However, we have taken long enough in getting with our Noah's Ark of a caravan to the Herat valley, and have left little enough room for a reminiscent sketch or two of some of the incidents of the eventful story which followed. That march to Kuhsán, west of Herat, included 226 miles of desert and 540 of foreign territory. The average length of the day's march was eighteen miles (exclusive of halts), and on two occasions distances of fifty-eight and sixty miles respectively were covered within thirty-eight hours. This reflects great credit on the infantry escort (drawn from the 20th P.I.), who always had heavy guard and other duties to attend to. For six days running they averaged twenty-two and a half miles per day. We entered the Herat valley with about 500 fighting men, 700 followers, and 1,800 camels, and Colonel Ridgeway issued his farewell order and reported the arrival of the Indian section of the Commission at Kuhsán on November 19th. It was a march of which he might very well be proud, and is probably still a record in frontier marching.

Then followed a weary wait, and what would have been a weary winter, but for the ever-growing extension of geographical exploration. We had met Sir Peter Lumsden and his Persian contingent from Tehrán. We had spread out a mighty camp in the district west of Herat, on the banks of the Hari-Rud; and we had heard all about the Russians. They had excused themselves from appearing as boundary demarcators on the grounds of the indisposition of the Russian Commissioner, General Zelanoi; but they had not failed to occupy Sarrakhs, nor forgotten to push their outposts southwards to Pal-i-Khatun, forty miles beyond Sarrakhs, nor to continue their reconnaissance up the Murghab river. They had tried the usual overtures, which were to lead up to a request on the part of the Turkman tribes who occupied Panjdeh to be brought under the rule of the White Czar—but the Turkmans as a people did not see it. The Merve Turkmans had, of course, submitted, but the Sariks had not. They dwell about that corner of the Murghab where it joins the Kushk after leaving the hilly districts, ere it shapes itself northward for the deserts leading to Merve. This section of the Turkmans was unresponsive.

The Afghans had not been idle. In June, 1884, the Amir had assumed the rights of a sovereign over that remote corner of Asia, and had appointed a Naib or Governor. The Sariks and others near by Panjdeh were unsettled and anxious, but they were not prepared to throw in their lot with either side till they could measure the prospective advantages to be gained thereby. Thus matters stood when we broke up camp at Kuhsán and spread over the country northward to take our measure of its capabilities.

By dint of daily labour, the labour of measuring a fresh base at the end of each day's march and triangulating therefrom, added to the labour of nightly observations of the stars, and of computing and projecting fresh positions to guide the daily topography along the route when all other work was done, we had arrived at Kuhsán knowing our whereabouts exactly. But we could now adopt more regular forms of triangulation (the delight of a surveyor's heart), and work with something of the deliberate and accurate system that is applied to all mapping in India. In this way we finally ran a "series" to Mashad, well within the Persian border, and there determined a longitude by means of the telegraph which confirmed our work so far; and in this way we also finally ran another "series" right through Afghan Turkestan, till it reached the Hindu Kush and was tied on to our Kabul surveys of 1879-80. This is anticipating a little, but it may as well be said here once for all. This is the basis still of all Northern Afghanistan mapping—for what was done then has never been superseded, and our geographical positions were accepted by the Russian staff as the basis of their work at the same time in the same regions.

Travellers before our time may have made their way from

the Hari-Rud valley across the long slopes of the Paropamisus, into the waste places of the Oxus valley, over the rolling Badghis downs. But they have left no record, and whether they travelled on our lines or not, I doubt if a cheerier and more eager party ever stepped over the line that parted Herat from the land of the Turkman than ours. It was late November then.

We had found out during the march up from India the meaning of the word "Shamshir." Shamshir is the "scimitar" wind which pierces like a keen-edged blade to the dividing asunder of bones and marrow. It is not only a concentrated essence of all the bitterest of north-easters known in England, but it whistles down with the force of steam, and the steady persistence of a regulated blast. I believe the Shamshir of Turkestan to be closely connected with the Shumál (the northern wind) of the Persian Gulf. Over the sea the intensity of its bitter cold is modified, but not its actual power. The heaviest seas known in the Gulf rise under the influence of the Shumál, which generally takes about three days to blow itself out. We noticed much the same process during the upward march to Herat; and a subsequent analysis of meteorological records certainly seemed to indicate that it was one wind spreading across a vast area, and leading to the same phenomena even on the frontiers of India. Badghis (the district north of Herat) is locally supposed to be the home of the wind. There is no mistake about the multiplicity and variety of the wind family which dwells there. There are wind devils, or "shaitáns," enough to people a universe. The air is full of them at certain seasons, and one's mouth and lungs are full of the effect of them. But late November is a little late for them. The temperature is falling and the skies are clearing in November. The lines of poplars which thickly edge the Hari-Rud had turned yellow and red; the wheat and barley fields, where they existed, were brown and hard; and over the dasht the little dried stubs of wormwood had no green about them, and the dried stalks of asafœtida and thistle stuck out aggressively from the ground.

Rising out of the Hari-Rud on to the slopes of the Paropamisus (a name which has been preserved from the classics in default of a better one, for the original Pa[illegible] was considerably further east, tho[illegible] water-divide) there was little variety of feature, the surprise to everybody being the fact that the range was so easy to negotiate. Lessar had already disposed of the myth of an impassable range north of Herat to some extent, but we were hardly prepared to find that it could be *driven* over, without taking the preliminary trouble of making a road. Then down the other side (for the water-divide is still of a respectable altitude in spite of its accessibility) we dropped on to the downs of Badghis, where runs the Kushk river and its tributaries. There is little to choose between the slopes of Badghis and the intricate maze of clay and sand hills which form that Chol country further east about which so many questions were asked in Parliament; the description of which seemed to oscillate between that of a prairie or a waste, according to the view which each speaker desired to advocate. The fact is that it is both prairie and waste at different seasons of the year, but can hardly rank as desert at any time. It is prairie in the greenness of spring and early summer, when these breezy hills lie knee-deep in grass and flowers—flowers of all descriptions, but consisting chiefly of scarlet tulips and gorgeous purple thistles. These are replaced later by poppies as scarlet as the tulips; and yet more thistles. But this is just by way of full dress for Nature's levée once a year. There is little water; and what little there is, is found at far intervals in the one or two river beds which intersect the Chol. When the spring rains cease, all this gaiety ceases too. The flowers wither and the stalks dry up and stiffen. Then comes the wind, and it just scrapes all the dry stalks from the surface of the downs. It blows them off, and then rolls them up into huge bundles which collect in the folds and gullies of the hills, a tangled mass of dry nothingness; which is, however, thick enough to conceal the shaggy-hided wild boar of Badghis—the biggest, the ugliest, and the most awe-inspiring of all the wild boars that ever I have seen. When the snows descend, and the floods finally come again, out goes all this mass of débris, sailing after the manner of detached haystacks, into the open plains that lie south of the Oxus. None of it ever reaches the Oxus, for none of the local streams ever reach that river. So the débris gets piled into the

 swamps, and there gives cover to countless pheasants

(for the Turkestan pheasant is quite as much of a water as a land bird), and finally becomes submerged. According to that excellent authority, Major Griesbach (the head of the Geological Survey of India), it is in this way that the coal beds of the Oxus plains must have been formed, there being no appearance of forest since Eocene periods, a period which is too far off for practical consideration.

Across these barren hills and valleys we rode during that cold November. Sir Peter Lumsden was anxious to see for himself how Panjdeh lay with reference to the proposed boundary, and to estimate for himself the value of the country under dispute. I was with him on this reconnaissance, whilst Gore and Talbot were busy with triangulation on the peaks of the Siah Bubuk, taking a more direct route to Bala Murghab which lay under the Turkestan hills to the north-east. As we dropped down from the Paropamisus into the head affluents of the Kushk river we had excellent opportunity for contrasting the Persian system of travelling (which the Tehran party had adopted) with the leisurely Indian methods to which we had been accustomed; and the contrast in that country seemed all in favour of Persia. The Persian mule is a hand or two higher than the average Indian mule. I do not know that he is much the better for that, but he certainly shows a marvellous capacity for getting over ground so long as he is on fairly level country and under favourable conditions as to food. The Persian muleteer is a strong-limbed, loud-voiced, truculent person in appearance, but his excessively bombastic style is no criterion of any real backing of grit. Behind the manners of a costermonger lie hidden the timidity and inoffensiveness of a schoolgirl. The smallest active demonstration is enough to bring him to a gentle reasonableness which is in curious contrast to his loud-mouthed objurgations before the value of a hunting crop is explained to him. There is no doubt about his physical strength. I have seen Persian muleteers who would stand for advertisements to Sandow. He heaves your belongings on to his mule with infinite ease, and an artistic eye to a final adjustment of the load which leaves nothing to be desired, not even a comfortable seat for himself when everything else is up. A Persian mule caravan always claims a certain ragged picturesqueness of its own which is never entirely wanting. There are tags and rags of carpets that once were bright with colour; there are little coloured tufts of wool about the harness, and cowries artfully applied here and there; blue beads for luck are to be found twisted into the mane and tail of the leading pony, and the latter always has a bell around his neck. It is curious that a crowd of mules will only follow a pony. Why a mule cannot be trained to lead, I do not know; but it is the invariable rule to leave the guidance of the caravan to a pony, who is dressed in a manner suitable to his responsible position, and who carries a bell to the sound of which the caravan behind him moves up in darkness, or in times of storm. It is a pretty custom, and a pretty sight. The leading pony's position in the party is by no means a sinecure. Being stout-limbed, and, to a certain extent, a select pony, he generally carries a select load; and so long as the road is clear he moves along at a walk or an amble which would leave a lumbering camel, with his two miles an hour of slow contemplative progression, far behind. It is not unusual to see the drivers of the caravan themselves at a trot, or a run, alongside the mules in order to keep pace with them; and it is a recognised custom that, no matter what may be the load that a mule may be carrying, the extra weight of the driver, when he is tired of running, may be added thereto. But I have never seen a driver on the leading pony. The latter is perfectly well aware of his responsibilities, and is exceedingly proud of them. The one thing which, as a rule, he cannot stand, is the sight of another pony leading another caravan. I have seen two ponies arriving in the same camp from opposite directions, after challenging each other with their hideous screams a quarter of a mile off, proceed to action at close quarters across a sea of mud caused by the irrigation of cultivated fields; stepping up out of the mud with their knees up to their noses, arching their necks and snorting defiance, although there must have been three hundredweight of miscellaneous property on their backs, and unknown depths of sticky, treacherous mud below.

It is this facility for moving rapidly which makes travelling in Persia a comparative luxury. From six to eight miles an hour is quite fast enough for your own comfort in the saddle; and your mules (if there are not too many of them, and they are not overloaded) will keep this rate up for thirty miles or so, leaving little chance of a weary wait in the sun till the baggage comes up, which is so often the bane of Indian frontier journeys. And the mule, obstinate as he may be under aggravating conditions, is by no means the ungainly, unresponsive, cross-grained brute that the camel is. The latter acknowledges no advances. He is ever the same to friend or foe. Nothing will disturb him from his querulous, discontented attitude when the time comes for work. Nothing can modify the unearthly gamut of evil sounds with which he salutes his driver, when, in the small hours of the morning as he sits in the moonlight casting weird, three-cornered shadows on to the sand, he watches that driver approach with the ulterior object of loading. All the same, setting aside his evil disposition, the camel, in good and familiar hands, and *in his own country*, can make really noble efforts. In order to appreciate such good qualities as he possesses you should see a Bactrian two-humped camel traversing the steppes of Turkestan with his master's house and his master's family on his back. His appearance, with sweeping long folds of deep brown hair on neck and forearm, with head aloft and majestic tread, leaves an impression of massive strength and dignity which the overrated African lion, "the king of beasts," may emulate in vain.

It is also instructive to watch a frontier khafila ready to file out from some Indian frontier fort in the chill hours of a winter morning, under the guidance of its own poshteen-clad people, who move along with their heads tied up in their turbans and their muscular bodies swathed in what might be mistaken for their bedding. Ten maunds (say 800 to 1000 lbs.) of well-packed cotton bales is the sort of load that one of the leading camels will carry; and there is nothing wanting, either, in impressiveness, as you find if you crane your neck to look up to his towering height as he stands over you ready for the march.

But we have gone away from Sir Peter Lumsden's reconnoitring party across Badghis, and we must get back again.

This land of the Jamshidis and Hazaras was not entirely deserted; but we saw nothing of its owners and population except when we neared the Turkman "kibitka" villages and towns about the Kushk river. Till then the rolling barren slopes and the narrow, reed-fringed streams appeared to be given over to the wild beasts of the field—here represented by marmots, rats, and pig. The former lived in marmot cities underground—cities planned with much ingenuity, but we only saw the interior of these devices when we descended into them from above along with our horses, ere we learnt to detect the rottenness of marmot architecture by certain little indications above. The marmot is a lively, red-backed, white-chested, inquisitive little animal; as big as a hare, and sometimes not unlike a fox as he sneaks away to his hole in a hurry. When not in a hurry he sits up straight at his house door, and he chirrups his impressions of strangers in the distance to other marmots, who come out and sit up on their small tails and compare notes. Occasionally his love of inquiry leads him to risk his precious little life till the sportsman gets within range; but it is very seldom that he does so, and he is, as a rule, exceedingly difficult to shoot. A marmot sitting up straight is a tempting object for a spear, and he has not the same apprehension about an approaching horse as he has of an approaching man. So our Lancers were often beguiled into an attempt to "tent-peg" a marmot, which attempt occasionally looked almost as if it would come off. But at the very last moment the little creature would reverse itself like lightning and turn a somersault into its hole, and the rider might think himself lucky if he did not turn a somersault and follow him. The rottenness of the superstructure over a marmot village is quite inconceivable.

My Jamshidi guide told a queer tale that the local dogs (who are as fine a breed in their way as the Tibetan mastiffs, and not unlike them) could catch marmots by an artifice which plays on that instinct of curiosity which is bred in every marmot like original sin. The dog would crawl slowly towards the marmot's quarters, and suddenly assume the appearance of falling down in a fit. The marmot's curiosity would at once be aroused, but tempered with a certain amount of apprehension; and his first general inquiry into the dog's proceedings usually led to his disappearance down his hole again. This was the dog's opportunity—a rush in for a few yards, and then another collapse. The marmot's curiosity would get the better of him this time, and after peering cautiously around, he would emerge for a yard or two from his fortress in order to watch the dog's dissolution. If he skirmished back again, after a brief inspection from afar, the dog would gain another yard or so; till finally the distance of the marmot from his hole became a trifle less than his distance from the dying dog. Then it was all up with the marmot, and his family at home would look out in vain for his return. I commend this story to Mr. Rudyard Kipling. Exactly when the marmot retires into hibernation I never could ascertain. I fancy it depends much on the altitude at which he lives (and he is found up to 15,000 feet) and the existence of his food above the snow.

But not only marmots lived and burrowed in these loess hills of Badghis. Countless varieties of rats and mice were there too, including the little singing, or chirruping, mouse, whom I have often watched sitting at his door, upright, sunning himself, and occupied in piping a little tune. The peculiarity of the rodents in this part of the world lies in their capacity to live without drinking. Moisture in some form or other they must, of course, imbibe, but their habitations are often miles away from any possible opportunity for a free drink, and it appears often as if they could live without any fluid at all.

But for the insecurity afforded by rat holes and marmot villages the sport of pig-sticking might be introduced into Badghis with advantage, for pigs flourish and attain a size which I can only call impressive. I never had the opportunity of measuring one (at least, I have had the opportunity, but I failed to take the measurement), but the individual specimens who occasionally shook the nerves of my horse by starting suddenly from the bundles of dry cover collected in the smaller ravines and nullahs appeared much bigger than their Indian cousins. The shaggy light hair which covers them, and the barrenness of the open country over which they run, no doubt adds to the impression of size.

Into a little reedy strip which lined the banks of one of the small affluents of the Kushk, the Nawab* disappeared

* Nawab Hassan Ali Khan, who was attached to the Indian Political Department.

one day in quest of pheasants. But his shooting was resented by a fierce old boar, who speedily put a stop to it. Out of that cover quickly came the Nawab again; and his running did credit to his early Persian training. Behind him came the boar, with curly white tusks and a nasty eye, which most distinctly meant mischief. Luckily some of the party were mounted, and his attention was happily diverted from his first quarry to a handsome little white Arab pony, ridden by that good sportsman, Ned Durand.* The boar was so big and so ugly, that the first movement of the pony was rapid and retrograde, and it looked for a minute as if he was to have things all his own way. But it was not long before the really game little Arab was induced to reconsider the position, and then there were no second thoughts; and no mistake about the result. Fair and clean, right between the eyes, Durand's spear took the plucky old pig; and he died on the steppes of Turkestan charging home as gamely as any member of his gallant fraternity who has died on the plains of the Ganges.

Thus passed those pleasant days—too short for a survey and too pleasant to last. The early morning found us in the saddle, and about ten we might usually be found out of the saddle again, stretched by the side of such water as there was in the wilderness, with a table spread on the sloping sandbanks amongst the little tufts of yellowing grass, and a breakfast ready such as only a Persian (or an Indian) cook can prepare without the accessories of a kitchen. And the ever-ready, genial welcome of our much-loved chief was never wanting. Go where we would, find ourselves as we might (and did) in never so unpleasant a tangle of difficulty and anxiety or cold discomfort, we were always sure of a kindly welcome and unfailing courtesy from our chief.

We went to Panjdeh, and we made friends amongst the weather-beaten Turkmans of the Sarik fraternity, who gave us good welcome, and were not above taking our rupees in exchange for their inimitable carpets and saddle-bags and silver-mounted harness. I have seen many carpets since, but I still think that those of the Sariks of Panjdeh are unmatched.

* Now Sir Edward Durand, Bart.

They have backs like boards; stitches infinite in number and minuteness; they are soft, but firm in pile, and harmonious (though a trifle monotonous) in colour. Some of the best of these Sarik rugs were to be found hanging across the doors of the "kibitkas"—those round felt tents which are called "akoi" by the Kirghiz, but which are exactly the same in construction whether you find them on the sands of Merve or the grass plateaux of the Pamirs.

Between wood-smoke and the tanning effects of wind and weather many of the door-rugs acquire a tone which is not to be matched by any other artificial process; and we took them eagerly whenever we could persuade the fierce, wrinkled old Turkman women to part with them. First advances were usually made through the rosy-cheeked, cheery little Turkman children. A present of a few beads would produce ecstacies of pleasure; but it wasn't always that the children were allowed to retain the beads by their parents. I remember one little damsel of six or eight whose delight was expressed in every line of her sweet little form when she first took a string of blue beads from my hand. Then she showed the beads to her grandmother, a wizened old hag who was watching proceedings with fierce but bleary eyes from the darkness of a kibitka interior. I don't know what passed between those two, but the young lady returned with an expression of infantile dignity that stiffened her little limbs, and curled her lips into the funniest affectation of disdain that ever was seen. She flung the beads down at my feet with a scorn that would have done justice to an actress. So far it was exceedingly well done, but she waited just a little too long. A childish look of longing stole into her eye; and it stayed there, and disturbed the theatrical pose of her head, and then a large, unbidden tear appeared. I did not wait to see any more, and I do not know what became of the beads.

The tumbled masses of rounded loess hills which slope away northwards from the Paropamisus plateau sink into longer, wider sweeps northward towards the junction of the Kushk and Murghab rivers; and it was from the slopes of one such sandy shelf of mixed sand and clay that I looked out over the plain of Panjdeh, and surveyed the scene of that historic contest which so nearly changed the destinies of the Commission. The white mound of Ak Tapa shone under the setting sun like silver. The long line of sandcliffs which bordered the Murghab on its northern flank were reddened into a vermilion streak along the far edge of the yellow plain; and across the plain, here and there, were dark streaks like the streak of forest, with a light blue smoke-haze above them, which showed where the Turkman kibitka towns held temporary positions. There was nothing else—not a yard of cultivation—simply an open sweep of plain, which melted away on the north-west into the hazy nothingness of the Kara Kum desert, and on the north-east was hedged by those cliffs which were but the southern edge of the Karabel plateau. It was in those cliffs subsequently that De Laessoe made his remarkable find of Budhist caves, and it was at the western edge of them, where they were lost in the plain, that the Kushk and Murghab rivers joined forces at the Pul-i-Khishti, an ancient brick bridge which spanned the united streams ere they sped away northward for many a desert mile to Merve. But we made no long halt at Panjdeh. We worked round eastwards by the Band-i-Nadir, the head of the irrigation system of the Panjdeh cultivation, and up the Murghab river past Maruchak to Bala Murghab, under the Turkestan mountains.

The Murghab river was flanked by a remarkable network of canals, and here and there it spread into wide, reed-covered swamps, which were full of pheasants. Pheasant-shooting was the beguilement of our spare hours after this—and some of us found more spare hours than we altogether desired in that Turkestan retreat. Here, on the Murghab, where in days gone by the ubiquitous Arab trader traversed high roads and founded great towns, where flourished the world-famed city Merve-ul-Rud amidst the scenes of a busy past (but of an absolutely deserted and profitless present), our unwieldy Commission was gathered together for the winter.

The idea of delimiting the boundary during the winter months had finally been abandoned by Russia on one pretext or another, and we knew by this time that there was nothing to be done but to abide, like Ashur, in our breeches, and await spring developments. The winter settled down fast upon us. Thick clouds gathered in solid banks on the Tirband-i-Turkestan. The grey outlook changed rapidly to gleaming white, as snow lay soft and deep on mountain and valley. The bare skeletons of the few fruit trees that lived their chequered lives about the mud walls of the old mud town of Bala Murghab were picked out in permanent white filigree; and we lined our tents with felt, and built up impromptu stoves, and made what cheer we could out of the situation.

Now it must be remarked that the situation was by no means deplorable, nor even altogether disadvantageous to our interests. We had travelled far, and we had travelled fast, and we had collected a vast mass of facts and figures which had to be reduced to order. Our native surveyors, in particular, had spread out over every square mile of country that could be effectually reached from the line of route. Between Quetta and the mountains of Turkestan there was a whole world of fresh geography to be turned into effective mapping, and a whole mass of information to be sorted and digested. We wanted the spare months of winter badly, for we already had our hands over-full of work without extending further observations. Meanwhile a gallant effort was made to find out the whereabouts of Khwaja Salar. It was an important position on the Oxus which was to be the termination of the boundary (when we found it), and ere we reached the depths of that Arctic winter, Peacock and Merk were sent out on the quest. They came back with a stirring tale of exploring ventures, but without any solid assurance that the "post" of Khwaja Salar yet existed. It had existed in the days of Alexander Burnes. What had become of it?

CHAPTER VI.

THE RUSSO-AFGHAN BOUNDARY COMMISSION

Winter amusements—Retirement from Bala Murghab—Position at Panjdeh—Gulrán Camp—Occupation of Panjdeh by the Russians—Retirement to Tirpul on Persian border—The blizzard on Chashma Sabz—Loss of life and baggage—Amir's attitude—Herat at last—Movements during the summer of 1884—Crisis—Collapse of Russian opposition.

AT Bala Murghab we passed our first winter in Turkestan. Days of gloom when the clouds were level and low, and we could hardly distinguish the white gleam of snow beneath the shadow of mists on the Turkestan mountains; days of bright clear sunshine and crisp biting air when the thermometer ran down to double figures below zero, and the scintillations of light reflected from the myriad particles of frozen moisture sparkled like the drops from a lamp-lit fountain. In spite of the low temperature (as registered by the thermometer) there was little discomfort from cold. Our tents were made snug by the introduction of felt lining, and the iron pan of hot charcoal embers that were replenished from time to time kept up quite as much artificial warmth as was necessary, or even desirable.

Pheasant shooting and camel fights were our relaxations from the monotony of map compilation, and were both remarkable in their way. We lived amongst pheasants and on them; and as they were goodly birds of the European type akin to the English pheasant, only larger, with more brilliant plumage, they not only afforded excellent sport, but excellent feeding also. The camel fights were but sham and meretricious engagements. The ferocity with which the huge, hairy, bubbling animals rushed at each other were but a poor criterion of the damage that resulted from the fight. For about ten minutes there was a whirling, heaving mass of hair and legs, and the dust would fly in clouds where the earth was not snowbound, whilst each champion endeavoured to crush the other by sheer force of physical preponderance. When one camel had fairly adjusted the full weight of his fore quarters on to the neck of the other, so as to force him to the ground, the match was over. The smallest camel boy could separate the two combatants, and the game was never played out. What would have happened eventually can only be a matter of conjecture, for we never saw a finish. But it is probable that both would have made use of their enormous jaws eventually. I never could see how a conclusive victory could be won by simply sitting down on an adversary.

This period of rest only lasted about two months. In the middle of February it began to be evident that the Commission must take up a fresh position. What led to this conclusion was the development of events on the actual line of disputed boundary at Panjdeh, which came about much as follows.

In November that ever-restless firebrand of the Russian frontier, Alikhanoff, appeared at Panjdeh. Alikhanoff had long ere this made his mark on the Russian border. His fine, commanding figure, his fair complexion and good looks identified him as an almost typical Caucasian. His energy and restlessness, which brooked no bonds of discipline, and his fiery temper marked him out as the sort of leader who would well serve Russian purposes amongst the savage peoples of the Afghan border. Doubtless he did serve his adopted country well, in spite of the irrepressible insubordination which periodically landed him in difficulties with his superiors. His real name is Maksúd Ali, and he is the son of Ali Khan, as the Russian rendering of his name implies. In November Alikhanoff had made a personal reconnaissance from Sarrakhs to the Kushk river and Panjdeh, which had met with a prompt response from Ghaus-u-din, the Afghan general, who commanded in the Murghab districts. Ghaus-u-din immediately moved up troops to Panjdeh, and Alikhanoff for the time retired. He was at Sarrakhs when Sir Peter Lumsden rode through, and an interview passed between him and Mr. Condie

Stephen, which apparently consisted in the interchange of guarded civilities. On the 12th December, when we went into our winter quarters at Bala Murghab (which is situated on the Murghab river and on the direct highway between Panjdeh and Herat), the Afghans were strengthening Ak Tapa (the "white mound," which lies about six miles to the north-west of Panjdeh), and making a fairly strong position of it. Thirty miles to the north of Ak Tapa, at a place called Sari Yazi, they established an outpost to watch the approach from Merve. Their total force at that time amounted to about one thousand men and two guns.

Early in February there was a general Russian advance all along the line of the frontier. It will be remembered that Pul-i-Khatun (forty miles south of Sarrakhs on the Hari Rud) was already occupied. The Russians now pushed their outposts (composed chiefly of local levies) to Zulfikar, twenty-five miles south of Pul-i-Khatun, and a force of one hundred Cossacks moved southwards on the line of the Murghab river (forcing the Afghan posts at Sari Yazi) to Aimak Jar, twenty-five miles north of Ak Tapa. Under British advice the Afghan posts were withdrawn, and Colonel Ridgeway with Captain De Laessoe moved up from Murghab and Panjdeh on the 6th February to watch proceedings.

Meanwhile negotiations on the subject of the boundary had been proceeding at home. In these negotiations M. Lessar, the engineer who had reconnoitered the border country so successfully in Russian interests, took a prominent part. Acting on the principle (as he himself explained it) that the political views of the average Briton day by day were guided by what he read in his morning paper at breakfast, he succeeded in obtaining great support from a section of the English press; and it may be safely assumed that his enterprises in the field of English daily journalism were hardly less effective in the interests of Russia than were his previous enterprises in the open geographical field of Turkestan. A new boundary line, involving an entirely new departure from all former traditions, was suggested by him as the line which would be acceptable to Russia. This new boundary was to run along the crest of the watershed between Herat and the Kushk drainage, and would, in fact, overlook the city of Herat at a distance of about sixteen miles. This proposal was declined by the British Government; but at the same time (March 13th) an intermediate line, which conceded much, was proposed by Lord Granville; on which formal assurances were given by the Russian Government that no further advance of her troops would be sanctioned. These assurances were repeated by Mr. Gladstone to the House of Commons on March 27th, but Lord Granville's proposal was declined. Three days later the Panjdeh action took place.

Meanwhile Sir Peter Lumsden had wisely resolved on withdrawing the mission from Bala Murghab. We were, as I have said, right on the highway between Panjdeh and Herat—a position that was obviously untenable in the event of an advance of Russian troops; unless, indeed, the advance were checked by the Afghan detachment, which was considered improbable. Gulrán, the site of an old town on the northern slopes of the Paropamisus and on the road to Kuhsán, was selected for the next encampment, and thither we directed our march in the middle of February. No one was sorry to leave Bala Murghab with the prospect of spring developments before us. No one regarded the actual work of boundary delimitation as probable; but the longer the work of delimitation was delayed, the more time and opportunity would be gained for exploring the vast expanse of unmapped and unknown lands that the district of Herat and the borders of Persia offered to us. No restrictions were placed on the movements of native surveyors by the Kabul authorities at that time. I was told that they might go where they pleased, so long as responsibility for selecting lines of exploration rested with ourselves. The Kabul Court was, indeed, most specially complaisant at that time, but such a concession as permission to survey Afghanistan (which has never been accorded before, or since) was so absolutely contrary to all traditional policy in that country that I have no doubt it was due to special representations which were made to the Amir on the subject. About this I may have more to say further on. Anyhow, full advantage was taken both of the permission accorded by the Amir, and of the delay caused by Russian proceedings at Panjdeh. We owe it entirely to Russia that we not only possess complete maps of the Afghan border country, but that these maps are completed on a scientific basis. Every available officer in camp was pressed into this service of exploration and survey. The Intelligence officers, Maitland and Peacock, were especially active, and some of the political staff (which included geographers such as Yate and Merk) were indefatigable in their efforts to amass information. The Russians had been before us in the work of exploration, it was true; but we were determined that, so far as in us lay, they should claim no advantage based on superior knowledge should boundary demarcation become an actual process.

Winter was hardly over by the middle of February. Snow lay about in patches, and the mud on the country tracks was knee-deep. It was bitterly cold, and the counter march through the Chol to Gulrán was not made without difficulties and some loss of followers. There was no time to be lost, and we pushed on through those wintry days with a weary, straggling line of half-numbed people, frequently finding it impossible to collect dry sticks enough for a fire to warm ourselves, or to cook our food. The lowering clouds still lay heavy on hill and plateau; the lanes which bordered the Kushk were but rivulets and streamlets in the general system of snow drainage; the admixture of clay and sand (clay, washed down as mud detritus from the mountains; sand, wind-blown, from the deserts of Kizil Kum) which composed the Chol hills cut up badly under the feet of our ponderous caravan as we dragged along, beguiling the weariness of the march with much mixed language anent the necessity of turning our faces southwards, instead of pushing on to assist the Afghans on the north, and together facing what might happen.

What would have happened had the Commission boldly taken up a position at Panjdeh and there announced that we were ready to commence the work of demarcation? It is always pleasant and easy to be wise after the event; but it must be conceded in this case that there were not wanting many opinions in the camp (if I said that those opinions were unanimous I should not be far wrong) which, before the event, held fast to the conclusion that *nothing* would have happened —not even the historically "regrettable incident." We were altogether in a false position. We did not mean to fight about the boundary—and we said so. As events have proved, it would have been the extremity of foolishness to go to war for Panjdeh, or for any other Russo-Afghan contention short of Herat itself. Whether Herat would have been worth it, we will discuss hereafter. But neither did Russia mean to go to war about the boundary; only she did not say so. She made as if she *did* mean it; and thus it was that steps were taken to remove the British Commission with its five hundred good fighting men from the risk of collision. Writing simply by the light of knowledge gained subsequently from Afghan and Russian officers who were serving in Turkestan at that time, and with no reference whatsoever to the representations which may have been officially made on either side, I may state my conviction that, had the headquarters of the British Commission, supported by that escort, been moved to Panjdeh instead of Gulrán, there would have been no blows struck at all—and for this reason. The Russians were not in a position to risk an attack on the combined force (small though it would have been) of Afghans and British. Numerically the Afghan force at Panjdeh was perhaps slightly superior to that of the Russians, although infinitely inferior in arms and discipline. The addition of five hundred well-armed troops behind entrenchments would have been enough to turn the scale in favour of peaceful proceedings, even if the absolute certainty of war with England, which would have been entailed by aggression under such circumstances, would not of itself have been sufficient to decide the question. But at the time we did not know their weakness, nor could we tell that a forward movement at Panjdeh would not end at Herat.

The position selected for the new camp was an excellent one for awaiting the tide of events, and it was a delightful one for the beauty of its natural surroundings. Next to Panjdeh itself nothing could have been better. Here, overspreading the site of one of the old Arab towns of mediæval times, were meadows and plains of grass now showing green in patches, as the snow gathered together its skirts and left ever longer and broader spaces of turf. A small yellow crocus and starlike white anemones thrust their heads up above the still sodden soil, and by the beginning of March the whole prairie was bright with the scattered gifts of spring. Down from the Turkestan hills came the wild asses seeking for their usual grazing, and occasionally indulging in a free fight with our baggage animals, who had taken possession of some of their best pasturage. Soon the red crags and scars of the lower hills ringed the camp with a warmth of colouring which was a delightful change from the everlasting grey tones of winter. Then, of course, did the little survey party scatter wide and far in search of fresh material for Central Asian mapping, and many were their adventures, and thrilling were the stories which were told when they rejoined headquarters.

Of a sudden the crash came—Panjdeh was occupied by the Russians! The Afghan troops were in full retreat to Herat, and we had to retire on to the Persian border and take up a fresh position of idle speculation as to what the next move in the game might be.

On the 13th March most explicit assurances had been given in the British Parliament that no further forward movement would be made by Russia. On the 22nd Komaroff and Alikhanoff advanced from Aimak Jar, twenty-five miles north of Ak Tapa, to Urush Doshan eighteen miles north of that place, with a large force and guns. On the 25th the Russians appeared before Ak Tapa, and took up a position between Kizil Tapa and the river.

The position may be described as follows. The Kushk river, which runs approximately from south to north, separates two conspicuous mounds or "tapas," Ak Tapa and Kizil Tapa (the White and the Red Mound respectively), which lie back from its banks about a mile or so. Ak Tapa is to the east and Kizil Tapa to the west, Kizil Tapa being a little north of Ak Tapa. Flowing in a most tortuous course with a general trend from east to west, the Murghab river joins the Kushk north of Ak Tapa, and about opposite to Kizil Tapa, and a large "jui," or irrigation canal, is brought from the south-east to join the Murghab shortly before the latter joins the Kushk. This canal is south of Ak Tapa, and skirts the slopes of the southern hills; Ak Tapa is thus dovetailed in between the Murghab and the canal. Old Panjdeh, as I have said, is about six miles south-east of Ak Tapa.

The road from Kizil Tapa to Panjdeh crosses the Kushk by an old brick bridge called the Pul-i-Khishti, and then runs across the intervening plain to the canal and follows its banks. Here, between the road and the canal, was the first Afghan encampment. As they moved forward from the right bank of the Kushk across the bridge to the left bank, and occupied earthworks there, they placed themselves in front of Kizil Tapa, and consequently in direct collision with the Russians, when the latter occupied that place.

Ak Tapa was held by Afghan levies, kassidars of the Chahar Aimák tribes, not by Afghan regulars. The Afghan troops * remained all night of the 25th in their trenches expecting attack—wet and weary, but confident withal. On the 27th the Russian Government formally declined the boundary suggested as a compromise by Lord Granville, and on the 29th Komaroff sent an ultimatum demanding the withdrawal of the Afghan troops from the left bank of the Kushk river. We need not follow the course of the local negotiations and interviews that passed between Captain Yate (who had replaced Colonel Ridgeway at Panjdeh) and the Russian generals and Turkman chiefs. On the whole the Sarik Turkmans behaved well. They were true to the last to their word and to their Afghan allegiance, but they were obviously waiting to see which side was the stronger, and prepared, as are all Asiatics, to declare for the winners. Captain Yate stuck to his post with commendable determination to do all that might be done towards preventing hostilities; but the Russians were not to be denied; and it was impossible to do otherwise than counsel resistance in case of attack. The pity of it was that our good offices ended with good advice.

It was 3 a.m. on the 30th March before Yate had quieted Turkmans and Afghans and got to bed. The morning broke gloomily over the damp plains of Panjdeh. The clouds hung low, and the drizzling mists clung to the saturated river banks, partially concealing the movements of the Russian troops from the sodden trenches of the Afghans. All night

* Afghan force—1 mule battery, 4 guns; 1 field battery, 4 6-pounders; Kabul Regiment and Kandahar Regiment armed with Enfields, no uniform; 800 Kabul and Herat Irregular Cavalry; with kassidars, &c. = 1,200 Infantry and 800 Cavalry.

had the Afghan soldiers remained on the watch for the Russian advance. Wet to the skin, with the damp permeating their rifles and ammunition, they had not long to wait. As the day wore on, covered by the irregular Turkman levies, the Russians advanced on the trenches at 6.30 a.m., and in an hour had cleared the left bank of the Kushk river from all further opposition. The chief loss to the beaten force occurred whilst struggling and tumbling across the Pul-i-Khishti bridge.

Confidently anticipating a sudden rush for Herat on the part of the Russians, the Afghan general wisely withdrew from his advanced position on the Kushk, and retreated to the Hari Rud. Two thousand Russian troops might then have occupied Herat without a struggle (for the Afghans were thoroughly disheartened), but there were not 2,000 Russian troops just then available for the movement; and the Russian Government contented themselves with Panjdeh—and explanations.

Meanwhile our political staff rejoined headquarters at Gulrán. Yate remained long enough at his post to send a letter offering Dr. Owen's services to the wounded. It was taken by two Sarik chiefs, but they were stopped by Alikhanoff, and directed by that too energetic official to attack the English camp. It is said that he put a reward of Rs. 400 on the head of each British officer. A Sarik chief finally brought a pair of dilapidated boots to Yate as a gentle hint that he had better be off. The British officers reached Gulrán (100 miles) in three and a half days, after falling in with a detachment of the 11th British Lancers that had been sent down the Kushk under Captain Heath for their escort and protection.

Meanwhile our area for geographical exploration had become considerably restricted. It was, indeed, very nearly limited to what we could see from our own camp. A rabble of beaten soldiery is not a nice rabble at any time, and it became a dangerous rabble when composed of Afghans all more or less prepared to lay their disasters at our door, and to swear that they were first instigated to fight, and then deserted by us. It was, as I have already said, a false position that we occupied—the sort of position that only an irresolute Government could be responsible for producing.

Without the usual professional openings for duly earning our daily bread, we surveyors were soon absorbed in other duties which were interesting enough in their way, and which kept our hands full of employment. Captain Gore and I proceeded, under Sir Peter Lumsden's orders, to prepare the way to another camp, which should be so placed as to be outside the Afghan frontier in case of further hostilities, but at the same time close enough to enable us to watch proceedings and recover lost ground the instant that opportunity again offered. Such a position was found on the Persian side of the Hari Rud, at Tirpul, where another ancient and rickety brick bridge spans the river. Tirpul is not very far from Kuhsán, that town in the Herat valley to the west of the city where we formed the first general rendezvous of the Commission. All this Perso-Afghan borderland was, before our time, the home of the "alamán," those destructive raids carried on by Afghan and Persian alike, which devastated the country and turned every village into a fortified position.

When Gore and I arrived on the river banks, we found a mighty change had come over the scene. Instead of a wide expanse of stony river-bed, with a trickle here and there of running water, a raging, tearing, red flood was boiling and swirling down the channel, and threatening to uproot the bridge altogether. The five arches were, however, all intact, only the superstructure of the bridge being of brick; the pillars were stonework, and the paving of the roadway stone slabs. True, there were gigantic holes in the roadway, but they could easily be made good for traffic if we could only reach the bridge.

But between the Afghan bank and the nearest arch a very fine and broad current was washing down at a rate that might have been twenty miles an hour, and a supplementary bridge was necessary in order to reach the Tirpul. However, as the flood subsided, little difficulty was found in arranging this stop-gap, and by this eventually all the camp was transferred to Persian territory. Although the gleam of no Cossack spears were detected in the distance indicating a triumphal Russian progress into Herat behind us, the passage of those usually easy and accessible mountains which lie between Badghis and the Herat valley was fraught with disaster.

Everyone who has travelled in Turkestan knows what is meant by the "shamshir," the blizzard of the north that occasionally wraps up men and animals in the cold embrace of blinding, freezing hurricane, and leaves them helpless on the open steppes. More than once we had heard of disasters due to the "shamshir." Our postal service was not altogether secure from them; and now and then a runner would be caught and frozen into a heap, along with his letter-bags and mails, whilst crossing the passes of the seemingly gentle Paropamisus. Such a disaster occurred in the early days of April, when the head-quarters and main body of the Commission camp moved out from Gulrán over the pass called Chashma Sabz, which led down southward to Tirpul.

Indications of a change from the bright clearness of that early spring were not altogether absent. The northern horizon had banked up with clouds, and there were scudding emissaries afloat in the skies that betokened the advance of a more serious contingent of wind and weather later. But there was no time to lose. Gulrán was an untenable position in the uncertainty which attended the next move of the Russian force at Panjdeh, and it was high time to make that strategic move to the Persian frontier which had all the appearance, and much of the general discomfort, of a retreat.

All went well enough till the ascent of the pass on the northern slopes commenced. The comparatively gentle slopes of the soft-sided mountains afforded pleasant enough ways for men and mules in the little watercourses and ravines which seamed its slopes, and the party struggled gaily on with its mule-bells ringing, and all the bustle and clatter of a free-moving Persian caravan. There were no camels, if I remember right, only the strapping, leggy Persian mules and their muscular drivers; and the latter had on the usual thin blue cotton tunics and round felt caps, which were their customary wear, and generally proved quite sufficient in the days of spring and summer. A gust or two of the north wind, freshly iced on the northern deserts, set them shivering, and sharpened up their pace a bit. It was not long before the gusts gave place to a wild, fierce shriek of blizzard and snow, darkening the air and blinding the eyes with its fury. It is impossible to give any adequate idea of the strength of the icy "shamshir" blast. Horses and mules would not face it, and man could not. The rule of the road, when it passes, is to stand fast and make the best of circumstances till it is gone. If it freezes the life out of a man before going, that is but a matter of detail; it would be frozen out, anyhow. Here it caught the caravan in the rear, and might have assisted to blow them over the brow of the mountain on to sheltered slopes on the far side, but for the melting process which set in on the hillsides under the influence of snow and sleet.

In the space of a few minutes the mountains ran down to the plains in rivulets and streams of mud. The mules floundered in and out, or sank helplessly in the yielding soil. The drivers lifted them up, and set them going again, for the process to be repeated within the next few hundred yards again and again. Such a struggle could not last long. Down went mule and driver at last, huddled in a heap together, embedded in mud, and helpless under the freezing tornado which searched out bones and marrow, and turned the heart of the not over-plucky Persian into pulseless stone.

It is this process of detrition, this "degradation" of the heights, which, going on at intervals for centuries, has made of the northern Herat mountains what they now are. They are certainly not such as were described by classical authorities two thousand years ago. In this way a vast amount of surface soil must annually be washed off the surface of the hills and spread over the plains. The formation of that curious feature, the Chol (the loess hills of Badghis), composed of mixed detritus and sand, is easily intelligible by the light of such a scene as was occasionally witnessed in Turkestan during the chequered progress of that Boundary Commission. I have stood on an isolated hill on the Perso-Afghan border whilst quite an ordinary hailstorm passed over; such a one as might occur two or three times anywhere during the spring. It was a weird sight. The lightning played disagreeably round about the hill; the hail streaked across the sky in gleaming white bands, as it drove downwards from clouds to earth; and finally a gathering, whirling cloud-mass above overshadowed another gathering heap below, and extended a corkscrew twist of attentuated tail to meet an ascending black finger pointing upwards, with the obvious design of forming a waterspout. Then I thought it better to go down, and although the distance was comparatively short and my descent was not delayed, I was up to my knees in a moving mass of liquid mud long ere I reached the bottom. By evening that mud had spread out in a thin, but very measurable sheet of surface soil far over the plains all around the hill; and the hill was definitely smaller, and the plains definitely higher than they had been the day previous.

But to return to Chashma Sabz. The European members of the party did all they knew to keep the caravan moving, and to secure for it the lee of the mountain sides. Some of them nearly lost their own lives. Sir P. Lumsden, Yate, Drummond of the 11th B.L., Merk, and others, reached the foot of the southern slopes, and succeeded in pitching a solitary little tent in the intervals of intermittent blasts; and into this tent they all huddled together, but not before some members of the party had nearly perished in their efforts to save the followers.

Here they passed a miserable night, ere the brightness of a clear morning broke on them, and they could crawl out and try back, and reckon up the loss of that fatal crossing. Help was sent from Tirpul, and all next day and the next there came crawling into camp lame, frost-bitten, and all but helpless units of that great company. Over twenty men perished and many mules. All the dogs with the caravan were dead, but so far as I can remember, no horses. Yet some of the 11th B.L. chargers got slowly on to their legs the day after the disaster, literally sheeted with ice, as an ironclad is sheeted with steel. It is a fact worth noting that a horsc will stand cold where a mule or a camel will not, and where a dog will die. There was some looting, of course, but not much, and there was a great reckoning up of the losses of that misadventure. As the days wore on, and the immediate effects of it wore away, it was surprising how the memories of the followers of the Commission were awakened when it was a question of compensation.

Day by day fresh articles of value were discovered to have been missing after further revisions of property, till it almost seemed as if each follower had been bound on a great financial venture, instead of being only a humble twister of tails, or a guileless leader of camels, whose worldly wealth was all on his back.

But, after all, if ill-luck attended that retreat of a peaceful Commission to neutral territory, it was not so much the manner of it as the necessity for it that was undignified and unworthy. Nor can I see that the matter was in any way improved by the Amir's candid statement that the loss of Panjdeh was not a thing of consequence to him. All England was then ready for an appeal to arms against the high-handed proceedings of Russia, and had the Amir insisted on what we conceived to be his rights, it is difficult to see how war could have been avoided. His attitude, however, practically made war impossible, if war were to be based on the violation of Afghan rights; but at the same time it left us in the position of having countenanced, if not advised, a resistance which had led to quite unnecessary bloodshed. Many people think that the Amir's complaisance on this occasion (which undoubtedly relieved us from a difficulty) was due to the recent influences of the Rawal Pindi Durbar. I doubt it. The Amir has always shown a wise reluctance to burden himself with responsibilities in the remote and inhospitable regions north of Afghanistan. I do not imagine that he cared then about the far-away Turkman desert, where Afghan sovereignty had ever been vague and shadowy, any more than he afterwards cared about extending Afghan domination into the region of the Pamirs. Jealous to the highest degree of any sort of infringement of his frontiers on the side of India, he has never exhibited any particular interest in the far north. It would almost seem as if he regarded encroachment from the east or south with much more apprehension than that which might arise from north and west. He possibly regards it as our business to protect him from the latter, while he must depend on his own resources to protect himself (should such a possibility arise) from the former.

But at that time we did not know (it was impossible that we should know) what was the exact disposition of Russian military resources on the Oxus frontier. Panjdeh was occupied, but days and weeks passed, and there was no sign of any further advance southwards; no appearance of any attempt to rush Herat, to capture that place by a *coup de main*, which would not, in truth, have been very difficult to accomplish then. Whether Russia was politically prepared or not to plunge into war with England was of course a matter of speculation; nor did we know with any certainty that the military force at her disposal at Panjdeh, though enough for the purpose of dealing with a small Afghan contingent, was, in fact, rather less numerically than the contingent with which it had to deal. It was considered advisable, at any rate, to send British officers into Herat to inspect its position and defences, and, if possible, to induce the Afghans to improve the latter under scientific advice.

Thus at last was the Amir persuaded to admit the presence of English officers in that frontier city. Hitherto no one had approached Herat (excepting Griesbach, who had taken advantage of a geological trip to obtain a closer view of the city than anyone else had secured so far) near enough to get even a general idea of what its strength for defensive purposes might be. The risk of untoward accidents arising from the fanaticism of the Kandahar troops which garrisoned the town (for it must ever be remembered that the centre of fanaticism and ghazidom lies in Western Afghanistan rather than in the neighbourhood of Kabul) was considered too great to admit of any free approach to the city by British officers. The Amir was careful of our safety in the highest degree, and he, no doubt, rightly considered that the further removed we were from the centres of all Western Afghan population the better. But now there were urgent reasons for the admission of Engineer officers to that historic city, and thus it fell about that, as the senior of the R.E. officers present with the Commission, I enjoyed the privilege of being amongst the first to visit Herat.

It was a bright, hot morning in early summer when three of us (Colonel Stewart, who was there on political duty, Captain Peacock, and myself) sat waiting at the end of a short march, within easy view of the mud walls of Herat, on the uncomfortable ends of certain Afghan graves in one of the local cemeteries which abound round every Afghan city. We were waiting for the inevitable "istikbál"—that ceremony of reception which always includes a few local notables and a ragged guard as a preliminary escort to a Persian camp or court. And as we waited we ate our breakfast and discussed the situation. We had ridden through the long western valley, with its intricate network of irrigation, its teeming villages and cultivation, keeping well up under the northern hills so far as we could; for there we gained the firm ground of the "dasht" and gravel of the lower spurs, and were above the system of canals. Everywhere we had met with civility from the rural population. The Herati of the agricultural districts is not a fighting man. In his blue cotton shirt and skull-cap he looks (what he is) a Persian of a Persian stock; and as he spends his days in digging and clearing his water-cuts with a triangular spade, or in heaving up water from the shallow wells, he is the typical agriculturist, the tiller of the soil, the slave, the hewer of wood and drawer of water to the Afghan community; standing absolutely apart from the truculent Durani soldiery of Kandahar, who (when represented by certain western tribes) are the most clearly objectionable people in the whole Afghan race.

The time for scarlet tulips to decorate the hillsides had come. They were there in patches of vermilion, and hung about the blue hill landscape in vivid contrast. Purple thistles and wild poppies and roses were of slightly later bloom; but there were, even then, beds of the graceful white opium poppy, varied with a slate-coloured beauty, massed in patchwork about the feet of old gateways and minars, and wasting a sleepy perfume over the acres of the dead. The villages of the valley were buried in orchards, now scattering their wealth of pink and white blossom idly to the passing winds. Lucerne beds were already knee-deep in luscious greenery, and the odour of scented willow pervaded the moist, hot air. One small whiff of that perfume would as clearly call up to me the vivid, yet sleepy, scenery of the plains about Kabul or Herat, as does the scent of soap revive visions of a corner of Bond Street.

Sitting lazily on those tombstones, and wondering idly what sort of a reception we should get, there suddenly appeared in

NORTHERN GATES OF HERAT

the distance a whirl of sand and dust, and then a vision of galloping horsemen and flying garments, which betokened that the ceremony of reception was coming off after all. We had begun to be rather doubtful about it; but our doubts were soon set at rest. Certain gaudily-dressed functionaries, well mounted on horses that did justice to Herat (which is saying a good deal for them), much over-decorated with silver embossed harness, and altogether sufficiently well turned out to show that complimentary attention had been bestowed on appearances, proceeded to conduct us by something of a détour past the north-western walls of the city, and beyond a maze of outlying buildings (which included a magnificent mosque and some stately minars), to the gate on the northern face of the town, which is known as the Kutb Chak gate. Here, for the first time since the historical defence of Herat by Eldred Potringer against the Persian forces directed by Russian officers, did British officers again find themselves passing its portals. The sun was reflected hotly from the white, baked mud walls as we crossed the bridge leading into the well-guarded, double entrance-way of the city gate. The guard tumbled out lazily from the dark recesses of the guardroom, and forgot to salute, and we were at once in the tortuous, narrow streets of a typical mud-built city of Afghanistan. They are all alike. The same crowd of irregular houses presenting bare flat walls to the narrow, unpaved gutters, which represent streets; and reached, as to their interior, by small doorways and long defensible passages. Here and there a street becomes a sort of burrow beneath the houses, and one rides in semi-darkness through an evil-smelling tunnel, lit by the white glare of sunshine at the far end. A huge rabbit-warren of unsavoury buildings, flat-roofed for the most part, but domed now and then; with no ostensible means of entrance, but with long, twisting gullies wide enough for a single rider to pass along winding in and out amongst them and all converging on the central bazaar. Such is the form assumed by the mass of the township.

Herat, like Kandahar, stands foursquare, covering about a mile of space, and right through the middle of it, from side to side, north and south, east and west, are driven the four main streets. Where they meet in the centre is the Charsu, or central square, and this, together with a certain length of adjoining streets on all sides, is roofed with beams and matting. Here are the shops—and the shops of Herat were a feature of interest. Bokhara silks and cloths, with vivid colouring and bold bright embroideries are most charmingly decorative when hung outside with fitful gleams of sunshine playing on them through the breaches in the matting of a sketchy roof. Silks and embroideries are the specialities of Herat; but there is all the variety of native craft-work which Central Asia can produce; all the marvellous variety of fruits of the trees and of the field that the most highly irrigated and most productive corner of Afghanistan can yield; besides Russian crockery and hardware, and probably, by this time, Russian produce of all descriptions, to be found in Herat. However, on this our first visit there was but little to be seen. It was a poor show of second-class trade that we then observed. Under the influence of the rupees of the Commission it was perfectly astonishing how that bazaar brightened up into life and vigour. But it took a year of free expenditure to brighten it.

Our first stay in the city was regarded by us as an indication of what we might expect in future. We were, of course, most carefully guarded on our visit to the Governor, but we met with nothing but civility and hospitality. We were comfortably quartered in one of the best houses of the local nobility, in rooms which were magnificently carpeted, bare of furniture, but which left nothing to be desired in the matter of fresh air. Our quarters lay beneath a flat roof, to which there was the usual access by steps—necessary enough in Herat, for Herat is low (barely 3,000 feet above sea) and hot, and life without the resort of the roof would at times be insupportable. Here Peacock and I made our way up for a general first reconnaissance of the surroundings. I had time to secure a hasty sketch of the citadel, the lofty walls of which faced us with something of impressiveness across an intervening space of ill-cultured gardens and domed roofs, when a warning message reached us from below, the intention of which was to request us to beware lest our observations of neighbouring harems should lead us into difficulties. We had no idea that there was anything so interesting in our vicinity—we had not seen the harems—but we immediately looked for them, and finding none, we came down without delay.

Naturally, it was with the deepest possible interest that, on the following day, we made careful examination of the defences and the surroundings of the city; looking across the eastern reach of the Hari Rud valley over the dark, massive lines of orchard trees, broken only by the white glint of village walls and towers; noting the packed blocks of buildings that stood close round the walls, reaching even to the foot of the glacis, interspaced with vineyards, gardens, and orchards; measuring the size of the stupendous earthen rampart on which the walls were reared, and estimating the distance of the nearest hills on the north, and the command of the city that might be obtained from thence. Northward, indeed, the hills run down rather close. From Herat city to the crest of the Paropamisus range (which is crossed by several easy passes, besides the Ardewan) is a distance of about sixteen miles; but between that range and the city is a low ridge called the Koh-i-Mulla Khwaja, which dominates the city from a distance of about three miles, only with a higher altitude of from 600 to 800 feet. The total fall from the passes of the Paropamisus to Herat is about 2,000 feet, the drainage of the mountains southward passing through the sub-range of the Koh-i-Mulla Khwaja. At the foot of these latter hills, nestling close under these southern slopes, is the last resting-place of the great Amir Dost Mahomed, the maker of the present Afghan kingdom. He lies peacefully under his unpretentious marble tomb in a pretty little garden called Gazagarh, some four miles to the north-east of Herat; and never, perhaps, was rest better earned. He died at Herat, just as he had restored that city to the Afghan kingdom, in 1863. Afghanistan of to-day is what Dost Mahomed made it; and we English people at least have reason to recognise the strong character of the man who held to his promise of friendship against adverse counsel when we were beset by the perils of the Mutiny, and when a bold bid for Peshawur might very well have ended in the retransfer of that ancient Afghan capital to Afghanistan.

To the north-west, at about a mile distance (as Peacock and

I looked over the walls that day), was the Masalla, a graceful group of buildings of regular Persian style, with a preponderating gateway leading into a court, two sides of which were occupied by the cloisters and buildings of the Madrasah (or college), and the end closed in by the mosque. Four minarets, or minars, stood at the corners of the paved platform on which the whole structure was raised. It is said to have been built by Shah Rukh somewhere in the last half of the fifteenth century. Shah Rukh's own tomb, with some ragged vestiges of the ancient beauty of its tiled ornamentation, stood about one hundred yards from the building. Of the effect of the encaustic tiled decoration which graced the face of the gigantic gateway, and which was introduced in plaques and panels wherever space admitted on the walls of the Madrasah and mosque, it is difficult to write in measured terms. The old Persian colouring of copper-green, golden brown, and rich turquoise blue with a straw-yellow ground, was employed in most exquisite harmony in graceful flower-patterns; and these were introduced with precisely such value in detail as befitted so vast a subject. It was a triumph of the Art of Babylon and Nineveh, preserved for centuries through Saracenic agency, applied to comparatively modern Persian architecture.

But all this was not visible from the distance of a mile. What was much more clearly discernible was the fact that mosque and Madrasah combined were in a position that was fatal to practical engineering in the interests of defence; and that the Amir must be advised to remove them. Looking west, nothing was visible but the long stretch of the Hari Rud valley, still highly irrigated and cultivated, but not so full of populous villages as were the plains to the east. South, at about four miles' distance, the river was spanned by the Pul-i-Malun, on the road to Kandahar. The bridge was in ruins, but the pillars and arches stood in measured line across the span of the river-bed, witnessing to the strength of Hari Rud floods and the inertness of the Afghan Public Works Department. Villages and suburbs thickly filled up the space between the city walls and the river.

Practical reminders of the last Persian siege were not wanting all round the walls. On all sides could vestiges of approaches

HERAT, IRAK GATE

be found; but on the south, where the accumulation of centuries of defunct Heratis in a graveyard had gradually risen to the dimensions of a vast mound, these parallels and approaches were as clean cut as if they had been driven through that mass of waste material only a month before. There they were, ready made for the next besieger. This was not the only graveyard which might serve a useful purpose to an enemy. Peacock's professional eye counted them out where they disfigured the surrounding landscape; and yet there were no signs of despondency discernible in his face. For my part, I did not quite see how to get rid of these unsightly and most objectionable obstructions to a fair esplanade round the walls of the city. We wanted a clear space, smooth and regular, across which not a rabbit might travel without being duly saluted by the garrison; and we got it—eventually. Not then, but months afterwards, when the war tension of Panjdeh had passed, and another tension arose, infinitely more dangerous and more critical; when we were actually told to make the best defence we could of Herat, and trust to Providence and an Indian contingent from Quetta—then those mounds disappeared as if by magic. The Masalla, alas! had gone before, and nothing but four slender minars were left of its splendour, and it was now the turn of these ancient and most sacred graveyards. Thousands of ploughs were collected from all the countryside, and the whole area of cemeteries was ploughed up as a field is ploughed. Bones of Persian, Afghan, and Moghul were scattered abroad like pebbles in the Bolán, and in the midst stood the grim old Ghaus-u-din and the gallant Colonel Rustom Khan, and there was nothing on their faces indicative of pious horror at this wholesale desecration. Talk of desecrating Moslem graves! Here was desecration, if you like; and remember that it was by the order of the Amir, not by the will of the engineers, that this was done. What the Amir objected to was the carrying off of relics. Tempting as was the beauty of that faience work which adorned the Masalla, it is needless to say that the Amir's wishes were respected. So far as I know, not a square inch of that historic tiling was removed from Herat.

But this, as I say, happened after our first visit. We returned again and yet again to direct the crowd of Afghan workmen who were laying out new outworks, new flank defences, new emplacements, and making a clear field for action. Our political officers paid them, and paid for all damage done to private property; and they rejoiced greatly, and Herat grew fat and rich, and its bazaars blossomed with Bokhara silk and the splendours of Asiatic broidery after a fashion that had probably not been known for centuries.

We were not molested. On the contrary, it happened more than once that soldiers fell out of the ranks to salaam to me and to claim the recollection of exploring work done in the north. Peacock, who unites all the outward and visible signs of a good practical soldier (such as an Afghan admires) with the inward grace of an exceedingly able Field Engineer, could do what he pleased with them. Is there not a solid tower of sun-baked brick or "pisé" work (puddled mud and straw), with the best of our guns (specially selected for Herat defence and despatched with all ceremony from India) on the top of it, which is called the Burj-i-Pikark to this day? We used to ride around the melon-beds which graced the glacis with the cheery military-works director, Rustom Khan, or take tea in the afternoon with Ghaus-u-din in his town house, which was a trifle cleaner and larger than most town houses, and gossip of past history. "Do you remember," he said to Gore one day, "a very old man, the last old man that was left in the farthest village of Baraki Rajan, the day you reconnoitered southwards to the Altimúr pass, during the Afghan war? Do you remember his appeal for protection to you as being too old and infirm to leave the village after his people had gone, and the excellent information he gave you on all matters on which you were pleased to question him? Well, *I* was that very old man; and if I gave you certain information, I did not fail to get some in return. I have grown younger since, and you have grown older, but I remember you perfectly well."

On these visits to Herat, which were periodic, not continuous, we used to live in a garden of roses outside the city walls. The garden was enclosed with high walls, and there was always a bodyguard in attendance, generally an imitation Highland bodyguard, clothed as to the upper man in tunic and kilt, the latter being of a tartan peculiar to the Herat bazaar, and the former, relics of British regimentals. The lower ends of these Highlanders were, however, encased in tights of dirty white linen, not tight enough to serve the purposes of a stage Highlander, nor loose enough to be classed as trews. But they were a well-disposed and cheery lot of men, drawn chiefly from the regiment called "Logar," with which I afterwards made closer acquaintance. They were at any rate north countrymen, Kabulis rather than Kandaharis, as is invariably the case where a European escort is wanted.

Meanwhile, before our connection with Herat had ceased, great changes had taken place in the constitution of the Commission. Sir Peter Lumsden had left for England, and with him the political detachment (Colonel Stewart, Mr. Condie Stephen, Captain Barrow, and others), who had originally joined from Tehran. So that the Commission party had recovered very much of the original form with which it had left Quetta nearly a year before, and was now once again under the command of Sir West Ridgeway.

We need not follow out the manœuvres of that summer. We were first blown to pieces in the Herat valley, where the wind and the dust and the heat combined to make life insupportable. The wind, which tore our light tents to rags, was a daily trial for months. It was like the winds of the Persian frontier far away to the south (but on almost exactly the same meridian), where Persia borders on Baluchistan. Indeed, I have no doubt that they were the same winds. The heat and the dust drove us northward through the valley of Korokh, to the cool heights of Zirmast, on the Paropamisus. Here we found a fresh atmosphere, and new fields for exploration at an altitude of 7,000 or 8,000 feet above sea-level, and here the headquarters could have passed the summer months in comparative comfort but for fresh and most disquieting rumours as to the Russian preparations for an immediate advance on Herat. In the state of tension which then existed between the two countries it seemed at that time almost impossible but that war should ensue, and the very first intimation of it that we should get would be the appearance of Russian troops in the Herat valley. As we were on the northern slopes of that valley, another movement, which should take us a little nearer the Persian frontier and a little more removed from the line of advance, was deemed expedient; and after a short enjoyment of the pure atmosphere of the hills, we moved down again through the Korokh valley to the west of Herat, where the Doshak hills offered a chance of keeping cool, and, at the same time, of keeping off the direct line of probable military movement. The heat of the valley at this time was excessive, but it was not, all the same, to be compared to the heat of the Indian frontier at the same season.

The Herat valley had assumed a new aspect. All the wealth of crops had been gathered in, and the fields were bare and sun-baked; the sun glared down through a dusty haze on a tracked and parched waste of little square fields cut up into sections by the now dry little irrigation channels. The poppies were reduced to a stiff and brittle anatomy of their spring splendour; and casual collision with a bed of thistles resulted in a cloud of pungent dust. The deep, thick shade of the grove of stone pines which adorns, in solitary glory, the ziarat of a departed Khwaja near Korokh, was an intensely grateful incident in a hot and dusty march. Even the roses had disappeared, and the sweet, low-spreading variety, which a month or so before had covered the western valley with spangles of gold and maroon, had dried up into dusty nothingness. On the other hand fruit had come in; great yellow peaches, apricots, melons, and early grapes were abundant; and life was as far as possible spent in retirement tempered with the refreshment of the orchards. Such retirement, however, was hardly practicable for surveyors, who found this just the best of all possible seasons for extending work. They wandered and worked over the surface of all the southern districts of the Herat province (the wilderness of hills peopled by Firozkohi, Taimani, Jamshidi, and Hazara, which lie between Herat and Kabul), the valleys of the Persian frontier around Mashad, and the long, straight course of the Hari Rud and its tributaries. The ancient Afghan capital of Ghor was unearthed, and all that remained of it was mapped. The sources of many of the rivers that, running south-west, help to swell the volume of the great Helmund lagoons, were traced out, and a good solid backbone of triangulation well connected with the Indian surveys was established, which would serve the purpose of scientific geographers of both English and Russian missions should we ever come to a boundary demarcation.

This glorious summer was not a lost summer. We may have spent rupees freely; but if we did, we were all that time gaining more than money's worth. It may be long yet before such an opportunity occurs again, and when it does occur again there will not be very much to learn afresh.

Then came the change of Ministry at home. Remote as was our position, there was nothing to complain of in the matter of postal communication. We got our telegrams a few days late, perhaps, but we got them regularly, and we followed the course of political agitation at home with an interest which can only be felt by those whose immediate future depends on it. What was it that caused the change? Was it a question of beer, or was it municipal government? I have forgotten; but it was certainly nothing that had the remotest connection with the chances of peace or war with a great Continental Power like Russia. The English public had had their nine days' excitement over Panjdeh, and the "regrets" that had been aroused in some official minds had been expressed and passed; nothing again could revive the dead agitation which certainly for a time did shake all England. But in proportion to its violence, so was the apathetic calm that succeeded. Lucky for us in some ways that it was so, for with the advent of the new Ministry and Lord Salisbury, there came a new procedure in the course of negotiations with Russia; and the new procedure, which was one which could be trusted to bring matters to a definite issue, ended at the beginning of August in a crisis which was actually more acute than anything which had preceded it. Never till then did we get definite instructions to suspend all survey work and be prepared to make the best defence we could of Herat. There was no excitement in England then, so far as we could tell; but there was a sudden, determined, business-like activity in the camp of the Commission that showed where the heart of everyone was set, and the hands of everyone were soon full of those last arrangements for perfecting the new defences of town and citadel which were to help us decide who was to be master in that far corner of Asia.

Then, perhaps for the first time, was the strength of that Indian escort reckoned up to the last man, and estimated at its full value. Five hundred sowars and sepoys in a fortress with four miles of walls to defend—what were they? Well, they might have been a great deal, combined with the Kandahari regiments of the Amir that formed the permanent garrison. Anyhow, they were all the reliable troops that we possessed. Too many for mere escort purposes, too few to fight the battles of an empire. I had the honour to be president of the military committee which reckoned up our chances of successful defence, at the same time that the Afghan generals were called on to put their heads together and form conclusions of their own. At the end of our deliberations we compared notes. We had but imperfect data on which to base our calculations, and we assumed a strength for offensive purposes on the part of Russia which was probably far in excess of the possibilities of the situation. But it is a curious fact that the two committees, English and Afghan, came to precisely similar conclusions. It was a question of how long we could maintain our position at Herat; whether we could last till reinforcements arrived from India to our assistance. As to the means whereby these reinforcements were to reach us—the preparations that were made both by the Amir and the Indian Government for such an eventuality—we had, of course, the best possible information, and having it, we had no misgivings as to the result. Herat was certainly no longer open to capture by "*coup de main.*" That had been placed beyond the field of possible contingencies by the energy of the Afghans themselves in the preparation of new defensive works. The enormous ramparts, above which the thick mud walls towered to a command of eighty feet above the plain (too much of a command), could be breached and removed by no artillery such as was likely to be formed on Russian Turkestan. Mud walls are proverbially difficult to destroy, and a regular "sit-down" siege would have been a long undertaking.

We need not speculate as to the possible results of such a siege. It never came off, and it may perhaps be doubted whether there was ever any real chance of its coming off. When all was ready, and the hopes of the military contingent of the Commission ran high, the front of Russian political opposition collapsed; and we heard that we were to demarcate a boundary after all, instead of defending a town. It is difficult to forget even now the feelings with which that news was received. The chance of a lifetime seemed to have slipped from our grasp. But if we had laboured to some little purpose to place Herat beyond reach of the clutches of the Bear, we had also laboured yet more persistently to prepare the way for a peaceful solution of the whole boundary question by extending our knowledge of the country. If we did not then map out the whole of northern Afghanistan, it was not because we were prevented by either Russian or Afghan. It was because the original strength of surveyors attached to the mission was quite inadequate to the opportunities encountered. We had taken all the assistance we could get from politicals and soldiers (and the assistance they gave us was not to be lightly reckoned either), but even then we were short of working power; and we lost much value that might have been gained had we been better supplied with trained workmen from the first. So it happened that whilst we were glad enough to hear that the change of Ministry at home had effected a change of programme in our proceedings—a change which would lead to the ends which we had purposed when we left India—there was a distinct shadow of disappointment that the opportunity was lost of testing the value of our practical engineering in Herat.

CHAPTER VII.

THE RUSSO-AFGHAN BOUNDARY COMMISSION

Commencement of demarcation—Work in winter—The Chol and the steppes of the Oxus—A blizzard in spring—Cordial relations with Russian camp—Khoja Salar—The Turkmans—Balkh Plain—The Oxus—Kilif—Native surveyors—Change of front on the part of the Amir—The march to Kabul—Hindu Kush and its passes—Closing the survey line—Ghorband Valley—Conclusion of Commission—What we gained by it—Railway to Herat.

BY November, 1885, just about a year after leaving Quetta, we were once again on the borderland between Afghanistan and Russia. We had met the Russian camp at Zulfikar; we had argued about the position of the first pillar; had watched the Russian topographer at work; had admired the foresight which had turned the whole Russian Commission into a practical survey party (with a small military escort) under one of the first of Russian scientists, Colonel Kuhlberg. We had interchanged hospitalities on a scale that for Turkestan was unprecedented, and we had found that we had to deal with hard-headed men of business, who were keenly aware of the enormous advantage in demarcation proceedings of a close intimacy with the geographical details of a country before commencing political discussions.

The winter was coming on again apace. The poplars and pistachios had turned red and yellow about the edges of the Hari Rud and the slopes of the Koh-i-Bubuk. The reedy banks of grass had again dried into excellent cover for pheasants and chikor; the thousands of little water-channels had been turned off, and bare acres of brown stubble land spread out where cornfields had been. All the host of green things, the asafœtida and the thistles and the strange plants of umbelliferous (I think that is the word) nature, which burst up through the moist earth of spring like mushrooms—or like the tortoises of the Peshin valley—were standing stark and stiff and dry, not yet scraped off the face of nature by the periodical blasts of Badghis. With the first touch of frost, all these spread out the delicate white tracery of a thin lace veil over stretches and sweeps of the low hills bordering our daily route. Such a vision of soft filmy beauty I have never seen again, not even in the salt mines of Kishm. But there was not much time to look about. The Russian party was strong in topographers, and every inch of ground they covered had also to be covered by our attenuated party. We, by this time, were strong in triangulation, on which we could base our topography—a fact which the scientific director of the Russian camp was not slow to appreciate. He did us the honour to accept our basis, and to work his own maps upon it.

There could be no retirement into winter quarters for surveyors this season. It was a keen race for the best information within those limits (or "zone," as it was called) which were to determine the bounds beyond which demarcation was not to be carried.

By December the cold was intense. I remember about Christmas setting out in the early morning from our camp, which was then near Bala Murghab again, to run our work through a district as yet unseen, which lay between the Murghab and the Oxus plains. From Zulfikar to the Murghab mapping had proceeded rapidly, as both sides had already been over the ground, and the boundary was after all only provisional. Both sides reserved to themselves the right of appealing to their respective Governments—a right which was so frequently exercised that it may be doubted if more than a few miles of that historic line were laid down without it. By Christmas we were on the Murghab again above Maruchak, and from that point we had to plunge into the unknown Chol country which spreads out towards Maimana, Andkhui, and the Oxus. The Chol hills were snow-covered, but only sparsely so; the intervening valleys are usually quaking bogs of salt mud, but were now freezing into a consistency which made it possible to traverse them; and every blade of vegetation had disappeared into the gullies and nullah beds. Daily the wind got up to put a little grip into the cold, which, without it, would have been easily bearable. The thermometer had suddenly dropped down well below zero, and as I rode out of camp the air was filled with little stars and spangles of frozen moisture which scintillated and danced in the gay sunshine. As I rode, I met the wind, and my face was soon icebound. Turning up a narrow little gully, which led to a low pass and a drop over into the Chaharshamba valley, the wind was projected down it like steam through a funnel, and I was not at all surprised when my horse positively refused to face it. The blue-shadowed sheets of snow on either side met on the pathway in a solid runlet of ice. Even without shoes (for I always deprived my horses of shoes in winter), and without wind, it would have been difficult to climb that gentle declivity; but now I was fairly beaten on a track that in ordinary circumstances one could have galloped over!

It might be asked why, under these uncomfortable circumstances, one did not walk instead of riding. It was because no Turkman or Jamshidi guide would ever dream of walking. Their high-heeled boots are not made for walking even if they would. But no man in that Oxus country with the slightest feeling of self-respect would appear on business on foot. And if your escort (possibly including Indian cavalry or Cossacks) as well your guides decline to leave the saddle, the advantage of being mounted yourself outweighs even the prospect of becoming a frozen image before the journey ends. Yet, in spite of the cold, it was a delightful expedition that will live in my memory to the end of time—my time. The cold was, after all, wholesome and bracing, and we made our way from point to point through a wilderness of hills, which were to one another as the waves of a vast frozen sea, with all the confidence which can only be attained by a very sure and certain faith that you know exactly where you are going. This is, at least, one advantage which a surveyor should possess over the rest of mankind. But the Chol hills were shrouded with snow, and occasionally buried in the sweep of low-drifting clouds, making it doubly hard to distinguish the slight, unimportant natural landmarks which made up our tale of survey fixings. On emerging into the plains of Andkhui, north of the hilly Chol country (which is, as I have already attempted to explain, a belt or band of loess formation which intervenes between the main range of the Band-i-Turkestan and the flat plains bordering the Oxus), it was possible to imagine what a journey across a Siberian steppe in winter must be like.

A wild, white, silent wilderness of untrodden snow; a thin, blue line of jagged hills in the far distance; a deep (intensely deep) canopy of blue sky above, and the glare of the sunlight off the snowfields. This was a sort of daily record, and it became a painful one to those of the party who were unprovided with blue-glass spectacles, or goggles. I rode on the trail of my little camp caravan, and caught it up sometimes in the midst of a snowfield. With his head bandaged up into a bundle, and blue goggles protruding therefrom, the guide of the party made first tracks in the immaculate expanse. Behind him, one by one, slow and stately, swung the camels (there was no lack of camels at this time; there had been a time when we would have hired all the camels in Turkestan had it been possible—not that we wanted them, but we thought possibly the Russians might), and on the top of the camels unsightly bundles of humanity and baggage went waving and bobbing in time with their long, slow step; and every soul in the whole caravan, excepting the man leading, was fast asleep. It was amusing to note the gradual process of drifting by which the horse of the sleepy orderly with the caravan would gradually sheer up alongside of mine. Like two bits of wood in a drifting current, our two steeds would inevitably collide. The monotonous click, click of spur and scabbard seemed to possess a soothing faculty, like the ticking of a grandfather's clock. It was the only thing to be heard, as the drowsy horses with their silent riders slowly drifted into collision. Then, indeed, all was instant alertness. Asleep! Oh, dear no—nobody was asleep! Were they not taking a bee-line for the next camp? And there in the distance was the smoke curling up out of a black blotch on the landscape that was certainly a kibitka; which showed how wide awake they must have all been, or they never could have found it.

On an intensely cold, hard-freezing night the smoky comfort of the kibitka was not to be despised. It was better than a tent. You could throw half a stack of wood into the fire and enjoy a good blaze if you could only stand the smoke; and by lying down close to the ground the effects of smoke were modified. The process of making red-hot charcoal embers, which is the only method of warming a tent without a properly constructed stove, was slow, and one was often too cold to wait for it. I frequently made use of the village kibitka, and I never found that those creeping things which no doubt were there, and which make night hideous for sensitive folk, ever troubled me.

The winter passed, and spring had well advanced, when one sunny day Yate and I took our way into the Chol wilderness east of Maruchak, intent on boundary business; and hoping to find amid the tangle of salt mud ravines and hillsides now slippery with rain and knee-deep in grass, some possible track which might lead us along the line of demarcation. Our Jamshidi guide was not very hopeful. We might reach a point on the boundary here and there, catching it, as it were, on the passage from hill to hill (for this part of the Russo-Afghan boundary follows no natural feature, but takes a course across the general trend of all the streams which drain from the Karabel plateau into the Chaharshamba river), but as for following it systematically from end to end, the conformation of the Chol topography rendered such a feat impossible.

However, we started with light hearts, and a Cossack escort. There was sunshine, bright and clear; the snow had nearly disappeared; the air was full of the song of birds, and the tulips, scarlet and black, or pink-striped and white, were just beginning to air their glory amidst the deep, rank growth of grass. Life of itself was a joy amidst those unspoiled gifts of spring. Our halt for roadside breakfast on the first day out was in an open space where no shade was (there are no trees in the Chol), and we agreed that, delightful as might be the unsullied brightness of sunshine in the month of April, it was better, if possible, to temper it with shade. We would carry a small tent with us next day. This we did for several days, and then followed an experience the like of which had not befallen us since the crossing of Chashma Sabz pass in the early April of the year previous.

With but little warning, the full blast of the "shamshir" was upon us again, but we were not caught on the march this time.

Black and thick it rolled up against our tents, and the snow fell in blinding whirls, piling up to windward, and shooting into thin drifts through cracks and crevices, speedily obliterating grass and flowers, and finally settling into a two or three foot covering of the whole earth's surface. The thermometer fell to zero, and we were once more in the depths of winter. Spring was annihilated, and the situation was all the more unpleasant for being absolutely unexpected and unprovided for. When we attempted to move we found ourselves snowed up. Our wretched horses were standing out up to their knees in snow, and the grass, which was to have been their provender and support, required digging out. Innumerable small birds, who had shown over confidence in a treacherous climate, lay dead about the snowdrifts. Some even took refuge in Yate's tent; and, to crown our sorrows, wood was not obtainable near our camp, and cooking became an impossibility.

Fortunately, we had a certain amount of grain for our cattle; but we could spare little for the Cossacks, whose horses, huddled together in Cossack fashion in order to keep life and warmth in their bodies, could not, or did not, assist themselves by scratching away the snow. It is curious that my Australian horse, who had probably never seen snow in his life before the previous winter, showed much more ingenuity in scratching snow away from underneath the scattered scrub, where it was occasionally thin, and thus gaining a few mouthfuls of grass, than did the Cossack ponies, who must have been far more accustomed to similar situations. When the blizzard was once over (and forty-eight hours probably covered the whole duration of it), the sun shone out with intense and blinding brilliancy; the atmosphere cleared as if by magic, and the whole of our world became a mixture of bog and steam.

The first step was to gain a position where wood could be found. Thanks to the unerring instinct of our weather-beaten old Jamshidi guide, this was safely accomplished; the next was to get off an Afghan contingent of ponies and drivers down some practical route to the Chaharshamba valley, from whence they might bring back a certain amount of provisions to meet us; whilst meanwhile we proceeded on the practical business of demarcation. It was all accomplished finally with no worse results than the effects of snow blindness on most of the party, and the loss of a few ponies. My Afridi orderly found his eyes so seriously affected that I had to lend him my goggles, trusting to a green gauze veil for my own protection, which I wrapped closely across my face. It did not finally prevent me from suffering in the same way; but I never became totally blind. Our camels (of which we had a few) suffered terribly; some of them went absolutely blind. But the horses escaped, so far as their eyes were concerned. Two or three Cossack ponies were lost from starvation, as well as some of the Afghan transport which was bringing material for pillar building; but this was the full extent of the damage done. It might well have been worse.

As we gradually pushed our surveys right up to the Oxus, Gore and Talbot worked with the forward Russian contingent, whilst I kept up triangulation. All along British and Russian surveyors had worked in peace and amity together. The acerbities of political discussion, such as they were, were not for us. I found the Russian topographer ever ready to welcome any English colleague in the field of geography, and only too glad to place his little *tente d'abri* and his really excellent camp cuisine at his disposal. I acquired a taste for vodka, rye bread, and salt fish, to say nothing of caviare, which has not been weakened by time and distance. Of course there was a certain amount of rivalry in the field, and there were a few little plots to secure the first information about wells and cultivation, and such other items of intelligence as might affect the position of the boundary; but they were all understood to be conducted on strictly business principles which in no way affected private social relations. In this sort of field the Indian surveyors were soon keen competitors. Not even the veteran Benderski (whom I met years afterwards in a very different field) was able to cover more ground than Hira Sing in the course of a day's run. The latter had had a good practical training in Turkestan fields during the previous year. He had taken to the saddle. Now, a Gurkha on horseback exists in an atmosphere of surprises, both to himself and his friends; and when Hira Sing was seen in Cossack costume, and with a seat which, for picturesqueness, might have been the envy of Sloan, chasing a Turkman horseman of suspicious appearance across the plain; and when he finally returned safe and sound with the Turkman's head-dress as a trophy, we were undoubtedly surprised that he had returned at all. But he would have led a cavalry brigade, or a battery of Horse Artillery with equal assurance.

The same cordial relations which existed between the surveyors of both camps extended to the military escorts on either side. Visits were interchanged between the officers, and the hospitality of the Russian camp was almost embarrassing in its fulness. In the early winter, whilst the headquarters of the two camps were pitched at some little distance from each other, ere the British political section finally retired to hybernate at Chaharshamba, a curious sight might occasionally have been witnessed apropos of these friendly reciprocations.

An afternoon's call at the Cossack headquarters had come to an end, and evening was closing in, grey and lowering, after the last glint of sunshine had been withdrawn from the valley, when a gallant representative of our native cavalry would tear himself from the civilities of the Cossack mess. He could not be permitted to return to camp alone; nor was it right that he should cut short the afternoon's entertainment at the outskirts of the Russian camp. So he made his way slowly back with a Cossack escort. In front of him marched a brawny soldier, with a deal table reversed on his head; the legs appealing to the clouds. On either side of him was a representative officer of Cossack cavalry singing hymns, and on either side of them again were Cossack orderlies, who were more or less officially present to see that they did not miss the road. The road was a little difficult to distinguish. Behind this picturesque party (which never moved too fast) was the chorus of the Sotnia—a certain number of Cossacks who are instructed in singing, and who beguile the march day by day for many a weary mile with most excellent vocal music. The chorus took up the burden of the hymn of welcome which was sung by their officers, and ever and anon a halt was called. Then down came the table on to its four legs in the middle of the road. A bottle of vodka was produced from somewhere, and a toast was proposed and honoured. Then again the party would move on, and thus it progressed intermittently to the gates of the British camp. Here I am told that the mingled emotions that expressed themselves on the face of our gallant comrade, the proud appreciation of the honour which was conferred on him, coupled with a certain sense of shyness at the prospect of passing down the main street of the British camp past his commanding officer's front door, was delightful to witness. But at this point he usually wished his entertainers a most cordial and impressive good-bye.

Political friction was perhaps not to be avoided, but, so far as I know, it began and ended with political business. Our social relations with the Russian camp certainly did not begin and end with the interchange of official hospitality. This, of course, was not neglected; and justice was at last done to the consignments of liquor and stores which had been bumped about on camels and mules for so many months. But it was the cordiality of the unofficial relations between the surveyors and the military on either side which made that last year's work a work of pleasure, as well as of the deepest interest. There was no reason why it should not be so. A considerable portion of the original Commission that started from India had already disappeared from the field and found its way back to Quetta. We were a smaller party and more closely drawn together. The immediate purpose of our work from day to day was to make maps of all the country under dispute. It was the purpose of both sides equally, and we were equally concerned in the matter. And so things lasted till we reached the Oxus.

Here occurred the great difficulty of the bouhdary settlement, a difficulty which led to the general break up of the Commission in the field; and the transfer of the scene of discussion from the plains of Turkestan to Petersburg. It arose chiefly from over-confidence in the ancient geography of the Oxus regions, and the acceptance, in the boundary agreement drawn up between the Governments of England and Russia, of Khwaja Salar as a "post," or point, on the river which was to define the termination of the boundary. This post undoubtedly existed in the days of Burne's travels, some fifty years before the agreement was drawn up; but, unfortunately, it had ceased to exist so long before our arrival on the banks of the river that not the oldest inhabitant could tell us what had become of it, or where it had once stood. A district called Khwaja Salar extends for many miles along the southern banks of the Oxus. It is narrow, never more than a mile or so wide, but magnificently fertile and highly cultivated by irrigation drawn from the river. The Ersari Turkmans (we had left Salors and Sariks far behind) who hold it, are good cultivators, and show quite as much aptitude with the spade as they do with the tools of the light cavalry raider. Indeed, I thought that all clans of Turkmans seemed well enough disposed towards the peaceful occupation of land development if they could only be certain of security. It must be unsatisfactory to dig deep "juis" (canals) and spread out a network of minor irrigation channels; to raise fat crops of wheat and barley, and grow the apricots and apples of the Turkman orchards, if others are to take the proceeds in the fruit season. It was rather a surprise to me to find such splendid agricultural development anywhere in Afghan Turkestan. There was much of it then, and there is doubtless more now.

The great plain of the Oxus which extends towards Balkh is mostly fallow and unculturable for the want of irrigation. Where the rivers flow down from the southern hills (the rivers of Andkui, of Shiburgan, and Balkh, which drain the Band-i-Turkestan and Elburz) there is always a delta of irrigation, and every drop of available water is utilised; but none of these rivers ever reach the Oxus; and the gradual upheaval of the plain and formation of an anticlinal which cuts short their northward flow, will ever act as an impediment to the restoration of that ancient system of canal irrigation which once made the Mother of Cities the centre of human civilisation and progress.

But to return to Khwaja Salar. At the eastern end of the district there was, indeed, a ziarat, or shrine, sacred to the departed Khwaja, which made a definite *point d'appui;* but it was not a "post" within the recognised meaning of that term. It was finally discovered that there was a disused ferry which had long disappeared, and which might have been sufficiently marked to be called a "post," much further west. It was supposed that it had been washed into the river at some period of flood; and that the ferry had been removed to Kilif in consequence of the unalterable nature of the river channel at that point, and remained there. Anyhow, Khwaja Salar could not be found in such outward and visible form as would satisfy both Commissioners that it was the "post" of the agreement; and we spent the summer in a vain search, supported by elaborate mapping of all the Oxus riverain.

It was hot—very hot; and the daily wind seemed to carry little refreshment into our stuffy tents; where I have seen the thermometer register 120 degrees on my bed. We built bowers of some prickly material, which answered the local purpose of the Indian "khus-khus," and by keeping these well watered we gained such comparative coolness as enabled us to get on with the enormous mass of mapping that had to be reduced to practical form. The flies were, perhaps, our chief annoyance in that Oxus camp. They swarmed in their myriads and millions—as they swarm occasionally on the Indian frontier. They positively ate the Indian ink off the paper ere it was dry, and absolutely destroyed all artistic claims to clearness and decision in our drawing. Then they clung, bloated and sticky, to the tent-poles and furniture of what we delighted to call our office. There they were occasionally raided and killed with a fly-flapper. There is a certain advertisement of somebody's ink, in which a magnificent black splash with a purple centre indicates the result of an artistic ink-spill. That is how the Oxus flies spread out under the executioner's weapon. It was a gruesome method of disposing of them.

The river rolled down in a wide, reddish, turbid flood as the snow melted, and spread over its banks into little lagunes and lakelets which were often very picturesque. Indeed, there was no lack of beauty about Oxus scenery. The Bokhara hills to the north made a wild and rugged background to avenues of poplar and willow; to groups of orchard trees surrounding the neat, stone-built houses of the Ersaris, and to the shimmering spread of cultivation.

The scene at Kilif was well worth remembering. Kilif Fort is a queer picturesque pile of red buildings hanging about an isolated rock bordering the northern banks of the river. Here

THE OXUS FERRY AT KILIF

the bed narrows considerably, and immediately opposite Kilif are some bold rocky hills, which contain many quaint relics of past days when the "alamán" was the normal method of enlivening existence. Across the river the heavy ferry boats ply all day long, bringing Bokhara merchandise to the great trade routes to Afghanistan, either Kabulwards, or in the direction of Herat and Persia. They are loaded down to the water's edge sometimes, these heavy, clumsy barges, and with the rapid current of the river setting strongly down between the Kilif Fort and the Afghan hills would not be very easy to navigate. The local ferryman, however, saves himself all trouble in the matter by making use of horses, or rather ponies, to haul his boat along. One, or sometimes two, of these rather insufficient-looking animals are attached to the boat by belly-bands or sircingles, which allow them to swim alongside, with the strain of the haul on their middles. They are, I believe, to a certain extent supported in the water by the ropes which attach them to the boat; but only their heads are usually visible as they strike out with measured pace, snorting with each stroke, being directed from the boat as to which way they should go. So powerful is their stroke that two small thirteen-hand "tattoos" will easily pull over a boat which might carry ten tons of dead weight. One almost looked to see if their feet were webbed as they struggled into the shallows of the river banks. It is a curious method of ferrying (unique, I expect), and it was a revelation to me as to the strength of a horse's stroke in the water.

As the summer waxed hot ere it shivered with the first shoots of cold air from the northern deserts, our limits for geographical exploitation became more and more restricted. It was not the heat alone which restricted them. We had our hands full with the detailed surveys of the Oxus riverain and the Herat valley at that time; but we had also an accession to our survey strength in the shape of three good native surveyors, who were sent up from India, and who did not arrive before they were sorely needed. Chief amongst them was Yusuf Sharif, a Mahomedan gentleman who has worked with me, and for me, for so many years in so many different fields that I feel it difficult to acknowledge his services adequately. He has received the recognition of the Royal Geographical Society since those days. He has become a Khan Bahadur, and he is an authority on the geography of so much of our Indian frontier that there is probably not another native in the service of Government who is so full of "confidential" information of a practical nature. Withal he is a loyal and true-hearted gentleman, a living type of a class of native employés of whom Sir West Ridgeway wrote, at the close of the Commission, that the Government of India had no better servants. May he live long to enjoy his honours!

With this addition to our party we could have spread again into geographical fields that might have extended through Badakshan to the Pamirs, but for a sudden change in the attitude of the Amir towards the mission. We only learnt afterwards what had happened. He had mistaken the meaning of a second mission which reached Badakshan from Gilgit, under Lockhart; and had considered himself threatened by the irruption of a handful of Balti coolies who had been engaged as carriers. This may have been the true meaning of his change—or it may not. Amongst those who were nearest to the Court at Kabul, and had the best chance of knowing, I have heard whispered the word "gout." Anyhow, the result was the same. Not only were we strictly confined to the business of the boundary as it lay immediately to our hands, but the attitude of our Afghan guardian, Saad-u-din, the Kazi, the nephew of the fanatic old Mullah Mushki Alam who lighted the bonfire on Asmai as a signal for the assault on Sherpur, distinctly changed for the worse. It had always been bad enough. From the first day that I called on him with Durand and found him cold and clammy—bathed in a perspiration induced by sheer fright at the prospect before him of acting as personal conductor to our expedition (responsible to the last bone in his body for the individual safety of some thirty Englishmen who had perhaps too little regard for their own safety), he had been a thorn in the side of the Commission. He possessed none of that charming affability and princely courtesy which distinguishes most of the nobles of Afghanistan. He was only a commoner, and he behaved like one. But doubtless he did his duty well by his master, and it is not for us to judge him. At this time, however, he became truculent and unpleasant in his demeanour, and he was imitated in servile fashion by all his Afghan retainers.

Fortunately this phase of policy did not last long. We had permission to retire by Kabul to India; and as soon as the boundary question was finally relegated to home decision we left the Oxus for good. We crossed the great Balkh plains to Mazar-i-Sharif and Tashkurghan, and passed the terrific gates and gorges of the hills which lead to Haibak. We could now take a wider field again into our geographical embrace. Gore, with Imam Sharif (brother of Yusuf), had left for Mashad and the frontiers of Persia, with instructions to make his way through Khorasan to Bandar Abbas, on the coast of the Persian Gulf, and to carry on a systematic survey *en route*. Talbot had been through the mountains that border on Badakshan. He had seen the gigantic Budhist rock-cut idols at Bamian; he had unearthed many a strange relic of Budhism in the Hindu Kush districts which must once have been closely connected with the centre and capital of that faith in the days when the valley of the Kabul was full of it, and the valley of the Kunar was in the hands of the Kafir. Now we all stood in line under the northern slopes of the Hindu Kush; and we subsequently passed that range by every pass that was open between the Khawák on the north and Bamian on the south, reckoning up the value of each, and placing each in its right position relatively to Kabul and the mountains which enclose it. It was a good finish. We were none too soon either. The storm signals were hung out over the highest peaks which bordered the pass of Chahardar when we crossed it. Thick, black, October clouds, bulging with snow, were heaped on the surrounding hills (which here run to something over 14,000 feet), and it hardly seemed likely that we should get the whole party over without difficulty. We did so, however, and dropped easily and quickly into the Ghorband valley. On the top of the Hindu Kush, from the summit of a peak adjoining the pass, a last view was gained of the Turkestan mountain tops which lay northward towards Haibak, and the first view of those snowy summits in Kohistan to the north of Kabul, which had been fixed in geographical position during the progress of the Afghan war.

Here, then, closed the long line of triangulation which, with so many vicissitudes, had preserved the connection of all its successive links from Quetta to Mashad and Herat, and from Herat to the Hindu Kush and Kabul. It was the final link in a chain of technical expedients. It was a test of the value of method and instrument rather than a testimony to the skill of the surveyor. It proved once for all what may be done with the smaller class of theodolites aided by the plane table; and it proved much more that we need not enter into here, for it all belongs to a chronicle of another kind. There was joy in the camp of the surveyors when they met again in the general gathering up of the Commission at Kabul, and found that all the great mass of patchwork fitted together with satisfactory exactness, and that the work of two years was closed with no displacement, and no corrections necessary in our geographical maps.

It is not possible to skip lightly over that march down the Ghorband valley. It lives in the memory apart from other scenes of interest and beauty as the crowning scene of all. We were still on the Amir's high road to Turkestan, which we had struck on the other side the Hindu Kush, and it was a road which reflected the highest credit on the Kabul Public Works Department. We could ride down it at our ease, and enjoy the scenery at our leisure. On either side rose battlemented cliffs, with now and then a crumbling castle watching over the pass below, fitting into the cliffs like a natural outgrowth. Trees of all the tints of autumn filled up the slopes between the roadway and the cliff basement; below us was the mountain torrent tumbling along in rapid and cascade between its rocky banks; and here and there a corner of alluvial ground reached out from the stream, yellow with autumn crops or deep in pasture. It was the scenery of Switzerland and of the Rhine combined. The little parties of Afghan gentlemen whom we met out for a day's hawking were quite mediæval in their costumes and their trappings. Any one of them might have stepped out of Early English tapestry. Occasionally the valleys widened considerably, and the sweep of the enclosing

THE GHORBAND VALLEY

hills was carried upward to snow-capped peaks on either hand, leaving a vista of orchards and villages, and the blue mist of a multitude of distances between them, whilst at the end there shimmered the far-away blink of perpetual snow. Afghanistan is beautiful throughout its northern districts, but nowhere else in Afghanistan have I seen the landscape of Turner's ideal combined with the grandeur of Kashmir mountain scenery. The Ghorband valley route leads northward from the direct line joining Haibak and Kabul, so as to avoid the necessity of traversing a second range or branch of the Hindu Kush, called Paghmán, which overlooks the plains surrounding the city. This secondary range we were already well acquainted with, for we had reached it previously from Kabul. All these northern routes across the mountains join at Charikar, in Kohistan, and here the survey party was mostly reunited. Talbot had come over the Kaoshán, or Hindu Kush, pass, for the pass really gives its name to the range, from the fact that it was here that a Hindu force perished in the snow whilst attempting to cross into Badakshan. Hindu Kush does not mean the "happy Hindu," as is often supposed, but the "dead Hindu"; and there is a grim significance about the name. This was the range, as it stretches northwards, which formed the Paropamisus of Alexander. He crossed into Kabul by the Kaoshán, but the name Paropamisus has for so long been adopted for the Herat extension of this northern mountain system that it is not convenient to displace it. Yusuf Sharif crossed by the Khawák pass at the head of the Panjshir. Peacock investigated the southern group of passes south of Chahardar.

This may be said to have closed the book of Afghan exploration in connection with the Russo-Afghan Boundary Commission; for although the transfer of negotiations to Petersburg opened up fresh claims which were based on geographical considerations outside the zone of the original agreement in the Kushk valley, advantage had been taken of a suspension of demarcating operations when nearing the Oxus, to obtain full topographical information about this new area.

It was indeed clear as our surveys progressed that a revision of the boundary agreement which confined operations to a certain zone would become necessary. There are certain considerations which must govern the existence of every boundary that possesses any pretensions to be of a practical nature, and these conditions were not to be found within that zone. The final result was that the Russian boundary was shifted to a position very much nearer Herat; but there was no difficulty in negotiating this new alignment at Petersburg by the light of the mapping already completed. Actual pillar-marking was all that was subsequently necessary.

At Kabul we were sumptuously entertained by the Amir. He had (or appeared to have) recovered from his feelings of indignation at the "invasion" of Badakshan; and when he arrived at Kabul, after some days' delay, there was nothing wanting in the fulness of his hospitality. It was with much interest that I revisited the scenes of our military experiences of 1879, and noted the changes that had taken place in six or seven years. New roads, new gardens and palaces had sprung up, and the bazaars and streets were full of life and energy. A review of the Amir's troops showed no neglect of War Office administration. There was a remarkably well-set-up and smart-looking regiment of household cavalry that, for equipment and mounting, would have done credit to any army in the world. The artillery was rough, but serviceable; and much the same might be said for the infantry, whose roughness, however, was more apparent, for it was due to a lack of uniformity in clothing. However, I have had the opportunity of testing the capacity of Afghan infantry in other fields, and I know that their powers of endurance are not to be measured by the smartness of their clothes.

Looking westward over the Chardeh plain from the Amir's new gardens, near Baba's tomb, it was hardly possible to recognise the scene of that memorable fight of December, 1879, in the poplar-covered flats which spread below us. In the matter of planting, as in administration, there was most marked development. In short, the keynote of the whole scene was progress—progress everywhere. But we did not stay long in Kabul. I had there an interview with an old surveyor who had been on my native staff during the campaign, and who had taken service with the Amir at the end of it, which was as interesting as his whole story is instructive. He was a Kashmiri who had risen from the position of writer and accountant to be a very able draftsman and plane tabler, and he finally developed considerable capacity as an explorer. It is only after many years of steady service in the Survey Department that these native surveyors acquire the professional skill which is necessary in a geographical map maker. They probably on the whole acquire it quicker than Europeans, as they are neater handed and more patient, and they give their whole time to it. Still, it takes long to make a good plane tabler; and Abdul Subhan was one of the best. Consequently his value was well known; he was a well-tried servant, and he was entrusted on several occasions with missions of importance and secrecy. He accompanied Trotter on the mission to Yarkand, under the leadership of Forsyth, and he was the authority for our mapping of all the Oxus region between the Pamirs and Badakshan. He is the authority for a good deal of it still. During the Afghan campaign he was a most able assistant, carrying on his detailed surveys from day to day whilst we were still shut up in Sherpur, when it would have been absolutely impossible for any European to have ventured on such service. At the close of the campaign he was deputed to undertake a very difficult and extensive reconnaissance right across Afghanistan. He is dead now, so there is no harm in these references. But unfortunately he was just at that time in a state of deep disgust at the refusal of the Indian Government to raise his pay by a few rupees per month, and his Kashmir instincts (to call a man a Kashmiri in the Punjab is much the same as calling him a liar) rose to the surface. He accepted my instructions, together with certain advances, and disappeared. We returned to India, and not long after there arrived in India evidence which was unimpeachable, that Abdul Subhan had taken service with the Amir at a high rate of pay, and that he had practically deserted from my party. Let me hasten to say that this is the one solitary instance in which such a lapse has occurred. Men have explored all over Asia year after year, and have brought back their tale of mapping together with information of the utmost importance—such information as might have found a high value if taken to a paying market—and not a single other instance can I recall of misplaced confidence. Ten times his normal pay had proved too much for his cupidity. The Amir had marked the usefulness of the man, and he had taken him at his own valuation.

Well; I saw him again in Kabul. He was then Brigadier of Artillery, Instructor in Signalling, Surveyor-General, and many other public functionaries all rolled into one. He had amassed wealth, and he wanted to make the *amende* to me (he was under the impression that the loss of the advances made to him was personal; which it was not), and restore all that he owed to my office treasury. He gave me his confidence, and I gave him mine, and advised him to walk straight in future and stick to his new career. Apparently he could not take that advice. In an atmosphere of Court intrigue he became as bad as the worst intriguer there. He doubtless intrigued against Sir Salter Pyne when Pyne had secured the royal favour. I can recognise him again under a thin disguise in Gray's amusing account of his Kabul experiences; and Gray has no good to say of him. He finally miscalculated his influence with the Amir, and came to an Afghan end. He may have been smothered (as I think Gray states), but I am more inclined to think, from certain internal evidence, that the story of an execution which reached India from Kabul referred to my old explorer and Trotter's right-hand man. He was called upon to ascend a machán, or elevated platform built up on high poles, and there await the Amir's pleasure. There he stayed with the glaring Afghan sun staring down on his starving frame, till the end came. Such, at any rate, is the tale that is believed by his own fellow-workmen; and possibly the moral of it is just as good in a frontier survey office as in the Court of Kabul. But whatever may have been the sins which he committed in his later career, he held his place for a time and made his influence felt. I have very little doubt that one result of that influence was the freedom with which native surveyors were permitted to traverse the untrodden parts of Afghanistan in the early days of the Boundary Commission; and another is the remarkable acumen which the

Amir has always displayed about maps. He not only knows the meaning of a map when he sees one, and can decipher its topography, but he has shown a shrewd appreciation of the part which a map may be made to play in the political arena of boundary agreements.

By the end of the autumn of 1886 this chapter in the history of the modern geographical definition of some of the oldest commercial areas in the world was closed. The Russo-Afghan Commission had given us very much. Some of our gain was premeditated and sought for; the rest of it was the accidental result of a long-extended course of proceedings which were neither premeditated nor desired. As the cost was great, we may conclude this chapter by summing up what we got for our money; and in what direction the knowledge that we then gained may influence the future of our frontier policy.

We gained in the first instance a boundary which definitely limited the territorial progress of Russia towards India. Of that boundary Sir West Ridgeway wrote afterwards that, although a war with Russia might lead to its violation, its violation would never lead to a war; that is to say that the gain to Russia of further advance towards Herat would of itself (apart from all other political considerations) never justify the extreme penalty of war with England. An advance on Herat would only form part of some far-reaching scheme of development, which would involve interests of much greater importance either further west, or further east. Under such conditions the actual physical nature of the boundary is not of vast importance. Local questions and disputes would never become the pretext for any substantial violation of the line agreed upon, and whether that line be sixty or eighty miles from Herat city is only a matter of comparatively unimportant detail.

The boundary from Zulfikar, on the Hari Rud, to the Kushk river, and from the Kushk to the Murghab, is an effective line following fairly prominent natural features which it is impossible to mistake. On the Oxus, again, there can be no question raised in future as to its exact *point d'appui*. But intermediate between the Murghab and the Oxus, where it passes through the monotonous wilderness of the Chol hills, crossing all the main lines of drainage from the Karabel plateau to the Chaharshamba valley, and again striking across a wide expanse of desert between the foot of the Chol and the Oxus riverain, it is little more than a "paper" line; for its practical demarcation on the ground in such a manner as to render it readily recognisable to the nomad inhabitants would have been impossible without prohibitive expense of money, time, and labour. The wandering shepherd from the Karabel plateau, who drives his flocks down the long, grass-covered valleys which run towards the Chaharshamba stream, knows that when he has reached that stream he has transgressed the boundary. Similarly, the sheep-grazing nomad, who works upwards, is only aware that he is beyond his rights when he finds himself on the plateau. But no danger need be apprehended from this want of definition. The country is too sparsely inhabited, and the grazing rights of too ephemeral a character, to be likely to involve any actual appeal to force such as might seriously disturb the peace of the border. Such a boundary might well have been attained by a mutual agreement between Russia and England, based on actual surveys made by a comparatively small party, working at comparatively small expense under the Amir's guarantee of safety, without raising any important political question locally; involving no risks of collision with Russia, and exciting little public comment. But had we adopted so simple an expedient, we should certainly have missed a vast store of geographical information such as should now enable us rightly to appraise the value of these transfrontier regions in the general scheme of economic development affecting the commercial interests of India equally with her military position. We know now what Herat is to us; what lies between Herat and India; what are the relations between Herat and Kabul; and we should be able to decide for ourselves whether Herat is worth the sacrifices that at one time we were certainly prepared to make for it.

It has always seemed to me that Herat owes much to the accidents of its geographical surroundings. North, south, and west of it there are huge stretches of unproductive country, which can hardly be called desert, but which only present facilities for development and cultivation over restricted areas. East of it the upper reaches of the Hari Rud valley wind away into the inhospitable mountain regions of the Koh-i-Baba; regions of barren hills intersected by narrow little valleys, and these valleys are as nothing in comparison with the width of wilderness which binds them. In fact, the actual wealth of the Hari Rud valley is all centred between Obeh and Kuhsán. There is not much more than a hundred miles of it in length; and it is hardly fifteen miles in average width from the foot of that secondary range on the north (the Koh-i-Mulla Khwaja) to the long, straight-backed ridges which divide it from the Taimani country on the south, and which run out to an end in scattered fragments near the longitude of Kuhsán. There are one or two important affluents of the Hari Rud (such as the stream which drains the Korokh valley to the north-east of Herat), and these affluents support fairly populous districts in their immediate neighbourhood; but it is the valley of the Hari Rud itself in the immediate neighbourhood of Herat, crammed as it is, with villages, and irrigated as it is, to the utmost capacity of the river to maintain irrigation, that has given Herat its extraordinary celebrity amongst the cities of Asia. It is the startling contrast between almost abnormal fertility and almost absolute sterility which strikes the imagination, and which has, in my opinion, tended to wrap round Herat a fictitious estimate of commercial value. The practical capabilities of its valley have been carefully reckoned up. Its resources are by no means inexhaustible. Its people are for the most part an inoffensive and most unwarlike race of agriculturists, who would prefer to be left in peace. The Herati would neither assist to defend Herat nor to take it. The city is a poor one, and its bazaar quite third-rate, as compared to either Kandahar or Kabul. The propinquity of a Russian railway may have done something to develop it. We found that it was very largely influenced even by the contiguity of a Russo-Afghan Commission; but at present it is not, nor has it been for centuries, on any great commercial highway of Asia; and it is only because the river affords the means of cultivating an oasis in the midst of a wilderness that Herat can claim any commercial eminence. In those far-off centuries of our era, before the great overland trade routes from the East to the West were blocked by the Turk; when the commerce of the East was concentrated on a line which included Mashad, Tiflis, and the Black Sea; Herat must have played a prominent part, if not one of the highest commercial importance, in a general scheme of khafila traffic, which claimed a trade connection between Herat, Kandahar, and Multan. It may do so again in the process of the world's economic evolution; but it was, for the time being at any rate, fairly knocked out of commercial existence by Moghul invasions, and it failed to recover its position before the sea route to India was established. Once again it *may* claim a high place amongst the cities of the Eastern world; but this will only be when the rail head, which now points to Kandahar from the little out-of-the-way station of New Chaman, is drawn out northwards, and passes Herat to the Russian frontier. There is no practical difficulty about this 500 miles of railway extension. Indeed, regarded as a feat of engineering skill, it would be so simple—so inexpensive—in comparison with any other connection by rail between Europe and India that could be seriously suggested, that it is difficult to conceive that it will not be ultimately adopted.

The geographical conformation of Afghanistan, east of the Herat-Farah-Kandahar line, is such as to render a through connection between the Russian and Indian railway systems prohibitive on account of the immense expense that would be involved in traversing systems of mountains of which the general main axial strike crosses the line of projected railway. There is the further difficulty of the high altitudes which prevail throughout northern Afghanistan, and which alone would render traffic impossible for months together, on account of snow. If there is one high-road between Kabul and the Oxus which might possibly be brought within the pale of practical railway engineering, it is that which now forms the khafila route across the Hindu Kush by the Khawák pass and the Panjshir valley; but the height of that pass is 11,640 feet above sea, and it is exceedingly doubtful if the measures which are taken to keep the pass open for khafila traffic would be equally serviceable in the case of an open line of railway. As for any possible connection across the Pamirs, it can only be regarded as absolutely chimerical. There is, indeed, no reasonable probability that any practical method of connecting Russia with India across the Hindu Kush will ever be discovered.

Turning to the west of the Herat-Kandahar line, we have all Persia before us. Here, indeed, the advocates of a through line to India have an open field for speculation. But the geography of that country has been almost as much misrepresented as that of Afghanistan. Assuming that the head of the Persian Gulf will finally be brought into connection with Europe by the Euphrates scheme, there are doubtless possible opportunities afforded by Persian topography for its extension eastwards to the Baluch frontier. But no practicable alignment has as yet been suggested; and it requires a close acquaintance with the mountain configuration of southern Persia to point out where such an alignment is possible. This, however, is a matter which will be considered further on. At present we are considering the possibility of a Kushk-Quetta connection through Afghanistan.

From the Russian advanced station of Kushk in the valley of the same name (which must not be confused with the Jamshidi capital of Badghis, also called Kushk, which lies considerably to the south), the surface of the loess formation forming the northern slopes of the Paropamisus sweeps up in comparatively gentle slopes to the main watershed. The height of the Russian station is about 2,000 feet above sea. The height of the crest of the Ardewán pass on the main water-divide is about 4,800 feet, and its distance from Kushk is, roughly, thirty miles. The back of the Paropamisus widens about the Ardewán, so that the pass winds and twists for some six or seven miles through the rounded summits of the range ere it reaches Kush Robat (3,900 feet) at the foot of the southern slopes. Sixteen miles of nearly level dasht (sand and gravel formation) intervening between the southern foot of the Paropamisus and the northern foot-hills of the subsidiary range of Koh-i-Mulla Khwaja brings the road to Parwána, a walled town commanding the main entrance to a pass, or gorge, through the Mulla Khwaja. Thence a winding nullah-bed, and eight miles of twisting through this insignificant mountain range, opens out on to the alluvial flats of the Herat valley, where canals and cultivation are the only barriers to progress. Herat is about six miles from the debouchment of the pass. The total distance to Herat from the crest of the Paropamisus, as indicated by the Ardewán Kotal, is about thirty-six miles; the drop from the Dasht-i-Ardewán through the Mulla Khwaja to Herat being about 1,000 feet. Herat is 2,600 feet above the sea. Three miles nearly due south of Herat the river Hari Rud is crossed by the Malún bridge; and beyond that river southward no further obstacle of any consequence to railway engineering is encountered through the 360 miles of road winding through Sabzawar and Farah to Kandahar. For twenty-eight miles the road, which turns the eastern end of the isolated Doshakh ridge, stretches over open uplands of dasht, encountering no great wealth of townships or villages after leaving the immediate neighbourhood of the river; but, on the other hand, encountering no engineering difficulties as it steers its course a little west of south to Chahgazak wells.

For the next forty-five miles the country is an undulating upland of the same dasht formation, with little cultivation, little water, and no villages of any size till it skirts the Adraskand river on its right (or western) bank, some ten miles above the populous town of Sabzawar (3,550 feet). For the next sixty miles to Farah (2,500 feet) there might be room for divided opinion as to alignment. The direct route would involve the negotiation of a considerable stretch of hilly country between the Adraskand and the Farah rivers. The hills belong to the tail of that vast stretch of highland country which, gradually increasing in elevation as it reaches to the north-east, is finally buttressed on to the central chain of the Hindu Kush and Koh-i-Baba, about the sources of the Helmund. Between the Adraskand and the Farah rivers it sweeps out into the plains that centre on the Helmund swamps with long, narrow, jagged ridges, running with a general north-east and south-west strike; nowhere (at this point of their strike) much elevated, or formidable, but ranged in a more or less serrated phalanx on the direct route from Sabzawar to Farah, and only tailing out to a single line of ridge some forty miles north-west of Farah. Here the whole mountain barrier is concentrated at Anardarra, a

THE PUL·I·MALUN

pretty little town perched in a transverse valley of the hills, called the Anardarra Gap; which is indeed but a short pass of a mile or so from side to side of a rocky ridge. An advantage in a westerly détour would be the inclusion of several flourishing townships, such as Sangbur, Zakin, and Kang. The villages hereabout cover considerable oases with cultivation and orchards; they are picturesquely scattered round the feet of the disjointed and broken hills which rise from the surrounding sea of scrub-covered plain and rolling dasht, like islands, with a sweep of wind-blown sand piled against their weather sides. The Persian windmill, built to catch the north-western blasts and to concentrate the wind by an artificial funnel on to the horizontal sails, is a familiar feature hereabouts. There is a pretty trade in carpets at Anardarra, and all round about Farah (the classical Phra) are homesteads, and wide fields, and a well-developed agricultural landscape. To call this a barren land, or an unpromising one for the developments that railways bring, is altogether misleading. As yet it is not a rich country; but it possesses natural advantages which might easily make it so.

From Farah to Gerishk, on the Helmund, is 150 miles of fairly level roadway, skirting the base of the northern hills, but crossing their lines of strike and drainage through the whole distance. Not much is known of the levels of this part of the route, but it is certain that very many small and comparatively insignificant nullahs would have to be crossed; and that on its northern flank, near the Helmund, lies the teeming province of Zamindawar, full of villages and thriving settlements, rich in pasturage and agricultural products, and swarming with a fierce and most untamed race of Durani Afghans. Even the Amir thinks twice before meddling with Zamindawar.

From Gerishk to Kandahar we need not particularise the route. It is well enough known to our military experts, and it presents no very insuperable difficulties to railway engineering. There are about seventy miles of it, making in all some 350 to 360 miles of line between Herat and Kandahar.

To sum up, there are no formidable engineering difficulties to be encountered, but there are three large and somewhat uncertain rivers (the Farah, Adraskand, and Helmund) to cross; the last of the three requiring extensive bridging; all three, as well as smaller intermediate streams, being liable to heavy floods. There are no severe grades, and only one narrow band of hills which need necessarily be traversed. There is an irregular distribution of populated districts, analogous to that of the Sind and Lower Punjab sections of the north-west Indian frontier railway—a railway which has certainly succeeded in paying its way, even locally.

The question of the Kushk-Kandahar connection is daily assuming more importance as a factor in Anglo-Russian polity. Whilst we are at a standstill in the matter of railway extension on the north and west of India, most significant progress is being made on the European side. The concession by Turkey for the construction of the Konieh-Bagdad-Basra line to a German Anatolian Company not only affects the military position of Russia with regard to Asia Minor, but foreshadows the possible contingency of a junction between German and British interests in southern Persia by the extension of a system of railways which might eventually unite India with the Basra terminus and shut off Russia from the Persian coast. Such a possibility has already been discussed by statesmen such as Lord Curzon, who have made a special study of the subject. The practical possibilities of railway construction in Persia will be considered later on. Meanwhile the theoretical possibilities, so far as England is concerned, appear to have been shelved by the Russian repartee to the German concession. The arrangement lately concluded between the Russian Bank and the Shah's Government, by which Russia obtains entire control of Persian finance on consideration of a loan of three and a half millions sterling, is a stroke of business which effectually precludes foreign interference (other than Russian) with Persian commercial policy. At any rate, British railways in Persia are at present beyond the pale of practical discussion, and they may continue to be so for an indefinite period. Farther north the promise of a direct connection between the Trans-Caspian system and the central railways of Russia is even more significant to India than is the Bagdad concession.

This latter scheme is already strenuously advocated, and seems likely to assume practical shape. The proposed alignment is from Alexandrop-Gai, where the Ryazan-Ural Railway at present ends, almost straight viâ Kungrad and Khiva to Charjui and Merv. This connection promises to be more important in political and strategical advantages than it would be commercially. Its strategical importance may be estimated by the fact that troops could be sent from Moscow to Merv in a hundred hours, and from Warsaw in less than six days. It would avoid the delay attending the passage of the Caspian, and (according to Mr. R. Long, who writes in the *Fortnightly Review* for last December) practically shortens the route to Central Asia "by the whole distance between Krasnovodsk (the terminal station of the Trans-Caspian Railway on the Caspian shore) and Charjui."

Thus a well-organised system, not unreasonable to expect on a great trunk line utilised for Indo-European traffic, would place the whole of the Trans-Caspian system within less than a week's journey from Moscow. Were the Kushk-Kandahar-Chaman line completed, it is estimated that a passenger leaving Moscow, and travelling twenty miles an hour, would reach Quetta in six days and Karachi in seven and a half, or, in other words, he could complete the whole distance from London to Karachi in something under ten and a half days.

The commercial interests of such a line are necessarily indefinite and intricate. It is impossible to forecast exact results. Russian commercial authorities assert that it would do more mischief by diverting the Central Asian trade from Russia to India than it would effect to their advantage by opening up Indian markets to Russian goods. They are not altogether in its favour. But although, as I have pointed out, there is no reason to suppose that it would prove to be a financial failure with respect to local traffic, it is unlikely that any great development of goods traffic of a "through" nature between India and Europe would result from its construction. No such extended line of railway could compete with ocean traffic, and the break of bulk necessitated by the break of guage at Kushk would be an evil only slightly less than that of transshipment for the Caspian passage. It is probably not as a commercial venture that it could specially benefit either Russia or India. It would, at any rate, be unwise to make any assumptions in this respect. The gain to India would be the shortened overland route and a possible diminished expenditure in transit between Europe and India. It can hardly be doubted that the vast majority of the passenger traffic between England and India would be diverted to the overland route, or that such traffic would enormously increase. The gain to Russia (and it would be a most substantial gain) would be the contract for carrying European mails and passengers, the value of which has been computed by an eminent Russian engineer as ample guarantee for the success of the through line (so far as Russia is concerned) independently of local developments. The gain to both would be the better international understanding arising from more frequent and more personal intercourse. The military aspect of the connection remains to be considered.

Doubtless the advocates of a policy for keeping our rivals and our possible enemies in Asia at a distance, and of avoiding all measures which might tend to facilitate an approach to our borders, have much to say for themselves. The line from Kandahar to Herat is a long line, and it would be impossible to guard its whole length with our present Indian military resources. But it is doubtful if such considerations ever ultimately stood in the way of an international project such as this; a project which makes distinctly for the advance of Asiatic civilisation, and, probably, far more for mutual friendly understanding between two peoples already *personally* well affected towards each other than for commercial disputes and rivalries. We shall probably make that railway eventually; and we shall find that the break of guage at Herat or Kushk is one considerable safeguard against the use of the line as a military factor in an advance upon India; and that the existence on its flank of a numerous, warlike, and fanatical people (for we could never construct the line without a complete understanding with Afghanistan) is another safeguard. Indeed, the value of a long single line of railway communication has already been seriously discounted by our experiences in South Africa. It was not an advance with the assistance of the railway that led to the occupation of Bloemfontein. It is far more probable that mutual financial interest in the maintenance of the line would prove to be important in tightening the bonds of peace than that the line itself should lend much assistance to our enemies in a war which, year by year, as the world grows older and wiser, acquires more and more political *vis inertiæ*, and is less and less likely to occur.

CHAPTER VIII.

DEVELOPMENTS IN BALUCHISTAN

What Sandeman first found in Baluchistan—Afghan and Baluch—Advance and Administration—Result of occupation of Zhob—Political expedition of 1889—Opening of the Gomul—Zhob expedition of 1890—Kidarzais again.

THE gradual development of Baluchistan into a province under British administration is inseparably connected with the career of Sir Robert Sandeman. Other able officers had entered the arena of Kalat politics before Sandeman's time, and had left their mark; but it was with Sandeman that the border policy of absolute "non-interference" changed to active interest in the internal affairs of that country. Thornton writes of him that "he found the tribal organisation of the Baluchis of his district in a state of rapid decay, the authority and influence of the chiefs and headmen waning, the different sections and subsections at loggerheads with each other, and some of the tribes at bitter enmity with tribes beyond the border; while still further west civil war was raging between the Khan of Kalat and his confederate chiefs."

The "close border" system, which had hitherto been applied almost as much to Baluchistan as to the Punjab, had the effect of keeping frontier officers absolutely ignorant of frontier geography, and prevented that intercourse between them and transborder chiefs which might have led to better mutual understanding. Previous political methods of dealing with the borderlands of north and south respectively had differed in degree, but both had resulted in shutting the gates of the frontier in the face of explorers, so that geographical darkness reigned over all the mountain tracts between the highlands of Baluchistan and the plains of the Indus. There are many points of difference, both physical and ethnographical, between Afghanistan and Baluchistan, and this may serve to explain, to a certain extent, the success of those methods of administration which Sandeman introduced. Perhaps a brief reference to the general characteristics of both countries will help to illustrate this difference.

The mountainous belt of independent country which forms the great barrier of the north-west of India extends from the extreme north of the Punjab right down the Indus frontier through Sind to Karachi (a distance of about 1,200 miles), and does not end even there, for it curves away westward through Makran, north of the Arabian Sea, to Persia, and then continues to form a vast series of steps leading up from the sea coast to the plateau along the eastern shores of the Persian Gulf. There is no real interruption or break in this long extended system, although it is pierced here and there by the rivers which drain through it from the highlands beyond, and which generally form more or less practicable transverse routes from the plains into the interior of the continent. But there is a remarkable feature in Sind, where a flat, triangular desert inlet from the Indus valley runs from south to north, penetrating the hills at the entrance of the Bolán and Nari routes to Quetta. This is the Kach, or Kachi, of Gandara; and it is, perhaps, the most highly irrigated and best developed corner of Baluchistan territory.

On the east of this alluvial inlet are the Mari and Bugti mountains, which here round off the Sulimanis, and bring them to a southern terminus. West of it is the elevated Kalat plateau. Northward from it one penetrates by the double line (the Harnai and the Bolán) to the upland valleys about Quetta and Peshin. This displacement in the general strike of the frontier mountain barrier results in the piling up of the highest and most massive peaks in the neighbourhood of the Peshin. Quetta is surrounded by great peaks, such as Murdar, Takatu, Zerghun, and Chiltán, all well over 10,000 feet high, and all possessing grand outlines and magnificent geographical independence. The cantonment lies low in the midst; an oasis of green trees surrounding pretty, well-built houses, and gardens gay with all the flowers of East and West. But he would be a misguided man who, looking out from the windows of the train which landed him at eventide at Quetta, surprised by the still, pastoral beauty of the landscape around, should imagine that this was typical Baluchistan. Quetta scenery is more than pretty, better than beautiful; it is almost a resurrection from the dead to those who remember Quetta of 1878; but it is not a fair sample of Baluchistan. Baluchistan, taking it as a whole, is a country of rugged, barren hills intersecting stony plains and plateaux, of arid deserts where the wind-blown sand spreads out in alternation with dry spaces of level "put" (alluvial clay, baked hard and cracked in the sun), or with gravel-strewn plains interspersed with those heaps of rubbish which the Baluch nomad maintains were shot down here at the creation of the world. Wherever there is a line of watercourse not too impossibly salt for effective use, there is also a line of thin cultivation and a growth of tamarisk trees, a species of vegetation which seems to thrive on salt.

Baluchistan contains much of large stone-covered plains and dry rocky mountains; of wastes which are more conspicuously desert than anything which may be found in northern Afghanistan. They are, however, repeated in southern Afghanistan, on both sides the lower course of the Helmund, where naturally we find much the same sort of country on either side the border. Much of northern Afghanistan approaches Kashmir in the beauty of its mountain scenery, and in the wealth of its cultivation, which is maintained by irrigation works so complicated and complete that it is difficult to imagine it to be capable of either extension or improvement. The wealth of fruit, too, which is grown in the northern valleys of Afghanistan is absolutely unknown in Baluchistan, excepting about Quetta and in lately developed gardens

The enormous extent of unprofitable Baluchistan seems to crush out of recognition those spaces which may be turned to good account. And yet these spaces (insignificant if compared to the grand total) are by no means a small factor in the economic development of the country. And it was this geographical fact which chiefly impressed Sandeman early in his remarkable career. He was never weary of insisting that agricultural Baluchistan was at least as big as England; and his interest in the gradual unearthing of the evidences of early occupation, and of the remarkable degree of commercial vitality which must have once existed in southern Baluchistan both before and after Sind was conquered by the Arab invader, was never weakened till the day of his death. When Sandeman first took Baluchistan in hand it was a wilderness—but a wilderness with possibilities of development far greater than even he ever dreamed of. Afghanistan was, and is for the great part, a country where such possibilities are rare, because so much of the profitable soil is already turned to good account.

As with the country, so with the people. There are very radical differences between the north border countryman and the south, although those differences do not appear to me to be precisely such as have been generally represented.

Into the innumerable ethnographical distinctions which beset those independent tribes who inhabit that long belt of mountain barrier which lies between the frontier of India and the frontiers of Afghanistan, or the highlands of Baluchistan, there is no necessity to enter. There are tribes and clans innumerable, and their manners vary as their origin. They agree in a united profession of the faith of Islam; but they are not all of them of the same way of thinking, even in this vital principle of existence. There are Shiahs to be found at various points of the frontier. As regards distribution, the one broad distinction, easiest to remember, is that all the Pathan (or Pushtu-speaking) tribes are to the north of Quetta, and the Baluch (or Persian) speakers are to the south. To the north are Afghans and aboriginal Pathans. To the south are the peoples of Arab extraction intermixed with people of Dravidian and Persian stock, all lumped together under the name of Baluch.

The Mari and Bugti tribes, those people who occupy the most southern buttresses of the Sulimanis, are Rind Baluchis, almost certainly of Arab extraction. They came to Sind either with the Arab conquerors, or after them, and remained there mixed up with the original Hindu inhabitants. The Arab type of Baluch extends through the whole country at intervals, and includes all the finest and best of Baluch humanity. Besides the Baluch Arab, we find all through Kalat, and, extending almost to the sea, a Dravidian people called Brahui, who are quite distinct, and probably very much older than the Arabs; relics possibly of those prehistoric Dravidian immigrations from the plains of Mesopotamia which have filled the central and southern Indian jungles with such communities of interesting people. Mixed with the Brahui is another people, who have never yet received sufficient attention from the ethnographer; a race who call themselves Mingal or Mongul (they say the name is identical), and whom I hardly believe to be Brahui in anything but association.

Then there is the ancient race of Bolédis, once the ruling tribe in Baluchistan, who may possibly have originally given their name to the country, but who are now fast dying out. They call themselves Arabs. If they are Arabs, then Arabs must have been in Baluchistan before the days of Herodotus. A comparatively recent Rajput importation called Gichkis; another Rajput race called Lumris (in Lus Bela); a powerful Persian race called Naoshirwanis; Tajiks and Kurds; Jats and Medes; all are represented in Baluchistan; the flotsam and jetsam of untold centuries of irruptions and immigrations; the stranded remnants of ancient hordes, who all have at one time or another sought for the promised land, the ultimate Arcadia of the Indian peninsula.

The races of the north are not less mixed than those of the south, so that when people write of the distinctions that exist between the Pathan of the Punjab frontier and the Baluch of the Sind frontier they almost invariably refer to two particular representatives of the respective geographical areas. If we take the Afghan, or Afridi, as the northern type, and the Rind Baluch (the Arab) as the southern type, then the distinctions drawn by late writers generally holds good. The Baluch is easier to deal with and to control than the Pathan, owing to his tribal organisation, and his freedom from bigoted fanaticism or blind allegiance to his priest. He respects and honours the chief of his clan, who possesses far greater authority in the tribal councils than is the case with the Pathan. The Pathan is a republican of the worst type. He is a law unto himself, and although he is very much under the influence of the Mullah, he has always an eye to business, even in his most fanatical outbursts. Both are warlike and predatory, but their methods of fighting differ essentially, even when engaged in intertribal warfare. The Baluch fights openly, and faces his enemy boldly. There is a rough form of chivalry amongst the Baluch warriors, who are in most respects worthy descendants of the Arab conquerors of Asia.

The Pathan will make use of any stratagem or subterfuge that suits his purpose. He will shoot his own relations just as soon as the relations of his enemy, possibly sooner—and he will shoot them from behind. Yet the individual Pathan may be trusted to be true to his salt and to his engagements. He has his own code of honour, a very crooked code, and one which requires to be well understood. Physically there is little to choose between the best representatives of either people. It would be difficult to match the stately dignity and imposing presence of a Baluch chief of the Mari or Bugti clans. When clothed in raiment which is decently clean (which only happens at a durbar), with his long hair well oiled and ringletted, and his trappings of war — knives, sword, and shield, all well polished and slung easily about him—he is as fine a figure of a man as can be found in Asia. His Semitic features are those of the Bedouin, and he carries himself as straight and as loftily as an Arab gentleman of Nejd. Yet some of the Pathan clans, notably Afghans and Ghilzais, can show thews and sinews which are living testimony to the survival of the fittest amongst them. The rough life led by the Povindah clan (the fighting khafila leaders of the Dera Ismail frontier) excludes the possibility of weakly survivals in their clans. As a class, these Suliman Khel and Nasir camelmen are magnificent specimens of the human race, but they are exceptional. The Wazir and the Afridi are by no means on the same physical level with the Povindah. As to language, they all, Baluch and Pathan alike, talk dialects of a tongue of which Persian is the root; excepting the Brahuis, whose original language was probably Dravidian. Arabic has entirely disappeared, and is now as dead as Greek in the Indus valley. The *lingua rustica* of Baluchistan is a form of Persian overlaid with Sindi and Punjabi words; and Pushtu, the language of the Pathan, is also distinctly of Persian stock.

It was with the intermixed races of the south that Sandeman

had to deal for the best thirty years of his life. He had already patched up a reconciliation between the Khan of Kalat and his refractory chiefs; had established a system of tribal levies; introduced law and order by organising jirgahs, or tribal meetings, for arbitration in matters of dispute; had founded a new Quetta on the ruins of the old; opened up the Bolán route for traffic, and made himself not merely Governor-General's Agent but practically king in Baluchistan, when I first joined the staff of military workmen under his control as superintendent of the frontier surveys. This was at the close of the Russo-Afghan Boundary Commission in 1887. I had been associated with Baluchistan at the close of the Afghan war nearly ten years before, and thus I had the opportunity of measuring and admiring the extraordinary change produced in that country by the energy and ability of one man. I found the surveys of the country already well advanced. Wahab and Wilmer had made their mark; Longe and McNair had been busy; and so also had many others, whose exploits amongst those frontier hills would be well worth a record were there space to include it.

It was with great satisfaction that I found myself once more a humble colleague of Sir Robert Sandeman in the field of exploration. His policy of "peace and goodwill" with the tribes; his methods of making his power felt, and the success attained by these methods without the aid of a single armed expedition of any magnitude, had always impressed me greatly. At Kohat, where I had superintended frontier survey operations in Punjab fields, I had witnessed the effects of what has perhaps been unjustly termed the policy of "close border tempered with expeditions," initiated by Sir John Lawrence. Whatever may have been its advantages, we did not reach the people that way; we learnt nothing new and made no friends. In Baluchistan the crowd of khans and chieflets who fluttered around Sandeman whenever he moved, or who waited upon him as if they had been personal retainers, always witnessed to the strength of his personal influence. They certainly believed in him, they knew him and probably feared him, but, practically, they represented a friendly alliance with all sorts and conditions of tribal communities. Nobody ever attempted this sort of thing in the north; and yet I soon perceived that the difference in the effects of the two systems of administration was not due entirely to the personality of our political representatives, neither was it due to the varying idiosyncrasies of northern or southern border tribes alone. It could be traced to the difference of our actual position in reference to the borderland. In the north we were in front of the border tribes—we are so still; in the south we were both in front of them and behind them. There were no back doors on the Baluchistan frontier for comfortable and timely retreat should matters go badly in front—no hidden means of communication with unseen supporters in the vast upland plains which stretched away to Kandahar and Kabul. Much was due to our strategical position; and no one knew this better than Sandeman. Very soon he perceived that what was true of the Maris and Bugtis and the Brahuis of Kalat, could be made equally true for all the mixed assemblage of Pathan tribes of the border fastnesses which reach from Quetta to the Gomul. The occupation of the long extended Zhob valley would secure them all, and it would bring under our direct control many more roads leading from the frontier to Kandahar than have yet been enumerated in any gazetteer.

It was about the time that I joined my headquarters at Quetta that practical effect was given to this new extension of British influence. Already one preliminary exploration had been made by Sandeman, but it had been of the nature of a military reconnaissance rather than of a definite advance, and no systematic surveys had been practicable; so that I was in time for the actual consummation of the scheme.

As the mountain railway which connects Jacobabad and Quetta by the Harnai (or northern) loop through the hills gradually works its way up the steep gradients which (supplemented by many engineering artifices) land it on the Kach Kotal (the water-divide which separates the Indus drainage from that of Peshin), it passes on its right an imposing mass of mountains which form the nucleus of the central Baluchistan system. In amongst them are the juniper-clad slopes which embrace the little mountain retreat of Ziarat, to which the overheated Quetta official betakes himself during the few really hot months of the Quetta year. From a point near this central elevation the Peshin valley starts westward and the Zhob starts eastward; but the Zhob soon assumes a twist to the north, which takes it parallel to the Indus frontier and fairly straight to the Gomul, which latter river runs out to the Indus near Dera Ismail Khan, and is (as all men now know) one of the great gates of the frontier leading to Ghazni or Kandahar. From this centre also drains off the Bori, running parallel to the early beginnings of the Zhob, but south of it with a mixed pile of rocky crags running in narrow ridges between. In the Bori valley, just outside the limits of the British districts (*i.e.* those districts which figure as British Baluchistan in the map, and which have been acquired partly from Afghanistan by the Treaty of Gandamak, and partly from the Khan of Kalat in lieu of a quit-rent), is the little frontier station of Loralai.

The Bori valley is a flat, comparatively uninteresting upland, with a certain capacity for cultivation. Its flatness commends it for cavalry occupation, although its resources both for pleasure or profit are limited. It has been called the penal settlement of the Bengal Cavalry. Unpopular as it may be, it is an important central post in the general scheme of frontier defence and security. From Loralai a series of narrow lateral valleys stretch up to the north-east, away from the main stream, which makes a countermarch through the hills at Anumbar, and gradually squeezes its way down to the Kach Gandava plain in company with the Nari. The scenery of these valleys is imposing. The comparatively low clay ridges, chequered with stones and boulders, which ornament the edges of the Bori, give place to much higher and more attractive-looking hills, though the green touches on them are always scanty, and they are seldom dignified by snow.

On December 19th, 1889, Sir Robert Sandeman left Loralai, and with an ample and decorative company of Baluch and Brahui chiefs, supplemented by the more humble and unpretending *entourage* of his own staff, made his way towards the Zhob. From the present post of Murgha (about four marches to the north-east) he struck off to his left, over two steep ridges and through a long intervening defile, which brought him into the Zhob valley, where we found ourselves amongst a new

TORGHAR FROM THE ZHOB VALLEY

people and amidst new surroundings. Thenceforward we either followed the Zhob river itself, or passed through lateral valleys of the Zhob basin, till we reached the Gomul.

As we made our way northward we had on our right the stupendous masses of the Sulimani hills and their extension southwards. On our left were a multitude of broken and craggy ridges, sometimes thousands of feet above us, sometimes hundreds, tossed and tumbled into a general appearance of ragged confusion, but in reality not only possessing a plan, but a plan of marvellous regularity—as we saw when the general design was pulled straight on a map by observations from some of their craggy peaks. In amongst them was the Kundar valley, a recognised route connecting the Gomul with Kandahar, and one which was deemed to be of special importance.

Nobody had ever seen the Kundar in those days. Beyond the Kundar lay more of the rough gridiron system of frontier ridge and furrow, and then the open plains of Central Afghanistan, on the far side of which stood Ghazni and Kalat-i-Ghilzai. But we did not arrive at this knowledge all at once. A political promenade moves slowly, and involves many important functions, and none knew better than Sandeman how to combine them all. It must, above all things, be imposing. Military display is essential, and it is essential not only for effect, but for safety; so we had two regiments (23rd Pioneers and the 6th Bengal Cavalry) with us. We had also a strong detachment of well mounted and serviceable frontier levies, and a goodly company of that miscellaneous tag-rag following whose *métier* it is to be always mounted, entirely irregular, picturesquely dirty, and to swarm in coloured patches over the dusty plains behind those chiefs whose "izzat" is to be maintained by their presence. It is hardly necessary to add that it is always well to ride a little ahead of these retainers.

We were not shorn of the comforts of tents and full equipment, nor restricted to the sketchy *menus* of commissariat cuisine. The shamiana (or large, square tent in which durbars and meetings were held) was roomy and airy, as need be for Baluch gatherings, and our own more humble lodgings collectively made a very fine show when ranged on both sides the street terminating in the durbar tent and Union Jack. The camp was in the hands of a camp-master, an official who plunged out into the darkness night after night, with a cheerful confidence that he would find the right place for next day's camp in that unknown wilderness, which was above all praise. If he had ever failed, it was probable that Sandeman's head cook and general factotum would have succeeded. I never knew "Mr." Bux to be at fault. The road might be of the vilest frontier pattern; it might be long, it might be wet and slippery with rain or snow—it was all the same to Mr. Bux; and even when occasionally our own guides lost their bearings, and long, weary hours had been passed in the saddle, twisting and winding about narrow paths blocked in by sun-cracked ridges and apparently extending through an interminable maze to nowhere, we would round the last jagged corner ultimately, and stumble over the last boulders, to find the shamiana pitched, and Mir Bux wearing an injured expression because breakfast had waited for us.

The highest points of the rugged mountains were often very difficult of access. It was absolutely necessary to reach them in the interests of geographical survey, and it frequently involved days of hard labour to compass the final pinnacle which overlooked the stupendous cliffs and offshoots of the Kundar hills. Some of the most conspicuous points were indeed finally abandoned as hopelessly impracticable; but this did not often happen. Captain Ranald Mackenzie, whose special mission it was to build up survey stations, and leave his mark on all points and places which adjusted themselves to a geometrical survey, was seldom to be denied, and where he failed, it was probable that no local mountaineer would have succeeded.

But long before we reached the Kundar events had happened which marked distinct epochs in the history of the frontier. It was on Christmas morning of 1889, when the air was still and clear, and the blue sky above the purple-shadowed hills seemed full of that peace and goodwill to man which has ever been so strange to the frontier, but which Sandeman, with all his determined methods and unflinching courage, had set himself to bear as the unvarying message of his mission, that I watched the first-fruits of it literally fall in fulness and truth over this far-off Zhob valley, so long shadowed with the clouds of misrule and border anarchy. We had ridden together through the quiet morning amidst softer and gentler surroundings than were often found, within view of the square-cut crags of the throne of Solomon, round the low, sweeping spurs of the hills which immediately overlook the river, and had emerged on to a wide stretch of open plain which ended at the river banks, under the small, piled-up village of Apozai. Here, on a little hill, village homes clustered and hung together like a beehive swarm. We were yet some distance off when a small company of people approached. They were unmounted, ragged, and unkempt, but there was a purpose in their movements which was visibly expressed by their actions, and we stood still, awaiting their arrival. Some four or five young men presently reached Sandeman's horse; they kissed his hand, they held his stirrups, and then they presented what appeared to me to be a very small and very dirty little scrap of paper. He read it, and I could see that he was moved. There were no really hard angles about Sandeman's nature. I can easily imagine that viceroys and secretaries may have found him a little too plain-spoken, a little obstinate, perhaps; and recalcitrant robbers did not like his looks at all; but his sympathies were with the people whom he sought out and governed, right to the very back of his heart. The little scrap of paper contained the last message—the will and testament of the departed Chief of Apozai.

Khanan Khan, Chief of the Mando Khel, had been a hard man and a robber from his birth. But he had met Sandeman before, and he had judged with that spirit of prophecy which seems to belong peculiarly to those who live beyond the working of the world's social machinery that a new era was dawning on the wild, wide wilderness of mountains and valleys which had overlooked his savage life and undeservedly peaceful death. He expressed the hope that the dawn of peace might indeed have broken, and he commended his country, his sons, his wife, and his family to Sandeman's care. He added that he trusted that his sons would not be detained too long from the ceremonial of meeting by staying to watch their father die. There was pathos and there was hope in that small scrawl—something of the hope which the first Christmas brought to the world of Judea, and which required no angelic choir for its announcement in Zhob. There are many ways of carrying the message to men, and Sandeman's was none of the worst.

How the Mandokhel have behaved since then I do not fully know. How the valley has behaved I know very well. Little patches of ragged cultivation have grown into well-spaced fields in terraces dropping down from the hills to the river. Rubbishy little villages have shot out offshoots, and sprung up into scattered towns. Groups of weather-beaten mulberries have expanded into orchards, and, to put it shortly, the Zhob revenues have increased threefold more than even Sandeman forecasted.

Between Quetta and the Gomul river, all along what we may call the back of the Sulimani mountains, there dwelt clans innumerable, the enumeration of whose names alone would fill a page of small print. But they all, or nearly all, belong to one great people called Kakars. These Kakars are a very ancient race, and it is probable that they were in possession of the Sulimanis and of these western slopes long before the advent of Afghan or Arab. They are (taking them as a whole) an energetic race, tillers of the soil rather than warriors, and they are more or less touched with a spirit of adventure which takes them far from their own country in search of employment. I think I have already mentioned that at the fight which took place in the Sanjao valley during the progress of the British forces from Kandahar to the frontier at the close of the first phase of the Afghan war in 1879, a prisoner was taken who possessed certificates of competence as an engine-room subordinate in the P. and O. service, and who could speak English as well as most cockneys. Some sections of the tribe send men in battalions to the plains of India, where they find employment on railway and road construction.

Covering the mountains which culminate in the Takht-i-Suliman are our old friends the Sheranis. To the north-west of the Zhob valley are the Ghilzai clans of Afghanistan—the Ghilzais being a people of Turkish origin, introduced into Afghanistan within historic times. They have no affinity, except in language and religion, with the Afghans. North of the Gomul are the Waziris (or Wazirs) of Waziristan. These latter have still the keys of their own back doors in their pockets, and give us trouble accordingly.

Such was the relative ethnographical position in which Sandeman's mission of 1889 found itself. Not far from the village of Apozai, to which I have already referred, was discovered a suitable site for a frontier post, and there the Pioneers at once set to work to prepare a place for a political residence. No time is lost on these occasions. The foundations were blasted out of the solid rock of a small isolated hill there and then; and on a fairly open plain reaching down to the river, overlooked by the prospective residency, was the selected site of the now flourishing cantonment of Fort Sandeman.

Here, then, a halt was called, and here summonses were issued to the surrounding clans and peoples to "come in" and attend a durbar. Meanwhile survey work was extended to the Kundar river, and the great collection of tribespeople already in camp were entertained with camp amusements of the gymkhana type, which are always intensely popular amongst them. One Bugti chief, Shahbaz Khan, who had just been made a Nawab (himself a splendid specimen of the Arab type of Baluch and an athlete from his youth), organised an athletic meeting on his own account, and gave really valuable prizes to the winners, amongst whom, naturally, the Baluch horseman was conspicuous.

Early in January a small party, which included Captain McIvor, as political officer, and a small escort of the 6th Bengal Cavalry, under Lieutenant Barnes, started from Apozai camp to reconnoitre the Kundar river, a river which joins the Gomul from the south-west at Domandi, and which has from time immemorial been reckoned as one of the chief trade highways between Kandahar and northern India. A very casual glance at the map will show that if one wishes to reach Quetta from Lahore, the present railway route down the Indus valley to Sukkur, and then up again to Quetta by either the Bolán or Harnai lines, is a very circuitous and clumsy route. The natural highway to Quetta from Lahore is *viâ* the Gomul and Zhob, and the natural highway from Lahore to Kandahar would follow the Kundar. So that it was of very great importance that we should obtain at least a look at the Kundar, and make something of a detailed estimate of possible railway construction through the length of the Zhob. Our exact surveys now not only include the Kundar but extend far beyond; but in 1890 no European had ever been known to have set eyes on the Kundar. Naturally we wished to be the first in the field; and we had (as usual) to be quick about it. So we mounted ourselves well, and putting up a light equipment on a fast-trotting camel which we expected to keep pace with our movements whilst the baggagers took their own time, we trekked away westward across the intervening hills and the narrow little spaces in between which can only by courtesy be termed valleys, till we reached a point from whence with one rapid rush we could reach the Kundar, and be back again within the hours of daylight.

On such occasions I usually mounted myself on a hired Baluch mare, as I found that the rupee or two which secured her services for a day's hard riding was always well expended. Baluchistan is a rough country, stony in most places, slippery in some, and the paths in the mountains generally are such as might be afforded by a highland burn with the water left out. So that an animal with legs and feet of iron and a capacity for balancing in narrow places was a great acquisition; and it was usually to be obtained cheap, especially as the bargain always included strict injunctions on the part of the owner that no food whatever, and *very little* water, was to be given until the day's work was done.

It was a clear, still morning when we mounted early for that memorable outing. Thin grey laminated clouds with pink edges stretched straight and level across the sky, parted by streaks of the clearest blue, at the back of the pinnacles and castellated crags of Sharán; and the foreground, deepened into shades of black and brown, was filmy with the smoke of the early camp fire. It was cold—cold, with a bright sharpness such as a small frost brings at high altitudes.

No startling episodes occurred as we spurred along at the best pace we could make, down one nullah, then up another, through defiles, and over the flat "raghzas," or spaces at the foot of the hills which intervened for our convenience between the slopes and the scarp of river-beds. But one little incident

THE KUNDAR VALLEY

was interesting. As we rounded a turn in the last twisting nullah which was to land us on the Kundar banks, we suddenly encountered a cavalcade approaching—a well-armed cavalcade; and as the rule of the road on these occasions is to shoot at sight, there was a rapid pull up and a general disposition to edge away towards cover. But the practical frontier political is never caught napping; and ten courteous words from the gallant McIvor resulted at once in due acknowledgment and a relaxation of the momentary tension. *We* were on the road to prospect the Kundar. *They* were evidently on the road to reconnoitre our camp. Our friend of this encounter (I forget his name, I am sorry to say) was a very well-known Ghilzai chief of the Suliman Khel clan, but even his ready wit was not quite equal to maintaining that he was merely coming in to meet us in friendly durbar. He was obviously and conspicuously on the war-path, and his display of breechloaders was quite enough to make us humbly thankful for an escort. The Ghilzai can be brute enough on occasions, but he can also imitate the gentleman fairly well, and nothing finally occurred to mar the harmony of our meeting. The chief was at last moved by McIvor's persuasive eloquence into promising to pay Sandeman a friendly visit, and he kept his promise.

We rode on rapidly to the Kundar after breakfast, and made the first hasty reconnaissance of the lower reaches of that river where it now forms a section of the boundary of Afghanistan, returning the same night to our camp near Sharán.

Another long day's ride, which lingers in my recollection, took Mr. Colvin (another political officer) and myself into the wooded valleys which underlie the great buttresses of the Takht-i-Suliman on the west. Never before had any Englishmen set foot in these valleys, although we had long previously overlooked them from the Takht peaks. We were anxious to discover the movements of a small local chief who lived in his feudal stronghold near the sources of one of those mountain streams which cut through the frontier hill barriers to reach the plains of the Indus. This chief had declined Sandeman's invitation; and it was not quite certain what attitude he might assume towards visitors. So we rode with a strong escort, both of Indian cavalry and Baluch horsemen, and we went warily through the narrow glens which led to his valley. Here, under the shadow of the Takht, Baluchistan blossoms into unexpected beauty. As we looked northward past the little four-square fortress which we had ridden so far to reconnoitre, we had all the impressive grandeur of the Kaisargarh cliffs and scarps above us to the right, and all the deep-toned pine-clad beauty of Shingarh on our left, shutting in a narrow little ribbon of cultivated plain, through which one might pass to those same mountain gateways to India which had given us access to the Takht-i-Suliman in 1883. Immediately on our left were the edges of the long sweeping slopes of Shingarh, clothed with olives from end to end. Amongst the patriarchs of this forest of wild olives were trees so large that we could put a sufficient cavalry escort into very convenient hiding under one single specimen. I have seen no olives in Europe at all comparable to them for size. There are, indeed, in sterile and barren Baluchistan, here and there, some remarkable forest features. The juniper forest of Ziarat is famous. The pistacia forest of Chahiltan, which is not far from Quetta, might possibly pass unrecorded, the few scattered and ragged trees which form it hardly justifying the dignity of its title, but the Forest Department assures us that officially it *is* a forest, and we must accept their view as the view of a final authority. There is a shisham (*dalbergia sissa*) forest in the Harnai basin, and there are pines in abundance (*chilghosa* and *longifolia*) on the higher spurs of the Sulimanis; but there is no such satisfactory forest of close-set thick shade trees to be found anywhere else that I have seen, as these olive forests of the hill country which lies north-east of Fort Sandeman. It was fully worth the fifty-mile ride to see them. We accomplished our purpose and rode back to camp that night—but it was a hard day's ride, and more than one gallant little Baluch steed succumbed before it was over.

By degrees the gathering of the clans waxed strong until all the important tribal divisions (especially those who had most to say to the Gomul pass) were represented. Our old friends, or enemies, the Kidarzai section of the Sheranis, held aloof, and had to be dealt with subsequently; but Waziris and Suliman Khel were there, so that finally, without further delay, a move was made northward to open out the Gomul pass to India. The Gomul is the most important pass between the Khaibar and the Bolán. It gives access to the very centre of Afghanistan from India. It is the regular highway for thousands of trading and fighting people who bring their khafilas yearly to India, and who pass unmolested through the length and breadth of the Indian continent. But the European official had ever been most carefully excluded. The pass had indeed been seen both by Macaulay and Broadfoot previously, so that we were not altogether without information; but the last political mission which had attempted to penetrate it had been most rudely scattered and repulsed. It was very doubtful what kind of a reception we might get, and it was all-important to secure the goodwill of all the more powerful "pass" tribes and their chiefs.

At the very top of the pass, where we camped just before we reached the two narrow hill tracks crossing the steep ridge of Gwaléri, which is one of a succession of kotals, or divides, which have to be crossed in avoiding the river route (which is indeed absolutely impracticable from the narrowness and steepness of its gorges), a havildar was shot. This might have meant little, or it might have meant a good deal. Were we in for a really bad time as we struggled through those precipitous defiles and over those narrow little hill paths; or was this only a casual expression of opinion on the part of an insignificant Waziri marauder? We assumed that it was the latter (indeed there was no other course open) and started for the pass. We were only twenty-six miles as the crow flies from the Indian frontier, and we knew our way. The surveys had been pushed ahead of the camp as usual, for in Baluchistan it is always easy to see ahead for a considerable space, and we reckoned that nothing need (or indeed *could* very well) stop us. On the 28th January the military caravan was set in motion and went slowly winding over the kotals, and half-way down the other side, to an open plain called Nilai Kach. On the 29th we resumed our crooked journey through the actual Gomul pass (a four-mile defile), and then, after topping a slight rise, we dropped gently down to the Punjab plains. We were locally under the guardianship of the Waziris as we executed this manœuvre. Shots were fired, but they were ineffective shots—mere protests against this new development of Feringhi inquisitiveness, and they did no harm.

Since then has this important pass been open to India, and since then have we been really made aware what is the straightest and best road to Quetta from the Punjab.

Thus by one well-planned and well-executed movement was all the stretch of frontier between the Bolán and the Gomul brought into subjection to the British Ráj; and thus were all the wildest Pathan races of the Indus borderland taught that the reach of the Sirkar was as long as its arm was strong. The lesson was commenced without bloodshed; but it was not learned all at once. An expedition in 1891, commanded by Sir G. White, and accompanied by Sir Robert Sandeman as chief political officer, was organised to convince those Sherani highlanders the necessity for accepting the new era of Pax Britannica which had replaced the old order. It was a most useful expedition, for it included another and more comprehensive excursion to the Kundar valley—in vain search for one Bungal Khan.

Bungal Khan had long outraged the peace and quiet of the Zhob border and had betaken himself to his rock fastnesses in Kundar to be out of the way of reprisals. On this occasion we worked down the Kundar to its junction with the Zhob at Domandi, and then back again to Fort Sandeman, ere starting for the eastern section of the Zhob frontier where dwelt the recalcitrant Sheranis. Here the force operating was divided into four columns, three of which blocked the outlets from the headquarters of the tribe, and the fourth, under Sir G. White in person, scaled the heights of Maramazh, and then dropped down straight on to the offending villages. There was no fighting to speak of. The force was too strong, and the arrangements too well planned. We next exhausted the Sherani country in explorations, and opened up one of the weirdest and most remarkable mountain byways that intersect the frontier. The Chua Khel dhana is now one of the military roads leading from the Indus. It was once a great trade route, but that was in long-ago days. It had been blocked by landslips and destroyed by floods many years before our time. This pass intersects the Sherani mountains and turns the southern end of the Takht-i-Suliman as the Zao turns the northern. When we passed through, there was nothing but a rough drainage line choked with boulders, slippery with sheets of polished limestone, shut in by gigantic and unscaleable cliffs, deep with pools of swirling water, and all hidden away in the very bowels of the hills. It is now a practicable road, and an important one, and the Sheranis with the rest of the Pathan tribesmen make good use of it. It was then that Sir G. White with a small staff ascended the southern ridges of the Takht and once again scaled the walls of that vast natural frontier fortress; but this was a venture which I was far too ill to join. From the day we left Quetta till the day that the expedition ended I never knew what it was to be entirely free from Baluchistan fever; and the end of the expedition was nearly the end of all things to me. Then followed a long dreary time of sickness and depression which lasted several months. It was well into February before I could look about me again—and we had started early in October.

CHAPTER IX.

SOUTHERN BALUCHISTAN AND PERSIAN GULF

Southern Baluchistan and Persian Gulf—Makrán and its people—Naoshirwanis and Azad Khan—Sir R. Sandeman's dealings with them and first reconnaissance through Southern Baluchistan—Surveys—Telegraph service—Coast scenery—Astola, the enchanted island—Persian Gulf—Bahrein tombs—Hormuz—Salt caves of Kishm—Bundar Abbas and Linjah—Gulf storms—Winter seas—Phenomena of phosphorescence—Ginao hills and possible Sanitaria, Kawait, and Arabian coast Arabs—Telegraph prospects—Persian railways—Through line to Europe from India—Russian projects.

BALUCHISTAN is cut into two very distinct halves by the railway from Jacobabad to New Chaman, the last little roadside station on the far slopes of the Kojak. The northern half is the long narrow strip of Pathan border mountain land stretching to the Gomul, and this is the part which is now dominated from Zhob. South-west of the railway, and of those districts which being originally Afghan, were assigned to us by the Treaty of Gandamak, is a vast square block of territory some 300 miles long by 300 wide, of which the southern border rests on the Arabian Sea coast, and the northern is lost in those deserts south of the Helmund through which the Afghan boundary has recently been demarcated. All along the eastern side of this block is the mountain region facing the Indus occupied by Brahuis and cognate tribes, which until lately was (with the exception of the Kalát country on the north) an absolute blank in our maps; a space of country to the conditions of which neither history nor tradition gave us the faintest clue, although the eastern ranges are plainly visible from the windows of the railway carriages as they roll up the Indus valley from Karachi to Sukkur. All that we thought we knew about the greater part of this region was that between the Mulla pass leading to Kalát, and an indefinite track, which was supposed to connect Las Bela, at its southern

REED BOATS ON THE HELMAND LAGOON

extremity, with Karachi, there was not a road into it, nor yet a staircase over its straight-backed ridges, which stood like a wall facing Sind. This was what we thought we knew twenty years ago. We know better now; but it may still be said that except for the surveyors who have worked out its topographical plan, no European has ever climbed that western barrier. Beyond it, filling up the rest of the square to the Persian frontier, is as strange a country as any in Asia.

Across this country, with a strike that has changed to east and west, the border ridges still run in formidable bands, with long narrow valleys between them. But these valleys gradually increase in width towards the north; the most northerly of them exhibiting wide spaces of sand and desert, very similar to the country which embraces the Afghan river Helmund. None of the northern or central valleys have an outlet to the sea. Their vicarious drainage is lost in central Hamuns or swamps. Only a narrow strip of the southern hills, barely one hundred miles wide, contributes anything to the Indian Ocean, and this strip is called Makrán, possibly from "mahi khuran," which is in Persian the same as "ichthyophagai," or "fish eaters." Makrán was once a country with a reputation for active and vigorous trade. It was a factor in mediæval political geography when Arab ships sailed the Persian Gulf, and formed a connecting link in the chain of trade communication between Europe and Asia. Yet earlier, in pre-Mahomedan days of Arab supremacy, when Semitic settlers were found in peaceful occupation of the western shores of India and the eastern shores of Africa, probably for six or seven centuries before the Christian era, and for six or seven centuries after it, Makrán possessed a trade status of its own, although the zenith of its prosperity did not arrive till the Arabs had swarmed into Sind, and held the north-western borders of India with Makrán as a highway between. It was the land of myrrh, spikenard, and "bdellium," a fact of which the Phœnician settlers who followed the tail of Alexander's army as he dragged it westward by slow steps and impossible routes towards Persia, were fully aware. Dravidian races passed through it from Mesopotamia to India in prehistoric days; Punjab people poured into it from the Indus valley, and established themselves as pirates and buccaneers in the Arabian Sea;

Greeks made their way home through Makrán; and Arabs and Zoroastrian refugees (Parsis) worked eastward from Persia to the promised land of the Indus by the same routes. They have all left their mark on the country—but chiefly the Arabs have done so. At any of the old mediæval coast ports, or sites of inland towns, which existed before the Portuguese first rounded the Cape to the Gulf and to India, glass bangles and beads, as well as Arab coins, may be dug up in such abundance as to suggest that before the days of the coins, glass bangles and beads must have been the currency of the country. And from end to end of it, mixed up with Dravidian remains and possible Parsi fire temples, are the great stone "bunds" of Himyaritic Arabs, built for water storage and irrigation, and the still recognisable revetments of cultivated fields, where cultivation exists no longer, and can never have existed within man's memory. The Portuguese wiped out, first the Arabs and then the Turks, from the Eastern seas; and with them Makrán lapsed into absolute geographical obscurity. Such is shortly the history of the country which has recently been brought again to the light of civilisation, and is now included, together with the hills and sandy wastes and flats which lie to the north of it, in the great Protectorate of Baluchistan which was practically welded together by Sandeman.

So many and so various are the tribes which occupy all these barren, baked, and sun-dried hills of southern Baluchistan, and the narrow valleys (some green with crops and thickly shaded by palm trees) which intersect the hills, that we had better pass them by and not attempt to enumerate them. In the long sandy valley of Kharán, which partakes not of the fertile nature of the narrower valleys of the south except as to its edges here and there, where it breaks out into patches of cultivation—and which stretches all the way from the Jalawán (or Kalát) hills to the Persian border—there dwelt, in Sandeman's early days, a chief of much local renown named Azad Khan. Azad Khan's people were of pure Persian stock. They call themselves Naoshirwanis, and possess quite a creditable history. As a fighting, raiding, restless clan they were perhaps unequalled on the border. They were, and are, as different from the modern Persian (who is not a fighting man) as the Sikh from the Bengali; and they are a living testimony to the possible existence of that true military instinct amongst Persians which might well have died out with Nadir Shah ere Afghanistan was independent. Azad Khan was quite the typical border chieftain. At ninety he was strong in the saddle, swift in resolve, fierce in action, and it appeared to be all the same to him whether he raided Persia, or Kalát, or the Quetta frontier. His hand was against every man, and a strong right hand it was. One of Sandeman's final measures towards the reviving and reorganising of the ancient confederation of Baluch chiefs was directed towards Azad Khan of Kharán; and, as usual, he seized on the earliest opportunity to effect his purpose in person. In the autumn of 1883 he left Quetta for Kharán, and there inquired into Azad Khan's grievances against the Khan of Kalát, and found means for adjusting the differences between them. Azad Khan was then ninety-seven years of age and Sir Robert thus describes him: "In spite of his great age Azad Khan retains his mental faculties unimpaired. Bowed by age, he is unable to mount a horse without assistance, but once in the saddle, his endurance is greater than that of many a younger man. Possessed of unflinching resolution, impatient of wrong, generous to reward, stern and relentness in punishment, Sirdar Azad Khan has above all things enjoyed a reputation for unswerving honesty. He is never known to depart from his word once given, and has a sincere contempt for chicancry or falsehood."* Azad Khan died in 1886 at the age of one hundred and one, after having proved the practical nature of his friendship with the British Government by rendering valuable assistance in the matter of transport to the Russo-Afghan Boundary Commission and "arranging in co-operation with our officers for the protection of trade routes."

From the open deserts of Kharán, Sandeman passed southwards through the network of the hills which separate Kharán from Makrán, and finally emerged on the sea coast, returning by sea to Karachi. This was a surveyor's opportunity, and then for the first time did we get an insight into the real nature of that maze of mountains which fills up all southern Baluchistan.

* THORNTON'S *Life of Sir Robert Sandeman*, p. 182.

I could not accompany the mission, for we were busy about that time with the Takht-i-Suliman, but two most able of all the many officers who have assisted to make geography on the frontier (Lieuts. Talbot and Wahab, R.E.) between them, drove a straight and connected triangulation right down from Quetta to the heart of Makrán, and filled up blank spaces in the map to the extent of 20,000 square miles in a few months. Systematic surveys have swept over the land since then, but they have never disturbed that preliminary reconnaissance, which well deserves to be numbered amongst the best records of frontier exploration. From that date we began to amass more exact information about the wild Kalát highlands, and the little Rajput state of Las Bela which nestles between their southern spurs and the eastern Makrán hills; about the long date-producing valleys of Panjgur and Kej, and the southern land of spikenard and "ichthyophagai," till we came to the Persian border on the west; unearthing the sites of mediæval Arab towns, and identifying tribes and places included in the marvellous records of Herodotus and Arrian as we worked.

It will be remembered that a line of telegraph stretches from Karachi first northwards to Sonmiani at the north-east corner of the Arabian Sea, and then westward along the coasts of Makrán and Persian Baluchistan to Jashk; from which point it takes to the sea-bottom, and emerges again at Bushire (or a little south of it) thenceforward to pass overland through Turkish territory to Europe. So much land line, and so much cable, demand attention both ashore and afloat, and consequently the Persian Gulf telegraph service comprises both the staff which is necessary to maintain efficient land posts at intervals—intervals which are often separated by dreary spaces of most abominable country—and a small naval reserve comprised in one ship and its crew, to look after the sea line. On the whole the sailors have the best of it. The hot, muggy, steam-bath atmosphere which pervades the Persian and (in a less degree) Makrán coasts, during certain of the hot months of the year, is indescribable. With the limpness of rags, and the complexions of blankets, the weary telegraph assistants drag out an existence on land which for a good third of the year is ruled by worse conditions than those which govern the worst of the hot plains of Sind or the Punjab.

The latter at least suffer from an access of dry heat; and those who know all about it usually assume that it is infinitely better to be baked than boiled. I do not know, but I can believe it when I am on the Persian coast. The telegraph steamer *Patrick Stewart* which picks up the cable now and then and cuts it in two, and restores it "faultless" to the depths of the deep sea, does not risk dissolution in the Persian gulf during the worst of the summer months. She only runs her busy course in the bright months of winter and early spring, when the temperature changes so much that it is occasionally necessary to provide for the contingency of hard frosts and bitter cold. The cold comes with the "shumal," the same northern wind which deals destruction in Turkestan, but the terrors of it are greatly modified by sea influences in the Gulf. When a "shumal" sets in with real vigour there is an uneasy time for all shipping between Arabia and Persia and occasionally much difficulty in landing at the open roadsteads of the Persian and Makrán coasts ports.

To the *Patrick Stewart* and those who control her movements, to the courteous assistance of the telegraph officials, and the ever cheery service of her captain and crew, I owe many most delightful months of voyaging. With their assistance I have been able to explore the harbours and ports and coasts of Makrán, Persia, and Arabia with a fair amount of method, and with a freedom which would have been hopelessly impossible had it been necessary to drag through the weary lengths of the necessary land journeys.

Viewed from the sea the iron-bound coast of Makrán is not inviting. The coast of Arabia about Aden is not unlike it; but exception must be made in favour of Makrán where gigantic headlands and massive cliffs form the seaward protection to the ports of Urmara and Gwadur, and, in a lesser degree, to Pasni also. These possess a grandeur that nothing near Aden can boast. The long narrow line of desolate yellow strand, pricked out with little clumps of tamarisk and bunches of salt grass, which reach out from the broader flats of Sonmiani where the Puráli (the river of Las Bela) enters the sea, is backed (as you approach Urmara from the east) by really grand mountains. Within a mile or two of the coast the Malán and Talar ranges run to 4,000 feet of elevation, and they break up into peaks and precipices which are quite majestic in their rugged dominance over the ocean. Makrán is, as a rule, an intensely dry and thirst-ridden country, where water is hardly to be obtained. Here, however, about the Malán are deep streams of pellucid blue, hidden deep between banks of most refreshing green—for where water is there is also abundance of vegetation. Nothing of this is visible from the coast, neither is it very much of Makrán that is thus favoured. Near where the most ancient and honourable ziarat of Hinglaz is hidden away in the clefts of the mountains (a ziarat so ancient that both Hindus and Mahomedans claim it without recognising its almost pre-historic Persian origin) ibex play about the scarped summits, and the hills are as full of life as is the sea which washes their feet. But this would be a very unfair picture to present as a sample of vast tracts of country which lie beyond to the west and the north—where the parched and fissured hills are moistened by liquescent salt; where even that ubiquitous nuisance, the common fly, finds existence insupportable; where the scanty shreds of vegetable life are too highly flavoured with salt for even a camel's approval. Not till we reach the valleys of Kej, and of the Rakshán, far away to the north-west, do we again encounter much besides the perpetual gridiron formation of baked clay hills alternating with narrow salt-fed gutters.

The coastline is not greatly changed from the coastline of the fourth century B.C., when the galleys of Nearkos slowly worked their way from point to point till they reached the Persian Gulf. Most of the primitive ports and landing-places of Arrian's story can be identified, although some have been filled up by sea-washed sand, or washed away altogether, as the case may be. Some of the coast islands still exist in their primitive form of sterile arenaceous simplicity, and some have obviously disappeared. The island of Astola (or Astalu) nearly midway between the Urmara and Pasni headlands, and possibly in geologic ages once forming a connected range with them, is as much an object of superstitious dread to the Med fishermen of the coast now as it was to the Greek sailors then; although the enchantress who once dwelt there, and turned her lovers into fish, is no longer recognised. It is probable that her unlovely story ceased to be told when the Karak pirates infested the coast and disposed of the crews of captured ships wholesale over the edge of its cliffs, till they finally drew down the vengeance of the Arabs upon their heads and were wiped off the sea. I landed on the slippery, weedy rocks of Astola one evening with a cheery party of sailors from the *Patrick Stewart*. We were told that the rock pools and shallows were infested with dangerous snakes, and we went armed with weapons of defence. It was a weird, wild shore that we struck, one quite suited to the bloody traditions which have always hung round it; and swirling eddies of the sea, as they broke into circles inside the outer rock barriers, were full of quaint sea-bred curiosities. That hedgehog of the ocean, the prickly echinoderm, was there in great force, and he lived with a large company of smooth, shiny, fat sea-slugs and a host of vicious-looking creatures which I believe to be the snakes of ancient tradition. They were there in vast numbers. Every little pool that was rimmed with rock afforded a home for a snake, and its protruding snout was usually just visible under the sea-worn ledge. But were they snakes? That was a point which we never satisfactorily decided. If there is any radical distinction between an eel and a snake I give in my adherence to the theory of eels. I left the enchanted island with reluctance. An hour's ramble ashore was just enough to give birth to an impression that the island of Astola, or Hashtalu, or Nuala (it has many names in history), would as well repay careful scientific study as any in the deep seas.

But this island is only one of many that must once have studded the coast, and which have now disappeared. I had the opportunity of witnessing that process of island demolition which ends in sand banks and sand bars, in the instance of a small island composed of hardened sand and clay, which once stood near the western horn of the Bay of Gwatar. In the winter of 1891–2 this little island stood up stiff and square and as apparently immutable as the white bands of the Pasa hills beyond it. Passing it again two years later I found it split in two, and in the narrow channel which divided the halves we measured three fathoms of water. This process of disintegration is no doubt partially responsible for the scores of sand bars which protect the coasts of Makrán, and which present an insuperable obstacle to utilising some of its best harbours. It is also probable that the filling-up process, which has resulted in wide spaces of sandy flat, protected on the seaward side by sand dunes and ridges, where once the sea penetrated far inland, may be due to monsoon influences acting on broken-up material of this nature. But this is conjecture, and it is impossible to linger amongst these marine records of Makrán.

The triangulation first carried to the Makrán mountains by Talbot and Wahab was gradually extended along another line, from the Indus valley to the Persian frontier, and beyond it. It even reached the coasts of Arabia across the narrow gullet of the Gulf, and where triangulation went, there in its wake followed the native surveyor with his plane table, making maps in sheets and leaving no peak unvisited, no point of interest unrecorded. Thousands of square miles of geographical work were turned out each season—sometimes 50,000 or 60,000 in the course of the winter's explorations, involving months of incessant travel and an expenditure which was ridiculously small compared to the results achieved. Such practical experience as was thus obtained is not often to be reached. Small wonder that the staff of native artists belonging to the frontier parties of the Indian Survey became some of the most effective geographical workmen in the world.

The Persian Gulf is the old wonderland of Arab story, and to no less extent is it the wonderland of mediæval history. Was it not here that the immortal Sindbad lived and died, and were the adventures of that fictitious naval hero more astounding, more full of tragic incident and dramatic force, than the exploits of the Portuguese heroes of the Gulf who annexed the Eastern seas, and all that in them is, during the early years of the sixteenth century? If you doubt it, read Hunter's *History of India.* Many points of surpassing interest lie about the southern shores of the Persian Gulf; and a book might be written about any of them.

The very earliest record of maritime enterprise, the birthplace of Semitic mercantile adventure, probably the cradle of a race of traders and navigators who spread over the world as Arabs or Phœnicians in widening circles until hardly a corner in the continents of Europe, Asia, and Africa remained untrodden by them, lies, as it would seem, near a group of tombs in the Bahrein islands. These islands (the ancient Tyros and Sidona of tradition), whose names were transferred to the Mediterranean coast with the Phœnicians when they settled in Syria, were civilised ages before the Semitic progenitors of the Phœnicians had turned out the yellow-skinned, round-headed people of Chaldæa, and sent them drifting southward through Persia towards India. The Phœnician tombs in them are mounds of consolidated gravel and sand heaped about chambers built up with blocks of conglomerate, rectangular and double-storeyed. They were first opened by Sir Edward Durand when he was on political duty in the Persian Gulf, and subsequently visited and described in fuller detail by Theodore Bent. They can be reached by an uneasy donkey-ride of about nine miles from the nearest coast landing-place. The shallow sea which washes the coral reefs of the Bahrein islands does not permit of even a small boat actually touching the fringe of dry shore, and the instant the boat grounds in the shallows a swarm of donkeys, and their usually naked attendants, charge down and take possession. It is necessary in the interests of peace and safety to secure a donkey speedily. Guiltless of saddle or bridle, long of limb, and strong of wind, these donkeys are directed from afar by the voice of the owner, as the war horse answers to the trumpet, and the rider has little to say to subsequent proceedings.

Across the gulf, on the eastern shores, lying under the lee of Persia, is the little island of Hormuz; and here one may study a surprising record of commercial enterprise and commercial decay. Hardly less astounding than the gigantic conglomerate blocks which are fitted together to shape the solid sepulchre of the Phœnicians, are the concrete blocks which have been used in the construction of the Portuguese fort at Hormuz. They are worth inspection; great branches of coral are embedded in them; they are varied in colour, and they face the blue seas in tones of pink and grey and green; they are as hard and sharp-edged as when the Portuguese engineers placed them in line in the early years of the sixteenth century. But apart from the wonder of this great relic of Portuguese supremacy is the wonder of the island itself. We know that it was a central emporium of Eastern trade long after Siráf (higher up the Gulf on the Persian coast, and now called Tahiri) and the mainland trade centres were ravaged and destroyed by Mogul invaders. We know that here was once a great city, with streets and squares, where awnings protected the bazaars from the sun, where fountains played, and the streets were watered to keep them cool. There is not only not a vestige of all this left, but it is almost impossible to conceive that it could ever have existed. A bare, wind-swept plain covered with gravel and boulders, and here and there the protruding corner of an ancient tank, backed up by lines of serrated, volcanic-looking hills, red and grey; baked sand and burnt clay, with streaks of white efflorescence, and the taste of salt permeating the thin yellow stalks of the stunted grass tufts; even under the bright sunshine of winter betraying symptoms of the fierce passionate oven heat of summer—such is Hormuz. As unlikely a spot for an important commercial city, the desire of the eyes of pleasure-seekers from all parts of the East, as one can well imagine. Occasionally a stray slab is washed out bearing a high-flown inscription in stilted Latin, denoting the spot where once lay one of those intolerant, domineering, but ever valorous merchant crusaders of the West, who, in the course of one short quarter of a century, made all the East their own. At Siráf I found vestiges of another race of Western traders (probably Venetian, or Genoese) where with deadly rivalry they held on to those overland communications through which the wealth of Venice had passed from India. All round the Gulf are relics in abundance; relics that may help to spell history out of tradition, and may teach us (if we are willing to learn) what part the Gulf played in that world's commercial see-saw, which has given wealth and power in succession to Phœnician, Arab, Turk, Venetian, Portuguese, Dutch, and English.

One bright December morning, when the line of white surf breaking on the coast was less aggressively distinct than usual, a small party landed on the island of Kishm to search for evidences of the great salt trade of the island. There are ranges of salt in Kishm, as there are in some parts of the

Punjab—whole mountains, which have been excavated without skill or method for untold ages, until a thin outside shell only remains between salt-pit and sky, and the mine has become too dangerous even for the followers of the doctrine of "Kismet." We wandered for hours seeking some trace of a footpath which might guide us to these ancient mines. We knew that we were in their neighbourhood—but nothing could we find of them. Paths indeed there were, but they obviously led in wrong directions, as some of our party were able to remember. They could say when we were wrong, but they could not put us right. And as the day wore on we got tired of making unprofitable guesses. The surf was getting up, too, as it usually does towards afternoon, and so most of that little party decided on a return to the ship. I remained ashore with one of the officers, and we proposed to try a fresh cast before finally abandoning the quest. Fortune favoured us, for we presently saw a little Arab boat stealing along the coastline, and there appeared on the shore a solitary figure staggering under a load which could be nothing else than blocks of salt. Our language was doubtless imperfect, but we learnt enough from this stranger to tell us that the salt had been extracted from some place where lights had to be used, and which, according to a plan which was drawn on the wet sand with a stick, involved a very artful arrangement of underground galleries.

This was exactly what we wanted, and the smuggler was soon on his way towards the hills to show us the mines. He dived straight into a network of nullahs, the end of which was a jagged rough stone-covered mountain side, with a hole in it. It was not very easy to climb up and into that hole, and the drop down to the inner recesses of the cave blotted out the bright warm light of the winter sky and reduced us to a dim cathedral twilight. We were in a gigantic cavern. Overhead the mountain side had fallen in, and through a broad clear space there streamed just enough daylight to make our surroundings visible and their extraordinary colouring fairly distinct. Underneath the open apex of the dome there was piled up a vast heap of the débris of fallen roof, and at top of it, pointing to the light, was a gigantic white glittering salt pillar, a shining natural obelisk to the perpetual memory of the company of miners who were said to be buried beneath. Round about this central pile were the smooth excavated walls of the dome, painted in every conceivable hue that salt is capable of assuming; from delicate shades of lemon or salmon colour, through tints of sea-green, to deep bands of maroon. In and about the irregularities of this marvellous excavation, where the salt had been split out, and small caves had been formed within the central dome, were wondrous side chapels filled in with salt tracery—the delicate lace-work which is formed by deliquescent salt in the moist steamy air of the Gulf in summer. I have looked down on a bamboo forest weighted and interlaced with snow; and I have seen the weird beauty of acres of wind-dried vegetation picked out with the delicate trinketry of frost, and gilt by the morning sun; but the smooth rounded grace of twisted salt pillars, and the fall of a salt lace curtain over folds of salt strata, is matchless amongst Nature's arts and handicrafts. Captain Townsend and I wandered round in silent admiration, till we came to a short and sharp declivity which led to an interior gallery. The mouth of it was as black as pitch, and the depth of it unguessable, so we suggested that our guide should precede us and show us the way down. Not so, however. The guide protested that the gallery was so full of the demons and sprites of the mountains that nothing would induce him to experiment further on their good nature. He would have to square matters with the local divinities, as it was, and he had brought us quite far enough. We might settle matters with "Jehannum" as we pleased. We therefore elected to go without him, and we dropped straight into a subterranean pathway that might very well have led to where the guide imagined it would lead.

The darkness was however unquestionably inconvenient, so Townsend proceeded to dive into his pockets for blue lights which would at any rate show us which way to move. With a splutter and fizz the ship's signal glared out into broad illumination. It lit up the gallery, and revealed a scene of such fantastic weirdness as no nightmare bred in the overworked brain of a master of pantomime could well have outmatched. We were in a long narrow disused salt gallery. Through it, here and there, moisture had either permeated, or else the humid Gulf atmosphere had first melted the salt and then twisted it into grotesque shapes and patterns, as it dripped and dropped slowly from the roof. A forest of twisted pillars covered with smooth round bosses of clear white salt efflorescence barred our way in an interminable crowd; the sides of the gallery were salt cascades, falling draperies of salt lace; the floor was frozen into a salt slide. In and out amongst the twisted and tortuous shafts of this crypt we made our way, whilst the intense blue glare of the light shimmered and broke into millions of quaint reflections. It was a dancing maze of blue lights, and jerking broken shadows; quite a typical home for all the goblins of Persia. We groped our way along for a distance and time that we quite forgot to mark, till far away ahead of us there glimmered the faint white light of day, rising like the white half-moon of the far opening of the Khojak tunnel after you have trollied through the first mile of it in darkness. But there was not much of daylight when we reached the end. The gallery had been blocked for ages by fallen débris from the outside, and it was with difficulty that we squeezed ourselves through the narrow gangway and out into the open. We then found that we had passed through, and under, the hill-side, out into a nullah bed; and the breath of the sea told us that we had only to follow down the nullah to come to the shore where we would be.

Truly the salt caves of Kishm are not the least of the wonders of this Eastern fairyland of fables and traditions.

Bundar Abbas and Linjah are two ports to which public attention has lately been much directed. They are both on the stretch of Laristan shore which lies immediately north of the Straits of Hormuz. Consequently both occupy commanding positions at the mouth of the Gulf. Bundar Abbas is the port for two great trade routes, one striking northward through Persia to Kirman and Mashad, and the other north-west along the highlands to Bushire. Linjah owes its importance chiefly to the coral and pearl trade; Bundar Abbas does an immense business in carpets, wool, and goats' hair, raw cotton, opium, drugs, etc., including bales of rosebuds for the manufacture of "ata." The bursting of an ill-sewn bale of rosebuds over the greasy decks of a British India steamer was quite an impressive incident in one of my voyages up the coast. I can never smell the smell of dried rose leaves now without visions of a flat white shining sea, and a black busy steamer, with a scrambling crowd of dirty coolies scooping up the sweet ill-used little rosebuds with hands as filthy as Persian coolies can make them.

The trade of both ports is rapidly increasing, the exorbitant dues charged on khafilas passing through Afghanistan no doubt throwing much of the Khorasan traffic on to the Kirman-Bundar Abbas route. Even the brilliant carpeting of far-off Panjdeh finds its way through Bundar Abbas to Karachi and Quetta. Possibly much of this will change with the opening of the Helmund desert trade routes between Sistan and Quetta, but Bundar Abbas will doubtless still continue to increase and multiply, spreading its feelers from the shore to the hills. I am pretty well acquainted with both Bundar Abbas and Linjah, and I have no desire to see them again. They are the filthiest ports on any coast between India and Europe. Both of them press close down to the seaboard, and both trust to wind and tide for a daily system of natural sanitation. There is no harbour at either place, only an open roadstead, and owing to the everlasting surf, goods are frequently transferred to the steamers through the medium of native craft. These "buggalows" (which are built on prehistoric lines and always look as if they had been cut in two and left tailless) receive the cargo at convenient seasons, and hold it ready for transhipment on the arrival of the steamer.

The coast seas are not often troubled by storms, but when cyclonic influences do prevail there is a truly tropical fury about them. I don't think I have ever been at sea in such a blinding, black, raging storm of thunder, lightning, and rain, as beset us one night when the mail steamer left Linjah for the north. We went out into the thick of the night with the sea hissing round us, and nothing but the glare of electricity to show us the way. I only hope I did not look as much afraid as I felt. The captain consulted a ragged and dripping bundle of clothes, with a human pilot inside, and together they took their ship through the labyrinth of unlighted islands which lie about the coast, fearing nothing and seeing nothing. It appeared to me likely enough that we should hit every one of them in succession. Had we done so, we should certainly have required a lantern to enable us to walk ashore.

But the winter seas of the Persian Gulf and the Arabian coast are for the most part smooth seas, and the ship slides along her smooth way on the rippling tides pulsing softly to the throb of the engines and leaving faint shimmering streaks ever widening from her stern. The nights are the nights of the Arabian Sea—soft and star-lit, the gently undulating surface of the smooth polished ocean rounded off by the girdle of a faint horizon and streaked with the glitter of star reflections. Then, of a sudden, out of the blackness of the silent night leaps the wonder of one of Nature's great transformations. First flashes out of the summer darkness little fire-lit streaks where each tiny wavelet curls itself down on to the ocean floor, and from the churning screw there spreads a milky way of efflorescence which shines out into wider and stronger breadths as it leaves the beating blades. In an instant the whole broad sea is alight, dancing with a shower of myriad phosphorescent sparks, aglow with silver flame from the ship to the horizon. The stars pale, and the edges of the heavens finish off sharply, a black canopy leaning down upon a shining sea. Then men look around, and then may now and again be seen the iron lines of the ship—stay and stanchion, rail and davit, aglow with pale wan light, whilst St. Elmo points the yards with dancing pencils of blue flame. And so the ship stalks on over the silver sea illuminated from stem to stern by Nature's artifice.

Sometimes electric wonders join hands with phosphorescence in the magic of these "Arabian nights." I have heard (but I have not seen) that from the depths of the ocean there occasionally rises a straight shaft of brilliant light which breaks and spreads in circles as it reaches the surface, pulsing with great beats, and moving with terrific speed, as it passes away into swift darkness. Eighty miles an hour was the pace estimated by the electricians of the *Patrick Stewart*, and eighty miles an hour is after all nothing in the region of electric possibilities.

Standing back from Bundar Abbas about the distance of a day's march is a mass of mountains called Ginao. The slopes of Ginao spring almost from the coast, and the whole mountain belongs to that system which forms the invariable first step upward from the low foreshore to the Persian plateau, near Bundar Abbas. This is a more prominent feature there than it is further north, where these "western ghats" break and recede from the coast line, leaving plenty of flat space for cultivation and palm growth. Ginao was carefully surveyed with a view to determining its capabilities as a sanatorium, or summer resort, for the perspiring political and telegraph officials of Bushire. There is no doubt that it would answer admirably, and, in view of the importance of the Bundar Abbas position over against the Hormuz straits, and of the certainty of its inclusion in the general telegraph system of the Gulf, no better place could perhaps be found. But the highlands abreast of Tahiri (where lie the ruins of the once famous commercial centre of the Gulf, Siráf) possess certain physical advantages which are not to be overlooked in comparison with Ginao. To begin with, Jam is not half or nearly half the distance from Bushire that Ginao is, and the connecting road is good. Nor is the position so isolated as Ginao, nor so difficult of access from the low coast line; and it lies in the midst of an important oasis in the generally empty land of Persia. It must once have been a position of great importance in spite of the usual difficulty of sea approach. There is not a port on the Persian coast (including Bushire) which can be approached in safety under all conditions of wind and tide, and Tahiri forms no exception to the rule.

Evidences of the importance not only of Siráf (which is nothing now but a heap of ruins) but of the hill towns abreast of it on the plateau, in the old-world scheme of Eastern trade as it existed in the days of Venetian supremacy, are very abundant. Amongst other survivals, Venetian gold coins are still current in Makrán and on the Persian coast. They have been found at Quetta, and they must have been the currency of the Persian and Baluch coasts long after Venice had been shouldered out of the field of Eastern commerce. It has always appeared to me to be probable that the vast quantity of glass beads and bangles which are to be found throughout these districts may be relics of Venetian origin rather than Egyptian, although a Venetian expert informed Captain Macdonald (of the Indian political service) that no such glass is now known. Nevertheless we must remember that Venice still holds the monopoly of the bead currency of western Africa. No Brummagem imitations have ever displaced them. The glass currency of a great part of the world is still in Venetian hands.

In striking contrast to the filthy Persian ports are the Arab coast towns of the Bahrein islands, and Kawait. Kawait is the proposed terminus of a line of railway to the East which is to traverse northern Arabia. It is a (comparatively) clean, white-walled town, with narrow shut-in streets, where one can walk without fear of offence to oneself, and the inhabitants of it are as refreshingly different from the thick, dirty Persian in his felt skull cap, his voluminous blue-skirted coat and trouserless legs, as are the sun-washed walls of these pretty seaside towns from the slimy embankments of Bundar Abbas. The town-bred Arab (and even the Beduin, on occasion) is a gentleman in outward presentation, and his flowing bernous and silk head-dress, with its little tricks of tassels and fringe, are as smart and as well put on as the dress of any Bond Street masher. It is usually a pleasure to talk to him, but beware of entering into personal negotiations about pearls or horseflesh. His progenitors were of the Semitic race (which included Jews and Phœnicians) at a time when yours were possibly Skythic nomads; and the trail of heredity is over us all. But about his manners I can only add my testimony to that of a crowd of other witnesses who have seen vastly more of Arabia than I have. Whether seated at a table as a guest and engaged in jugglery with knives and forks the like of which he has never seen before, or entertaining as a host a small crowd of visitors who have to sit on the floor and perform clumsy tricks at breakfast with their fingers, he is equally master of the occasion. Whether you know his language, or do not, is a matter of polite indifference to him. He will entertain you with general conversation with equal facility. And to meet an Arab gentleman in his best clothes, on his best horse, twirling his delicate little cane and intent on entertaining you with his best ability, is an education in manners such as one knows not in England in these days of high schools and "kitchen" lancers. I have been entertained at Babylon, and I have been put up in the country home of the chief mullah at Kerbela, the headquarters of the Shiah sect of Mahomedans, and the one impression which lingers still is an impression of undeviating courtesy intermingled with the same frank hospitality that I once before found in the house of a Pathan gentleman under the shadow of the Hindu Kush.

But to return to Kawait. The harbour is distinctly indifferent and difficult of approach, but at the same time it more nearly approaches the conformation desirable in a terminal port, and possesses larger possibilities than any other harbour of the Persian Gulf. If the projected line which is to cross Arabia is foredoomed to follow the fate of so many other projects for reaching India, it need certainly not be on the grounds of an indifferent terminus.

Another project which has already found expression in voluminous reports and correspondence would result in the transfer of the line of telegraph from the coast of Makrán, and the sea-bottom, to an inland position which would carry it through the date-growing valleys of Makrán, Panjgur and Kej, to Kirman in eastern Persia, and Bushire. There cannot be a doubt about the advantage of an overland line such as this, although it would at once increase our political responsibilities in southern Baluchistan; but there may be many doubts about the wisdom of abandoning the coast-line and cable. So long as we hold the seas the latter is infinitely more easy to protect than is the long line of internal communication, the support of which might involve military movements of a most complicated description; neither is the political influence on the coast which is maintained by the constant visits of the telegraph service steamer a factor to be altogether ignored, unless the maintenance of this influence by other methods and new political appointments is to be recognised as part of the new programme. The present representation of British naval power by warships in the Persian Gulf is not impressive; there are not enough of them; and the coast-trading steamers of the British India service are more likely to have to appeal for protection themselves than to assist in maintaining political influence. The telegraph steamer is, on the contrary, recognised throughout the whole length of the Gulf coastline as a Queen's ship carrying officers who are charged with local political authority, and as her movements, if not rapid, are regular, and directed to points which would often otherwise remain unvisited by any British representative whatever, there is clearly a good purpose secured by her existence which lies apart from all telegraph or commercial considerations, and which it might be a mistake to lose sight of.

The question of railway extension through Persia and Makrán has received a new impetus lately from the Turkish concession to the Anatolian Company for the Bagdad-Basra line, which again brings to the front speculations on the possibility of a connection between European systems and India by way of the Persian coast. The activity of Russia, too, in the matter of explorations southward from Mashad, and her well known anxiety to secure a port in the Persian Gulf, added to the facts of Persian concessions to Russia for railway and road developments which effectually block the way to enterprise on the part of other countries, when taken together with the control lately acquired by Russia over Persian finance, have stirred up anxious inquiries as to what may be the possible outcome in eastern Persia and Khorasan. All railway developments must be more or less governed by geographical considerations, so it is worth while to consider by the light of newly acquired geographical knowledge, both what is possible, and what is improbable (if not impossible) in this connection. In the latter category must be included a coast line from Basra and Bushire which should skirt the eastern shores of the Persian Gulf and the northern shores of the Arabian sea to Karachi and Sind; and this not so much on account of the natural obstacles (which are formidable enough to render the cost of the line prohibitive) as the insufferable nature of the climate. No first-class passenger traffic along such a line could be maintained for at least half the year, nor could there be, in competition with the sea highway, any very great promise of goods traffic at any time. The carriage of mails and of the local coast population would hardly justify the outlay on a line which would have to be constructed somewhat as follows. I regret that the only trustworthy maps for reference are those which emanate from the Indian Survey Office which are not at present given to the public. The public must consequently take my word for the nature of the route.

From Basra to Bushire it would be found necessary to make a considerable inland détour in order to avoid the low marshy flats of the Euphrates and Karun delta. It would probably be found advisable to carry the line to Awaz and to bridge the Karun at that point before turning southward to Bushire. The bridging of the Shat-el-Arab, of the Karun, of the Kurdistan, Tab, etc., would make the Basra-Bushire section (about 300 miles) expensive. It is unlikely that the line could be carried actually through Bushire. A branch of about ten to fifteen miles would be necessary to connect the seaport with some point on the main line to the east of it. From Bushire to Bundar Abbas is a distance of about 400 miles, through which a coast line touching Tahiri (or Siráf) and Charag could undoubtedly be engineered without more difficulty and expense than the bridging of several shifty, expansive, and troublesome rivers, of which the Mand, Narband, and Dargabind are the chief. Probably also one comparatively insignificant ridge of hills would have to be tunnelled, or surmounted. It would be almost impossible to approach the port of Linjah, so shut in on the landward side is it by extensive swamps and hills, so that Linjah again would be connected by a branch line, if connected at all. It is from the Linjah swamps that most of the firewood supply of the Gulf is obtained. But as far as Bundar Abbas a better line (if more expensive) than the coast line from Bushire would be one which takes to the highlands *viâ* Jam and Hormuz instead of the coast. Although this line runs in and amongst the hills for the whole of its length, it must be remembered that it follows the strike of those hills (which is approximately parallel to the coast), and the transverse water-partings which are encountered are comparatively insignificant. There would be nevertheless a considerable amount of construction on this route along the mountain skirts. The advantage of altitude, and consequent gain in climate thus far, would however render such a line possible to a degree which cannot be claimed by the coast line. From Bundar Abbas to

Jask (200 miles) no high-level line is possible, and the wretched traveller would thenceforward have to run the gauntlet of the worst that Makrán can do in the blazing, blistering days of unshadowed sunshine.

No one would travel that way for the pleasure of a summer trip! The crossing of the Minab delta between Bundar Abbas and Jask would be a work of difficulty, possibly involving a wide inland détour; and there would be further crossings (eight of them considerable, and the rest troublesome) between Jask and Charbar in the next 200 miles. Still there is nothing involving great engineering difficulties in this section. After leaving Jask we may take the Indo-Persian telegraph line for an approximate guide. It follows the coast, and is carried along the most practicable route. From Charbar to Pasni is another 200 mile section, which includes the port of Gwadur about half-way, and the crossing of the delta of the Dasht river; but no great obstructions. Pasni to Urmara (another port, like Gwadur, with a double bay, east and west of a hammer-shaped headland) is another 100 miles, and then follows the great block of the line, a block which would require careful and patient technical examination to determine any possible means of surmounting it. This is the Ras Malán, which protrudes its gigantic 2,000 feet headlands into the sea, and supports those headlands on the landward side with a vast and imposing mass of scarped mountain buttresses. There is a way over them which the telegraph takes—and the linesmen follow; but it is not a way which would commend itself to a railway engineer, and the expense of outflanking or surmounting that barrier would be enormous. On the eastern side of the Malán is the Hingol river, and the two together with a subsidiary mass of hills present about sixty miles of solid barrier to roads or railways. Once beyond the Hingol, eastward, the last 140 miles of approach to Karachi offers no difficulties that can be called important. The line would touch Sonmiani, crossing the Purâli high up towards Las Bela and the Hab river. The total length of line from Basra to Karachi would be not less than 1,600 miles, and would probably be more.

Although the coast alignment, in so far as it follows the line of strike of the main ranges, and runs parallel to the hills instead of crossing them, fulfils those geographical conditions which indicate the least expense in construction, it is doubtful if it could ever be commercially successful. It could never compete with sea-borne traffic between the head of the Persian Gulf or the Persian Gulf ports and India; and, on the other hand, it taps no considerable area of productive country. If we could find the same geographical conditions admitting of easy construction farther inland, supporting an alignment which passed through the centre of highly developed and promising districts, and entering into no local competition with sea traffic, there might be greater hope for a future "grand trunk" for Persia. Such a line really can be found, and all our recent geographical surveying in Persia tends to support the proposition that it is the one line in the country which promises to be worth construction. I refer to the route which connects Tehran with Kashan, Yezd, and Kirman, and which, passing south-eastwards from Kirman, might be carried through Dizak to the Rakshán valley, and so brought to Kalát and Quetta; or connected by a transverse line with Las Bela and Karachi. Tehran possesses no immediate prospect of connection with European systems; otherwise this 1,200 miles of unhampered line, crossing no great water-divides and no great rivers, which brings the rail head to the head of the Rakshán, could not possibly remain long overlooked. From the head of the Rakshán to the Kalát plateau some twenty or thirty miles of careful (though not difficult) construction would be necessary; when once again there would be 100 miles of unobstructed open way to Quetta. As the level of the line never falls below 3,000 feet, it would never be unbearably hot. The strange feature about it is the fact of its running easily amongst mountains for so great a distance. A transverse line from the Rakshán valley to Las Bela and Karachi at once departs from the ruling conditions which govern the alignment from Tehran. It crosses the strike of the hills, which though neither high nor formidable at this point, would still present a most serious obstruction to railway making for about 100 miles.

Much irresponsible discussion has lately arisen about a possible line to be projected by Russia across the width of Persia to a port on the Persian Gulf coast, which might give her Central Asian trade an opening in the Eastern seas. Bundar Abbas is usually denoted as the port of her aspirations. From what I know of the energy of Russian official exploration, I am certain that the geographical aspect of the question has been well considered long ago, and that full reports on eastern Persia are in official hands. From what I know of Russian astuteness I am equally convinced that no such line will be projected for many a long year to come. It possesses all the disadvantages, from the engineering point of view, that any line directed across a rough mountainous country, taking each range in succession almost at right angles, can possess. The cost would be enormous. The 750 miles of direct measurement from Bundar Abbas *viâ* Kirman, Tarbat-i-Haidri and Mashad to the Trans-Caspian line would probably expand to a thousand; and that thousand would cost five or six times the amount expended over any thousand miles of Russian railways elsewhere in Asia. About three-fourths of it would not only be a mountain line—it would be a mountain line working at the greatest possible disadvantage, with but little base for gaining gradient on the hillsides, and little room to turn round in the intermediate valleys. If, instead of directing the line on Bundar Abbas, it were directed on Charbar these physical disadvantages in the geographical conditions would largely disappear; but it would on the other hand be strategetically weak from its exposed position with reference to the Afghan frontier. Bundar Abbas has not the makings of a great trade dêpot. There is no harbour (harbours are not to be found on the Persian Gulf coast), there is nothing but an open roadstead and a dangerous surf. Trade is often carried on locally by a process of transhipment from native craft anchored off the town—and in bad weather it is frequently suspended altogether. It is improbable that Russia (even if she possessed a free hand) would commit herself to such a doubtful financial undertaking as the opening up of a Persian Gulf port for purposes of trade only by means of a railway across the width of Persia. The trade of Central Asia might possibly be turned southward to the seaboard by such a line, if undiverted by any rival system to the east (between Herat and Kandahar, for instance), but when once the disadvantages of the present transhipment of goods for the passage of the Caspian is obviated, Central Asian trade is far more likely to flow northward through the cheap and easy channels of the Trans-Caspian system than southward to the Persian coast. The mere possession of a trade port at Bundar Abbas could hardly be considered as a menace to England in itself; for so long as England holds command of the sea, such a port would be more of an objective to her superior naval power than a menace; and if England ceases to command the sea the want of such a port to Russia would hardly affect the question of the vulnerability of India. The political danger no doubt arises from the prospect of a trade port developing into a naval station. But it would take not merely the occupation of Bundar Abbas, but the further occupation of the islands of Kishm, Hormuz, and Larak to the south of it, and the construction of costly permanent fortifications on these most undesirable islands, to render the position strong enough to constitute a distinct menace to British interests, either in the Persian Gulf or Indiawards. Such developments as these may safely be considered as beyond the reach of Russian political enterprise at present.

CHAPTER X.

THE "DURAND" BOUNDARY

The boundary agreement with the Amir of 1893—What led to the agreement—The Amir's position relatively to the independent tribes on his frontier—New Chaman—The Durand mission—the Amir's attitude—North-west frontier expedition previous to 1893—Kuram delimitation—Wana love-story—Delimitation south of the Gomul—Native surveyors' work.

WHILST Baluchistan was thus rapidly settling under British administration, the tide of progress on the northern frontier was being recorded in a succession of events which brought us into direct political dealings with the Court at Kabul, and finally led up to such a wide sweep of frontier reconnaissance—such a gathering in of the fag ends of geographical information where the first-fruits had already been collected, that it was much more difficult to find workmen for the field than to open up fields for them to work in.

During the progress of that farther delimitation which divided off the northern territories of Afghanistan from Russia, and temporarily, at any rate, put a limit to Russian expansion across the Himalaya, the Amir had shown himself to be in practical agreement with the Indian Government. It is true that the agents he selected for duty with the Boundary Commissions were not always gifted with that unfailing tact and courtesy which usually distinguishes the Afghan Sirdar, and it is also true that under the influence of unfounded impressions created by the advance of a mission into Badakshan in 1886 he had shown us what a disagreeable process delimitation might become if unillumined by the smiles of the great autocrat of Afghanistan; but he had, on the other hand, relieved us from an unpleasant (if not absolutely false) position by his action immediately after the affair at Panjdeh, and he had cordially supported our efforts to render Herat defensible, and to insure means of relief should we have been forced to defend it. If there were indications that he would rather not be burdened with the responsibility of safeguarding a large European party through his capital to India on the return of the mission (a feeling with which it is not difficult to sympathise) there was at least nothing wanting in his hospitality and courtesy when the mission reached Kabul; and no flaw in those admirable arrangements which he made for guarding against casual surprise, or attack, during its return march to Peshawur.

But strong as the Amir has shown himself to be in the government of his miscellaneous assortment of tribes and peoples, neither he nor any other Amir could possibly be successful without extraneous help financially, and without the maintenance of a powerful standing army. Now the army of Afghanistan is much beyond the resources of the country to support it, and always has been so. It is not as are other armies with which we are acquainted. It is, as a whole, ill-conditioned, half-paid, and only quarter disciplined. It includes some of the finest natural fighting material in the world; and yet it is in the habit of deciding for itself its own course of action on the field of battle, and its traditions and history are one unmixed record of disloyalty and independence. So also was the history of some of the best fighting races in India, until the British officer was introduced. So that two of the leading principles of the government of Afghanistan were (and are) still what they had ever been since the Durani Empire was first founded, *i.e.* attainment of power to raise funds from extraneous sources for the payment of the army; and the making of opportunities to keep that army sufficiently well occupied.

The natural outlet for the superabundant energy of the Afghan army is on the frontiers of Afghanistan. The unconquered independent tribes that fringe its eastern (and our western) borders have always been regarded as affording a legitimate hunting ground for Afghan intrigue and Afghan military practice. For some years after the accession of Abdurrahman to the Kabul throne the Afghan army was well occupied, first with a campaign in Afghan-Turkestan against the Amir's cousin, Ishak Khan—which campaign was fought out in true Afghan fashion within a network of unintelligible intrigue; and next with the subjugation of the sturdy race of Hazaras, that Mongul people who occupy a very large slice of central Afghanistan, and who would (were they only sufficiently well armed and properly led) prove a match for the whole Afghan army.

But internal difficulties all being disposed of, it was inevitable that the military instincts of the Kabul Court should be directed towards those outlying tribes who never yet have been subdued from either side; who are intensely proud of their independence, and who look on the vicarious phases of frontier fighting as a normal condition of existence. Such are the Kafirs of Kafirstan and their Pathan neighbours, Mahmunds or Mohmands, Bajaoris, Swatis, Afridis, and Waziris. They are all alike in their indomitable spirit of independence, but very unlike in their tribal constitution and idiosyncrasies. It is the greatest possible mistake to mix them all up together, as if there were any possible spirit of combination amongst them—even on religious principles. The Kafirs are regarded as infidels and outcasts by the rest, and between them and the Afghans there can be no dealings founded on any basis of common faith, common tongue, or common advantage. Swatis and Mohmands are themselves chiefly Afghans, talking the same language, boasting the same descent from the tribes of Israel, imbued with the same faith, acknowledging the Amir as their spiritual head; but practically independent; although they are much more Afghans of the ruling race than the great majority of the people of Afghanistan. Afridis and Waziris are allied in tongue and religion with Afghans. They are all Pathans, talking Pushtu, but they admit no sort of race affinity. With the exception of the Kafirs who claim a far-off European strain of blood none of these people have the faintest race sympathies with Hindustan, or the ruling people of Hindustan. Excepting the Kafirs, all of them would appeal to the Amir as arbitrator in their disputes, adviser in their military ventures, supporter and provider of refuge in distress, spiritual guide in their religious counsels. All mere sympathetic bonds however would not, and did not, prevent the Amir when he had nothing better to do, from intermeddling with their affairs to the extent of threatening their independence; and in the case of Bajaor, of entering on a serious campaign which included the Kafirs on one side, and the Bajaoris on the other, and seemed designed to bring dominant Afghan control right down to the borders of Peshawur.

To put the situation into political language, "relations had been strained" with the Amir for some time before actual aggression led to the consideration that a boundary was necessary between Afghanistan and these independent tribes. The selection of New Chaman as the site of the Sind-Peshin railway terminus on the far side of the Khojak was a source of irritation and offence that the Amir could not get over. Possibly the situation was aggravated by the silent significance of the rail-ends pointing towards Kandahar; anyhow the Amir considered that we had trespassed gravely on his preserves, and had violated the Treaty of Gandamak which placed the boundary between Afghanistan and British Baluchistan at the foot of the Khojak mountains, on the Kandahar side of them. Where the steep slopes of the mountains end, before tailing off into long sweeps of wormwood-covered "dasht"—there is the site of the fort of Old Chaman; and as the railway passes by zigzags down to Old Chaman after passing through the Khojak tunnel (the necessity for constructing which the Amir could not see), there at any rate he considered that the line should end. But Old Chaman was not a desirable terminus for more practical reasons than I need enter into, and so the rail was carried on for another seven miles or so, still on a downward grade, to New Chaman, where has now sprung up a pretty little cantonment, with gardens and buildings all on the approved Indian pattern.

It was after all only the open question of what should be considered the "foot of the mountains," but it was enough to raise a very solid grievance in the mind of the Amir, and almost produced the same effect with him that the Sistan boundary decision created in the mind of Sher Ali. Indeed it is not too much to say that when the question of a boundary to eastern Afghanistan was pressed on the Council of India it was a question either of a boundary or of war with Afghanistan. Nothing short of this could have justified a measure which was so likely to raise a frontier hornets' nest about our ears.

Our first negotiations for a mission to Kabul were not altogether successful. The mission was to have been placed under the chief control of Lord Roberts, and at first it seemed as if the Amir was satisfied with the nomination of so distinguished an officer as British envoy. But a period of delays and procrastinations set in, and after the apparent commencement of the necessary arrangements for collecting supplies on the route, the mission fell through. Next Sir Mortimer Durand was nominated as envoy, and with his nomination, the mission took practical shape. In October, 1893, a distinguished company of officials left Peshawur for Kabul, there to enter into a boundary agreement with the Amir which should for ever settle the responsibilities of the Kabul Government as regards the outlying independent tribes on our border. No survey officer was permitted to accompany the mission, on the grounds that his presence might raise suspicions in the mind of the Amir. This proved to be a mistake. No one was better aware than the Amir that the road from Peshawur to Kabul had been thoroughly surveyed, and indeed far beyond it; and no one but a survey officer on the other hand, could possibly give an authoritative opinion on the subject of the maps which were to illustrate the line through 1,300 or 1,400 miles of boundary. This book has served very little purpose already if it has not shown that the methods of acquiring geographical information are as many and various as are the nature of these opportunities for geographical surveying which military, political, or commercial movements may give rise to. And the quality of the work varies with the method which necessity indicates as the one to be adopted. Geographical survey is at best a patchwork, and it requires an expert to appraise rightly the true value of the miscellaneous patches when there is question of details along an extended line dividing them in the midst. There is also a certain value in the proper use of technical expressions in formulating an agreement which is (and must always be in the case of boundaries) based on geographical considerations. If all the time and all the money, and the bitterness of dispute which have been wasted over the failure to recognise these simple considerations in the matter of political geography in England alone were collected together, and could be represented by a total cash value, it would go some way towards settling our national debt.

The reception accorded to the mission at Kabul was magnificent, and the arrangements made for its safety were perfect. The Amir received our representative with that hearty cordiality, that frank courtesy which always distinguishes him, and which has warmed the heart of many a traveller. The spirit of personal good-fellowship and even of affection is strong in the Afghan; so strong that it is often said that had Lord Mayo lived, Sher Ali would never have tempted his fate. With all this readiness for the recognition of personal friendship, it is hard to realise that behind the open geniality of the Afghan manners the door is shut to any real intimacy. We never get to the back of the Afghan's mind; never measure the depth of the race antipathy which furnishes the real motive power of his political action. But the fanatical spirit of the destroyer of Amalek is there even when the superficial spirit of geniality and human friendship conceals it, and overlies it for the time.

But cordial as was the reception of the mission, business proceedings undoubtedly dragged; and it was not without much patient attendance on the Amir's humours, much persuasion from his one trusted friend, Sir Salter Pyne, that the agreement was finally signed and sealed after weeks of waiting.

However the great end was achieved. The Amir had signed the agreement. His subsidy had been increased by six lacs of rupees yearly—and he had omitted to sign the maps which were supposed to be illustrative of the agreement; but he had signed the agreement itself. The mission returned to Peshawur with great rejoicing and was accorded honours such as no mission has received before or since.

It requires no great strain of the imagination, and not much reading between the lines of official correspondence, to conceive that the Amir disliked the boundary exceedingly. There was indeed no reason why he should do otherwise. The independent tribes interfered very little with him. And they might at any time be brought under his sovereign control. It is true that he had all Kafirstan on his northern border where he could not only exercise the military energies of his commanders, but where he could himself pose as a prophet of Islam, the instrument in the hands of Allah for the conversion of the infidel to the true faith. But the Kafirs were an awkward people to deal with; their country is remote and inconceivably difficult, and except on the edges it leads to nowhere. North, west, and south of Kafirstan the land was already his. There was little or no military glory to be won in Kafirstan. But Bajaor and Swat and the Mohmand country—were they not full of his own people, who being already allied to him by ties of faith, of language, and of kinship, should learn to recognise his direct authority? Peshawur had gone from Afghanistan hopelessly; but the dream of Peshawur, once the capital of the Durani Empire, lingers still in royal slumbers, and the independent Mohmands spread down right to the very edge of the Peshawur plain. He claimed at least to be lord of the Mohmands. An army under the command of Ghulam Haidar, Charki, one of his most trusted generals, was already in the Kunar valley (the valley which runs up from Jalalabad to Chitral and to the Hindu Kush, bounding Kafirstan on the east) and had taken signal vengeance on the Jandol Chief, Umra Khan, who had had the impertinence to come over from Bajaor and occupy tracts of country within that valley, which he (the Amir) considered to be Afghan territory. It was, in fact, the success of the Afghan arms in Kunar and the doubt as to ultimate ends of that success, which formed one of the strongest reasons for a boundary settlement with Afghanistan. But now the Amir was to be compelled to hold his hand.

In the far south, too, his outposts had pushed forward into Baluchistan, and had occupied positions which gave them command of the trade routes between Sistan and Quetta which it was most desirable that we should open without Afghan interference and Afghan imposts. Here again he must not only stay his hand, but actually withdraw his troops. That he should *like* this curtailment of his power, this lowering of his "izzat" in the eyes of his own durbar, is quite inconceivable. He did not like it, but he signed the agreement all the same (and accepted our offer of six lacs per annum further subsidy), silently reserving to himself the right of disputing the boundary in detail when it should come to the process of actual demarcation.

As for the independent tribespeople themselves, they probably knew very little till the matter was explained to them by their mullahs. Their general view of the situation (as I gathered, not from one, but from every tribesman whom I have questioned) was that the Indian Government meant annexation. Hitherto there had been no very definite ideas about a boundary between themselves and Afghanistan. Their back doors opened on to the Afghan country, and they could pass through them in times of difficulty occasioned by their own lawless proceedings on the Indian border, and be certain of that asylum which no true Mahomedan can refuse to a brother in distress. Possibly they might even get active assistance in opposing the Sirkar. Under any circumstances they were connected by ties of faith and brotherhood with the West, and not with the East. The Hindu bania of the plains had been their lawful prey from historic times; and from such times Afghanistan had been their refuge from pursuit. They were not afraid of Afghan annexation. They had held their own from time immemorial, and could hold it still (or believed they could), but they were afraid (speaking generally that is, for there were small communities who officially protested that they wished to be taken under British protection) of the ever-advancing overlap of the red spaces in the map of India, to which the astute old prophet Ranjit Sing had alluded when he said "Soon it will *all* be red."

This much is necessary in explanation of the subsequent difficulties that arose in the progress of boundary demarcation; but we must not altogether overlook the series of military operations on the north-west frontier that filled up the space between 1886 and 1893 and which themselves had much to say to the necessity for defining the area of our administrative responsibilities all along the border. A punitive expedition was rendered necessary by an outrage on the part of the Black Mountain tribes to the east of the Indus in 1888. This expedition added much most useful geographical information to our store of knowledge, which was largely increased during subsequent expeditions in the autumn of 1888 and the spring of 1891, all acting in the same direction. The extreme difficulty of administering a satisfactory thrashing to a mountain-bred people who have ever an open door behind them was very well illustrated by these three Hazara campaigns. The first thrashing being incomplete entailed the subsequent operations, and even now it may be doubted if the wild Indus clans are thoroughly satisfied that they cannot defy us with impunity. Another punitive expedition in 1891 was directed against the tribes living in the Orakzai hill borderland (now so well known in connection with the Tirah campaign) which fringes the Meranzai valleys connecting Kohat with the base of the Kuram. This was followed by a second in 1892 and led to the occupation of the Samana range (the outer ridge of the hills overlooking Meranzai) by the construction of those forts which proved to be such a source of irritation to the Orakzais and of such doubtful utility to ourselves. It was during these years too that the series of operations in western Kashmir were conducted which ended in the subjugation of Hunza and led to the occupation of Chitral; the story of which has been so well told in Mr. Knight's enchanting book. Truly they were busy years, and as they were years of great financial depression as well, we can fully realise the welcome relief which the prospect of a final settlement of Afghan pretensions by the definition of a boundary afforded to the Government of India.

The Durand agreement was signed in November, 1893, and early in 1894 a new Viceroy came to rule over India. The Viceroy is, as all men know, the official head of the Indian Foreign Department. There is no Member of Council for Foreign Affairs as there is for Finance, for Public Works, for Military or Home affairs, or in the interest of Legislation. The Viceroy is his own Foreign Office member, and in the periodic intervals which occur between the departure of one Viceroy and the arrival of the next the responsibility for advising the conduct of foreign policy rests with a secretary. He is not the executive, he is simply the adviser. And his views and advice must largely determine the conduct of Indian foreign policy (so far as it rests with the Government of India) even after the advent of a new Viceroy; for it is seldom that any Viceroy can take up the reins of Government in India with an independence of opinion based on such wide knowledge of Indian foreign relationships as Lord Curzon possessed when he lately succeeded to that high office. It is well to bear this in mind, in relation to the immediate political action which was taken on the frontier at the commencement of this most critical period of frontier history—the period which followed the advent of Lord Elgin to India. A few months only after Lord Elgin's arrival, a division of opinion in the councils of the Indian Government occurred about the desirability of forming a military post at Wana. Wana is a barren desolate plain lying north of the Gomul river at the south-western corner of Waziristan, south of the Gomul river, in Baluchistan. I have already pointed out that all the independent tribes of the Baluch frontier are dominated from the Zhob. Wana would afford much the same sort of key to the back doors of the ever-restless and turbulent Waziri tribes that Zhob did for those of the Pathans of Baluchistan. It is also conveniently placed for dominating the Suliman Khel and other of the strongest of the Ghilzai tribes, and it absolutely commands the greatest high road for trade between Ghazni and India. In short, Wana is a strategical position of more than usual importance. Between Jalalabad on the north and Quetta on the south, it may be doubted if there is a stronger one anywhere on our frontier. But Wana is a wild and desolate stone-covered plateau; it possesses none of the beauty of those grassy uplands dotted with deodars which grace Birmul to the north of it; nor the grandeur which distinguishes the rugged scenery of the lower Zhob and Kundar to the south; and the very same arguments which might be advanced in its favour as a position of exceptional strategic value, have been adduced to prove that it would be difficult to hold, difficult to keep supplied, and constantly exposed to attack. Strategically it might be regarded as a link in the line of Zhob communications, but politically it would fall under another local government (that of the Punjab) and it would remain an isolated, expensive, and unreachable outpost, if it depended on the Punjab alone for its base of supply. So the councils of India were divided, and it was only by the casting vote of the Viceroy, who had been but a few months in India, that it was decided by a resolution passed on the 10th July, 1894, to occupy the plateau with a brigade. Under any circumstances the support of such a force was considered essential to a delimitation of boundary west of Waziristan.

Meanwhile all efforts had been made to give effect to the Durand agreement. In February, 1894, I received instructions to find surveyors for the three detachments that were to commence the work of delimitation from Lundi Kotal northward to the Kunar valley, and from the slopes of the Safed Koh southward through Kuram; and from Domandi at the junction of the Zhob and the Gomul, through Baluchistan, to the Persian frontier.

Only the Kuram detachment was able to take the field at once. The usual period of procrastinations set in as regards the other two sections, and active proceedings hung in the wind thereafter for many weary months. The delimitation at the head of the Kuram valley presented little difficulty. It may be taken as a fact of some significance perhaps that the occupants of the higher slopes of the Kuram (the Turis) are of the Shiah sect of Mahomedans, with whom the Sunnis (all the inhabitants of Afghanistan except the Hazaras are Sunnis) have no dealings. Here at any rate the terms of the agreement were very fairly observed and our agents had comparatively little difficulty. But in the midst of it, came the Waziri protest against the occupation of Wana, and their protest was in this wise.

Collecting silently and secretly from the southern valleys of Waziristan (where this scheme must have been hatched under the very noses of our political officers), the Waziris massed themselves by night in two dense columns for the attack of our camp. The position selected for this camp was not above criticism, and careful arrangements were made by Waziri spies (by lighting fires beyond the camp) to guide the attacking column, which, provided it kept straight, would hit upon a weak corner and, missing the political encampment which was on one side, would penetrate straight into the lines where they might expect to find treasure and stores. It was admirably planned, and was carried out with more than partial success. The Gurkhas, who held the outposts on the side attacked, heard nothing in the silence of the night—till suddenly the tramp of many feet shook the earth. In an instant the wave closed over their heads. Their comrades in the encampment had barely time to seize their arms and to collect in fragmentary groups, when the Waziri attack burst full upon them; and then ensued one of the wildest, weirdest fights that our fighting frontier has ever witnessed. In scattered groups, or in solid line—fortunately it was all the same to the stout little Gurkhas. They never budged from their position, and although the wild yelling mass of Waziri braves broke through and passed shrieking into the midst of the camp, cutting horses loose, looting tents and slaying all unwary victims, like frenzied demons, till they were turned out at the bayonet point by Meiklejohn's Pathans (who swept them back as a housemaid disturbs blackbeetles with a broom), they never moved from their own lines. Had that first column been followed up by the second with equal determination, there is no telling what the end might have been; but I was informed long afterwards by one who was there, that the cutting loose of the horses by the first column and consequent stampede, produced the impression amongst the "reserve" that the cavalry were after them. The effect of the word "cavalry" on the frontier mountaineer who is caught in the plains is magical. He has but one idea left in him, and that is to make his way back to his broken hills as rapidly as circumstances will admit. He is for the time utterly demoralised. Anyhow the second column never delivered their attack in support of the first, and the camp was saved from the hands of the enemy.

But it was secured with much grievous loss. It was then that I lost one of my best and most promising assistants, Lieutenant Macaulay, R.E. He had been sent to join Major Wahab's detachment from work on the Kuram delimitation, where he proved both his pluck and ability. He went, poor fellow, with one of those curious presentiments of death before him which one sometimes reads of, but seldom actually encounters, and he was found dead at the close of the action, with more than one Waziri foe lying near him, the victims probably of his revolver.

Some strange stories were afterwards told of that eventful night, one of which is perhaps worth recording as a sample of the ethics of frontier tribal existence.

A young Pathan who had risen to the rank of havildar in a well-known border regiment had fallen desperately in love with the daughter of another member of the same regiment, who either by right of superior caste or position, considered the young man's claims to the girl's hand as preposterous. Entreaties proving of small avail, the suitor backed his proposal with the usual offerings, increasing his offer of rupees with each demand, till he had offered all that he could by any possibility scrape together. It was of no use. The father's heart remained obdurate, and his face was full of scorn for the suitor—when suddenly a strange change came over him. He appeared to listen to the young man's proposals, and with a sudden (too sudden) change of demeanour, he told him that at last his long suit and weary crying after the girl had sickened him. He could stand it no longer. He would give up the girl for 100 rupees. "Give me 100 rupees and take her," he said. "You will find her at —— village." So the enraptured lover paid over the coin, and went after his sweetheart. He went to the village named by the father, and he found his girl; but he found her *dead*. The poor child had sickened and died while her lover knew not of it. Let us hope he buried her! I do not know—but this much is certain. He went straight to the father and demanded his money back again, and we may presume that he used the purple language of the Pathan that is suited to such occasions. But he got nothing for it—not a rupee. "Could you imagine that I should part with a good-looking, high-caste girl to such a swine as you for 100 rupees if she were *alive?*" said the father. "Go to, you ought to have known better." In wrath and bitterness the young havildar turned away, and the first chance he got, he deserted. He deserted, and joined the Waziri ranks at Wana, and when the rush came that flooded the camp he made straight for the lines of his old regiment and the tent wherein dwelt that man whom he had so earnestly desired to make his father-in-law. But the old man was wary. He was away from home, and the young man it was that died. And so the moral of the story did not turn up at the end as a good moral should. It got mislaid in the turmoil of that Wana fight.

Thus was the very first attempt at delimitation between Waziristan and Afghanistan frustrated, and not till the episode of Wana led to an expedition the following winter under Sir W. Lockhart, which swept the country from end to end (at a cost of twenty-eight lacs), was Major Wahab's survey detachment able to take the field in the interests of demarcation about Birmul and Shawal. There was no suspicion of concerted action about this affair at Wana. The Waziris had heard of the boundary that was to be placed between them and their refuge (in fact, between them and some of their pleasantest summer resorts), and they saw nothing short of annexation in the military occupation of Wana. How could they think otherwise? It was a strike (and a strike which produced new impressions of the fighting capacity of the Waziris) for their independence, and every Wazir of the Gomul districts will tell you so to this day. This, however, did not interfere with some lively demonstrations of satisfaction on the part of a particular section of the Darwesh Khel Waziris in the north (the Mada Khel, about whom more presently), when they saw the great stone pyramids set up which divided them from Afghanistan. *They*, at any rate, declared that they elected for British rule, and they also accepted those pillars as outward and visible evidence that they were to come under that rule.

Thus dawned the year 1895, and meanwhile demarcation southward from Domandi had made progress, even if demarcation in the north seemed to hang fire. There was no great eagerness displayed on the side of Afghanistan for the settlement of their Baluch border. The Afghan commissioner who was appointed to meet Captain McMahon on the borderland below the Gomul, came to the rendezvous, inspected the arrangements, and went away again. Whether he objected to the junior rank of the British commissioner (whose ability was certainly not to be measured by the length of his service), being himself a sirdar, and a connection of the Amir, I do not know. It has been said that he did. He at any rate indulged in all the usual oriental forms of procrastination, and advanced all manner of reasons for delaying progress. This mission actually took the field in March, 1894. It was officially estimated that the demarcation of a line drawn through 800 miles of country, mostly desert, to the Persian border would take four months. It did actually last two years, being completed by the erection of the last trijunction pillar on the top of the Malik-Siah-Koh mountain on the Persian border in June, 1896. Captain McMahon's party escaped the attention of the Waziris who, during the early stages of its existence, were too much immersed in their usual occupation of robbing the passing khafila traffic through the Gomul to spare time for less profitable employment. They could hardly have avoided being drawn into collision with the Afghan escort of the Kabul commissioner, and they had moreover no personal interest in a matter which, so far, only concerned the Pathan tribes of Baluchistan. So they let McMahon alone until he had moved beyond reach of their attentions. The demarcation of that section of the boundary was a notable achievement; for it was carried through a country of "barren hills and mountain ranges and vast open plains, where in most cases want of water or the unsettled state of the people has prevented the cultivation of the soil. Rocks and stones varying from the size of the huge gigantic boulders on the mountain-sides to that of the small pebbles and shingle of the strands of the dry torrent-beds, cover a great portion of the surface of the country, while another large portion is given up to deserts of deep soft sand." And the water was scarce and indescribably filthy. But the people were Baluchis rather than Afghans, "a fine manly race, whose love of independence is as rugged as their hills, and whose stubborn bravery is unquestionable. With fair complexions and splendid physique they form for the most part a magnificent race of men." Captain Ranald Mackenzie and Mr. Tate between them gathered in about 30,000 square miles of geography in this weird country, full of volcanic remains and horned snakes; and in spite of the continued interference of the first Afghan commissioner, who was succeeded by a second of much more favourable disposition, the boundary was actually defined throughout its length. It is, however, defined by a line which at one point is at least seventy miles south of the position assigned to it by the Kabul agreement. Concession was the ruling spirit of the demarcation.

Beyond the responsibility of general superintendence and of providing for the survey necessities of this long-stretched-out line of demarcation from the Safed Koh range south of the Khaibar to the Persian frontier on the far side of Makrán, I had no personal share in the proceedings. Capt. Macaulay and a staff of native surveyors (which included the veteran Hira Sing) took the field with Mr. Donald, the political officer in charge of the Kuram section; Major Wahab and his assistants were responsible for the Waziristan line under Mr. White King; and Capt. Ranald Mackenzie and Mr. Tate completed the demarcation survey with Capt. McMahon. Wherever demarcation was carried there also spread the network of triangulation binding the tops of mountains together and trellising the plains with its invisible threads, reaching out long arms to the far-away hinterland, and fixing the whole into geographical position. Then followed the native surveyor, making maps of the land surface, and searching out hidden topography. It is impossible to say too much for the value of these native artists in such a field. They work silently and indefatigably, never hurrying, never resting, never talking, and seldom complaining. One of them was once lost amidst dust storms and haze in the desert south of the Helmund. In that red-hot land of volcanic rocks and earthquake cracks, of snakes, lizards and poisonous water, it is usually fatal for a man to lose his way. For five days he wandered about without a guide, living on leaves and roots until he struck the camp again. Luckily he came across water or he would have died there, and we should have had a gap in our mapping.

GHULAM HAIDAR, THE AMIR'S COMMANDER-IN-CHIEF

CHAPTER XI.

KUNAR VALLEY

Preliminaries to demarcation in the Kunar valley—Nature of boundary—March to Jalalabad and meeting with the Sipah Salar—Ghulam Haidar—Roads up the Kunar—The Amir and Umra Khan—Umra Khan's career—He declines to "come in"—Description of Kunar—A ride with Ghulam Haidar—Asmar—A review of Afghan troops—Umra Khan blocks the way—Change of attitude towards Umra Khan on the part of Ghulam Haidar—Afghan hospitality—Surveying—Chitral refugees in camp—Umra Khan goes on the warpath—Our views of the Chitral position from Kunar—Failure to communicate with garrison—Ghulam Haidar's attitude.

IT is a pleasure to turn once more to the cool shadowed valleys of the Himalaya and to trace the progress of the Durand boundary in the far north. On December 3rd, 1894, a compact little boundary commission party under the leadership of Mr. Udny,* Chief Commissioner of Peshawur, were received at Landi Khana, at the foot of the Landi Kotal on the Khaibar route to Kabul, by Col. Mahomed Ali Khan (a near relative of the Amir), who was to conduct them to Jalalabad and into the historic valley of Kunar for the purpose of delimitating the Afghan boundary from the Hindu Kush to the recognised frontier at Landi Kotal.

The circumstances under which the boundary party took the field were not altogether promising.

A preliminary meeting had taken place in Afghan territory between Mr. Udny on the part of the Indian Government, and General Ghulam Haidar, the Amir's Commander-in-Chief of his eastern army, for the purpose of arranging the conditions under which the party was to work, and of arriving at some sort of understanding as to the position of the line to be

* The Commission included Mr. Udny (now Sir Richard Udny) as Chief Commissioner, Mr. C. Hastings Assistant-Commissioner, Lieut. Coldstream, R.E., on survey duty, and Dr. McNabb in medical charge. I was chief surveyor of the party.

R

demarcated. It would naturally be supposed that all this had been included in the agreement of November, 1893, and that the definition of the frontier in this, the most intricate and difficult of all the disputed sections, was fairly exact. But it soon became clear that, so far as this part of his responsibilities was concerned, the Amir had no intention whatever of adhering to the text of the agreement; that he repudiated the maps which had been hastily prepared for purposes of boundary illustration at Kabul, and had determined to advance fresh views of Kunar geography. In the first place he declined to yield an inch of Kafirstan territory, and in the second boldly claimed control over all the Mohmand tribes right down to the Peshawur valley; so that, as a matter of fact, he repudiated the whole section of the boundary that it was our object to demarcate. Nor was his position at all shaken when we took the field; but he did, under pressure, guarantee our safety so long as we were under the protection of Ghulam Haidar, excepting as regards the Mohmand part of the boundary between the Kunar valley and Lundi Kotal, through districts north of the Khaibar. There he would guarantee nothing whatsoever.

This was not exactly a promising outlook, but it was hoped that an examination *in situ* of the main features of the position might lead to further consideration, and to a definite settlement of some sort, which, if it did not actually maintain the exact terms of the agreement of 1893, would be sufficiently near it to be acceptable to both sides. Practically the outcome of the mission justified the venture. A boundary was found between Afghanistan and the independent tribes to the east, from the Hindu Kush to a point in the Kunar valley from whence it diverged to Lundi Kotal; and although at that point it had to be temporarily abandoned, and has remained undemarcated, enough was secured to lead up to a better geographical knowledge of the whole position, on the basis of which it was possible to effect a subsequent agreement which has rendered actual demarcation through the Mohmand country unnecessary.

No part of the boundary defined south of the Hindu Kush was the actual boundary of the agreement, but it must be allowed that in the absence of fairly exact geographical knowledge (without which no boundary agreement whatsoever is worth very much) it was something to start with an agreement which was elastic enough to admit of reasonable concessions. Better use of such geographical information as did exist might possibly have been made, so that during the process of demarcation (or rather of definition, for no pillars were set up) it should not have been possible for the Amir to base his objections on geographical grounds; but beyond this it is doubtful whether any agreement drawn up at Kabul could have been made which would have met the situation better.

Once again we traversed the well-worn old route to Kabul, and it was interesting to observe that the last eight years had brought little change to the dusty, stony, sun-baked districts which lie between Lundi Kotal and Jalalabad. Beyond Dakka, indeed, there was a refreshing stretch of cultivation, refreshing in spite of the fact that at this season of the year it was only a waste of dun-coloured fields. The fort at Dakka looked ruined and neglected, gaping at us with gaps in its mud-built walls; the road appeared more stony than ever to us, although the variegated and motley bands of "Kachi" nomads, marching down to India with their wives and families for the winter tour in the plains, seemed to find it a broad and pleasant path. The same mud Mohmand villages nestled close under the same mud-coloured hillsides, hardly recognisable but for the black squares of door and window which spotted the distant slopes. It was all familiar and unchanged. Sikarám, the white giant of the Safed Koh, hid his head in the clouds, but the Kafirstan peaks beyond Jalalabad (the peaks where Noah's ark found its refuge when the deluge had passed) were white and clear; and the Kabul river ran thin and muddy as is its wont in winter time.

We were met at Jacobabad by the great Ghulam Haidar, Sipah Salar to the Amir. Great he certainly was, for he stood a giant in his boots (or out of them), and when mounted on his coarse-bred "waler" there was an appearance of solid momentum about him which did not end with an impression of physical solidity only. He met us with the full force of a cavalry band (including his largest drum) and conducted us with all honour to the new palace at Jalalabad—an imposing structure in chunam and stucco, without one single redeeming architectural feature, and only saved from absolute vulgarity by a surrounding garden of roses and cypress.

Two days we halted here, and then crossed the river Kabul by the deadly "ford" of history for the Kunar valley and a look into an unknown corner of the northern frontier; a corner which promised to be full of interest, and which did not fail of its promise.

The Kunar river rises in a blue lake called Gaz Kul, or Karumbar, under the southern slopes of the Hindu Kush. This at least is one of its sources. Many a mighty glacier standing about the head of the Yarkhun river offers its contributions. The Yarkhun flows past the fort of the Baroghél pass (of which more presently) over pebble and boulder-covered flats and through terrific gorges, with here and there the snout of a glacier protuding (or even temporarily blocking the valley) till it reaches Mastuj. From this point you may call it the Chitral river, or Kashkar, for it now flows past Chitral, and through the district known to hill people as Kashkar. It does not become the Kunar till it reaches the neighbourhood of the ancient kingdom of Kunar, which occupies the last fifty miles of its course before it joins the Kabul river.

The Kunar valley is of exceptional interest for many reasons. The ancient high road from Kabul to India through the Laghman valley ran across it to Bajaor. Consequently former conquerors of India (Alexander and Babar for instance) who advanced from Kabul, and were always much concerned in reducing the hill tribes about the Kunar before they entered the plains of India, knew it well. It was in fact a necessity of their advance that the powerful coalition of hill tribes who have ever dwelt between the Kunar and the Indus (even before the Afghan Mohmand and Yusafzai appeared) should be thoroughly well thrashed before further operations in the direction of Lahore and Delhi could be undertaken. So that we have much old historical matter about these regions which may haply be set in order by the light of its new geography. Until a comparatively recent date the Kafirs spread through the lower Kunar, and occupied a large section of Bajaor to the east of it. Thus we find none of those Budhist remains in the

Kunar valley which are such a remarkable feature about eastern Swat and the Nangrahar valley near Jalalabad, for the Kafirs were never Budhists. They have now been driven away from the Kunar westward into the Kashmund mountains bordering the river; there they still hold their own, and from these hills northward the whole country is in the hands of Kafir tribes till you reach Badakshan.

No European officer in modern times had succeeded in penetrating far up the Kunar valley. Colonel Tanner, during the Afghan war, made a gallant attempt to reach Kafirstan, and he partially succeeded, but he only reached that part of Kafirstan which is represented by the Kashmund mountains. Here he was robbed and ill-treated, and he effected his retreat from the country with difficulty.

The Amir had long cast his eyes on the Kunar valley. It afforded him a right of way from Jalalabad into Kafirstan and Badakshan. Here he could find opportunity for the construction of a road which should unite the Oxus in the far north with Jalalabad and India, passing across the backbone of the Hindu Kush. One such road he already possessed which, traversing that range by the Khawák depression and following the Panjshir valley to Charikar, unites the rich districts of Andarab and Baghlan in western Badakshan with Kabul. In spite of the altitude of the range about Khawák (11,650 feet), where we crossed at the conclusion of the Russo-Afghan Boundary Commission, it is, in ordinary years, possible to keep it continually open for khafila traffic. The snowfall is not usually great on this part of the Hindu Kush. The Kunar valley and the valley of the Bashgol, or Arnawai, together lead up to the Mandal and Dorah passes, either one of which is the gateway to the rich valleys of eastern Badakshan, and opens up a direct line to Jalalabad from the Oxus which does not touch Kabul at all. These passes are high (14,000 feet to 15,000 feet), difficult, and very much more buried under snow than those further west; but a well-constructed road across them would still be a passable trade route for many months in the year; and would offer a far more direct connection between the Oxus regions and India than any which now exists.

When a freebooter from Jandol named Umra Khan, therefore,

first threw himself across the dividing watershed, and descended into the Kunar valley, the Amir was exceedingly angry, and he took prompt measures for his repression. Umra Khan has been sometimes represented as a noble savage of the true border type, ruling by right of moral superiority as much as by physical ability, a pent-up eagle of the mountains pining for a wider scope for his activities. A bird of prey he undoubtedly was, but there is little of nobility to be found in his career, even if we admire his savage energy. With a following of 130 men (only half armed) he is said first to have commenced that career by disposing of the Khan of Jandol, and seating himself in his place. But 130 men could hardly keep him there. Mahomed Sharif, Chief of Dir, descended upon him with thousands, and Umra Khan was obliged to seek an ally in one Mian Gul, son of the famous Akhund of Swat. Together they disposed of Dir, and having defeated him, Umra Khan, for reasons of his own, at once allied himself with his late enemy, and turned on his late ally. Then was Mian Gul with his Swat army defeated in turn.

A year later the Chief of Dir heard that Umra Khan had once again changed round and was descending upon him in force. In his despair at finding no one prepared to face the redoubtable robber, he resorted to that invariable refuge of distressed frontier tribesmen—Kabul and the Amir; and this policy succeeded for a time, but no sooner was the Amir well occupied with his cousin Ishák Khan in Turkestan than Umra Khan seized his opportunity and overran Dir, forcing Mahomed Sharif into exile. Then he rose a little beyond himself. Inflated with the pride of success he trespassed into the Kunar valley and occupied Asmar. There he fell foul of the Amir. The result was that Ghulam Haidar, the Amir's Commander-in-Chief, fell upon him and crushed him. Then did Mahomed Sharif, Khan of Dir, regain his own; and one Safdar-Khan of Nawagai helped him to disperse Umra Khan's army.

But a man of Umra Khan's make is not easily disposed of. He reorganised his army (such as it was) at Jandol, and when the time was ripe, he played his old diplomatic game on the same old victim, Mahomed Sharif, as of yore. Mahomed Sharif's simplicity, for a Pathan, was phenomenal. Once again he joined Umra Khan in a joint effort to dispose of the Chief of Nawagai. Once again his rôle as a catspaw having been played out, did Umra Khan turn on him and rend him, thus establishing his rule over Nawagai and Dir, both. He also managed to retain a good stretch of the Kunar valley north of Asmar and south of Chitral. His garrisons intervened between us and Chitral when we entered the Kunar valley, and Ghulam Haidar was only stayed from the process of ejectment by our arrival on the scene. Umra Khan had clearly established the claim of the man in possession over a certain portion of the valley which the Amir claimed as his own, and he thus became a factor in the business of boundary demarcation; so he was accordingly summoned by the commissioner to "come in" and attend proceedings.

But whether Umra Khan foresaw that in the course of settlement he would inevitably lose the results of his conquests in the valley, or whether he really thought he had a substantial grievance with the Indian Government in that he had been promised arms to enable him to maintain his position in Bajaor and that the promise had been subsequently withdrawn—I do not know. But it is certain that he failed to comply with Mr. Udny's request; and from that time forward the relations between himself and Ghulam Haidar appeared to undergo a change.

"That accursed pig Umra" was still the object of the Sipah Salar's revilings, but there was a want of genuine spontaneity about the anathema that did not fail to strike so perfect a Pushtu linguist as the commissioner. Umra Khan never "came in," and it seemed more than probable that after strict Pathan precedent, he then found it expedient to patch up a truce with his former enemy in order to work out some new diplomatic end against us. What this scheme developed into all the world knows; but how far the Amir's Commander-in-Chief was in the counsels of the Chief of Jandol; what mutual understanding really existed between them; whether promises of assistance under certain conditions were actually made by Ghulam Haidar—I was never able to discover; and I feel confident that it is not in the power of any frontier official to say. Correspondence certainly passed between them, and there came a time a few months later when Umra Khan openly and boldly requested Ghulam Haidar's help.

We crossed the Kabul river on the 10th December and rode over the long stony slopes of the "talus" which spreads itself from the hills into the angle formed by the junction of the Kunar and Kabul. It is a comparatively short cut from Jalalabad to Shewa (the first considerable group of villages in the Kunar valley), passing under the cliffs of our old survey hill-station of Besúd. From Besúd we prepared for as comprehensive a survey of the route before us as circumstances would permit of our making; but we soon found that this was not an extensive prospect. The eagle eye of the Sipah Salar was on every member of our camp, and his knowledge of the exact limits of our previous work (within which limits further observations were of course unimportant) was accurate. Beyond it, not an observation was permitted. Discretion prevents me from unveiling the artifices which such conditions oblige one to adopt. They are necessarily inferior in their results, and comparatively unsatisfactory. It is sufficient to observe that the Sipah Salar did his duty. The Amir had set his face against any mapping of his country which did not bear directly on the matter in hand—*i.e.* boundary delimitation; and the Sipah Salar knew only too well what did bear on it, and what did not.

But the Kunar valley, as its mysteries were gradually unrobed from day to day, held much that is worth remembrance amongst the valleys of the Hindu Kush. The open width of the sloping stretches of corn-growing land which sweep down to the river on either hand for the first ten or fifteen miles of the lower valley, rapidly narrow into a fringe on either side the river, a river for the most part unfordable, and often with steep rocky banks. The Amir's high road (which would rank in official India as a "second class" military road) is on the whole excellently well engineered up the right bank, although the long spurs of the snow-capped Kashmund hills actually abut on the river in places, and narrow the facilities for road-making into inconvenient tightness. On the far side is the low line of the water-divide between Kunar and Bajaor, with the settlements and villages of the old Kunar kingdom extending

CHITRAL RIVER AND ROAD

sometimes in lines of unbroken walls and orchards for miles. All this part of the valley is vigorous and wealthy, but sixty miles up the river at the junction of the Péch dara (a river of Kafirstan which comes in from behind the Kashmund mountains) its nature changes. It becomes contracted between high, rugged, pine-clad hills, and gradually assumes those characteristics which cling to it between Asmar and Chitral, *i.e.* a narrow cleft with the river running deep and rapid; a broken line of flats on either side affording an interrupted foothold for villages and cultivation in terraces; and spaces where the rough slopes of spurs are carried right down to the water's edge, over which (or round which) it is necessary to climb by sheep tracks in order to pass from one patch of village cultivation to the next. When these sheep tracks are specially bad, zigzagging in uncertain lines across the face of steep, slippery, smooth, shining rock, they are called "paris." There are many of them along the river edge, although the Amir's high road has displaced them on the right bank so far as it extends.

At the junction of the Péch dara and Kunar I had the privilege of being called in as consulting engineer on the matter of irrigation. Ghulam Haidar (like his noble master) was a practical engineer of no small ability, and he had conceived the idea of irrigating a tract of barren alluvial flat which lay high above the river some five or six miles below the Péch dara. The idea had taken practical shape. Companies of the Amir's Hazara sappers were already at work. We rode up the Dara past Chagan Sarai to the irrigation head, and found a mile or two of the canal already constructed. Water was let in to test the grade, and the solid masonry aqueduct which carried the stream round the bold rocky headlands of the Kashmund foothills was found to act perfectly.

But the interest of that day's ride to me was Ghulam Haidar himself. He was in an outward mood of cheery good-fellowship which could hardly have been all assumed. If so it was exceedingly well put on, and a more courteously charming companion for a day's outing it would have been difficult to find. He told me tales about the Court at Kabul; he enlarged on the vast improvements that had been effected in the country by the Amir's capability as director general of public works.

Knowing our maps well, he was aware also of the probable extent of my own geographical knowledge. He supplemented it freely, and (as I have since discovered) accurately. We talked of the new khafila road connecting Afghan-Turkestan with Kabul—of that between Kabul and the Oxus, and the new alignment from Kabul to the Kunar which follows the Kabul river; of the Amir's hopes and intentions as regards Kafirstan,—nor did he conceal the fact that the road we were then traversing was destined to reach Badakshan eventually by a route which could not be decided till the Boundary Commission had completed its work. He was well mounted on a powerful roan Australian, and as I was equally well suited, and most of the road was good, I felt that fortune was treating me well that bright December day. The pines and deodars of the higher slopes showed black against the white snows of Kashmund as we turned up the valley of the Péch. Privet, oleander, and brambles filled up the spaces between the boulders on the banks and ran into tangles with wild vine and pomegranate. Marjoram and mint fringed the edges of the rushing stream, and scented the air with their crushed-out sweetness. That unexpressed (perhaps unrecognised) sympathy with the many moods of nature which is strong in the natural man (and gets squeezed out of the cockney) was certainly influencing Ghulam Haidar then. He could tell me the names of every plant which grew, and what it was good for; he wandered into reminiscences, and told me of battles fought and lost, supplementing his tales with enlargements and embellishments which were as interesting to me who knew most of the actual details beforehand, as were his estimates of the characters of those two distinguished Indian officials Lord Roberts and Lord Curzon. In fact we talked about everything from the lost tribes of Israel, of which he claimed to be a representative, to the effective shooting of the Highlanders at Charasia, and the latest little contrivance for range measurement, of which he was exceedingly anxious to secure a specimen. May I never encounter worse company than that of Ghulam Haidar, late Commander-in-Chief in Afghanistan.

As there have been theories hazarded about the Budhist character of certain remains at Chagan Sarai I may as well say that the present graveyard that there exists is full of remnants and scraps of Budhist origin—but they are merely the débris of some destroyed building which have been brought from elsewhere, and built into the tombs for the purpose of ornamentation. At the same time there are visible evidences of the former existence of buildings underlying the present structures which might prove to be Budhist. Our cursory examination was not sufficient to decide. It is an interesting question. We know that Chitral (Kashkar, or Kashgar) was Budhist when all Swat was Budhist; and probably when the sand-buried cities were still in existence which have been lately unearthed by Sven Hedin in the Takla Makán. But south of Chitral, in the same valley, how far did Budhism extend—or in other words what was the limit of Kafir occupation in Budhist times?

On the 18th December we reached Asmar. Asmar is the headquarters still of that eastern army of Afghanistan which Ghulam Haidar commanded, and which was placed in the field for the double purpose of a religious crusade against Kafirstan, and of forwarding the Amir's interests in Bajaor and Swat, where the formidable progress of Umra Khan had to be reckoned with. It may also have served a third end in finding suitable employment for many of the restless spirits in the Amir's army. Asmar is the most unattractive corner of the Kunar district. A narrow three-cornered patch of dusty valley over which the wind comes dancing and sweeping from all sides at once, with the river running deep in a rocky gorge below; steep pine-clad hills to the west and more reasonable slopes to the east, amongst which there winds up one of the chief routes into Bajaor—such is the general view of Asmar; and here, on the left bank of the river, is packed a tight and dirty camp which was said (when we were there) to hold 6,000 troops. A very fairly well-constructed bridge (on the usual cantilever principle with a small guard-house at each end) crossed the river, which separated our camp from that of the army.

We were not permitted to cross this bridge nor to approach too closely the military cantonment of the Afghan army. This was probably a wise precaution for more reasons than one.

But we were indulged with a review of the assembled troops which was really instructive. The risk of too close an association with such a mixed company as an Afghan army presents was avoided by keeping the troops under review on one side the river, whilst from a rocky eminence on the other side we looked down, like the king at Salamis, on the men of many nations who manœuvred below. All movements were executed to the sound of the bugle, which rang out from the rocks about us with no uncertain sound. There was no mistake about that bugler. He was quite first-rate. And the manœuvres, considering that they were executed across ground of which the natural slope had been utilised by terracing, and that from one terrace to another was an occasional drop of five or six feet, were certainly executed with most commendable precision. There was one movement which was almost surprisingly effective. At a bugle call which was unrecognisable (many of them were the ordinary British calls) the whole army disappeared. It was almost magical. There was no apparent means of gaining cover. So far as we could see from our half-mile point of vantage, the flat spaces between the terrace revetments were all of the uniform pattern, dry, bereft of vegetation, and open. The whole parade was one unbroken space of open unirrigated ground. But at one instant it was swarming with troops and the next it was miraculously empty. How did they do it? I have seen a similar manœuvre executed by a horde of rabble Afghan soldiery in front of a cavalry charge. The cavalry charged over ground that had but just before been alive with men, only to find nothing left of the foe. But there were cracks and fissures here and there and that ground was much broken, flat and open as it looked. If there were cracks and fissures in the field at Asmar it was impossible to detect them at a distance, and the manœuvre was so surprisingly effective that I have often thought of recommending it to the consideration of the War Office. There were I should think 3,000 or 4,000 troops on the ground—certainly not 6,000.

Asmar was considered to be far too risky a situation for a European camp—besides we were not wanted at Asmar—so we moved on to Nashagaon, a critical point in boundary operations—the last village occupied by Ghulam Haidar's troops before touching territory garrisoned and claimed by Umra Khan. This was, after all, the *crux* of the position. But we officially objected to commencing boundary operations without seeing that point of the river, a short march further up (though still forty miles below Chitral), where the boundary would touch the junction of the Bashgol, or Arnawai, river of Kafirstan with the river of Chitral; for it was there that in all probability it would leave the right, or Kafir, side of the valley, and cross to the Chitral, or Bajaor side.

At Nashagaon, then, we pitched our camp provisionally, about Christmas time, and then events occurred in rapid succession which finally put further direct progress up the valley out of the question.

We first made a tentative effort to get the survey party up the direct route towards Chitral in order to secure some mapping which was essential to the work of delimitation. This was a failure. Lieut. Coldstream was informed that his party would certainly be fired on if he attempted to pass the first fort occupied by a Jandol garrison, and he wisely returned. Meanwhile certain representatives of Umra Khan had appeared in camp. They were men of no particular standing or authority and officially they remained unrecognised. They held out no prospect that Umra Khan would appear in person.

At that time Ghulam Haidar would doubtless have solved all difficulties by advancing against the small bodies of Umra Khan's people who still held the valley in front of us, and clearing them out; and he would have been delighted to put the exigencies of boundary survey forward as an excuse for resuming hostilities against his old enemy. What the result would have been had he done so it is hard to say. It would probably have altered the whole course of subsequent events, and have saved us the cost of the Chitral expedition. But the instructions of Government were clearly to the effect that our proceedings were on no account to involve a collision between Afghan troops and Bajaoris; and it may very well be doubted whether under any circumstances a policy of trusting to our Afghan allies to fight our battles for us could possibly be a wise one. We should not have saved the Chitral imbroglio, but we should have kept Umra Khan out of it by placing a hostile force at the debouchment of the Lowarai pass on to the Chitral valley. This was absolutely the only way he could reach Chitral at the time he did reach it, and it would have been impossible to cross that pass with an Afghan force awaiting his arrival below.

However we adopted the last resource of indecision—we did nothing—and seeing that nothing was to be done, there is no doubt that Ghulam Haidar improved his position with Umra Khan. If he was not to fight him, he might turn him to good account by supporting him on a venture which could only possibly end in his final discomfiture, and the transfer of the whole Kunar valley up to Chitral limits to Afghanistan. It might even end in securing Chitral itself. Who could tell?

Such appeared to me to be the political position at Christmas, 1894, and with it we had to be satisfied. As for Ghulam Haidar's treatment of us, he behaved as an Afghan gentleman always does behave, when he is on his good behaviour. We interchanged formal visits once or twice a week. We obtained permission to shoot in the neighbourhood of the camp (always under a guard, *bien entendu*), and we shot chikor, and enjoyed the enforced picnic. But we were not allowed to go and look for the markhor with which the hills abounded. And here I may inform all good sportsmen that a country still exists where the markhor dwells in security, with no worse enemies than the Kafir bowmen who are good shots with an arrow but who cannot shoot far, and that he multiplies abundantly. Lower Kafirstan will be a future sportsman's paradise.

Ghulam Haidar insisted on providing us with dinner, and he sent us "pillaus" daily which for the excellence of their cooking would be hard to beat. In order to save us from unworthy suspicions this dinner was usually placed before us on one of those time-honoured Celadon china plates which are recognised throughout the East—in Turkey, Persia, and Afghanistan—as capable agents for detecting poison. They crack under it, and altogether refuse to sustain the weight of poisoned food. No one can exactly say what the age of this antique china may be. There were bits of it at Kabul in the Bala Hissar when that fort was destroyed. There are, of course, bits of it in museums and collections all over England—but still it is rare—and some authorities maintain that its age must be reckoned by hundreds of years. One certain fact about it is that it can be found in sherds and pieces all along the coast routes from India to Babylon. I have found it in Baluchistan, in Makrán, on the Persian coast, in Arabia and Mesopotamia. We may consequently assume that its value as a chemical analyst in cases of poison has been known from very ancient times indeed. The particular plate which adorned our mess from night to night was a gigantic one. I have never seen the like.

Efforts were constantly made to reach the hills adjoining the valley for the purpose of extending the boundary survey. It was impossible to give any effect to the agreement of 1893 without clearly ascertaining whether the geographical conditions of the country admitted of a direct interpretation. For the most part they did not. The boundary of the agreement was partly a geographical impossibility, but for a great part there was no obstruction in the way of carrying out its intention, except a new and varied interpretation which the Amir put upon the text of it.

So stringent was the safeguard put upon the European members of the mission that it was chiefly with the assistance of the native surveyors that such mapping as was absolutely indispensable was secured. Later, Lieutenant Coldstream was permitted to ascend some of the hills, and he made excellent use of his opportunities, but he was at first hampered with a detachment of Afghan troops who were not in all respects fitted for the purpose of hill climbing. The "Ardarly" Pultan (orderlies) who were clothed in scarlet and white, were the old soldiers of the force; respectable, quiet men presumably (so far as Afghans can be either one or the other), who would give little trouble, and who, in spite of their infirmities from age, would be good enough to keep pace with any Sahib over any hills whatever. So the Sipah Salar thought at least. But he soon discovered his mistake, and a change was afterwards effected. We had nothing to complain of eventually as to the quality of the troops on escort duty, as I will show presently. These reconnaissances were carried out sometimes with great difficulty, and they always entailed much rough work and no little risk—

but they were successful in providing us with such data as we wanted in spite of the restrictions placed on our movements.

So week after week passed on whilst all the world was astir with events which were taking place about fifty miles north of us. Early in January a running, panting band of Chitralis broke in upon our camp and claimed the protection of the British Commissioner. Amongst them was Dastagird (a member of the royal family of Chitral), who being himself out on a sporting expedition heard of, if he did not actually witness, the sudden murder of the ruling prince of Chitral (the mehtar) by his brother, and fled for dear life; well knowing that episodes of this familiar nature did not usually pass in Chitral without a clean sweep being made of the whole family of the chief. He was a small-made gentle-looking man, accompanied by his son, a boy of singularly intelligent and prepossessing appearance, and a few immediate followers and servants. The Chitrali has been so much before the public lately, and has been so generally described, that I need say no more than that he was a representative member of that idle, good-for-nothing, and happy-hearted people, who have a deadly propensity for wholesale murder and family butchery, combined with many attractive, and almost lovable, qualities. They are not a fighting people, but in a country such as theirs (so full of natural pitfalls and difficult pathways) a race of monkeys could make themselves respected as foes if they took to defensive tactics.

I need not enter into the story of Chitral. It has been often told, and told well, and I have nothing to do with it further than as it affected our proceedings in connection with boundary delimitation. Who first instigated the murder, or what may have been the precise share in the plot which could be traced to Umra Khan, does not concern this narrative. Dastagird and his attenuated following remained with us until the clouds rolled by, and they proved an interesting addition to our camp. He performed the duties of chief mullah at evening prayers, laid out a small enclosure which answered the purposes of a mosque, and so infected our camp finally with the spirit of ritualism that Udny's head syce (whose normal duty it was to look after his stables) took to calling to prayers at eventide. He was only stamped out of his priestly vocations by his master, who understood that part of the Moslem ritual a great deal better than he did himself, and positively forbade its being undertaken by an inefficient amateur.

We had been waiting for Lieutenant Gurdon, at Chitral, to signify his intention of coming down to meet us in order to represent the interests of the little Chitral state on the Boundary Commission. But Umra Khan's occupation of the valley between us, no less than the murder of the mehtar, seemed destined to prevent him from moving southward. We could get no certain news. From thenceforward we were mainly dependent on such information as seemed good to Ghulam Haidar to give us A letter was received by the Commissioner from Mr. Robertson a little later, by which we learnt, to our surprise, that Gurdon had not withdrawn from Chitral, and that Robertson was himself preparing to join him there. Boundary proceedings seemed to be indefinitely shelved so far as any active participation in them by the Chitral agents was concerned.

The next step in this curious little Himalayan drama (in which we were destined to play the part of the gallery) was the advance of Umra Khan northward through the Lowarai pass towards Chitral. This was a movement which, at the time, seemed to us to be incomprehensible. Equally incomprehensible did it appear to the Sipah Salar and to Umra Khan's own agents in camp, who assured us, with round eyes, that some species of madness must have seized Umra Khan to induce him to commit such exceeding folly. His following of Pathans was of no great dimensions. About a thousand men may have crossed the Lowarai with him, and some of them were lost in the pass in the bitter winter weather of January. "Umra Khan is an ass," said the Sipah Salar; "there is no telling what he will do." What he *did* was to attack Drosh, and his subsequent proceedings—until, anticipating stormy times many weeks later, he wrote to the Sipah Salar and requested him to be kind enough to afford an asylum for his wives and families in our camp—more nearly concerns the history of Chitral than that of the boundary. From the northward tales of disaster came down to us by degrees.

The Sipah Salar, with much apparent sympathy and commiseration, told us from time to time of the destruction of the little party in the Mastuj defiles; of the supposed annihilation of Fowler's detachment; of Robertson's advance to Chitral; of the curiously apropos escape of Sher Afzal (the favourite of the people, then and always) from durance in Kabul, and his appearance on the scene; of the mistake made in the abortive action which preceded the retirement of the garrison into the fort, entailing the loss of an officer killed and the still more fatal loss of prestige.

This we declined altogether to believe; all the more that Ghulam Haidar could not tell us the name of the lost officer, who was, he said, most certainly dead and buried. We never learnt his name till we reached Jalalabad, on our way back to India. Next we were told that the garrison was shut up in the fort "as in a box," and that they would probably stay there until relieved. Even then we failed to realise the gravity of the situation. We knew that there were four hundred good Sikhs inside the fort with provisions for some months, a number that appeared to us sufficient to deal easily with all the Chitralis that Sher Afzal, or all the Pathans that Umra Khan, could possibly bring into the field against them. We knew also that there were two guns with ammunition in the fort, and knowing the profound respect that all these hill tribesmen have for guns, we did not believe in a very close investment, or in any great pressure on the beleaguered garrison.

We had ourselves most excellent arrangements for communication with India, and although there seemed to be difficulties in the way of communicating with Chitral after the siege had once begun, there appeared to be none at all in the way of Chitral communicating with us. Our camp was on the river banks some sixty miles below, and the current of the river runs strong and free through that sixty miles. Any closed receptacle thrown quietly into the river below the walls of the fort at Chitral would have come to us in half a day's journey, and there was nothing that would have arrested its passage, nor would any difficulty have been experienced in stopping it at our camp, without detection, even should Ghulam Haidar have made it part of his policy to prevent us from getting news direct.

It was not till long afterwards that we learnt that no use had been found for the guns, no attempt had been made to send us information, and that the fort had been so closely beset that sangurs had been erected within forty yards of the walls.

I am not aware that any statistics have as yet been made available that will give a reasonable explanation of the persistency and success of the besiegers of Chitral. Of the gallantry of the besieged Englishmen and Sikhs we have heard enough to make us proud of our soldiers; but who were the besiegers who in so short a space of time reduced such a garrison to absolute extremities? The fierce fighting that subsequently took place at Malakand may tell us what a half-armed and undisciplined mob may do in a frantic effort to rush a position peculiarly susceptible to attack; and the history of the Tirah campaign tells us again what a few well-trained and skilful marksmen may effect against an overwhelming force under conditions particularly well suited to their tactics; but Chitral came to us as a surprise. The fort at Chitral was subjected to a sustained siege so well organised that, in spite of the lack of artillery on the side of the enemy, the garrison were absolutely shut helplessly up inside the walls.

We were free, and not very far away, but the intervening hills shadowing the Kunar on one side and parting us from the uplands of Bajaor and Swat on the other, quite shut us off from any close watch on the scene that was being enacted so near. We had however in our camp, officers who were well acquainted with the frontier and the strength of frontier armaments—who could give a very fair estimate of the fighting capacity of Chitralis, and of the Pathan following of Umra Khan. We knew exactly how many followed him over the Lowarai pass into the Chitral district in the first instance, and we knew that the strength of the attack was not at first formidable. It was not till we heard the final story of the relief that we heard also of perpetual fighting against well-armed Pathan soldiery; of Afghan troops actually caught red-handed in the enemy's ranks, and of other similar indications. Then we could spell out something like an answer to the riddle.

Then, indeed, it occurred to us that possibly the brave army of Asmar which we had so lately reviewed, was well occupied during that busy time. We were not allowed to go near Asmar. We could not tell whether there were 1,000 or 6,000 men still in that weary cantonment, but we did know that with a fight in progress on one side the Kunar hills, and an idle Afghan army seated on the other, it was little likely that the Afghan would contain his soul in patience and stay at home in peaceful contemplation of the dividing barrier.

And what could the Amir do to prevent this? As he wrote pathetically to the Indian Government when it was suggested to him that his general Ghulam Haidar did not sufficiently restrain his men, "If I had an army of 20,000 men and disposed of it in parties along the peaks of that frontier it would not prevent the "badmashes" of the valley districts from crossing the line." Perhaps not, but there are other ways well known to Afghan rulers of preventing contingencies of this sort, besides blocking the road. But this was written later, when it was impossible to deny the fact that Afghan soldiers had been found on the wrong side of the hills. I do not suppose that it is officially recognised that the Afghan army (*our* safeguard) assisted to besiege Chitral. I only believe that it did so. It was so simple; the position was so tempting; it was so exceedingly probable, in fact, that it would be much of a surprise to me to learn that it did not.

All through the Chitral difficulties, as through the subsequent more formidable frontier risings which culminated in Tirah, the Amir stoutly denied that Ghulam Haidar ever showed active hostility to the British Government; but the evidence that exists is difficult to set aside. The following statement is taken from the *Pioneer* of April 22nd, 1898: "Sir Bindon Blood in a report to Government dated Panjkora, September 28th, wrote as follows concerning the negotiations with the Mahmunds: 'The jirgah told the native political assistant that the Sipah Salar had encouraged them to attack the troops, and promised ammunition as well as compensation in kind for any loss of grain. This corroborates the information I received previously. I hear that special concessions have been promised the leading maliks who have property on both sides the boundary.' Major

Deane on October 6th asked permission of Government to address the Sipah Salar direct, calling upon him to prevent the Amir's subjects from crossing the border, 1,000 of them having appeared by way of the Ghakki Pass. Two days later he telegraphed, 'Two mule loads of ammunition arrived from Kabul this morning from Umra Khan to Uslad Mahomed and Said Usman, his followers, who are at present in the Mahmund valley.' This ammunition must have been passed through Asmar by the Sipah Salar's orders; it was escorted by twenty of Umra Khan's men armed with Martinis. When the Mahmunds of the Watelai valley finally submitted, they asked to be protected from interference on the part of the Amir or his representative the Sipah Salar. They evidently dreaded punishment from the latter owing to their having made terms with the British Government. There is this strong evidence to show that the late Sipah Salar actively assisted the Hada Mulla and encouraged Mohmands, Mahmunds, and Bajaoris to wage war. All this was of course subsequent to the Boundary Commission proceedings, and after the Sipah Salar had got rid of us from the Kunar valley, but there was little doubt in the mind of any member of that Commission that Ghulam Haidar and Umra Khan were already playing the same game to the same ends whilst we were still there, and that had a review of the Asmar troops during the Chitral siege been possible, it would as a military pageant have been but a thin and unsatisfactory show. Leave of absence—or absence without leave—was epidemic just then.

But it was clearly our duty to communicate with Chitral if that were possible, and to learn exact details of those early days of the siege when the garrison was first shut up. Our position was peculiar. We had Umra Khan's official representatives in our camp—but we could not trust them. We had the Chitrali refugees—but it was as much as their lives were worth to leave the precincts of the camp. We had our Afghan guardians, but we knew not what they were up to—and we had a tag-rag assemblage of Kafirs from Kafirstan who were collected as hostages for the good behaviour of their people during demarcation. We decided at last to try the Kafirs as the medium of communication. Amongst other hangers-on of the camp was a Chitrali interpreter, an intelligent and active man, who had come from Chitral armed with excellent recommendations from those officers who had employed him there, and he was our negotiator with the Kafirs. Ghulam Haidar entered with outward and visible enthusiasm into the scheme. The Kafirs were to take letters from us to the garrison and to deliver them by the simple process of attaching them to arrows to be shot over the walls of the fort. The Chitrali was to accompany them and to explain their presence in the camp of the enemy if discovered.

We reckoned that they would cover the intervening ground in three nights and that the letters should be delivered on the fourth day. There seemed to be every prospect of success provided only that Ghulam Haidar was sincere in his protestations of sympathy. He got his own information from Chitral with accuracy and regularity. In the early nightfall two Kafirs and the Chitrali disappeared into the darkness, and we expected to hear nothing further about them for at least a week. In the morning, however, the Amir's trusted agent (a man who went by the name of "the Hakim," and who was one of that most repulsive class in Afghanistan — the paid spy) appeared at Mr. Udny's tent and demanded urgent audience. With a face of horror and dismay he told how our Chitrali go-between had been murdered during the night—shot down by Umra Khan's men who were on the watch for him so soon as he set foot in Umra Khan's territory. He was asked what had become of the Kafirs. "Oh, they escaped in the darkness and are off to their native mountains." At any rate they were not on the spot to give evidence. There was no mistake about the murder. The body of the unfortunate interpreter was brought into camp, riddled with bullets, and he was buried a short distance down stream in a graveyard overlooking the river, that night. That night too it struck Mr. Hastings, the political assistant, that it might be well to visit the scene of the murder. He found, as he surmised, that it was within the official limits of our own camp that the deed was done—and if Umra Khan's men had anything to say to the murder, they were on our side the border when they did it. Thus did we lose a very useful servant and gained nothing in the direction of Chitral. It remains but to point out how fortunate it was for the Sipah Salar that neither of the Kafirs was killed by mistake. A blood feud might have been set up that would have been exceedingly *mal-à-propros* just then.

CHAPTER XII.

KAFIRSTAN

Boundary settlement—Why the Bashgol valley was given up to the Amir—The Amir's roads—Kafirs—Expedition into Kafirstan with an Afghan escort—Darin—Amir's dealings with Kafirstan—Over the mountains and amongst the snowfields—View over Kafirstan—How the boundary settlement stood when we left—The last of Ghulam Haidar—Break up of Commission.

MEANWHILE it might well have been supposed that all boundary demarcation would have been in abeyance, and that our continued residence in the camp of the Sipah Salar at Nashagaon on the extreme frontier of the Amir's possessions (possession by right of recent conquest) was uncalled for. This was by no means the case, for it was exactly whilst the garrison at Chitral were making what fight they could against the ever-gathering crowd of Chitrali and Pathan assailants, that the boundary between Chitral and Kafirstan was defined; and this boundary was within sight of the Chitral fort.

So far as the boundary of Afghanistan is defined by the Hindu Kush there could be no immediate (if indeed there may be any ultimate) object in demarcation. The watershed, or main water-parting, of that range is sufficiently well known geographically to admit of no subsequent dispute as to its exact position along the line that stretches from the Pamirs to the Dorah pass which leads from the Oxus valley into the upper affluents of the Kunar. Farther than this (through the unmapped mountain wilderness of Kafirstan) it is unnecessary to follow it; for from the neighbourhood of the Dorah pass the boundary turns southward from the Hindu Kush to follow an offshoot, and adopts the crest of a gigantic range called Shawál. This range actually faces Chitral. It is the western limit of the Chitral valley, and its crest is but fifteen miles or so from the fort. It is a well-defined and generally snow-clad line of peaks dividing the Bashgol or Arnawai valley from the valley of the Chitral river. The Arnawai stream joined the Chitral at a point about fifteen miles above our camp and forty-five below Chitral.

But, inasmuch as the Bashgol valley was included by the terms of the agreement of 1893 within the territories that lie on the Chitral, or Kashmir, side of the boundary, a few words about the reasons for ceding it to the Amir may not be out of place. The valley is known by many names, but the three most generally recognised are Bashgol, Arnawai, and Lundai Sin (which means "chief affluent"), and it entirely depends upon the nationality of your informant by what name he may elect to call it. It was originally named Arnawai in our maps by that gallant explorer McNair of the Indian Survey, who, disguised as a Mohamedan Hakim, and accompanied by a native explorer and two Kaka Khel Meahs, made his way right through Swat and Chitral to the foot of the Baroghél pass over the Hindu Kush, and thence homeward by the Darkot pass to Gilgit, in the spring of 1883.

At that time all this country was in outer geographical darkness, and the journey was one of the most adventurous that any European could well attempt. McNair's intimate knowledge of native character and language carried him through, and he returned to submit a most valuable report to Government. It has been generally assumed that when our relief force from India advanced through Swat to Chitral they were traversing unexplored and unknown ground. This was not the case. With but a small exception the route followed by our forces was that which was first followed by McNair. He named the valley Arnawai. But it was subsequently much more fully explored and mapped by Woodthorpe, when he accompanied Lockhart's mission in 1885, and traversed it nearly from end to end. He named it Bashgol, or Arnawai, attaching both names to it. It was found to be inhabited by a section of that miscellaneous conglomeration of mixed races called Kafirs, who received Europeans with something like cordiality, and were disposed to welcome the protection of the British Government against the encroachments of the Afghan.

By the name Arnawai was this valley designated in the

agreement of 1893, which however failed to define its geographical position by any technical references. The Amir consequently declined altogether to admit that the Arnawai of Kafirstan was the Arnawai of the agreement. He ignored the maps which had been hastily constructed for his special benefit, altogether, and insisted that the Arnawai of the agreement was a short and insignificant mountain stream which joined the Chitral river at the village of Arnawai, from the east instead of the west, and which had nothing whatsoever to do with Kafirstan.

Now it was clear that the village of Arnawai which gave its name equally to both streams (because both joined the Chitral river, the one opposite, and the other through it) was on the eastern banks, so that it was perhaps more in accordance with the fitness of the geographical situation that the river which actually watered the village of Arnawai should have the better claim to the name; and there was accordingly a certain amount of justification for the Amir's plea.

But apart from all geographical considerations he absolutely declined to surrender a "single house" in Kafirstan, or to admit that any portion of that interesting country could possibly join Chitral as an appanage of Kashmir. The Kafirs were his to do with as he pleased. It was for him to redeem the race and to bring them into the fold of Islam. For him was the apostle's mission reserved, and the apostle's reward hereafter, if he could but lead them to the true faith; and as for the methods by which this high aim should be achieved that was for the consideration of himself and his Sipah Salar—not for the Indian Government.

And there was yet another reason for his desire to retain the Bashgol valley. It promised to give him the means of establishing a great trade route between Jalalabad, or India, and Badakshan. Could the difficulties due to the altitude of the Mangal pass leading into the central Badakshan valley of the Minján only be as successfully negotiated as had been those of the Khawák at the head of the Panjshir, this high-road would soon be in existence. There were difficulties no doubt in connecting his Jalalabad-Asmar road with the lower or southern end of the Bashgol; but these were merely engineering difficulties, to be encountered successfully with dynamite or gun-cotton. As for the preliminary measure of conquering the valley, his well-armed troops could hardly find a really formidable foe in people who put their faith in bows and arrows, and appealed to an unknown god whose name was Gish.

On the British Commission side of the question (being neither in the counsels of the Government of Kabul or the Government of India) I may perhaps be permitted to suggest certain reasons which appeared to me personally to favour the Amir's contention. They may or may not have influenced the Government of India in deciding to concede this point; probably they did so more or less.

We had not then officially assumed the risky responsibility of a political occupation of Chitral. We were then in Chitral certainly, but it was not then decided that we should remain there. We could only effect a direct political control over any part of Kafirstan by adding it to Chitral. It would become in fact, together with Chitral, a dependency (an outlying and troublesome dependency at best) of the Kashmir state—and the Kashmir state wanted none of it. Gilgit was already quite a sufficient burden on its never-too-well furnished treasury, and the occupation of Chitral would seriously (*did* seriously, eventually) affect the State finances. To which may be added the well-worn old argument against the distribution of troops in far-distant outposts, weakening our frontier military strength, and offering coat tails to the restless foot of the frontier tribesmen. For it was certain that we should have to look after such outlying positions of observation ourselves. Now of all undesirable localties for a small isolated body of troops, the Bashgol valley might be reckoned the most undesirable. Amongst all the restless, unstable, uncertain tribes of our remotest frontier the Kafirs may be placed in the very front rank—and this is nearly all that we know about them. No European has ever had personal dealings with any but the Kafirs of Kamdesh and the Bashgol valley. Some of these, we have good reason to think, may claim an early Greek (pre-Hellenic) origin, and those that have been personally associated with Europeans have expressed a desire for British control over their country—but this only refers to the edge or fringe of that wild Kafir wilderness where each valley may, for all we know, hold a people of a nationality distinct from that of all surrounding valleys. Kafirstan is geographically separated from Chitral by a most imposing and difficult range of snow-capped mountains, a range which is impassable for many months of the year; and the one way which exists into the lower Bashgol valley leading round the southern spurs of these mountains instead of over their crests is absolutely impossible to any but a foot passenger; unless indeed by grace of the Amir's determination to bring the Bashgol into his scheme of frontier trade routes, his Hazara sappers have already made a road.

It is difficult to conceive how any part of Kafirstan and Chitral could have been rolled together into one political *ménage*. Even if this could have been possible, what was the high political end to be thereby achieved? Should we have prevented a highway being made into Badakshan? It was scarcely necessary to occupy the valley to do that, even should military considerations outweigh the manifest advantages to trade which such a road would bring with it. Should we have secured a body of capable and trustworthy allies? Against whom should we employ them? Against the Amir, or against advancing Russians? Russians will never seriously trouble themselves about either Kafirstan or the Pamirs, until we (or the Amir) make a road to help them towards India. An independent, untouched Kafirstan is about as solid an obstacle between ourselves and the Oxus basin as could well have been devised, as indeed Tamerlane found, and recorded for the benefit of his successors. We cannot improve on it, but we may very easily weaken it. What may have been the political reasons for the inclusion of the Bashgol valley originally within the British line of boundary I do not profess to know. If there was any sentiment at the bottom of it (which is hard to believe of the Indian Government) it is a misplaced sentiment. The Kafirs are not Christians, but Pagans, and if they are to be redeemed from the outer barbarism of their present existence, it will best be done by the gradual development of more civilising influences amongst them which already exist on their borders. The Pathan Mahomedan is certainly not the brightest emblem of spiritual development in this unfinished world, but compared to the Kafir Pagan he is an angel of light.

There really seemed to be no reason for insisting on the retention of the Bashgol valley on the British side the boundary stronger than that afforded by the Amir's absolute decision not to part with it. And he had a geographical entanglement to help him. He *might* have mistaken one Arnawai stream for the other, and he received the benefit of the doubt. With it he secured all that part of the valley of the Kunar between the Arnawai and our camp which was previously held by Umra Khan's people. Umra Khan's contentions were no longer admissible, so the boundary was brought down to a point opposite to us from the Hindu Kush by a series of natural features in the shape of well-marked ranges and ridges (except for the short space where it crossed from the right to the left bank of the Kunar river) which rendered artificial demarcation unnecessary.

From the point opposite our camp it followed the watershed which hemmed in the river southwards till it reached yet another fixed position from which it was to take off and divide the Mohmand country ere it reached Lundi Kotal and the Khaiber pass. Here however Ghulam Haidar was obdurate. Neither would he agree to one single acre of Mohmand territory being placed beyond Afghan limits, in spite of the clear expression in the agreement, nor would he admit of any survey or reconnaissance which might assist to bring our differences of opinion to a conclusion. Here then, in April, the proceedings of that Commission came to an end, and it was not till the close of the frontier campaign, which settled the Mohmands as well as Afridis and Bunerwals, that the boundary was finally adjusted.

If artificial demarcation was unnecessary, it was very much otherwise with surveying, and it was absolutely essential to insist on our being permitted to visit such peaks and mountains as would at least enable us to obtain a clear view of the whole line of country that the boundary was to follow from the Hindu Kush to the Kunar. In the depth of a severe winter it was difficult enough to reach points of sufficient command for our purpose in our immediate neighbourhood, even without the necessity for preliminary triangulation. Fortunately we were spared that. It had already been effected from the Punjab by long shots to far-away snow peaks in Kafirstan during clear weather. The points thus fixed were all part of the system which is called the Great Triangulation of India, but as is usually the case, peaks which stood out clear and sharp, silhouetted in white against the blue horizon when seen as part of a far-off range, became excessively difficult to identify when we stood in the midst of them. As we looked at them from this new point of view all appeared equally snow-covered, all about the same height, and the perspective of distance was absolutely destroyed by the universal snow-sheet of winter. It was impossible to estimate their relative distances. This is one of the perplexities of the professional surveyor, though it never seems to trouble the amateur mountaineer who is always cocksure that he knows exactly where he stands.

But as spring advanced, and the snow-sheet was folded gradually upwards; when the valleys were adopting tints of green, with purple and pink splashes where the almond blossoms showered down to the river on every passing breeze; when Hastings came back each morning with a new sort of lily, and the honeysuckle was twined about the tent poles; then we thought we might venture further afield and insist on an exploration up the Dàrin darra of Kafirstan, to the crest of a range from which we might rake the Bashgol valley, overlook Arnawai, and sketch something of the hills round about Chitral. We had made friends with such Kafirs as we could find in the Afghan camp, and it was whilst questioning them on their national customs, and persuading them to sing hymns to their great war god Gish, that, aided by the Chitrali interpreter of whom I have before spoken, we made the surprising discovery that they were singing psalms to Bacchus which may have been 3,000 years old.

Elsewhere (*Geographical Journal*, January, 1896) I have stated my reasons for believing that the Kamdesh Kafirs who sent hostages to the camp of Ghulam Haidar are descendants of those very Nysæans who greeted Alexander as a co-religionist and compatriot, and were leniently treated by him in consequence. They had been there, in the Swat country bordering the slopes of the Koh-i-Mor (" Meros " of the classics) from such ancient periods that the Makedonians could give no account of their advent; and they remained in the Swat country till comparatively recent Budhist times. I need not repeat the story here. It is much to be regretted that none of the subsequent military movements in that country admitted of a careful survey of the lower spurs and valleys of the Koh-i-Mor where the ancient city of Nysa (or Nuson) once stood. Apparently it exists no longer above ground, though it may be found in the maps of thirty years ago figuring as rather an important place under its old name. These were the people, at any rate, whose goodwill it was essential to secure before promenading their hills. On the 10th March we all, arrayed in uniform, and assuming our best durbar manners, made our way by the sloppy and slippery little pathway which connected our camp with that of Ghulam Haidar for an important interview with that functionary. We found him, as usual, seated in his reception tent (small, but quite sufficiently well appointed for durbar purposes) dividing his attention between his faithful attendant the Hakim, and his prayers. It was "Roza," the great fast of the Mahomedans, a period of special sanctity and frequently of special ill-will and fanaticism towards Europeans. Hunger and discomfort are doubtless bad for the temper, if good for the soul; and the Sipah Salar with his usual amiable frankness confessed that his temper was often a bit short during these religious trials. We had to obtain his sanction to an expedition into Kafirstan which should take us far enough, and high enough, to enable us to get a good view of that most remote and inaccessible wilderness of mountains which lies south of the Hindu Kush and north of Jalalabad, and to trace out the continuous line of water-parting which was hereafter to represent the boundary between Kafirstan and Kashmir.

I can easily understand the Sipah Salar's hesitation. He was bound to assist us to these ends if he could; but he had on one side of him a most uncertain neighbourhood peopled by a mixed race of unbelievers who counted Mahomedan heads as a special means of grace, and who were not entitled to address their war god Gish with the full liturgy of their quaint ceremonial unless they could show a fair record of Moslem victims; and on the other was his uncertain ally, Umra Khan—just then well occupied in the siege of Chitral but never to be trusted at any time. And it was certain that nothing would involve him personally in such utter and complete ruin as an accident to any of his European guests which might occur through any want of precaution on his part. It is a notable fact that our transfrontier neighbours have learnt at last the value of the white man's life. Afghans, Swatis, and Afridis alike take the utmost care nowadays that whatever disaster may accrue, they must look as carefully to prisoners as to guests, if these prisoners wear a white skin. Nothing would have been easier in the wild mountains of Kafirstan than for a chance arrow from a Kafir, or a chance shot from a marauding Pathan, to have put an end to our most annoying system of personal inquiry into things. But we found our friend as cheerful as circumstances would admit, and fully prepared after a little consideration to undertake the responsibility of the expedition. To this end he had, as a preliminary, secured a batch of Kafir hostages—wild-looking, sinewy men of Aryan features and doubtful tint; with prominent noses, straight eyes, wide, but expressive, mouths, no hair on their faces, and the hair of the forehead pulled back over their ears in a feminine fashion. They were rather well clad in thick felt or blanketing, with woollen socks reaching half-way up to the knee. But their limbs were bare and free, and they were the limbs of athletes. I have seen mountaineers of many sorts, but never any to equal the Kafirs in the extraordinary freedom and grace of their movements over hills. No hill-bred Pathan or Afridi is within a stone's-weight of them. Their favourite pastime is racing up and down hill (usually across terraced fields where there is an occasional drop from terrace to terrace of ten to fifteen feet) on *one leg*. This was the amusement in which they were indulging when, on the following day, Lieut. Coldstream and I paid our farewell to the Sipah Salar just before starting on our quest. A few of them accompanied us as guides, and were almost inconveniently affable and friendly. The Kafir is not a clean animal.

But besides, and beyond, the need for hostages, was the

necessity for a strong escort. It is not every general who would plunge with confidence into the heart of such a country as Kafirstan with an unexplored wilderness ahead, guiltless of roads, with hardly even a passable track, no possibility of utilising transport, no artillery, no equipment, no medical arrangements, no commissariat, and it is unnecessary to add no tents or cover of any sort. It was a cold country too. We were going up to any height between 11,000 and 15,000 feet and should live in snow for some part of our time. Yet this is what was done by an Afghan force of about 1,000 men, half of whom were Kassidars (irregulars) and the rest sepoys of the line. I have never seen such an experiment tried elsewhere, and it struck me as a revelation—this mobility of a force unaccustomed to luxuries. The Kassidars were but half-trained troops armed with jezails. They were to precede us and act as scouts. They subsequently proved useful in treading out a path through the soft snow up to some of the higher peaks. The regulars were drawn from the Asmar army, and they were carefully selected. The "Zabardast" regiment, and the "Ardarly pultan," and the Heratis were discarded. The former were old and too well stricken in years for hill climbing, and the latter were not to be trusted. Maybe they were engaged elsewhere.

The 500 men who accompanied us, who were before us, behind us, and all around during that most difficult climb through the hills, who stood thick and close at night, and who never let us out of their sight, were men of Logar and Baraki Rogán, south of Kabul—old friends, some of them, who had been with me on escort duty both at Kabul and Herat—men who strangely enough (if Bellew is correct) may trace an origin to the ancient Barkai settlers of the Trans-Hindu Kush, and thus claim amongst their remote pre-Hellenic progenitors affinity with the Kafirs themselves. Whether or not these men of Logar have ancient Greek affinities, I have frequently observed that they are trusted on escort duty with Europeans beyond any other Afghans. I like them, even as I liked our doubtful friend Ghulam Haidar, Charki, whose little country seat is itself perched in the Logar hills. Chief amongst them (by reason of his personality rather than his seniority) was

"Bumbo." I have reason to think this was a nickname, but it could hardly have been more artistically applied than to the broad-faced and broad-figured Afghan officer, bulging and beaming with jocular good humour, who, whether reducing his burly weight in a severe struggle over the slippery mountain-side, or plunged up to his neck in a snowdrift, still smiled around in broad good nature. There was a stout-limbed bugler too—square of cut, with most effective calves for hill climbing, ever cheery, possessing an inexhaustible supply of wind, a most admirable performer on the bugle and excellent company on the march. He had been christened "Woodthorpe" in our camp for the many good qualities he possessed in common with that never-to-be-forgotten surveyor and mountaineer.

As for the rank and file of that redoubtable detachment, when they were drawn up for the casual inspection of their commanding officer in the wan and misty grey of the early hours of morning, they were but a sorry company to see. Uniform was scarce (they were not sent on duty in their best clothes any more than our own soldiers are), and such of it as brightened the straggling line with a patch of colour here and there was all of British make. Cast-off English uniform is very popular in Afghanistan, and there is a good deal of it to be seen in that country. Perhaps the gunner's blue and red is the most in demand, and it is to be noted that whatever the regulations on the subject may be, many of these discarded remnants of the Indian cantonments retain their buttons. Having no commissariat arrangements for them, each man carried his provisions (Afghan "roti") for the week's supply on his back together with his ammunition and his bedding. They were armed with Enfields, Sniders, and a few Martinis, so far as I could see, and free use was made of their ammunition whenever an unobservant markhor crossed the line of route. But if there was lack of regularity in our guard there was no lack of energy and good humour. All seemed delighted to be off on service of some sort or other. Neither was there any want of discipline or prompt attendance to the bugle-call, and I do not think that a single man fell out or was left behind during the whole expedition. It is possible, however, that I should not have known of this even if it had happened.

KAFIRS ON THE WAR PATH. DARIN

Thus we fared forth on the morning of the 2nd March, and thus it fell out that we were guarded, supported, and helped along by a detachment of the very army that was probably contributing usefully to the siege of our friends in Chitral. Our first day's march was hot and steamy, and we crawled but slowly over the slippery limestone crags and the crumbling schistose rocks that bordered the close little valley of the Darin. Every now and then we dropped into the river-bed and took to wading, and again we climbed up the stiff staircase, often but a few inches wide, that carried us over a projecting spur whose solid snout of rock pushed out into the river-bed and made progress that way impracticable. Up and down those ragged spurs, and through the undergrowth of thickets which were but a tangle of reeds and briars shadowed by wild fig trees, olives, pomegranates, vines, apricots, and oaks, we pushed our slow way for the livelong day, till evening brought us to the foot of the rocks on which was perched the village of Darin. Here one might have expected the road to widen a bit; but it was exactly here, below the village, and within easy shot of a handy stone from the house-tops, that the road was worst. It twisted in a narrow ledge round the face of a cliff, and although but 100 feet of sheer descent would have landed one on a smooth grassy slope, there is little to choose between 100 feet and 1,000 when one's neck is in question. As, however, we were not called on to perform any gymnastic feat in absolute defiance of the laws of gravity, we got safely over it, and thereafter we encountered nothing but what may fairly be called very stiff climbing. We camped that night on the roof of a house which presented the only flat space a yard or two square to be found in the neighbourhood. Far below us in the depths of an oak forest the smoke went up which betokened that the advance guard of Kassidars were having their supper; and all around, pinnacle on pinnacle and peak beyond peak, were the great thrones of the Kafir gods burnished by the western sun, bright with crimson radiance where their heads touched the sky, and deep shadowed with impenetrable purple mystery where their feet were washed with snow-fed rivulets, and wrapped in forest wreaths. Just below us, so close that we might almost have fallen inconveniently into its midst, was a Kafir graveyard; the wooden boxes placed side by side, with a lid knocked off here and there, and the briars and thorns looking in for the remnants (which happily were not recent) and reverently closing up the ugly gaps. Here was silent witness to the extraordinary irreverence and indecency of Kafir ceremonial in connection with their dead; whilst hard by—only on the other side the village—were the neatly arranged tombs of departed Mahomedans, with headstones carefully placed and all the usual little embellishments in loving evidence of the care of the living for the lost. It is a mistake to suppose that the Kafir's hatred of the Moslem is based on any feeling of religious antagonism. The antagonism is one of race, not of religion. There are Kafir Mahomedans as well as Kafir pagans, and the Mahomedan villages are planted in the midst of the general community and hold their own, respected and secure. Nor has the spirit of fanatical virulence which in early days animated the military prophets of Islam (as it animated the Crusaders, or the Portuguese invaders of the western coasts of India) been manifested so far in the Amir's dealings with the Kafirs. If one might talk of the extension of Islam on modern Christian principles, that would really appear to be the ruling spring of action in this Kafir reformation. Such at least was the impression which I gathered on the spot, and nothing which has since occurred has in any way modified it.

At Darin we introduced ourselves to the Kafir at home, and it was into a most uninviting home that we intruded ourselves. A singularly ugly and unfeminine Kafir girl was nursing quite the most repulsive baby I have ever seen, whilst a grisly and ferocious old woman took stock of us from the corner of the shanti. It was doubtless not to be accepted as affording a type of the Kafir home community, although I believe the dirt and squalor to be not only typical but universal; still there are no doubt good-looking Kafir girls, as there are fine manly men to be found amongst the race, only we were not fortunate enough to meet with any.

Next morning we were off betimes for the day's climb. The grey cliffs were still wet with mist, and the white blossoms of the wild almond fell heavy on the riverside path, which was patched and spotted with cups of pale anemones. The dried reeds stiffened themselves in bunches against the moist still air, and the oaks and thorn bushes with last year's dress still about them, wore the November air of an English woodland. Spring had hardly caught these upland gullies yet.

As we trod the deserted grass pathway that ran by the riverside we found traces of long-abandoned cultivation. There was the ineffaceable evidence of terracing here and there, and a broken line could be detected along the foot of the cliffs which was suggestive of irrigation—but it was irrigation of a date so long ago that no remnants of canal cutting were left. Nevertheless there was a crude resemblance to what might once have been a riverside makeshift for agriculture extending for at least two miles. The walnut trees seemed to tell a tale of better times; blackberries and briars had overgrown what was once a well-used pathway, and where spaces of their tangle, tied up with trails of wild vine, stood clear from the forest growth of oak, there might once have stood a hut or two. It had all disappeared, possibly with the advance of the Afghan, but more probably at a date considerably anterior to that of the army of Asmar. So we wandered along over the flat, only too thankful for the respite from the everlasting toil of clambering over rugged limestone spurs, even for an hour or so. We could breathe and look around, and gather crocuses and violets from the shade of the bushes, or speculate on the age of the clinging, climbing masses of ivy which spread deep and thick up the perpendicular walls of rock which hedged in the narrow "darra." Our progress was not rapid. Our guard was heavily handicapped, and the severe march of yesterday was beginning to tell. Often the bugle sounded a halt, and the notes of the call were tossed in and out amongst the hills till twenty bugles seemed to be calling from the summits of twenty cliffs. Then would the weary sepoys sit down "all in one piece," dropping on to the nearest bank or stone, and slowly unwinding the interminable twists of their puggris if perchance there might be a piece of yesterday's "roti" tied in at the end. But such a luxury as flat grass was not for long, and the rest of that weary day was much the same as the day previous—one unending "getting upstairs" to descend again to the bottom landing. One or two comparatively modern "Bandas" or clusters of old huts were passed with their roofs knocked in, and the charred ends of the uprights sticking out. About these there was no legend. We were told that they had all been recently wrecked by Bajaori invaders.

Our political agency and intelligence department on this occasion was the Hakim. He had discarded the flowing garments of a wazir (or head adviser to the Sipah Salar), and had tied up his legs in putties and boots like an ordinary subaltern. He carried an alpenstock, and though he no doubt cursed the exploring Sahib from morn till dewy eve, he stuck to his post like a man, and never showed the smallest sign of giving in. That evening we camped in the valley below the peak we desired to ascend, amidst a deodar forest which was notable for the size of its timber. Indeed from this point to the end of our journey, the one remarkable feature about the country was the magnificent forest growth. I do not pretend to know all the trees we there met with, but there were oaks of several varieties and all of the true European pattern—not the inferior ilex of the Himalaya, but growing the good old crinkly leaf of the oaks of England, and some of them scattering acorns of enormous size. The trees were themselves gigantic, giants amongst the oak tribe, overlapping and overlooking the cypresses the blue pines and firs, which usually shadow the oaks of India. Although we had already accomplished enough climbing to have carried us up Mount Everest, we were hardly 6,000 feet above sea-level at the second day's camping ground.

The third day's march involved a stiff ascent up the sunburnt slopes of the mountains to a ridge which was within a few hours' climb of our final destination. It was there that we passed through those forests of oak and fir which appeared to dwarf the forests of the more southern hills, and it was there that we encountered such abundant evidences of the existence of markhor and other light-footed mountain game. Now and then a pheasant shot out over our heads and dropped with heavy wings into untold depths below, as we clambered slowly along, twisting and winding round the interminable spurs. One of them however ventured within reach of an Afghan bullet, and found his billet in the hands of our cook. It was a glorious day, and to men untrammelled with ammunition and commissariat it was a glorious climb—but our escort was showing signs of wear, and we were obliged to make a comparatively short day's march. We pitched camp for the night on a ridge, in a forest of fir and deodar.

The last day's work was a straight up-and-down climb of 5,000 feet to the Bozasar, a peak which overlooks the lower reaches of the Bashgol river and the Chitral valley—from whence we might view that promised land which we were not ourselves to set foot in. The Bozasar is hard by a very distinct and somewhat remarkable feature in the landscape of this part of the world, called the Bozagat. It is not a very high peak—11,000 feet is nothing for a peak in Kafirstan—but it is well marked by the square solid block of the Bozagat which stands like a cathedral (being of the size of all the cathedrals in Europe put together) above the surrounding snowfields. Its smooth and almost polished sides are too steep to retain the snow, and thus it makes a square-cut black patch on the white face of the landscape, difficult to overlook, and impossible to mistake.

Notwithstanding the labours of the crowd of kassidars and coolies who were despatched in gangs to make a way through the snow, we found it troublesome climbing on account of the early thaw. Very early in the day the melting process set in, and long before noon every rivulet was spouting and tumbling gaily down the hillside, and all the larger streams became impassable. A few thousand feet of climbing under such conditions offer a much greater amount of physical labour than double the number over frost-bound snow. We were fairly well pumped before we reached any point where we could get the plane table into action. Then, when we had time for a look round, this is what we saw. All the whole world ringed with snow—line upon line, ridge upon ridge of snow-bound mountain-top encircling the horizon in one vast sea of snow-billows. No very prominent peaks near by—only the smooth flat slopes of snowfields, and the broken outlines of snow slopes, with black patches of outcropping rock here and there, and the snouts of glaciers protruding. Opposite us was the long valley of Bashgol, reaching down from the Hindu Kush, and the long line of the Shawal ridge twisting southwards, and ending abruptly with the cliffs which overlook the turn of the river where it joined the Kunar. North-westward, lost in a maze of snow perspective, was the main backbone, the water-parting of the Hindu Kush, and although we could not trace it with the certainty that we could wish, we saw enough to lead to the discovery that its position was far enough from that which has hitherto been assumed in the maps. Northward the square peaks of Tirach Mir stood up solid and grand, dominating hills and valleys which radiated from the foot of this monarch of the western hills, and amongst these valleys was Chitral. We could trace the course of the Chitral (or Kunar) river without difficulty, although we could not see down to its level, or actually discern the fort wherein our friends were fighting for their lives. This, however, was not what we expected to see; Chitral was geographically already a well-fixed position. Then for the first time we ascertained that there was indeed another Arnawai, besides that which is the river of Bashgol; that the Shawal range was straight and unbroken, and that after once crossing the river from the foot, or point, of that range, further definition of the boundary southward to the country of the Mohmands could be well sustained by a strongly marked and unmistakable range of hills. This was all we wanted. We could see as it were the upper story of all Kafirstan. We could recognise the peaks fixed by the Indus triangulation, and could connect them together and make out the orographic outline of that strange wilderness; but we could see nothing of the valleys, nothing of the inhabited portions of the country, neither could we gather any very precise information as to the value of the passes and routes which intersect it. Nothing, however, of what we had claimed as indispensable information was wanting, and we could but admit to our guide and councillor, the Hakim, that he had directed our goings in the right way.

Then, after a few hours' careful work, came the getting down, and it was infinitely worse (as far as our camp) than the getting up. However, we had been blessed with that last great boon of the surveyor, a bright, clear day, and nothing else much mattered. We were up to our necks in snowdrifts now and then, and we were wet and stiff and fagged before we got to dry blankets and a night's rest.

The road back to the Commission camp was the same as the road out. There was no other possible. But commissariat had run low, and it was downhill (comparatively), and so our four days' march was reduced to three on the return journey, and we were able to relieve the anxiety of the Commissioner and Sipah Salar within a week of starting. I do not know that anyone was the worse for it. A few days were necessary to make up the mapping, and then, when mutual agreement (after much discussion) had been arrived at as regards the boundary to the edge of the Mohmand country, we lifted our camp for the return to Asmar and Jalalabad.

It was the 11th April when we left our winter camp at Nashagaon. Three months had passed on the terraced slopes of the Kunar river, and they were three months of expectation and waiting, crowned with success so far as the settlement of one of the most awkward sections of the Afghan boundary were concerned. How far they had contributed to bring about those frontier complications which culminated in the siege of Chitral, it is difficult to say. Umra Khan had by this agreement lost his footing in the Kunar valley. Whether he hoped to retrieve his position by a Chitral campaign is known best to himself, and how far the Sipah Salar acted on his own initiative in reversing the previous policy of antagonism, and in abetting this movement which for the time imperilled all boundary settlement, is also amongst the secret records of the Kabul Foreign Department. We must not forget that at a most critical juncture Sher Afzal, the popular hero of Chitral, was let loose from Afghanistan; nor, on the other hand, can we ignore the fate of the Sipah Salar himself. The Commissioner, Sir Richard Udny, once asked him where in all the wide world he would most prefer to live. "In the presence of my king," was his courtly reply. But when his king subsequently summoned him to his presence, he did not find it convenient to attend—at least, so rumour says—and thereafter he sickened and died. "There is no hope for him," said an Afghan official to Colonel Ottley at Lundi Kotal. "He is so ill that the Amir has sent his own doctor to attend him." I believe that with all his apparent genial good nature and never-failing hospitality the Sipah Salar was at heart an intensely bigoted Mahomedan.

He had not the smallest doubt that he was of the seed of Israel, and that the God of his father Abraham would bring about the final conversion of the whole world to the one true faith. Perhaps his political methods in dealing with Umra Khan were a little crude, and a trifle too openly hostile to British interests; perhaps he erred in showing a little too much of his hand. But it is far more probable that his popularity with the army, and his high position and influence at Kabul, were his undoing rather than any injudicious excess of zeal on the frontier. He was too big a man; his head stood too high in the poppy field. There were times when he showed a distinct disinclination to accept instructions from Kabul; as when, at the close of our Commission, he was ordered on escort duty with Nasrullah Khan, then on his way from Kabul to represent the Afghan Court in England. Nasrullah Khan is not a popular member of the Kabul Court. I will not repeat what Afghans say of him, but his own manners and disposition are certainly not typical of the true Afghan sirdar, and Ghulam Haidar did not spare us the expression of his own opinion on the subject. I have not forgotten that he is dead. When there was no object in deception he sometimes spoke the truth fearlessly, and he was obviously speaking the truth when he gave us his opinion about Nasrullah Khan.

The Chitral relief force was mobilised on the Peshawur frontier by the 1st April (much to the Sipah Salar's astonishment, for he did not believe in our mobility), and whilst we were making our way down the valley (hindered more or less by the same severe weather which set in about that time and made the crossing of the passes so difficult for Kelly's advance) it was slowly pushing its way across Swat to Kila Drosh. We saw nothing of all this. We were not permitted to touch Mohmand country—we could not even examine the southern passes from Kunar into Swat—but I was allowed to visit the quaint old-world town of Pashat which lies hidden amongst cypresses on the left bank of the Kunar, just at the foot of one of the best known of them. Now the beauty of Pashat lies in its quaint old garden, certainly not in the mud and wattle débris of dilapidated constructions which now form the town. Through a gap in a broken mud wall we climbed into this garden, this wilderness of tangled jungle and indifferent horticulture, and the instant we were in it we were seized with a feeling of suffocation from the overpowering scent of orange blossoms. The air was thick with the heavy odour, till it clogged one's senses and turned one giddy. The remnants of a quaint summer palace stood at one end of the garden, an edifice chiefly remarkable for the Kashmir lacquer work which embellished it all over, both outside and in. This is a form of oriental art which is often as exquisite in detail as it is ineffective and trumpery in general effect.

The usual rows of black cypresses standing stiff and straight pointed outwards to the main entrance, and the smooth, white footways which bordered the line were blotched with black patches, as of ink, where they passed from the parterres to the shade of the mulberrry trees. It was in fact but an ordinary Mohamedan garden, a trifle more unkempt than usual, but it struck us (being fresh from the wild mountains of the north) as a thing of beauty—a most sweet luxury; and so it will live as the joy of a spring afternoon on the banks of the Kunar amongst memories of the frontier.

CHAPTER XIII.

PAMIRS

The object of the Pamir boundary—Necessity for exact surveys—Formation of the Commission—Through Kashmir—Over the Darkot pass and the Hindu Kush—Process of surveying in such regions—The sources of the Oxus—Nature of the boundary—Climate and scenery of the Pamirs—The Afghan delegates—A Russian feast day—Excursion into Chinese territory—Stopped by force—The Kirghiz—Break up of Commission—Recrossing the Darkot—What is gained by the Pamir boundary—Impossibility of Russian forces reaching India from the Pamirs.

THE work of the Pamir Boundary Commission formed the most remote, and, in some respects, the most satisfactory, of the many phases of boundary demarcation to which the Kabul agreement of 1893 gave rise. Here, amidst the grassy valleys and glacier-freighted ridges of the world's roof, a boundary was actually demarcated, mile by mile, which followed the terms of the agreement fairly closely; and here at last was laid to rest the ghost of years of apprehension as to possible invasion of India from the extreme north.

The object of a boundary in these altitudes was not quite the same as that of a definite frontier line in lower and flatter regions. Hitherto we had been placing a buffer of independent tribes between ourselves and Afghanistan. Here we reverted to first principles, and defined a buffer between ourselves and Russia. It is not an imposing buffer—this long attenuated arm of Afghanistan reaching out to touch China with the tips of its fingers. It is only eight miles wide at one part, and could be ridden across in a morning's ride. It presents no vast physical obstacle to an advance of any sort; physical obstacles, however, are not wanting, but they lie on the Indian side, and they are rude enough and difficult enough to answer all possible purposes. It is a political intervention—a hedge, as it were—over which Russia cannot step without violating Afghanistan, and the violation of Afghanistan may (or may not) be regarded as a "casus belli."

The Amir was never keen in maintaining the integrity of this far-off and most inhospitable corner of his variegated kingdom. He was not keen about maintaining a frontier beyond Panjdeh; and this out-of-the-way wilderness is infinitely more unapproachable and more difficult to garrison than Panjdeh. In fact it may be doubted whether the Amir ever meant effectually to garrison it at all. His demands for assistance to enable him to do so were so preposterous, that it may almost be taken for granted that he regards these back premises as only useful to him so far as they might afford an excuse for further demands ultimately.

We were however not greatly concerned with the Amir's views on the subject. For years the danger of Russian intrigue and possible Russian advance from this direction had been preached in the military councils of India, not only by theoretical strategists who did not know the country, but by men whose energy and enterprise had carried them up into the wilderness to see for themselves, but who had nevertheless to work under restrictions and difficulties which denied them anything like exhaustive inquiry. It was thus of special importance not only that we should lay down a fixed and definite line limiting Russian dominion and the unsettling processes of Russian exploration amongst the border highlanders, but that we should acquire a complete survey of all the various hill tracks and mountain paths which intersect these rugged highlands, in order that we might better appreciate the relative value of the far northern lines of approach to Central Asia.

This was not at first sight an easy problem to solve. Following, more or less, the pioneer footsteps of McNair, a large number of officers (including Woodthorpe and Younghusband) had made their way to the Pamirs, and had followed down the many broken mountain staircases which cross the Hindu Kush, or contiguous Himalayan chains, and landed them on the flats of India. And all of them had contributed something (several of them much) to our general geographical knowledge of these regions; so that what we wanted was not so much the further reconnaissance of particular routes, but a strong framework of measurement to pull the patchwork together. This was all the more necessary as geographical definitions had been made use of in the terms of the agreement. "The latitude of Lake Victoria" was a factor in the general scheme.

This at first sight might not appear a very difficult matter to deal with. Most sailors will tell you with confidence that they can obtain latitudes by direct observation of the stars to a second or two of value, measured on the world's surface, which, as it only means a few hundred feet, is usually good enough for all practical purposes. But this is not (or may not be) the case in the Himalayas, or any other great mass of mountains. The enormous mass of a big mountain system protruding above the general level of the earth affects the direction in which gravity acts—that is to say, it upsets all levels, and plays the mischief with most observations. As an instance, I may refer to the deviation which exists at the headquarters of the Indian survey at Dehra Dun, which is just under the shadow of the Himalayas. Here the results of latitude observations are displaced by nearly a mile; and a mile is not a negligible quantity in dealing with boundaries. The only way to circumvent this inconvenient effect of mountain masses on the level is actually to measure all the way across them (*i.e.* to triangulate) from some known base. The Russians might, or might not, have carried their own triangulation to the Pamirs. We could not tell. If they had, there would be a series of most interesting problems solved in the process of uniting the vast Russian chain of measurement extending from Petersburg to Central Asia with another great system which embraces all India, and is itself dependent on Greenwich for its origin. Petersburg and Greenwich had long been connected, and so the last link in the vast circle of measurement would be forged on the Pamirs.

As it turned out the Russians had not quite completed their triangulation. There was a gap of about eighty miles. But this gap was so scientifically bridged by traverses, that there can be but the most minute variation in the results when it is completed. Thus the interests involved in the Pamir Boundary Commission's labours were not of a passing character.

They fully justified the most anxious care in the arrangements of all details which might ensure their accuracy.

We could not reckon on crossing the Kashmir passes into Gilgit till early in June, and beyond Kashmir there were the passes of the Hindu Kush which we knew to be usually closed in October. So that a bare four months from start to finish was all that we could safely assume to be available for the work before us. Experience had taught us that one great source of delay was the difference of opinion likely to arise in the interpretation of any ambiguous or uncertain term used in the draft of the political agreement, such as might involve references to the supreme Government on either side. So the terms of the agreement were anxiously scanned. It had also taught us that in order to effect rapid and satisfactory progress the Commission party should be as small as possible, and carry with it as little as possible. The lesson learnt by the experiences of the unwieldy Commission that invaded Turkestan in the days of Panjdeh was one that could not readily be forgotten.

The route to the Pamirs which lay through Swat and Chitral was practically closed by the field operations for the relief of Chitral, then in progress, so that an alternative had to be adopted; and we decided to travel *viâ* Gilgit and the Darkot pass.

On the 22nd June, 1895 (we had left the Kunar valley in the preceding April), the Commission party as detailed below* left Baramulla on the shores of the great Kashmir lake, for the Pamirs. The whole party numbered about 100 souls, including drivers; and some 600 Kashmir ponies had been requisitioned for transport. It must be remembered that provision had to be made for a possible six months' supply on the Pamirs. The prospect of passing a winter there was not so remote that it could be disregarded with safety.

* Major-General M. G. Gerard, C.B., Commissioner; Colonel T. H. Holdich, C.B., C.I.E., Major R. Wahab, R.E., Survey Officers; Captain E. F. H. McSwiney, Intelligence Officer and Secretary; Surgeon-Captain A. W. Alcock, I.M.S., Medical Officer in Charge. Ressaidar Zahirulla Khan, Central India Horse, accompanied as attaché, and Khan Sahib Abdul Gufar and two native surveyors on the survey staff. Escort, ten native N.C.O.'s and sepoys of the 20th P.I. with a few orderlies, amounting in all to a fighting force of nineteen men.

The political object of the mission was, briefly, to demarcate about ninety miles of boundary between the eastern end of Lake Victoria and the Chinese frontier. The much-disputed question as to which was the source of the Oxus was decided, for the purposes of the agreement of 1893, by adopting that which was supposed to be its source when the agreement of 1873 was drawn up—the only rational conclusion which could well have been adopted—and Lake Victoria with the Panja stream flowing therefrom was officially announced to be a part of the northern boundary of Afghanistan, which was continued thence for hundreds of miles to Khamiab by the main Oxus channel.

The journey up to the Pamirs afforded no special incident. It was during June, and the passes of Kashmir were full of the beauty of early summer. The snow-veil had been partially withdrawn, and it was replaced on the smooth rounded slopes of the Tragbal and Burzil by a bright carpet of many-tinted flowers—primulas, orchids, cowslips, and a whole tribe of sweet little groundlings, infinitely rich in wealth of colour, and infinitely varied. The scenery was the scenery of Kashmir in early summer. Surely there is none like it! The Burzil (13,500 feet) was crossed without any mishap, in an interlude between one stormy period and another. The slippery, muddy slopes, where a road might be recognisable, and the soft snow-drifts where none was to be seen, were matters of equal indifference to our independent-minded little Kashmir ponies. They are the best transport that I have ever travelled with. Over good roads and bad, up the face of a mountain, or down its shelving spurs, they managed to keep up a tolerably level three miles an hour; following each other with such persistent determination that if the leader plunged with mistaken zeal into a hole in a river-crossing all the rest would make for the same hole, in spite of the vivid interjections of the Kashmiri driver.

Through the valleys of Astor and Bunji, to Gilgit, we followed the road which has so far made the way plain between India and the far north. Beyond Gilgit, through the Yasin valley to the Darkot pass, we had no road. It did not much matter. The track occasionally ran in a narrow ledge over a slippery shelving "pari"—a steep declivity reaching down from the cliffs to the stream-bed. Occasionally it twisted its crooked way amidst the débris of mighty masses of fallen rock; and then, of a sudden, would wander through close-set lanes bordered with hedges of clematis and passion-flower with the blue cornflower and poppies decorating the fields on either side, till the sweep of green meadows and the shadow of orchard trees told where a village lay hid.

The village of Darkot lies at the end of a thick jungle-growth of trees and brushwood, only traversable by means of the numerous rivulets and channels which intersect it from a neighbouring river. One wades knee-deep in ice-cold water for a weary hour or more before reaching Darkot. Once there, a magnificent amphitheatre of towering granite and limestone cliffs (up which there wind at intervals some of the grandest glacial staircases of the world) closes the valley with grim grey determination to bar all further progress northward. One stands on a little green flat at the end of all things, and the beyond seems to belong to eagles and things that float in the air.

But there *is* a way out of it, and it is a dangerous and wearisome climbing way, over broken moraine and fissured glacier till one arrives at the snowfields of the Darkot pass some fifteen thousand feet above sea-level, ere plunging or sliding down again to the Yarkhun river. Nearly all our party were snow-blind by the time we had got across that pass. On it we found the débris of our advanced transport-party scattered up and down; the drivers hiding in holes and clefts, waiting, as is the wont of the Kashmiri, for the gods to come and help them from the clouds. A day was spent in collecting the fragments, fishing them up from the depths of crevasses or out of the snowdrifts, and in restoring sight to the blind. Long strings of sightless folk, holding on to each other's coat-tails, were led up to Dr. Alcock's tent for treatment, the result of a sudden blinding glare which blazed on the pass after a fresh snowstorm.

But we surveyors had on the whole a lucky time. Across the cloudless blue to the southward we could see the great array of Gilgit peaks freshly whitened with new-fallen snow, and far to east and west we could recognise the pinnacles of the mountains which were the farthest landmarks of Indian triangulation. It was a glorious scene. Sound seemed to be muffled in a thick white wrapper, except when the thunder of an avalanche broke the stillness and a wreath of white snow-smoke went upwards to the sky. Nor was the joy of it diminished by satisfactory reflections on a sound connection with India for our surveys.

The advantages we gained on the Darkot lasted us across the Yarkhun river and the main chain of the Hindu Kush (which, as all the world well knows, is not a difficult range to cross at this point) into the Wakhan valley, and there for a space we were completely nonplussed. Up the valley of the Wakhan we worried and twisted our way, day after day, along the devil's pathway which flanks the river gorges. There were no flat spaces, and no reasonable footpaths along that route. If we were not engaged in a rocky scramble upstairs, we were zigzagging down into depths measuring thousands of feet merely to make a fresh start on another climb after stumbling through a river at the bottom. It was a Pilgrim's progress, unbroken and unrelieved by any Christian alleviations; and out of that valley to the right hand or the left it was impossible to get. There was no scaling the gigantic icebound spurs which shut us in—no reaching any point of vantage from which once again we might see both backwards and forwards, and tie up our survey connections in scientific sequence. But the end came at last.

As we emerged on to the more open Pamir plains we were met by indications of Russian occupation. A mounted Kirghiz orderly (jiggit) in the white sheepskin hat of Turkestan, and the beflowered and baggy breeches of Bokhara, met us at Lungur with the welcome intelligence that the Russian Commission had arrived at Lake Victoria; and he took himself off straightway to make his report. Next day, at Bozai Gumbaz (the historical spot from which Captain Younghusband was turned back by the Russians) Captain Katotinski with a detachment of Cossacks rode in to meet the English party, and forthwith despatched a messenger across the perilous Burgotai pass (which crosses the divide between the Great and Little Pamirs) to report to the Russian general. Two days more (and two long days) were required to bring the two Commissions together. The British party rode by the Lake of the Little Pamir (Chakmaktin) to the foot of the Benderski pass, which is the easiest and most practicable of all those connecting the two Pamirs, and thence by a long forced march of forty miles they reached Lake Victoria on the identical day (22nd July) provisionally fixed by the Foreign Office for the meeting. This was in spite of the selected rendezvous having been shifted sixty miles from Bozai Gumbaz to Lake Victoria. It was a weary, dirty, travel-stained little party that halted on the grass slopes overlooking the white felt *akois* of the Russian encampment, planted on the edge of the turquoise-blue Dragon Lake. But the Russian general would accept no excuses pleading the necessity for waiting till the baggage arrived, and smart clothes could be dug out therefrom. The English party were forthwith escorted into the Russian camp by Cossacks bearing torches at the end of their lances, and entertained with all that cordial hospitality in which the Russian official is never found wanting. It was a right hearty greeting, and it initiated a feeling of good-fellowship between the two camps which was never thereafter disturbed, whatever might be the changes and deviations of the political weathercock.

But Major Wahab and I saw none of this. We were striving still and hoping against hope that we might find the opportunity of turning the flank of our heart-breaking difficulties in the narrow Pamir valleys by obtaining a clear view on a clear day from a point sufficiently high to see across the Hindu Kush back to Indian landmarks, and forward to Central Asian ranges. And we found it—at least Major Wahab (to whom a few thousand feet of altitude more or less is a matter of small consideration) did so, from an 18,000-feet peak near the Benderski pass. And having got it once, he got it again; and thus our anxieties ended, and we enjoyed the satisfaction of feeling that we knew the exact spot on which we stood on the earth's surface within a margin of error which might possibly be represented by figures, but which was far too minute for maps. And here I may say that when a scientific crisis supervened, and we had to compare our values with those of the Russian staff before commencing local demarcation, we found ourselves in such close agreement as to be inseparable by any amount that could be made appreciable in any scale of mapping applicable to the Pamirs. Further I may add, for the information of those interested, that the possible error due to local action of the mountain masses on the level (which we had provided against by carrying our triangulation with so much pain and tribulation over the Hindu Kush) was found to be quite insignificant.

The Russian staff included amongst others General Pavolo Schveikovski, Governor of Ferghana, as Chief Commisioner, with M. Ponafidine as political adviser, and Colonel Zaleski of the Russian Engineers as Chief Survey Officer. The topographical staff was headed by that tough old veteran M. Benderski, who was an old friend of the Panjdeh boundary days. They were all most comfortably quartered in Kirghiz akois (round felt tents), and some of these camp residences were something more than comfortable—they were luxurious. Bokhara silks and Central Asian carpets and divans all helped to make up an interior which, with artistic arrangement, was made most effective both as to colour and convenience; and in the general's akoi a portrait of the Emperor Nicolas II. graced the walls. The English camp, of much more modest pretensions, was pitched close to the Russians, with a river, which formed the eastern affluent of the lake, between them.

Then followed the setting out of a programme for marking off a boundary which should reach from the end of the blue lake to the uncertain regions of Chinese occupation. The giant peaks of the range which we had crossed by the Benderski pass (the range which divides the Little Pamir from the Great) answered the purpose of the boundary well enough as far as they went. In that eternal wilderness of snowfields and glacier which has now been named Range Nicolas after the Russian Emperor, and which looks down on the placid sheet of Lake Victoria (the name which Russian courtesy has finally adopted for "Woods'" Lake) on one side, and the swampy irregularities of Chakmaktin on the other, no one is ever likely to question the exact line on which he may set his foot and say he is passing from Russia to Afghanistan. No living soul has ever been there yet—or is ever likely to be there.

level of Lake Victoria has now been trigonometrically . at 13,400 feet above sea-level—400 feet higher than Lake ..akmaktin, the source of the Aksu; and the Nicolas range towers some 6,000 to 8,000 feet above this again. From its glacial sources, out of the mouths of green ice caverns, ice streams flow down on either side to the two lakes, and feed them. The two lakes were long rivals in the field of Oxus sources, Chakmaktin heading the larger, and Victoria the broader and deeper, affluent. But they both spring from the Nicolas glaciers. Not only so, but the stream which furnishes the main arterial supply to the Chakmaktin on the Little Pamir, breaks up and divides in the swamps at the western end of the lake, and sends down a considerable affluent to the Wakhan westward, as well as to the Aksu eastward. It is this Wakhan river which Lord Curzon claims as flowing from the real source; but this again owes its birth originally to glaciers—mighty glaciers which are held in the embrace of the Hindu Kush; but whether they are greater, mightier, deeper reservoirs than those of Nicolas who shall say? They are all equally immeasurable.

From the Benderski pass eastward natural features suitable for definition were not so easily found, and there came a crisis finally when the terms of the agreement could no longer be fitted to the geography of the Pamirs. Then there followed the inevitable discussion, and those references to Government which bid fair to prolong our occupation in the Pamirs till the beginning of winter should force us into the lower altitudes of the plains about Kashgar. There we should have stayed till summer came round again. Happily this was avoided. The ambiguity in geographical expression which might have resulted in such delay had been made the subject of reference to Government beforehand—so that the last pillar was set up on its base on about the very last day that we could have maintained our ground (9th September), and the boundary thence officially projected into a space where (as at its beginning) no pillars or markstones could be raised to witness to it. Amidst the voiceless waste of a vast white wilderness 20,000 feet above the sea, absolutely inaccessible to man and within the ken of no living creature but the Pamir eagles—there the three great empires actually meet. It is a fitting trijunction. N[illegible] Hindu mythology ever occupied a more stupendous thron[illegible]

Through this process of demarcation we need hardly fo[illegible] the Commission in detail. English and Russian topographe[illegible] worked side by side, and shared equally in the rough and tumble of the demarcation. The climate was at most times suggestive of a wild and unsettled English spring. Sudden were the changes which fell on those grey-green Pamirs. Clinging to the sullen sides of the purple mountains a cloud at first no bigger than a man's hand would gather and roll itself together from the light mists of the morning, sweeping upwards from the plains, and in a short space that might be measured by minutes, the whole wide dappled landscape would darken into gloom, the blue mirror of the lake would deepen to a leaden hue, little frills and froths of white would chase each other across; and then solid and resistless the black squall would descend upon us, blotting out our poor little attempts to make a record of nature's landmarks, and reducing our own half-frozen bodies to a feeling of pulpy insignificance. And then of a sudden the world would again leap into light; without so much as the introduction of a rainbow, quivering streaks of sunshine would dance on lake and river, and the chasing sunlight would sweep the shadows out of the valley ere the raindrops had ceased to drain from off us. When there was anything approaching to settled weather it included a settled wind. Either up the valley, or down it, cold blasts were perpetually whistling, peeling the skin off one's face already half-raw with the effects of snow-glare, and piercing even to the bones and marrow through the thick sheepskin coats and Kashmir cloaks with which we bound ourselves round. But yet there were many ameliorations. I have seen the Pamirs look quite beautiful. From Chakmaktin lake, looking across the sweeping slopes towards Kizil Rabat, there is a vista of narrow green plain bordered by yellow-grey dunes which spread themselves outwards on either side from the foot-hills; and in the midst there meanders with uncertain steps the infant Aksu, occasionally breaking into small lakelets and marshes. On the north the rugged peaks of Nicolas range culminate in the round white head of Peak Salisbury which overlooks the Benderski s, keeping silent watch and ward. East of Kizil Rabat, and beyond it, are the savage outlines of the great range which we call Sarikol, which here stiffens itself into a series of impracticable precipices. Towering above this line is a magnificent peak (20,720 feet high) which rests on a spur running north-east towards Tashkurghan, beyond the Sarikol. The southern mountains bordering the Pamir which are all part of the same Sarikol range (that great meridional range which has sometimes been called Taurus, and more lately in the world's history was probably known as Bolor) present to view nothing but the butt-ends of enormous spurs, ranged with such remarkable precision, and repeating the same outlines with such perfect architectural sequence, that the conviction is strong that the same forces of nature must have originally shaped them all to the same ends. The scattered boulders dotting the green expanse of Pamir tell their own tale of what the nature of this force must have been. It can only have been glacial. Between every pair of contiguous Sarikol spurs there is a glacier, which, according to such superficial observations as we were able to make, appears to be slowly diminishing and withdrawing towards the crest of the range. Under the influence of a bright sky and freshly-fallen snow Pamir scenery is exhilarating. When the glory of sunset touches it and tints the hills with scarlet and purple it is impressive; but under ordinary everyday effects of light and shade it is distinctly monotonous.

Snowfalls were so frequent that it perpetually happened that our efforts at reconnaissance were defeated by them. On the 17th August the first severe fall occurred. It broke down my tent in the middle of the night. In the morning not a blade of grass was to be seen, and the mountains sloped down in smooth white undulations to the river, without a break of colour. A small party of Russian and English officers who had attempted to reach the Sarikol valley by the Beyik pass were snowed up and forced to return. Food was unprocurable and the pass itself waist-deep in snow.

Much has been said about the want of fuel on the Pamirs. It is true that there is nothing in the shape of timber, not even an ordinary specimen of brushwood; but there is a very extensive supply of "burtsi," which is a sort of wormwood scrub, the roots of which answer well enough for cooking purposes. It is astonishing moreover to what excellent use as fuel the argols or droppings of yaks and wild animals may be put. I think the natives rather prefer this sort of fuel to wood. We were at any rate never reduced to extremities. We could not warm our tents efficiently (and they were probably all the more wholesome in consequence), but we never heard complaints from the kitchen.

As for the Russian *ménage* it was beyond reproach. It was not of course to be accepted as an illustration of the experience which ordinarily befalls the Cossack officer on outpost duty. The Russian staff were on their own ground on this occasion, and whilst they took care to impress upon us that we were more or less in the position of guests, they filled their rôle of hosts with all the courtesy of high officials backed by an irreproachable cuisine. It was good for us to be there on any one of their high days; but it was doubtless also good for the education of the Kirghiz nomads, who, rough and uncouth as they might appear to be, could not well fail to appreciate the effects of a display and liberality on the Russian side which was hardly reciprocated by the representatives of the Court of Kabul.

The Afghan Commissioner, Sirdar Ghulam Mohiudin Khan, had left his high position as Governor of Faizabad (the capital of Badakshan) for the rugged experiences of the Pamir highlands with a regret that he did not take much pains to conceal. He was a nephew of that Mohamed Jan whose name was in all men's mouths during the fighting days at Sherpur. Mohamed Jan led the national movement against us, and headed the attack on Sherpur—and survived; but he has long since joined the roll of those whose influence in Afghanistan has led to their own undoing. The Afghan delegate and his political adviser, Mullah Mufti Ashur Mahomed Khan, were always included in the official entertainments given by the Russian chief, who on these occasions maintained the impression of the vast dignity and resources of great Russia, in the Pamirs, in a manner worthy of his own high position. The Kirghiz were duly impressed, and the impression will last. It is nonsense to suppose that the small remnant of these nomadic tribes who may nominally remain under Chinese or Afghan suzerainty in the Pamirs and pitch their tents in the Tagdumbash, or about Chakmaktin, are not really as much Russian as the rest of their people.

The 3rd August was a high feast day in the Russian calendar. It was "Marie" Day, the saint's day of the ex-Empress of Russia and of the Duchess of Edinburgh, and it afforded us an excellent chance of witnessing the ceremonial reverence attached to all such semi-religious festivals in the Russian army. An open-air religious service was followed by the solemn ceremony of drinking to the health of the "Maries," a toast to which the Cossacks responded by a cheer in line;. a well-drilled and well-executed cheer. No service in Russia is complete without music. The grand hymns and anthems of their band sounded doubly impressive amongst the wild surroundings of that outstanding corner of the great Russian Empire, and it was curious to watch the imitative reverence and awe that expressed itself in the faces of the Kirghiz audience. Time was (and not so long ago either) when High Asia was a Christian country, and amongst the Kirghiz are to be found tribes who under their old names, are reckoned in history as once Christian tribes. Christian symbols still exist in scattered fragments, even if Christian graces are wanting; and it is not so far from where we were standing on that day, that the marriage ceremony is still conducted by the priest with the opening inquiry, "Wilt thou have this woman," and closes with the adjuration, "Those whom God hath joined together let no man put asunder."

That manly, outspoken, clear-sighted race of men, with their fresh-complexioned, blue-eyed wives and daughters (who in appearance, at least, show but little trace of Mongolian affinities) always seemed to me as if they *ought* to be Christian rather than Mahomedan. I doubt if there is much of the fanatical spirit of the Mussulman in them.

Kirghiz followers of the Russian camp were then collected for their national game of "Ulak"—a game which is known as "Buzgala bazi" amongst the Turkmans and which seems to be common to all High Asia. It is a simple game, and consists in a savage fight by mounted men for the possession of a goat, which, dead or alive, is carried at the saddle bow of one of the performers. The object of the goat-carrier is to retain the possession of the carcase, and to ride clear of all opposition, till he reaches a sanctuary (usually a selected space of clear ground) where he deposits it. At Jarti Gumbaz, where the festival was held, there is a rapid stream with a most uneven and dangerous bottom of slippery boulders, and the sanctuary chosen was a small patch of clear grass on the banks of this stream just opposite the officers' "gallery," where we all sat in a row to witness the sport. Each horseman who succeeded in avoiding all rival goat-snatchers, and who dropped the goat on to that patch of grass, forthwith left the mêlée, and was placed by the side of the Russian general's chair to receive his reward in due time.

The game was fast and furious, fully as reckless as any Turkman performance I ever saw, and the dust rose in thick clouds over the spinning horsemen. We soon found that our protecting river was no protection at all. In the heat of this Kirghiz fray horses and men went into it headlong, and it seemed to be due only to some special Kirghiz providence that they ever came out again. The game ended when one of the handy and hardy little horses had his leg broken. He was forthwith killed, skinned and preserved for the evening feast.

Meanwhile there were races for boys (mounted, of course, for no Kirghiz infant would think of *running* a race), and races for yaks and camels, and the usual Cossack "jigitovka" (feats of horsemanship), which included amongst the performers not merely a few selected men, but the whole Cossack escort. All winners were rewarded by the Russian general, and the prizes (rouble notes and "khilats" of Bokhara silk) were bestowed with an amount of ceremony which doubled their value in the eyes of the prize-winners. The lunch which followed was really a magnificent banquet, and it lasted till the shades of evening fell upon the Pamirs.

There is no doubt that the readiness shown by the Russians in supporting the national games and festivities of this nomadic race of people with whom they are rapidly assimilating themselves in Central Asia, the apparently valuable prizes which they bestow on those who distinguish themselves, and the careful observance of all due ceremony and etiquette on these occasions, impresses the native mind greatly; and if this was all that the Kirghiz saw of the Russians it would lead to great popularity. A Russian Commission headed by a distinguished general is not, however, a usual feature on the Pamirs. But it was distinctly effective whilst it lasted.

There is not much to tell of the ordinary everyday business of surveying and demarcating. Having once agreed as to main principles, the details of the Pamir Survey were rapidly filled in. It was not until we reached our last camp that any difficulty arose as to the interpretation of the agreement. The short delay which occurred was not unprofitable. It offered an opportunity for an extension of our reconnaissance to the Tagdumbash Pamir, and the passes leading thence to India on one side, and into the district of Sarikol and Tashkurghan on the other. Major Wahab started Indiawards, and I took the nearest and most obvious route into the Chinese district of Sarikol across the Beyik pass, each of us intent on gaining information. Our way for some distance lay together.

During the progress of the Commission so far, the chief social events of interest had been the arrival of certain distinguished travellers in our camp. Dr. Sven Hedin, whose name all the world knows by this time, joined us fresh from his explorations in the Takla Makan, and Mr. Macartney, who had long been resident in Kashgar, came to us officially to represent Chinese interests. Dr. Sven Hedin, accomplished as linguist, artist, and geographer, was a most welcome addition to the social circle. Whether making his way through the sands which hide the cities of the past, or telling tales in the reeking tobacco atmosphere of the round felt tent which the Russians called their club, he seemed equally at home, if not equally happy. To be born with a keen appreciation of one's environment in all circumstances and conditions of life—this is a gift which is not granted to all men, and it is given chiefly to great explorers. Dr. Sven Hedin is one of the lucky few.

Mr. G. Macartney, our other visitor, was our authority on matters affecting China, but not even he could say how far the Chinese authorities on the border had interested themselves in our proceedings. None of them had appeared to put in any claim, and none of them seemed in the least concerned where we put our pillars up, or whether indeed we put any up at all. The delay in settling the final details of the line gave us the opportunity of finding out. So with General Gerard's instructions, I started to turn eastward into Sarikol from the foot of the Beyik pass, whilst Major Wahab should explore westward up to the head of the Tagdumbash.

It was the 4th September when we left our camp in the Little Pamir near Kizil Rabat, and there was a break in the weather. The pass had been reported impracticable only a week or so before, but such is the variety of Pamir climatic conditions, that we had no difficulty whatever in crossing. The road up to it lay across great rolling grassy slopes shelving to the Beyik river on our left, and abutting on red and grey cliffs and precipices on our right. The soil was soft and swampy after snow, and as we rode gently along, not a sound broke the silence of the wild unfinished waste, except the chirrup of the marmots who sat bolt upright near their holes to watch the unaccustomed visitor at a discreet distance. Far away, well up the mountain sides, we could see black spots which we knew from experience were grazing yaks, so that we also knew that there was Kirghiz occupation of the ground, though the Kirghiz encampment was hidden in the folds of the "dasht." The altitude of the pass, when we reached it, was found to be moderate (for a Pamir pass), being about the same as the Benderski, 15,000 feet above sea; but it is high enough to lead to difficulties on account of snow, even in the summer season. It is not a difficult pass; the southern side of it being steep and dangerous, from the treacherous nature of the material beneath, for a space of about 500 or 600 feet only. The view looking southward from the pass is very grand.

The mountain track falls steeply away to the little camping ground of Ganjabai beneath, where a stream curls in from the west, and twining round the foot of the gigantic red cliffs overhanging Ganjabai, points straight away in a thin streak of blue for the snow peaks of Muztagh. The glaciers and snows of that terrific range shut in China (as we look across to them from the rim of Russia) and shut out a great space of mountains which borders northern India. From nowhere near the trijunction can one look into the three empires at once. For a day or so we trekked down the Ganjabai valley, which wore all the tattered apparel of autumn. The wild rhubarb was curled and blackened by early frost and all flowers had died at the first touch of winter, except the hardy monkshood and a few primulas. In amongst the willow bushes (the first we had seen for many a week) fat camels were grazing contentedly. The debouchment of the valley was deep in the embrace of the rugged snow-topped peaks which form the base of the two great ranges of Sarikol and Muztagh. Here was a Kirghiz encampment; and here too was the first Chinese outpost.

A dirty-looking Chinese soldier, whose grimy clothes were obviously uniform, in spite of the griminess, came out and grinned at us. His post, or station, was a dilapidated cabin of mud and stone—but this was enough; it signified permanent occupation. Round about it were no "premises"; only a few draggle-tailed cocks and hens, with pessimistic mien, scratched out a scanty subsistence from a gigantic dust-heap. This was interesting, because the domestic fowl will not grow on the Pamirs. There was no sort of interest expressed in our movements outwardly and visibly—but as the shades of evening fell about us, two more of the unkempt detachment stole out of the shanty and made off hastily in the direction of Tashkurghan.

On the 7th Major Wahab started up the Tagdumbash to its head at the Killik pass, and I started down (with Mr. Macartney) to follow out the Karachukar (or Tagdumbash) stream to its junction with the Tashkurghan river, so as to see what the other side of the mountain wall which was set up between China and Russia might look like. Two or three very pleasant and very interesting days followed in Sarikol. We found ourselves amongst brushwood (willow) and timber (juniper) and in a perfect warren of rabbits—or hares—for I really do not know how our naturalist finally classed them. The roads were easy, and evidences of Chinese occupation abundant. From Ujadbai where the streams unite, we made straight running northward for Tashkurghan with the great dome of the Muztagh Ata (the "Ice father" of Sven Hedin's story) before us, and a splendid line of snow to the east. Westward was the great living Sarikol mountain wall—as impenetrable and unsurmountable an obstacle as anyone need wish to see.

The Muztagh Ata (which belongs to the Sarikol—not the Muztagh system) is reckoned the highest peak north of the Himalaya. It is now connected with our Indian triangulation, and we know its height to be about 24,000 feet, but there is still a doubt whether a more northerly peak may not be higher. Trotter fixed a peak at 25,000 feet—but his data have been called in question. We ourselves saw no higher peak than Sven Hedin's Muztagh Ata. Ripening crops, water-mills, and stone-built hamlets gradually multiplied on our right hand and on our left as we proceeded, and we came to the conclusion that the Sarikol valley, though narrow, was fertile and consequently desirable. Here and there the valley narrows almost to a gorge, and the road strikes over a stony bit of "dasht." It was at a waist of this description that our reconnaissance suddenly terminated.

In the early morning, just as we started on the 8th, I had observed on the far side of the river a little cloud of dust following a little black shadow that moved rapidly southward in our direction (still having the river between us), and it seemed advisable that we should push quickly along if we would make a fair day's run in spite of what that shadow might portend. It rapidly resolved itself into a small band of horsemen (about twenty-five or thirty), who travelled in such close order, and moved with such a curious scuttling action, as to resemble a gigantic beetle chasing across the plain far more than any living form of light cavalry. Abreast of us the detachment suddenly took to the river. This was certainly most unexpected. Cavalry do not usually, without any preliminary notice, take straight headers into water as if they were spaniels. This cavalry did, and they emerged dripping on to the road just in front of us. I could see no apparent ford—but it may very well be that it was there all the same. Our way at any rate was effectually blocked. Then ensued a roadside "pow-wow." Macartney recognised an old friend in the commandant of the detachment, and they sat on the ground together, and argued the question of my proceeding to Tashkurghan without a passport backwards and forwards for an hour or so (with intervals for pipes and tobacco), whilst I sketched the Chinese light horsemen.

There was much in them that was worth observation. On the whole I was astonished at the smartness of their equipment and turn-out. At such an extreme corner of the Chinese Empire I had not expected anything better than unkempt local levies, or militia, but these troopers were evidently of a much superior class. They were clad in black velvet double-breasted coats with scarlet lettering indicating that they existed for the preservation of peace on the border. This information extended from collar to skirts. A scarlet border some three inches wide edged with a narrow white stripe set off the black breastpiece. The sleeves were of an unadorned grey, and their pantaloons tucked into their boots were purple. The boots had the usual tip-tilted toe, and the feet looked abnormally small. The coats extended in lappets down the thigh; and on this part of the uniform no legend was visible, the ornamentation being of geometric type. The head-dress was simple; a blue kerchief twisted round and knotted behind the ear. The individual uniform was suggestive of fancy dress, but massed together it was certainly smart and effective. On the march the detachment moved in very close order at a rapid run—hardly a trot—which was maintained from start to finish. The impression left on my mind was that, whatever the strength of the Chinese force in Kashgar may be, the troops selected for the service were efficient as frontier escorts, and good for irregular service.

There could be no doubt that a careful watch was kept on the border. Macartney soon discovered that not only were our movements on the Pamirs perfectly well known, but that the position of the boundary—even the last decision affecting the Chinese frontier—was known also. Presumably the frontier officials were satisfied and content to leave matters in our hands.

We had eventually to turn our horses' heads and retrace our steps—but not before we had gone far enough to verify the accuracy of Russian mapping, to determine the position of Tashkurghan, and make a junction with previous Kashgar surveys; all of which has since been more completely and satisfactorily rounded off by the efforts of that energetic explorer, Captain

Deasy.* On the way back we found our Chinese commandant an entertaining companion and as hospitable as circumstances would admit of his being. This was of course due to his personal acquaintance with Mr. Macartney. His views of life were cynical, and his description of Chinese military administration most amusing.

At Beyik I enjoyed the opportunity of breakfasting in a Kirghiz akoi, and of observing a Kirghiz interior under favourable circumstances. Excellent cream and butter were forthcoming, and one member of the family (a pretty girl of about eighteen) was sent out to scour the hillsides for a sheep as an offering—which we did not accept. A certain air of dirty comfort pervades the Kirghiz akoi. A strong colouring of smoke harmonises the interior, and is not altogether absent from the otherwise fresh and fair complexion of the Kirghiz ladies, whose clear blue eyes and attractive manners are very pleasant to the European wayfarer. Their outward and visible dress is a long close-fitting gown reaching to the ankles of a pair of top boots. All men, women, and children alike wear these long Russian boots; but they are guiltless of the high heels affected by the Turkmans, which render walking barely possible. The head-dress of the Kirghiz women is so distinctive that one would like to know its origin. It is not unlike the long pointed cap and streamer of the women of Tartary, which by some eccentricity of fashion in mediæval times, was temporarily adopted in Europe, and may be recognised in illustrations of early English history; but the conical shape of the cap has disappeared, and Kirghiz fashion shapes it into the semblance of an inverted milk-pail. The streamers remain, almost down to the heels in the case of matrons, but the maids braid their hair into long tails, and are not so fully developed in the matter of turban. The men wear small caps with fur edging, or else the felt Kashgar hat. Round about the interior of the akoi rugs and felts were scattered, and a portion of it was screened off for dairy purposes. Here milk in various stages was set in wooden vessels. Most of the domestic utensils were wooden. I observed several excellent milk-pails, a sieve, many bowls,

* Captain Deasy has proved that there is no higher peak than Muztagh Ata in the Sarikol.

a gigantic wooden spoon, and an iron pot, or cauldron, that would contain about twenty gallons. Some half-dozen Snider rifles, with bayonets fixed, and a few swords, hung on the walls. Very pretty saddle-bags were scattered about, the smaller ones containing women's gear, amongst which there appeared to be neither scissors nor thimbles, but there were dark glasses for protection against snow-glare, and many little products of Russian civilisation.

On the 10th we recrossed the pass on our way to head-quarters, and were delayed by a snowstorm. On the 11th we arrived to find the last practicable pillar set up on its base, and all arrangements made for our return to India. General Gerard had arranged to proceed to Europe through Russian territory, and the command of the Commission thereby devolved upon myself.

The last night we spent on the Pamirs was a memorable one for us all. We had not trusted to the chance of so speedy a termination to our work. We had reckoned that a winter up on the world's roof was an exceedingly probable contingency—and we had accordingly, with much difficulty and some expense, stacked up a wood-supply which was collected from the Kanjut valleys. We had, in fact, utilised our Kashmir transport (which was otherwise only eating its collective head off, on Pamir grass), for this purpose. We were in a position therefore to arrange for an illumination and a bonfire on a large scale, and to issue invitations for a dance. And a most effective dance it was. Never, even in the viceregal halls of Simla, have I seen a dance go so well. The night was intensely cold, but clear, and the witchery of moonlight was over it all. It glinted off the ice coating of the lake, and sparkled in little scintillating shafts on the slopes of the snowdrifts that still lay about us. In the midst was the roaring, blazing bonfire, such a bonfire as the Pamirs had never seen before, and never will see again; and it shot its red glare through the camp where the akois stood around, making black shadows of the mixed multitude of great hairy camels who sat stolidly blinking in the background.

Round about the fire either sat, or danced, the company, and they danced with a will; Cossacks and Kirghiz, men of Hunza and Kashmir, Russians, English, French (there was one Frenchman, who was responsible for the grammar of the protocols) and Afghans—they were all well in it, and the music was as wild as the dance. "Orpheus" was the leader of the band. He played a pipe, the same pipe with which he usually enticed the sheep along the mountain paths as he drifted slowly ahead of them. I have forgotten his other name, but he was a man of the hills, and a model for his Greek original. A Cossack supported him with a concertina, and there was a kerosine tin drum in addition. Nothing was wanting—certainly not refreshments. The grog was brewed in a vast Russian cauldron by my native cook and a Cossack orderly, and they warmed to their work as the night sped on.

Next morning we parted company, feeling assured that the Pamirs would remember us. The Russians packed their baggage on camels and trekked eastward, following the course of the Aksu. We stirred up our Kashmir ponies, and disappeared in the offing of the long plain to westward, and the Pamir wilderness was again left to the eternal silences and the blackened fragments of the still smoking bonfire.

Of the homeward route there need not be much written, though it was in some respects a hazardous march. As we stepped down the first slopes from the Pamir level to Lungur, we were met by a storm of sleet and snow that was little short of a veritable Asiatic "shamshir." Nothing but the conviction that our passage across the Darkot pass was a matter of days, if not of hours, would have induced me to drive the caravan full in the face of it, along those desperately evil tracks which overhung the Wakhan river. But there was not a day to be lost, and we pushed on over slippery snow-sodden paths (which soon became small channels for the surface drainage of the mountains) down into the depths of the valley, where we were dragged wet and weary through the local torrents, which now came rushing down in full "spate" from the highlands; then up again in an eternal see-saw of gradient over the worst hill-track (to call it a track at all) that I have ever seen between Persia and China, till we were once again at the foot of the northern slopes of the Hindu Kush. Here we encountered no great difficulty. A few feet of snow on the summit of the pass (a local pass near the Baoghel, but not that pass itself) made but little difference after our recent experiences, and we dropped down into the valley of the Yarkhun with feelings of thankfulness that so far all had gone well.

Then were we face to face with the great Darkot obstacle, and though we were now but a lightly-laden party, in excellent training for any effort of mountain climbing, the thoughts of that pass ahead cost me many an anxious quarter of an hour. Nor was my mind much relieved when I found at the Yarkhun that the pass had been closed for some days, and that it was reckoned more than a man's life was worth to attempt it in uncertain weather. It might not have been absolutely necessary to cross the Darkot. There was an alternative. Now that we were south of the Hindu Kush, we were in the Indus basin. We had therefore only to follow down the Yarkhun river to Chitral, the Kunar valley, Jalalabad and the Khaibar, or else pass through Swat country, to attain the plains of the Punjab where we would be. But it was an alternative the adoption of which nothing but actual desperation would have justified. We should have abandoned our base of supply, and our line of communications, and we knew nothing whatever of the conditions of the route between ourselves and Chitral. It is true that it had been reconnoitred and reported on by officers who had ridden through it under more or less favourable conditions, and it had been pronounced practicable—but nothing is more certain about these northern hill routes than their uncertainty. A path which is open one year may be closed by the protruding snout of a glacier the next. A bad season or a good season makes all the difference between impracticability or possibility; and we had no reason to expect much in the way of good weather at our time of the year. We should at any rate have been lost for many days to the ken of all the world outside, and we had no desire to create a temporary excitement in India by any such manœuvre. Still, when I looked across the grey whirling torrent of the Yarkhun, almost fresh from its parent glacier and filled with the milky scum of ice-ground silt, to the deep black gorge up which our path lay, where rolling purple and brown mists hid the glacier from view, I was very doubtful about transporting so large a company through those gates into that sullen cloudland.

I finally turned into my tent at night on the 20th with the intention of facing the unknown and striking for the Chitral route, should snow descend at night, and no fresh information be forthcoming before morning. But late that evening my invaluable intelligence officer Captain McSwiney came to tell me that Zahirulla Khan, our native attaché, had discovered a man from Yasin, who had but just come over the pass to rescue the bones of his sister (who had died somewhere in our neighbourhood), and carry them back to Yasin for burial. He offered to guide us should no heavy fall of snow intervene. But he did not fail to point out that it was one thing for a single individual unencumbered to make his way safely through the now hidden maze of glacier crevasses, and another for a large company which included many four-footed beasts. However, here was the one chance of success, and I soon arranged terms with him. Yaks were collected from a neighbouring "aul" with a view to driving them ahead to make a way through the snow, and the details of the next day's march duly arranged.

In the early morning of the 21st September I awoke to hear the muffled tread of the sentry through fresh-fallen snow, and to find snow coming down silently and thickly and winding all the camp in a smooth white sheet! I confess I thought that our last chance was gone. But the yaks were started off, all the same; and by nine o'clock there was distinct evidence of the thinning out of the clouds, and I could judge that the storm was but local after all. Accordingly the order was given to load up—wet as we were—and to make the start. Presently the sun broke through the mists, and we crossed the river to the foot of the glacier, with hope inspired by sunshine and the prospect of getting dry. It was but a short-lived respite, but it saved us. We found the slow lumbering yaks with heads down, shoving their ungainly way through the snowdrifts (which were not as deep as we expected) with a patient contempt for the fleeting hours which was quite inadmissible under the circumstances; and we promptly passed them by and made our own tracks. Our guide (with his sister's remains in a handkerchief on his back) proved to be thoroughly capable, and he was accompanied by two others of his own sort. Between them they drove a goat and a donkey, and with their aid, they diagnosed the position of fissures and cracks with great success when we were once on the glacier. I followed, mounted on a veritable steam engine of a pony—as untiring as he was determined to push ahead. On many (indeed on most) occasions the excessive redundancy of Dunmore's energy was fatiguing, and even annoying. On this occasion it served a most useful purpose, for where one pony treads there will all well-conditioned and self-respecting Kashmir baggage ponies follow. The donkey really made the first footprints. How *he* knew where to go is a mystery to me still. Occasionally the goat relieved him. Then came the guides, and when my steed had added his efforts towards making the way plain there was no further doubt about it. Dangerous points were marked off on the snow as they occurred.

McSwiney and Sergeant Stoddart brought up the rear, well armed with brandy and other necessaries for restoring exhausted vitality, and with such success did they undertake the ungenial part of whipper-in that there was never half an hour's interval between the head and the tail of that column through that memorable day's march. About 1 p.m., when we were almost within sight of the crest, a thick, snow-laden, bulging black cloud came up, with an ice blast of wind, and dumped itself on to the pass. In a few seconds one's moustache was frozen to one's face and one's limbs were numbed so that sitting in the saddle became an impossibility. For a minute or so (a very bad minute) all view was blocked beyond a few yards on either side, and a general halt all along the line was imperative. Was it going to last? Had we been caught after all? A few hours of it would have been quite enough for most of us.

No, it did not last. It cleared away almost as it came. It was but the advanced guard, the forerunner, of a great army of blue-black snow-laden clouds which swept up an hour later, settling down heavily on peak and ridge, blocking the glacier and taking possession, setting the annual winter snow barrier, and barring that pass (for all we knew) for the next eight months to all comers. But what cared we? We were over the pass by 2 p.m., speeding recklessly down the southern slope over glacier and moraine, sending the loose boulders spinning into the depths below, whilst songs broke out from the ragged crew of Kashmiri drivers, and the ponies scuttled along as if they were on a turnpike road. By 5 p.m. we were at the head of the Yasin valley, once again in sight of the Darkot poplars and willows, and the lanes and orchards of Kashmir.

There is nothing more to tell. We journeyed by Gilgit through the enchanting pleasure grounds of Kashmir, where the fingers of autumn had been busy with colour. Who can really paint the beauty of a Kashmir autumn in words? Not I. I must leave it to better artists.

It is however well perhaps to explain before we leave Kashmir for other fields, what we gained by that Pamir boundary. We know that we have put a narrow slice of Afghan territory all the way along, between Russia and our independent frontier tribes, till it touches China; but what else did we gain by this Commission? Incidentally we gained a considerable store of historical and geographical information (some small account of which may be found in the *Report of the Pamir Boundary Commission*), and if we put the two together, we get a reasonably accurate appreciation of the bearing of those remote regions on the great question of Russia's proximity to India. The geography shows us that between Russia and China there lies the great central meridional range, or mountain system—for it really embodies two distinct and parallel ranges—of Sarikol. This was once known as the "mountains of Bolor." It now figures in the maps under the collective name of Sarikol, but the eastern range of the system is perhaps better known as the Kashgar range. This eastern range is the more prominent. On it are the great peaks Kungur, Muztagh Ata, etc.; but it is not the water-divide between the Oxus and the Kashgar plains. This great mass of mountains forms a splendid natural barrier (throughout its southern parts) between Russia and China. It abuts southwards on another yet vaster system of mountains running almost at right angles to its own general strike, which form the northern outliers of the Himalaya and of the Hindu Kush. But it does not close with them in quite such simple form as that of a perpendicular to a straight line. It bends off westward with a sudden sharp bend, and forms a loop at its southern extremity; which loop is the Tagdumbash Pamir. Consequently about the head of the Tagdumbash we may say that the geographical junction between the gigantic Muztagh range north of the Himalaya, on the east, the Hindu Kush on the west (training off to south-west), and the Sarikol on the north, is to be found. Still Russia can reach China in a variety of ways. Well marked and magnificent as the Sarikol configuration may be, there is an open way into the Tagdumbash across it by the Beyik pass, and once in the Tagdumbash, the road into the flats of the Sarikol province is easy. And there are other passes further north which are yet more direct. The Nezatash pass from the Aksu valley is perhaps the best of them. Thus between Russia and the Chinese New Dominion there are no insuperable obstacles placed by nature. If Russia therefore occupied Sarikol and the Tagdumbash (which she could easily do), would she be any nearer India? Not in the least; for she would still have the gigantic peaks of the Muztagh to the south of her; and no living European (except Younghusband) has ever made his way across that barrier. But she would to a certain extent be paving a way towards Tibet. We may, however, safely leave that corner of the world to take care of its own interests and ours, unassisted. Russia could never by any conceivable effort reach India either by Tibet, or by the Muztagh.

Further west, when we come to the much-discussed passes over the Hindu Kush leading to Hunza and Gilgit, and to Chitral, and Jalalabad, we have interposed an Afghan barrier between them and Russia. But without that barrier there never need have been the smallest apprehension of any dangerous aggression on the part of Russia Indiawards. Here history steps in to the aid of our maps. We can now trace out with more or less success the routes of the Chinese pilgrims of early mediæval times—those pilgrims who came to India in search of religious teaching—and we can also faintly discern through the misty obscurity of past ages what must have been the routes taken by those countless hordes from Central Asia, be they Sakæ, Yuchi, Jats, Goths, Huns, or Monguls, who have overrun India from time to time, and left their impress on the ethnography of the country. Seeing that many of them must have started from regions far to the east of the Pamirs, they would naturally have swarmed through the nearest routes to the promised land, had these routes been possible. None of them ever did so. There is evidence that the attempt was made, and that it ended here and there in the upspringing of a most curiously diverse and mixed race in certain remote corners; but they never got through the mountains south of the Pamirs, and, so long as the mountains remain as they are, no military force of any consequence whatever ever will get through. All these ancient invasions were by way of Kabul. Chitral was never on the high road to India from High Asia, and never will be—unless indeed we or the Amir make it so; which can only be done by constructing a high road past it to Badakshan. It has been decided that Chitral must remain as an outlying channel for the spread of British political interest in the mountain districts northwards. As a military outpost it has little to recommend it. Indeed there is no position in the narrow cramped space of the Chitral valley that could offer much opportunity for good defence; and with a weak garrison all such hill-surrounded positions are but the ends of trailing coat-tails, admirably suited to the ordinary tactics of tribal aggression; but as political centres they are valuable, and as such, Chitral, like many others, must be maintained through the effective channel of a good road. Thus do the rough places and natural defences of nature become wasted, and we ourselves remove stumbling-blocks from the path of our enemies.

But whatever excuse we may have for the making of trans-frontier roads where none before existed, the Amir has yet better ones. He looks to good roads as a means of commercial development; and so long as he brings wealth to his capital, pays little heed to such military considerations as (for instance) would weigh with us in barring a railway connection between Quetta and Herat. The maintenance of the integrity of Afghanistan is our business; his is the introduction of that wealth to his treasury which Afghanistan has never yet been able to raise from internal resources. So he has made a first-class road from Turkestan over the Hindu Kush to Kabul from the west, and from the Oxus to the same capital from the north, and he has developed roads already existing in the Kabul valley—has reached into Kafirstan, and was (when we were in the Kunar valley) actively engaged in constructing yet another great central line of communication which should bring Badakshan into direct touch with Jalalabad. All the world knows this, and seeing that all the world does know it, what conceivable fatuity would lead any Russian strategist to plan an advance to India that should pass by Chitral or Gilgit when an open door lies further west?

So that one of the lessons we learnt on the Pamirs was this—that whatever may be the advantage of establishing political relations with the people who dwell in the secluded valleys and gorges to the south, we may well afford to place the Pamirs themselves outside the pale of strategical consideration.

CHAPTER XIV.

PERSO-BALUCH BOUNDARY

Object of Commission—Country to be traversed—Makrán—Kohuk disputes and raids on date groves—Gradual extension of surveys westward—Crossing Makrán—Arrival at Kohuk—A lady in camp—The Persian Commissioner and his staff—Question of first call—Kalagan and Jalk—Rapid boundary settlement—Persian sociability—Concluding gymkhana—Going into "bast"—Persian climate—Return to Quetta—What is the value of Makrán to us?

THE delimitation of a boundary on the far west of Makrán through the very remotest provinces of Baluchistan where Persian and British interests meet, had little or nothing to do with Afghanistan or the Amir. It was a political legacy bequeathed by the Sistan boundary arbitration of Sir F. Goldsmid, dating from a period previous to the Afghan war. It was this arbitration which set Sher Ali's teeth on edge, and was as an evil savour in the nostrils of the Shah (which sufficiently attests the impartiality of the arbitration), and which was undoubtedly one of the causes of the Afghan war; but this heritage thencefrom had nothing to do with more recent frontier troubles, although it was, to a certain extent, confused and mixed up with the Afghan boundary delimitation. This confusion was but the natural result of two Commissions working in the same corner of Asia at the same time, and pivoting their boundaries on the same point. The Perso-Baluch Commission (of which I had the honour to be Chief Commissioner) arose out of a direct agreement between Her Majesty's Government and the late Shah, and referred to a part of Asia which lies between the Arabian Sea and Afghanistan. But during the winter of 1895–6 an Afghan Boundary Commission under Captain McMahon was also in the field, delimitating the southern border of Afghanistan south of the Helmund, and both Commissions ran their demarcations to a common terminus on the peaks of

THE MALIK SIAH KOH

the Malik Siah Koh, a rugged and remote mountain at the south-west corner of Sistan. Here the three "empires" of Afghanistan, British India, and Persia meet.

Something has already been said about Makrán in these pages, but a trifle more of detailed description may not be out of place to render the story of the Commission intelligible.

North of the steamer route between Karachi and the Persian Gulf (which may yet be an ocean-way between Europe and India) there lies a long strip of southern Baluchistan, bordering the Arabian Sea, which belongs partly to Persia and partly includes outlying districts of the Kalát province of Baluchistan under British agency, and which on its shoreward edge offers to the voyager such uninviting ports as Urmara, Gwadur (which port belongs to Muskat), Charbar, and Jask. These have all been historical places in their day, but their day has passed long since, and they are now but stations of the Indo-Persian telegraph line, or fishing villages inhabited by a mixed race of people as ichthyophagous in their habits as they were in the days of Nearkos. By various routes northward from these ports an interior region is reached which is by no means so hopelessly barren and unattractive as the brazen outlines of the coast scenery might lead one to expect. This country is Makrán proper, with long narrow palm-filled valleys running east and west, and abundant reminiscences of a highly civilised past condensed within the narrow bounds afforded by the gridiron formation of ragged, shaly, knife-backed ridges which hem in contracted valleys in monotonous succession. Beyond the northern edge of the Makrán highlands (say 200 miles from the sea, and due north of the centre of the coast line between Karachi and the Gulf) you look down upon and across the great "hamún" (or salt swamp) of Mashkel. But this Mashkel country is not absolute desert. The "hamún" is the ultimate bourne of several big rivers, including the Mashkel and the Rakshán, which between them drain an enormous area of Makrán south of the "hamún"; and the Bado, a periodic river of some force which flows through Kharan from the east. Round about this "hamun" stretch an infinite series of sand and gravel-covered undulations, without much deep sand, but with occasional patches of "put" (bare, flat alluvium) interspersed with a scanty scrub vegetation everywhere struggling for existence. It is probable that water may be found anywhere in this pseudo-Mashkel desert a few feet below the surface. Herein lie its future possibilities in economic value.

Close on to the south-western edge of the hamun (which is nothing but a vast level expanse of salt-encrusted plain, in winter), and separated by twenty-five to thirty miles of waste from all inhabited districts, is a group of palm groves, the dates of which were said to be of very fine quality. Southern Baluchistan is famous for its dates. The dates of Panjgur are locally considered to be superior to any grown in the Euphrates valley, but the dates of these Mashkel groves by no means sustain the reputation of Panjgur. The groves are not inhabited. They are only visited by their nomadic owners at seasons of fertilisation and harvest, and as these nomadic cultivators (Rekis of Kharán on one side, and Damanis, a tribe of Kurdish extraction from Persia, on the other) are partly subjects of Kalát and partly dwellers within the recognised limits of eastern Persia, they form between them a fine natural field for the propagation of periodic raids and permanent intrigue.

It would be useless to enter into the intricate history which has enveloped these groves during the last fifty years. Matters had arrived at a free-fighting stage when the Government of India stepped in to propose demarcation and arbitration as the panacea for border strife and ill-will.

Nor were these unwholesome date groves the only subjects of dispute between Persia and Kalát. There is a small province called Kohuk closely underlying the southern slopes of the Siahán range south of Mashkel, the ownership of which had long been disputed. Upwards of twenty years ago Goldsmid endeavoured to solve the problem by means of the Sistan Commission. The story of that Commission is a part of Indian history. The difficulties encountered by the British representative in dealing with an arrogant and factious Persian colleague, whilst dependent on Persian sources of supply, and camped on Persian soil, were found to be practically insuperable.

So that whilst the limits of Persian ownership in Sistan were defined, and a line was also drawn from the coast northwards between Persian Baluchistan and Kalát, Kohuk still remained out in the cold. The Shah would not accept the arbitrators' decision, and the final agreement with the Tehran Court left Kohuk and Mashkel, together with a long stretch of frontier to the Helmund, including in all some 300 miles of frontier, undefined and mostly unmapped.

In the history of the unsettled borderland of India twenty years is a long time. Since then the Persians practically settled the question of Kohuk by military occupation, and they had gone on pushing their claims and their raids further and further east until a definite limit to their aggressions became a political necessity.

Meanwhile British sovereignty in Baluchistan had become consolidated and extended. Twenty years had rendered it possible to approach the Persian frontier, and to live on the Persian border, without Persian assistance, and had evolved a new order in that crude and unfinished stretch of Asia which lies between Quetta and Persian Khorasan. All this country had been closely reconnoitred, if not actually surveyed in detail, by the frontier surveyors, and more accurate geographical knowledge revealed many little facts which were neither known, nor even guessed at, twenty years ago. A consulate had been formed at Kirman (the most important town in eastern Persia south of Mashad), and the establishment of this political link between Tehran and India had been attended with the happiest results. It is to the political influence thus acquired, as well as to the possession of sound geographical knowledge, that the rapid success of the efforts of Government to settle once for all the vexations of border disputes with Persia must be ascribed.

Such was the position of affairs when Lord Elgin resolved to add this Persian question to the many boundary anxieties connected with Afghanistan which had been bequeathed to him in so liberal a measure by his predecessor in India. The agreement drawn up between the Persian Government and Sir Mortimer Durand in 1895 was a model boundary convention, involving the minimum of reference to uncertain geography, and permitting the maximum of elasticity to local arbitration, but it left little time to spare for the settlement of so lengthy a line in the brief space of a field season. The Commission was only formed late in January, and it seemed unreasonable to hope that so remote and inhospitable a corner of Baluchistan could be reached, and 300 miles of boundary laid down, before the advent of the hot weather in April rendered further active proceedings in the field impossible.

I do not mean that mere physical heat (although Persians say that eggs can be cooked by setting them on the sun-baked ground in the genial spring months of that climate) would have prevented field work, but that the clear atmosphere which is more or less indispensable to survey observations would give place in spring to haze and duststorms, which would effectually bar further progress.

And it *would* have been impossible, but for the fact that completed maps even of this remote region were already secured, and that their accuracy only required verification. Steadily, year by year, westward from Quetta across the great Kharan desert, over the ragged Makrán peaks, and along the line of Arabian Sea coast, triangulation had been pushed by Tate, Yusuf Sharif, and others; and close on the heels of the triangulators followed the little company of native plane-tablers, climbing over the hills like ants, and leaving no peak, no gully unvisited or unrecorded. It was often dangerous work, and always difficult. A later attempt to carry a more perfect system of geodetic measurement over the same ground was met by a savage attack on the surveyors' camp in which seventeen men were killed. This arose from no real feeling of hostility to the surveyors; it was merely a convenient method of calling attention to a family quarrel in which our native political agent (being but a Hindu amongst Mahomedans) had backed the wrong side. It answered its purpose. A small force was despatched under Colonel Mayne, which for the remarkably prompt and effective manner in which (making light of really formidable difficulties) it settled the dispute and dealt out even-handed justice to the leaders of the attack on the survey camp, deserved far more credit than many a frontier expedition which has made much more noise in the world.

On the 26th January the Commission left Karachi for the Makrán coast. Its formation was compact, its escort most efficient, and the commissariat arrangements organised by the Baluchistan political agency for its support in the field were admirable. There was no excuse for delay and none was wanted. The voyage to Gwadur was made in the telegraph steamer *Patrick Stewart* which faced a stiff "shumal" in quite her best form; and the whole Commission party, men, horses and mules, were rapidly disembarked on the awkward Makrán coast without hitch or accident. Camels were collected with difficulty, but there were enough of them brought together in the course of two days to justify a start northward.

From Gwadur to Kohuk was a twenty days' struggle, in which the record of one day was much the same as that of any other day. The underbred mangy-looking Makrán camels, whose natural flavour is not improved by the traffic in half-rotten fish which is carried on along the coast with their assistance, is not such a fool over the difficult stony tracks of southern Baluchistan as his aristocratic cousin of Sind would be. It is true that he is small and weak almost to inefficiency, but he jerks himself along after the manner of his kind at no very contemptible pace, and he can live on anything, from dried fish to last year's stubble, and still be happy. Insufficient and bad water was the worst trial of the route, and in a dry and thirsty land it is perhaps the most patently aggressive of all trials. But the most persistent and damaging feature of the route was the wear and tear caused by the monotonous recurrence of ridge after ridge of sharp-edged sandstone and clay rock; never very high and never very difficult, but always sharply aggressive, and occasionally bringing the caravan to a halt whilst the Baluch pioneers worked a way either through or round some impossible obstacle.*

The mountain scenery of this part of Makrán is not exhilarating. A dead monotony of laminated clay backbones, serrated like that of a whale's vertebræ, sticking out from the

* The Commission included the following members:—Chief Commissioner Colonel Holdich, C.B., C.I.E., R.E.; Assistant Commissioners Captain A. C. Kemball, I.S.C., Captain P. M. Sykes (Consul at Kirman), Queen's Bays; Survey Officer Colonel Wahab, R.E.; Medical Officer Surgeon-Lieutenant Turnbull; Officer Commanding Escort Lieutenant C. V. Price (now Major Price, D.S.O., who has so greatly distinguished himself in Africa); 120 sepoys 30th Baluch Regiment; 16 sabres 6th Bombay Cavalry.

smoother outlines of mud ridges which slope down on either hand to where a little edging of sticky salt betokens that there is a drainage line when there is water to trickle along it; and a little faded decoration of neutral-tinted tamarisk shadowing the yellow stalks of last year's forgotten grass along its banks—such was the sylvan aspect of a scene which we had before us only too often.

But there were also bright spots where the oleander grew, and pools of water that looked none the worse for being salt; and here and there, a few date palms, where a certain regularity about the setting of the boulders suggested the prehistoric existence of a small hamlet and a few acres of cultivation. This sort of scenery carried us far inland; but as we progressed northward the rule of the road as regards landscape was broken by the broader cultivated valleys which intersect Makrán from east to west. Had we been following up the length of these valleys instead of crossing them at right angles our way would have been plain, and much of our path beautiful. For Makrán is a country of most surprising contrasts. In the direction in which we were travelling (*i.e.* northward from the coast) we only lit on such valleys as Kej, and Bolida, at long intervals. When we did so it was hard to recognise that we were in Makrán at all, so different was the aspect of the country. Instead of the serrated outlines of jagged and barren clay hills, and the white twists of a narrow little pathway woven amongst the rocks, we found ourselves surrounded by palm groves set in the midst of emerald-green crops of young wheat, with here and there a white-crowned citadel overtopping the palm plumes and looking as pretentiously feudal and aristocratic as if it had been built of Scotch granite instead of underdone mud bricks.

The fact is that Makrán is a country about which a man may write much as he pleases and never stray far from the truth. The physical aspect of the land varies so greatly from many points of view, that one ceases to wonder at the equally extraordinary variety of its historical records—records of armies lost in its deserts and perishing from thirst; of triumphant forces marching through the length of it to the conquest of India; of hot, brazen waterless wastes where no living things (not even flies) are found; and of large flourishing cities with the trade of empires passing through their streets. But after all Persia, Baluchistan, Arabia, and Afghanistan are all much the same in this respect. It is not more difficult to evolve in imagination the magnificence of such Makrán cities as Ibn Haukel describes (cities as extensive and as famous in their day as Multán) than to reconstruct the ancient capital of Assyria from the sand heaps of Nineveh; or the mediæval affluence of Hormuz out of the bare, salt-swamped, heat-stricken desolation of the Gulf island shores that now bear its name.

On the 20th February the little Commission party pitched its camp and hoisted the "Jack" just on the borders of the disputed district of Kohuk, a mile or two from that much-discussed village, whose palm groves and towers were just visible amongst the broken ends of the Siahan range. Here they awaited events. The first event to happen was the arrival of a lady in camp. This was not altogether unexpected. We knew that Captain Sykes would be accompanied by his sister, and we were all delighted to welcome so charming an addition to our little company. Miss Sykes has told the tale of her adventurous ride across Persia so recently and so well, that it is not necessary for me to explain that our welcome to a lady as a member of our mess was, in this particular instance, free from all those misgivings which might, under ordinary circumstances, have detracted from its warmth. There are ladies who can face the roughnesses and inconveniences of travel in uncivilised countries as well as, if not better than, most men, and Miss Sykes is one of them. The staff of the Persian Commission were not far behind Captain Sykes and his sister. On the 25th the distant echoes of a brazen trumpet (an instrument of torture with which we rapidly became terribly familiar) announced that the main body of the Commission had actually reached the rendezvous, and that another day would decide the question of mutual agreement (or otherwise) on the terms which should govern the process of demarcation.

The members of the Persian staff who met General Goldsmid on the historical mission of 1873, have left behind them an unfortunate reputation for obstructiveness that is perhaps unequalled even in the annals of Afghan Commissions. Consequently it was with no small interest that the arrival of the representative of the Shah-in-Shah was awaited by us on the banks of the Mashkel river.

Readers of Major St. John's narrative of his reconnaissance along the proposed boundary line from the sea coast to Kohuk may remember his description of the unhappy young man whom he found seated on his baggage on the deck of a Persian Gulf steamer, making his way, penniless and destitute, to join the reconnaissance as co-surveyer on the Persian side. From this description it would have been difficult to recognise St. John's friend in the Itisham-i-Wazireh, Mirza Ali Ashraf (they all have long names in Persia), who now represented His Majesty as Chief Commissioner for the Perso-Baluch boundary settlement. The Itisham was a gentleman of fine and soldierly presence, whose usually grave demeanour was frequently relieved by the light of a passing smile. Clean-shaved, and well set up in his neat uniform of dark frock-coat with ample skirts (short coats are an abomination in Persia, as in Russia) with a close-fitting fez cap of black astrakan, he looked every inch the courtier and the statesman. He wore but one order besides his badge as Sartip (or General) and that order was a Russian one. His training with St. John had not been thrown away; he understood a map well; knew the country he had to deal with, and his criticisms on our surveys (the Persians had none of their own) were always to the point. From first to last he showed a sincere wish to conduct negotiations in a spirit of good-fellowship, and to work as close to his Tehran instructions as circumstances would admit. It is satisfactory to add that the end which he so cordially assisted to promote was altogether satisfactory, and that his subsequent reception at the Court of Tehran was considerably better than that which he experienced on his return from St. John's mission. On that occasion his hard-won records were thrown at him!

Zain-ul-Abadin, the Asad-u-Dowlah and Governor of Persian Baluchistan, entered largely into the composition of the Persian Commission. He was a small wiry man with no teeth and a passion for Worcester sauce. As the practical master of ceremonies; the provider of troops, of supplies, transport and equipment; as warden of the marches; the counterpart (as he was fond of explaining) of Sir James Browne at Quetta, he was doubtless an important personage. At least he had no doubt about it himself, and he possibly felt himself in danger of being overshadowed in his own domain by the Itisham, who was, so to speak, the "shadow of the Shah." Precedence is everything in Persia, and the "Asad" was careful to maintain his dignity. He rode with his horse's head a yard or so in front of the Itisham's steed; he received all the local honours of "istikbál"—that miscellaneous show of led horses, mounted beadles, irregular camelry, and general turn-out of the population which meets a great man before he arrives at his destination and precedes him thither; and he, and he only, possessed a private band.

This is an item in the support of the proper dignity of a Boundary Commission which the British Government has always strangely overlooked; but it is usually a distinguished feature of the "opposition," whether Russian, Afghan, or Persian. In this instance the band was of quite unusual force. It was clothed in a fore-and-aft raiment of red and black, *i.e.* it was half red and half black (with a perpendicular division) in front, and the same when viewed from the rear; but the fore-and-aft halves did not correspond. On the whole it was effective, especially at night, when lit up by red lights on the banks of a clear running stream, surrounded by all the glamour of an *al fresco* Persian entertainment. As for the music of that band it would take a better pen than mine to describe it.

> "It was wild, it was fitful, as wild as the breeze,
> It wandered about into several keys;
> It was jerky, spasmodic, and yet I declare
> There was something distinctly resembling an air"

now and then, but chiefly when "God save the Queen" was played.

The cavalry of the "Asad's" retinue was really too irregular to be classed as cavalry at all, but the infantry and artillery possessed uniform enough to admit of official inspection. The former were an active-looking and well set up body of men armed with breech-loading rifles. The latter consisted of one breech-loading mule gun of complicated construction, but I forget of what nationality. It was useful for saluting purposes only.

Next in local rank to the "Asad," but first in social dignity, was the Shah's cousin, Prince Suliman Mirza, a Persian of the Persians, student of the *école militaire* at Tehran, speaking French well, and dabbling in the sciences. The French polish of his irreproachable manners was perhaps more perfect than his Parisian accent. He afforded an excellent example of that *rapprochement* between French and Persian in their social methods which is so marked a feature in the Persian aristocracy. Prince Suliman Mirza in full uniform was a whole constellation in himself. His collection of decorations, which blazed from shoulder to shoulder, bore testimony equally to his diligence as a scholar, and his valiant bearing as a soldier. With all the affability of a true courtier, he never forgot that he was a prince.

Haji Khan, the good-natured medical adviser of the Persian staff, deserves to be had in kindly remembrance for his cheery good humour, and his knowledge of the English language "as she is spoke" in London. He passed through certain medical schools in England, and was taught dancing at a ladies' establishment in Notting Hill. Haji Khan's reminiscences would add an entertaining chapter to those of the immortal Haji Baba.

In such company times could hardly have been slow even if official business had failed to progress. But as a matter of fact official relations were on the whole all that could be desired, and not an unnecessary day was lost in demarcating the boundary from Kohuk to the Helmund. The progress of the Commission from the day that the first marks were set up at either end of the line (the one on a high and barren hill overlooking the Mashkel river, and the other on a peak of the historical Koh-i-Malik Siah) till we crowned the final edifice in the midst of the sandy wastes north-west of the "hamún," was uninterrupted when once the great question of precedence had been decided.

This is indeed a matter of immense, almost paramount, importance to every Persian, from the Shah to his cook; and in this case, on the first meeting of the joint Commission it involved most serious consideration. I had not forgotten the difficulties involved by the dependence of the Goldsmid Commission on the goodwill and support of the local Persian authorities whilst they were camped on Persian soil. So I took care not to be on Persian soil, but kept the broad sandy bed of the Mashkel river between my own camp and the Persians, until this knotty point had been settled. The Persian camp had not been pitched a day over against the British camp, before it was whispered amongst the tents of Iran that Captain Sykes (the Consul at Kirman) had visited the tent of the Commissioner at least three times and that his visit had not been returned. Now Captain Sykes, well knowing Persian ways, had specially warned me *not* to return his visit. Evidently then from the Persian point of view the Consul at Kirman was not a magnate of such dimensions as the Commissioner. What then? Would they all of them, Itisham, Governor of Persian Baluchistan, and Prince of the royal blood, be expected to pay the first call on the British Commissioner! Thus did a great social question assume a critical phase even in the remotest wilds of Baluchistan. It was debated in the Persian camp with much warmth and fervour of language, the debate lasting through the length of a blazing day, and extending to the small hours of the night-watches without any satisfactory conclusion being reached.

It was argued that I was but a common colonel who made obeisance to the Great General (Browne) who ruled in British Baluchistan, and that the "Asad" (it was always the Asad who was in opposition) was at least as high a dignitary as General Browne. To this there was but the simple statement (duly represented by those who watched proceedings on behalf of the British Commission) that whatever my rank might be, on this occasion I represented Her Majesty the Queen, and on no consideration whatever could I descend to the impropriety of paying the first visit. Here was a deadlock threatened at the very outset! Finally the Asad-u-Dowlah asserted with much emphatic declamation that whatever happened *he* was not going to call first; but the Itisham (the Commissioner, that is to say, with whom alone I was officially concerned) consented to call provided his visit was returned the same day, and in full uniform. To this I assented. I knew what would happen. It was not long before the brazen tones of that most discordant trumpet announced that the whole Persian official staff down to the bandmaster (the Asad could not bring himself at the last moment to be left out of the "tamasha"—no Persian could) was winding and twisting its way across the boulders and white sand drifts of the Mashkel towards my camp. Thus was the rule of British precedence maintained so far, and great care was taken to ensure its maintenance thereafter by never accepting from the Persian side anything whatsoever beyond those courtesies and civilities which each occasion of meeting demanded.

If the first interviews were formal and official they were certainly amicable, and they were at once followed by the first invitation to dinner, which again emanated from the British camp, and was accepted by the Persians. When this last entertainment (which with the assistance of Captain Sykes and his accomplished sister passed off exceedingly well) was over, and the Persian guests rode away in the bright moonlight behind one of the largest paper lanterns ever seen out of a pantomime, it was felt that a sound social basis had at least been secured, and that no further difficulties need be anticipated for the present.

The first official durbar, or meeting, to discuss the business of the Commission took place on the 27th February, leaving space which was certainly little enough for the demarcation of 300 miles of boundary ere the full blast of the fiery heat of a southern Baluchistan summer was turned on us. It was necessary to adopt a *modus operandi* that would ensure the least possible delay. We knew that of all physical terrors that of great heat is predominant in the Persian mind. Persia, as a whole, is not a hot country. It can in certain remote borders like those of Baluchistan and on the edges of the Persian Gulf, hold its own for heat against the worst passages of Sind, but the high level of the greater part of the interior of Persia ensures moderation in temperature, and even tends rather to extreme cold than to extreme heat, where extremes are recorded at all. It was not in the least necessary to urge the disadvantages of a summer demarcation. We could indeed almost pretend that we rather liked the idea of it, than not, and that on the whole we were quite prepared to stay in so charming a locality for such indefinite period as might suit the convenience of our Persian colleagues. If they were prepared to commence surveys of their own, we were prepared to wait for them; but as we had already completed our own mapping we should be able meanwhile to take things easy.

On the other hand, if our Persian colleague would be content to accept our mapping with such examination *in situ* here and there as he might judge to be expedient in order to assure himself of its accuracy, we could begin pillar-building at once, on the basis of the agreement. Not only so, but we could point out a splendidly definite and well-situated topographical line throughout the greater part of its length which would meet the terms of the agreement, and (excepting only the disputed tracts in the Mashkel hamún where the date groves grew) we might commence demarcation from both ends at once. Would he accept the mapping, and could we come to terms about the chain of natural features which we should adopt to represent the boundary? It was a hot day even then. The sun glared and blazed with unremitting fervour on the cracked clay slopes and the shiny black surface of the volcanic rock which split them here and there. Little spiral columns of dust (the "shaitáns" of the desert) sped across the flat, and the whole world slept an apoplectic sleep, while the horses cracked the hard knots of the dry "dharm shok" grass, and chewed the resulting toothpicks with half-closed eyes. I think the heat settled it—that and the fact that the Itisham had been on survey duty before with St. John. He knew what climbing up red-hot hills meant, and he also knew that accurate or not as the sahib's maps might be, it was not in his power to quarrel with them.

So he bargained for a strict examination into detail which was to be conducted by His Highness Prince Suliman Mirza, and provisionally decided that we should begin at both ends. Before next evening two surveying and demarcative detachments were off. One under Colonel Wahab, to which Suliman Mirza was attached, made for the jagged crest of the Siahán. The other under one of the ablest of my native surveyors, with a Persian colleague who was added for the sake of appearances (but who gave up any attempt at appearance soon after), trekked away northward on fast camels for the Koh-i-Malik Siah, where the Persian boundary ran itself to ground in Afghanistan.

So far as the northern section was concerned no further difficulty arose. Black and straight the outer line of ridges forming the western limits of the Helmund desert runs, from north to south, broken once or twice by the drainage which breaks through from the westward, but split by such narrow rifts as to form no practical break in its continuity. And where this ends, a hill-born nullah twists itself outwards through the sand drifts and dunes of the waste and barren desert till it touches the disputed Mashkel date cultivation. Barren ridge and broken nullah-bed, set in the midst of an uninhabited, almost untraversed wilderness, are as good a definition of where Persia ends and Makrán begins as this imperfect world could devise. It only remained to set up a mark here and there.

So with the southern end, once we had done with Kohuk. The Siahán is an admirable provision of nature in favour of boundary makers, and it carried us westward and northward till we came to the great debateable ground. This we reserved for future consideration. No time was lost in shifting the scene of operations, and on the 28th the combined camps started for the districts of Jalk and Mashkel, which lie north of the Siahán range.

For full three days the route lay across the stony undulations of the southern foot-hills of the Siahán, towards Isfandak. At Isfandak we were again gladdened by the sight of green cultivation and palm trees. Isfandak is one of the small oases of southern Baluchistan, and a pleasant refuge from diurnal dust-storms. The Persians made the most of it. Wherever there grew a good tree on a shady bank there would certainly be pitched one of the quaint tents of the Persian staff. No matter that by this means room could hardly be found for three tents in a straight line. They got the shade, and they could perchance enjoy the ripple of a stream at their tent doors. We could not. Our notions of military smartness prevented us from enjoying such amenities of camp life, and our tents stood in stiff straight lines out in the sun-glare.

From Isfandak, over the Bonsar pass, and through the date groves of Kalagán to Jalk, there was a variation from the monotony of stony hills and stonier plains. Water was running with refreshing abundance in the Kalagán valley. There was no haunting suspicion that it might run dry in a week or so, for it spread out into swamps with tall reeds and grass, and snipe in the midst of it. At intervals down the Kalagán valley there appeared forts protecting a small cluster of white mud-built houses surrounded by palms, and rich with fields of wheat and beans encompassing orchards of pomegranates, figs, and mulberries. Kalagán is as picturesque in detail as some of the Himalayan valleys; the pity of it is that there is so little of it.

But of all the surprises that awaited us on our journey, perhaps Jalk itself was the greatest. From the debouchment of the Kalagán into the Mashkel plain, wide, arid, gravelly "dasht" stretches away towards Jalk, streaked with the usual vitreous and volcanic-looking hills (there is probably nothing volcanic about these subsidiary ranges, although, from the summits of some of them, the smoking volcano of Koh-i-Taftán, or Chihiltan, may be descried in the far north-west) and this plain slopes gradually to the great central hamún of Mashkel. On closely approaching Jalk, after a blazing ride of some twelve miles across the open gravel plain, some point is given to the landscape by a few square-built ruins which are all that remain of the tombs of those Maliks who governed the Kaiáni kingdom till they were ruthlessly driven out of it by Nadir Shah. They appear to be standing as a solitary and desolate group in the midst of unending plain. On approaching the tombs, however, some care is necessary, as with a few incautious steps beyond them one might almost tumble headlong on to Jalk.

In a hollow depression worked out by ages of erosion, and extending over many square miles, lies this extraordinary oasis. Down the middle of it flows an abundant stream trained here and there into canals for purposes of palm irrigation, and spreading into wide grassy spaces of swamp land through which it is impossible to trace its course. The river runs out far beyond the cultivated fields of Jalk into the open Mashkel plain for a distance of ten miles or more, and affords a supply of sweet clear water far in excess of the requirements of the whole inhabited district.

This extraordinary abundance of water locally is difficult to explain. It appears to be a survival of a far more extended condition of water supply in southern Baluchistan than now exists. There is widespread evidence of former cultivation by an elaborate system of irrigation in so many parts of southern Baluchistan (where it is vain to hope that such cultivation will ever exist again) that it seems as if some mighty change must have come over the land thus to render so much of it waterless. It may be due to forest denudation and cessation of rainfall, but, more likely, it is due to the gradual exhaustion of those subterranean sources which seem to be still prevalent throughout more northern districts.

The Jalk water comes to the surface again after being lost in the desert in the Mashkel date groves, thirty miles away to the east, on the edge of the hamún, and would probably be found a few feet below the surface in any part of the intervening plain. Some dozen closely packed villages are scattered throughout the Jalk depression, some hidden amongst date palms, others asserting themselves by tower or citadel overtopping the trees. The inhabitants of these villages know little or nothing of the rest of Baluchistan, spending their lives in tilling their fields of wheat and beans, collecting their fruit in due season, and paying up taxes heavy in proportion to the extreme fertility of their remote oasis.

Under the palm trees of Jalk, by the waters of the canals, the Persians pitched their camp. Here they built up small enclosures, and, by damming the canals, they formed little artificial lakes or ponds by the side of which they could smoke the "kalián" of contentment, and leave business to take care of itself, or to be taken care of by the sahibs. They were philosophers to a man.

From Jalk the British Commission party spread out in detachments to complete the surveys in detail, and to demarcate through the date groves and waste places of Mashkel. This was the most difficult knot to unravel in the whole proceedings. It was these date groves (which proved to be vastly inferior to those of Jalk owing to the saline nature of the soil in which they maintain their precarious existence) which formed the real bone of contention between Kharán and eastern

Persia. With some difficulty, owing to the persistent interference of the Asad-u-Dowlah, an understanding was at last effected; and then came the question of demarcation, for here, at any rate, artificial marks were a necessity.

It is not easy to devise an artificial mark that is quite satisfactory in a desert subject to wind-blown sand. Any small obstruction is likely to form the nucleus of a sand dune, and to be lost to sight possibly in the course of a few months. So we were obliged to raise mounds large enough to be recognisable even amidst sand drifts, and to arrange with the local authorities for their preservation and protection as far as might be possible. All this meant time and labour, and much endurance on the part of the officers who had to carry it out; but with the willing assistance of the sepoys of the escort and of a small army of workmen who daily turned out from Jalk, it was finally accomplished, and the division between Persia and Kharán was at length effected.

For about three years all southern Baluchistan had suffered from drought. The rainfall had been scanty, and such crops as were not supported by irrigation had failed, whilst the want of water had nearly destroyed the flocks of the nomad Baluchis. It would have been almost impossible for large parties to move far from the line of water-supply, and most difficult to cover so large an area destitute of water and forage had it been necessary (as is usually the case on Boundary Commissions) to make the maps *ab initio*. Fortunately it was not necessary; and thus, in the course of a few weeks between the 25th February and the 24th March, when the final maps and agreement were signed, very nearly 300 miles of boundary (divided in its course between mountains and deserts) was laid down.

The headquarters of both Commissions were concentrated at Jalk for about a fortnight, and during that interval the interchange of hospitalities, regulated by the strictest etiquette, was frequent. The Persians are well-known artists in all matters affecting their cuisine, and their entertainments were excellent. The accessories and allurements of music and illumination were always carefully arranged. Nothing could have been prettier than the fantastic effects of red lights and Chinese lanterns flecking the palms with a coloured patchwork, and glinting on the surface of the little artificial ponds which framed round the central pavilion. The scarlet tent with its lettering of blue and its blue fringes took up tints of purple and orange, and the antique clothing of that immortal band, when artfully illuminated, was equal to the setting of a whole *al fresco* ballet.

Either Horace was wrong, or times have changed since he wrote the song commencing "Persicos odi."

The settlement was not effected without strong opposition, in spite of all my efforts to keep the whole Persian staff perpetually busy, and to allow as little time as possible for the hatching of obstruction. Delay is the root of all evil when dealing with Asiatics. The particular Satan who finds mischief for idle hands is much busier in Persian councils than in European nurseries, and one great secret of our rapid success certainly lay in the fact that references to Government on either side were unnecessary, and irritating delays were thus avoided. For this we had to thank Sir M. Durand, the framer of the agreement at Tehran.

But the strong position taken up by the Asad-u-Dowlah in the Persian Commission was distinctly inconvenient. He was always ready with an objection, and always suspicious. He carried his suspicions even to the extent of bringing his own chair with him when he sat in durbar; and when, on one occasion, his own selected seat collapsed with him, no one smiled, but we all regarded it as a righteous retribution. He finally threatened to leave the Persian Commissioner stranded and solitary in the desert if he signed the final agreement. It then became necessary to take measures to secure the Itisham from personal inconvenience, which we could never have done had we ourselves been dependent on Persian support for our existence in the desert.

The deep-seated animosity which existed between Gujjar (or Persian) and Baluch was also a source of occasional anxiety, although it was not always apparent. But it broke out at last when the labours of the Commission had ended, and the two camps were associated in a local gymkhana. There was but a day to spare before we finally parted for east and west, and so I thought that a friendly meeting might be permitted for the purpose of witnessing the well-known skill of the Persians in all athletic pursuits. It would have passed off well enough but for the wrestling. It happened that special point had been made of this particular contest, as each side boasted a local champion. To the credit of the Persian it must be maintained that he was not only a fine "figure of a man," but a real sportsman. He was prepared to take on the belt-holder of Sind on any terms he pleased. But the Sind champion finally declined the trial, and a less renowned wrestler took his place. What the result would have been I know not, for long before the umpire's decision could be given the atmosphere became thick with sticks and stones, and there was a passing prospect of a free and dangerous fight. Fortunately this little interlude was speedily brought to a conclusion by the officers on either side, but not before the Asad-u-Dowlah had been rudely crushed by one of his own bandsmen. The proceedings finally closed harmoniously—but there was an account to be squared between the Governor of Baluchistan and his escort which afforded us an excellent insight into Persian methods of maintaining military discipline.

The outraged chief issued orders that the whole of his force was to be bastinadoed, and the whole force thereupon went into "bast." "Bast" means "sanctuary," and "going into bast" is taking refuge under the protection, it may be, of a flag (as for example the British flagstaff of the Persian Gulf telegraph stations is always "bast" for runaway slaves) or a gun, or within the limits of some specially reserved portion of a town. In this instance there was happily a recognised "bast" near the Persian camp. This was a member of Captain Sykes' stud, a cantankerous Australian horse, who had often acted in a similar capacity before at Kirman, when one of the Consul's servants was called upon to "eat stick." He apparently knew his position, and was always prepared to take protective measures in favour of his friends. So the Persian force went into "bast" as well as it could behind this "waler"; and the Governor was powerless to get it out again! It only remained for Captain Sykes to maintain the inviolable nature of his "bast," and a formal proclamation of forgiveness had to be issued. Thus we all parted company finally on terms of mutual friendship and goodwill.

The march back to Quetta through southern Baluchistan was eventless. Southern Baluchistan had by this time adopted the dead-level monotone of neutral "khaki," merging into the undecided tints of a faded scrub vegetation. The hills were only surprised into streaks of transient glory when sunset turned their jagged lines into visions of scarlet and purple. But sunset can do anything in that way.

Passing through the oasis of Panjgur we gradually rose to the level of the Kalát highlands, and from here to Quetta late spring had dressed up the fields and orchards with all the beauty of wild flowers and fruit blossoms, and our daily march became a daily delight. We were thankful to leave behind us the desiccated wastes of southern Baluchistan, in spite of the interest which ancient relics of the early Arab occupation of the country never failed to arouse, and the speculations to which they never failed to give birth. We were cool once again, and we were also beyond the range of the wind fiend.

The climate of Baluchistan is made up of eccentricities and strong contrasts, but there is one phenomenon which we had always with us, and that was wind. There is a country to the north-west of Herat which is justly called Badghis (the home of the wind). There the yearly vegetation is actually scraped off the surface of the soil by the autumn blasts, and finally rolled up and washed into the great Oxus plains. And there are the Pamirs also, where at certain seasons if the wind is not shaped by the hills into a wild shrieking blast down the length of the valleys, it is only because it is shrieking up them. One way or other it is ever on the move. But I regard the wind of southern Baluchistan during the spring months as worse than either. It has no respect even for the hours of the night.

There was one memorable night in the valley of the Kalagán when it really seemed as if the historic contest between Hiawatha and Madgikeewis were renewed, and that those two immortal heroes, once again on the warpath, had selected that remote valley for the final conflict. It was night, and our tents rocked and swayed with the blasts, straining at the doubled tent pegs, until we decided that the camp could not possibly last till dawn. Sadly we packed up all our traps in the dark, and bitterly thought of the morrow, when we should be left tentless and homeless in that inhospitable land. We crawled into the mess tent which was reckoned to be the most secure, and the tearing howling blasts rocked it to and fro, whistling in under the edges of the kanats and ever and anon inflating it like a balloon, as we huddled as far to windward as we could to avoid the weight of the pole when the final collapse should arrive. But it never arrived. The fury of the gale suddenly subsided, and the riot finished with a hissing shower of rain.

On the morrow we went round to gather up the fragments, and found that so far as the British camp was concerned the damage was comparatively small. Sholdaries had been ripped to pieces, and a good many inferior bamboo poles had been smashed; and the one lady who graced our camp was hunting for various articles of her toilette in a neighbouring wheat field; but all the larger tents had been spared. This was probably due to the extra precautions that experience had shown us were necessary. The Persian camp had gone. The angels of the wind had borne it aloft, and the inhabitants of it were sitting huddled together, and sad, on the banks of the Kalagán.

Daily gales, and daily dust and sand deposits, became a familiar feature. When they ceased we missed them. Possibly we gained by the moderation of temperature which the wind effected, but it was an alleviation with which we would gladly have dispensed.

It has generally been considered that Makrán and southern Baluchistan is a country unsuited to horses and mules, so it may be worth recording here that we did not find it so. It was a particularly dry season when the Commission took the field. There had been no rain to speak of for three years, and yet from Gwadur to the Persian border, and from the Persian border to Kalát, we never failed to find a fair supply of a certain kind of grass called "dharm shok," which camels and sheep refuse, but which is, in spite of its most unattractive appearance, nourishing fodder for horses. Above a certain altitude this grass is not to be had, and throughout the plateau regions there was much difficulty about fodder; but in Makrán itself, and in desert places beyond Makrán, where sheep were dying for want of food, we still found supplies of "dharm shok."

What was far more deleterious to the well-being of our horses was the extreme roughness of the country. From the jagged, ragged, crag-crowned hills to the stony desolation of the wearisome flats, it was all the same—an unending struggle against sharp-edged sandstone strata, flinty boulders and three-cornered limestone nodules. No ordinary hoofs can stand it, and travellers will do well to observe that the Persian shoe, which has a wide protecting overlap for the heel, is the one which answers best in Makrán, though it is possibly not to be commended elsewhere.

When one turns to the ancient history of the first attempts to explore that far-away frontier and define the limits of Persian authority, one can but wonder at the change which has been wrought by a quarter of a century of progress on both sides—and prophesy a new departure in local border politics. In no part of north-western India from Persia to the Pamirs have I heard expressed such a thirsty longing, not only for the "pax," but for the "lex" Britannica; and such confidence in the power of the British Sirkar to remove the yoke of misrule and anarchy from the necks of the people. Nor can there be a doubt that the same sentiment extends far over the Baluchistan border into Persia. Whilst so much of the savagery of human nature remains, it would be idle to expect a radical change all at once; but as time moves on, and local responsibilities become recognised (that is to say if we insist on their recognition), we shall hear less and less of raids and reprisals, of the cowardly murder of defenceless shepherds on the hillsides to make up the balance of a blood feud; no more sneaking pillaging of date groves or destruction of scanty crops; and the full benefits of boundary demarcation will become very much more apparent here than they have hitherto been elsewhere on the Indian frontier.

With a political representation at Mashad and Kirman, and an open road for trade between Quetta and Sistan, south-eastern Persia is well safeguarded from an overflow of Russian influence for the present: but it still remains for us to make better use of our opportunities in Makrán. So far as the geographical position of Makrán affects the question of frontier strategy, it is very obvious that so long as we retain command of the Persian Gulf, Makrán lies outside the area of possible military significance. Thus it becomes merely a matter of preserving law and order in border districts, of avoiding the necessity for such local campaigns as that which was lately conducted by Colonel Mayne, and of developing the economic resources of the country. Makrán is capable of such development. The date cultivation is important, rather for the excellent quality of the fruit, than for its extent. Makrán wool has been famous from the Middle Ages; and Makrán is one of the few districts left where camel-breeding might be maintained on a large scale. None of these possibilities are unimportant or undeserving of consideration, but none can hope for any permanent development without security; and that security can only come by the introduction of British political authority in some higher form than that which is represented by a native assistant. There is no "forward policy" about this. Makrán leads to nowhere in particular, and is already subject to British control more or less, but it is capable of being made very useful to India at a very small expense by the introduction of British knowledge and energy properly applied locally. It will be applied in time, no doubt, but it is a pity that we should wait so long.

CHAPTER XV

NORTH-WEST FRONTIER

The rising on the north-west frontier and Tirah campaign—The Amir's attitude—Causes of rising—Misapprehension about the boundary—Turkish influences—The Tochi disaster—Rise of Swatis—Malakand—Rise of Mohmands—Shabkadir—Orakzais and Afridis—Lundi Kotal—Samana.

BY the summer of 1897 (the year of the Diamond Jubilee—and surely one of the most troublous years in all Indian history) the whole north-west frontier from the Gomul river to the hills south of Chitral was in a condition of seething irritation. South of the Gomul the independent tribes of the Baluchistan borderland remained peacefully unaggressive. The new boundaries of Afghanistan were nothing to them. We were already beyond and behind them, keeping guard over their back doors. Already the way was closed to intrigue and mischievous philandering with Afghanistan; and their sanctuary, in case of unsuccessful conflict with the British Sirkar, was shut off for good. But from the Gomul northwards, the paths which ran westward were still open, although a boundary line indicated by piles of stones had been drawn across their hills to show that theoretically they were shut, and that beyond that line they might appeal no more to people of their own faith and their own language in times of difficulty and disaster. How should they understand that their independence was not only not threatened by such a line, but actually more effectively secured to them? All they could see was a boundary placed between themselves and Afghanistan; and they assumed that it was a British frontier boundary as surely as it was an Afghan boundary. And undoubtedly they were carefully taught by their priests that this was so.

Beyond them amongst the far-away hills of Kabul, looking

westward from the shadow of Baba's tomb over the rich and varied landscape of Chardeh, sat the great autocrat of Afghanistan, deep thinking how best to instigate a policy of artful interference with the hated boundary demarcation, which damaged his high prerogatives and lowered his prestige in the eyes of the faithful, without committing himself overtly or perilling his boundary subsidy. He had lately written a book called the *Twakim-ud-din* setting forth the essential characteristics of a jehad or holy war as enjoined by the Korán. It was a harmless book enough under ordinary circumstances—a book which merely rehearsed doctrines already laid down by the prophet—but it was inopportune. It was not the time for one of the greatest Mahomedan rulers in the world to put a new interpretation of that part of the Mussulman creed which specially enjoins the extinction of the infidel. Further he instituted a religious convocation, assembling at his Court all the chief mullahs and religious men of influence in his kingdom. What was it that he wished to teach them at that special time?

But, after all, the demarcation of the boundary was not the only disturbing influence abroad, though it was the one which appealed most directly to the passions of the frontier tribespeople. At Wana, where the northern demarcation commenced, the Waziris had shown us what they thought about it; at Chitral the active agency in the whole complicated plot was Afghan, and the boundary was again at the bottom of it. Afghan soldiers had helped in the siege; Umra Khan (himself an Afghan) had at once patched up a truce with Ghulam Haidar, and Sher Afzal had been let loose from Kabul. These things were not accidents. Those who say that Ghulam Haidar (the "Red Prince" of the Kunar) was acting in direct hostility to the Amir's good intentions towards us are strangely ignorant of the length of the Amir's arm and the weight of his blows. Ghulam Haidar went, perhaps, a little too far—and paid for his temerity.

But there were still other widespread and far-reaching influences abroad at that time—influences which touched not only Afghanistan but the whole Mussulman population of the world, and they all spelt unrest and disaffection.

It is hard, very hard, to get to the back of the Mahomedan mind when questions of religious import are at stake. How far that belief in the final universal domination of the Crescent which many profess to entertain, is a popular article of faith on the border, I doubt whether any living soul can tell. But if ever there has been a time in late Indian history when there appeared to be a faint indication on the horizon of a glorious uprising of the planet of Islam, it was during the year preceding the frontier troubles. Wholesale massacres of Christians had undoubtedly taken place at the hands of the Mahomedans, and still the great Mahomedan potentate of the world retained his balance on his uneasy seat in spite of his responsibility for the massacres. I have heard it said that had England made a bold move at that time and deposed the Sultan, no combined Mahomedan action would have occurred on the Indian frontier. I do not believe it. Local irritation was far too acute for that; but such retribution would certainly have deprived the preaching mullahs of one of their most effective texts; and it should be remembered that the fanatical fervour of that preaching lost nothing subsequently by the success of Turkey against Greece.

There was undoubtedly a spirit of religious crusade in the air which unsettled the minds of men who had yet to wait for the crushing blow of Omdurman. Turkish emissaries are said to have left Constantinople for India, and correspondence between the mullahs of the frontier and the mullahs of Delhi is known to have taken place. Still it was a half-hearted, disjointed, undecisive effort if it is to be regarded as a religious revival. No well-educated Mahomedan believes in the Sultan as Khalifa to begin with; he is not of the Khoreish tribe. The Amir does not acknowledge him as Khalifa, and he officially promptly discredited the idea of a jehad, in spite of his book. But the mullahs preached jehad all the same, and they took for their text the late success of the arms of the prophet in Europe, exaggerating the details and clothing the actual truth in such disguise, that many of their ignorant hearers believed that the time was ripe for the downfall of British sovereignty in India.

The next outbreak after Wana and Chitral was in the Tochi valley, which lies just north of Waziristan and south of Kuram.

It has usually been supposed that the Tochi valley affair was not part of the general plan of protest against any threatened loss of independence, but the result of a wretched tribal quarrel, involving a story so complicated with deceit that it is impossible to unravel its mysterious threads. There is much to support the view that the Tochi rising was more or less unpremeditated. Not even the ethics of Pathan existence admit of such gross treachery as was practised then. The crooked code of honour which the Pathan maintains does not admit of an invitation to breakfast being followed by a volley, so that it certainly seemed as if some plot had miscarried which had not been matured with deliberate murder in view. But the murderers were Waziris, and we cannot overlook Wana (a Waziri fight) and the Waziri deputations to Kabul; or ignore the significance of such an outbreak at such a time.

Happily it furnished the opportunity for one of those brilliant displays of courage and endurance on the part of our native troops which go far to balance the temporary eclipse of British political prestige. The treacherous murder of our brave officers at Maizar in June was to a certain extent avenged at the time; for it is said that the Mada Khel lost 100 of their clan, including four mullahs and one chief, during the retreat of the Sikh detachment. It was subsequently punished by an expedition which lasted through the summer and finally occupied their country, under General Corrie Bird. But the Mada Khel made straight tracks for Afghanistan, where they lay snug till the tyranny of the British reprisals was overpast. There was a safe asylum for them beyond the border, and the existence of a boundary pillar more or less made no difference to them—though it made much to us. They probably got more punishment from the Sikhs whom they surprised, than from the army that went in search of them. And that army endured the most harassing and wearying of all campaigns, watching and waiting for an enemy who was never to be seen, through the long sickly summer and autumn season; until at last the promise was made to the blood-stained clan that no one should be hanged for the deadly work of June, if only they would leave Afghanistan (where we could not follow them) and surrender on our side of the newly-made boundary.

A month elapsed, and then the smouldering embers of Pathan hostility broke out in a new quarter.

No part of our Indian frontier is so full of the mystery of romance as the highlands of Bajaor and Swat to the north of the Peshawur valley. It was through this land that the ancient roads to India ran from Kabul; it was here that the great conquerors of India, who slew kings and established dynasties, first interested themselves in the subjugation of outlying tribes before descending from the hills to gather the wealth of the plains of India. And yet, some ten years ago we knew nothing of Swat or Bajaor, or the country of the Mohmands, or of Buner, beyond such reports as were brought to us by a few intrepid native explorers, and the tale that McNair had to tell after his journey to the borders of Kafirstan. Since the Khaibar had become the recognised high road to Kabul, all that lay north of it had been left in geographical obscurity.

And yet from Peshawur the three-headed peak is distinctly visible which marks the mountain once called Meros (now Koh-i-Mor), the mountain of the wild vine and the ivy, where Alexander sacrificed to his gods, and on the slopes of which lay Nysa, that city of a people who claimed him as a compatriot. From Nysa, in days that were traditional (even in Alexander's time), issued Bacchanalian processions, with skin-dressed votaries, waving spears encircled with ivy, chanting hymns (as indeed they are chanted to this day by certain of the Kafirs) to Dionysos, the god who sprung from the three-horned mountain. Here afterwards, in the plains of the east, were concentrated the wisdom and philosophy of a great Budhist school of teachers; when monasteries and stupas and all the magnificent structural symbols of that great faith crowned the hills, and looked over the peaceful valleys. Then came the destroying angel of Ghazni, and he swept out the infidels and laid waste their high places, and turned their cities into a wilderness and a desert—and so it remained for hundreds of years whilst the rhinoceros dwelt in the swamps of the Indus, and wolves took possession of the fields.

To us, some ten years ago, it was all a geographical riddle; but much was done to disentangle the confusion which existed in our maps during the Chitral relief expedition. Much however still remained to be done at a later season.

All had been peaceful in Swat since 1895. The country had prospered since then; roads had increased the traffic and the Afghan (*i.e.* Yusafzai) population had accepted the advent of the British, after one fierce struggle, with calm philosophy—especially when the British disappeared again from the plains and contented themselves with overlooking Swat from the heights of Malakand.

Towards the end of July, 1896, however rumours began to circulate in the Malakand bazar. A fakir, or mullah, had arisen in the northern hills (called sometimes the mad fakir, sometimes the bareheaded one), and he had concealed behind him a vast array of chariots and horsemen in the valleys and glens—a host such as no man might number. These he fed with miraculous food, and with them he was to uproot the infidel and thrust him back into the plains of the Punjab. The mad fakir was real enough, though his army was lacking. He was a preacher who had spent many years in Afghanistan and had lived at Kabul. He was a friend and ally of Hajab-u-din, the mullah of Hada (Hada is a pretty village which may be seen to the west from the walls of the fort at Jalalabad, and was once a Budhist centre of some importance in the Ningrahar valley), who also came from Kabul, but who was busy just then in the Mohmand country north of the Khaibar. They both started on their pernicious pilgrimage from Kabul. Who started them? This no man can say.

The mad mullah did not receive much encouragement at first, and his following was but a mixed crowd of unarmed peasants and boys when he first appeared at Thana. Thana is a big village piled onto the slopes of the hills over against Chakdara—the advanced post of Malakand, down in the valley beyond the pass.

Here his following rapidly increased. He is said to have declared boldly that if he could get no one to fight with him he would go by himself to the capture of the infidel position; he boasted that he was supported by high heaven, and that presently Allah would send him legions of angels who would descend on the fateful fort of Malakand and utterly destroy it. But of course if the Thana folk were unwilling to join him they could not expect to share in the plunder. That settled it. The mob behind him speedily numbered thousands, and, striking while the iron was hot, he went straight for Malakand. It is said that the Khan of Thana discreetly followed in a tonga along the British road to see what might happen. Chakdara was to be rushed in their progress.

Neither Chakdara nor Malakand are irreproachable if regarded as military positions—the latter especially favoured a sudden attack, for its immediate front is hampered with gigantic masses of rock and boulders, behind which a whole army might be easily concealed. The story of that night attack, and the gallant defence which followed, has been better told than I can tell it, for I was not there. So fierce was the fanatical fervour of that half-armed mob that General Meiklejohn has told me that he saw unarmed boys and men actually turning on the cavalry and attacking them with sticks and stones. And General Meiklejohn was always in a position to see well. One can understand Peter the Hermit and the Crusades better by the light of the story of Malakand.

But it was not long before the plains of lower Swat were swept clear again by General Blood; and then it was already time to turn one's eyes in another direction.

The Hada mullah and the mad fakir hardly worked effectively together. It is possible that they were not meant to do so. Anyhow the Hada mullah was comparatively late in the field when he prompted the Mohmand rising. The Mohmands, like the Swatis, are Afghans by right of kinship. They belong to the same people as the Duranis—the true Ben-i-Israel, as they delight to designate themselves. Their allegiance to the Amir was but shadowy, at least on the part of such clans as dwell nearest to the Indian border. All the country (half barren mountain, half flat riverain cultivation) that lies between the Kabul river and the Swat, even as far west as the Kunar and south of Bajaor, is theirs; and they claimed the distinction that no conqueror had ever set his heel on their necks since the days when their progenitors trekked eastwards from Laghman (which I observe that the Amir always spells after the old fashion—Lamkan). But the Amir's claim to sovereignty over the

Mohmands was by no means shadowy. His forefathers had held Peshawur till the Sikhs took it from them; but he admitted no rights of possession to the British beyond the old Sikh boundary. He could not claim Peshawur, much as he longed to regain that brightest jewel of the Durani Empire. There was no chance of that. Yet, in spite of the fact that many of the Mohmands had settled across the border and held strong financial interests in the Peshawur valley, he claimed to rule the whole people.

"Not a foot shall you set in Mohmand territory" wrote Ghulam Haidar to the British Commissioner, who was seeking to find place for that part of the boundary agreed upon between Durand and the Amir in the 1893 Convention, which split Mohmand territory in twain. It was rude, but it was provoked by the suggestion that he himself should not set foot in Chitral territory, and it was sufficiently to the purpose at the time. We had to leave that part of the boundary alone.

Rumours had been afloat that the Mohmands contemplated rising for some days previous to the actual outbreak, but they were discredited by the Peshawur authorities, and it was not till Shabkadar (a fortified post eighteen miles north of Peshawur) was attacked, and the old Sikh town of Shankargarh pillaged and burnt, that a movement was made to check the outburst. The glare of the burning village could be seen from Peshawur on the 7th August, and that evening a small force marched out to disperse the enemy. On the 8th occurred that memorable fight which was specially distinguished for the gallant charge of the 13th Bengal Lancers. Through and through the over-confident hosts of Mohmands did they charge. It is not often that hill-men are caught in the open by cavalry. They were caught then, as they had been caught previously by the 11th Bengal Lancers—and on both occasions the result was utter and complete discomfiture. This was one of the most brilliant cavalry charges in recent British military records. It settled matters for the time, and allowed breathing space for the formation of a punitive Mohmand field force, which subsequently swept through the land. The Hada mullah was for the time discredited.

Hardly had the Mohmand rising been set agoing when

rumours again circulated through the air to the effect that a joint rising was contemplated on the part of Afridis and Orakzais. This requires a little explanation. The Kabul river lies between the Mohmands and Afridis—so they were near neighbours. Immediately south of the Afridis dwell the Orakzais, with nothing between them and the Afridis but a mountain watershed. How could the boundary disturb the Afridis? It is true that the newly devised line did actually pass behind them, dividing them as much as it divided a part of the Mohmands from Afghanistan. Moreover it included all the Afridis (and not merely a few sections) on the British side of it. But it was not a demarcated line. No Commission had been up to the snowy peaks of the Safed Koh, planting pillars along that magnificent range, for the excellent reason that they were not wanted there. And it was the actual demarcation that set the teeth of these independent mountaineers on edge. Though Afridis are not Afghans (I say it with all diffidence, for I know that some weighty authorities are against me) their connection with Afghanistan is real enough. Deputations were constantly sent to Kabul—have been sent to Kabul ever since we were in that country—and the Amir was always appealed to for assistance in extremity. Much salt, too, is carried across those wild break-neck passes over the Safed Koh into Ningrahar (where Hada is situated), and across those passes the hard-pressed Afridi can constantly find refuge for his family, and sanctuary for himself, amongst the Durani tribes who dwell on the northern slopes of the Safed Koh. In fact he had his back door still open in spite of any boundary—just as had also the Mada Khel in Tochi. Thus whilst Afridi mullahs (notably Saiad Akbar) preached jehad with eloquent ferocity, and their Orakzai neighbours besought their assistance, the Afridis themselves did not neglect certain weighty considerations which induced them to pause. The land of the Afridis is not large. Maidán is the centre of it, and the best of all the cultivation is to be found in the Maidán uplands—but this does not amount to twenty-five square miles; and it may well be doubted whether the Upper Warán, the Bazaar, Bara and Khaiber valleys could contribute another twenty-five. But they were wealthy—rich in arms and rupees, the total annual payments in subsidies and pay which passed from British treasuries to Afridi pockets being nearly 200,000 rupees. The Afridi must have known that so far from possessing a fighting strength of 40,000 or 50,000 as was generally supposed he could number only a fourth or fifth of that strength. And out of this a very large number had served at one time or other in the ranks of the British Army, so that there were pensions to lose—besides the subsidies granted to the Afridi militia who garrisoned the Khaiber pass for us, and whose large allowances would certainly perish if they mutinied. As for the grievances of the Swatis or Mohmands, the Afridi cared no more for them than for the grievances of so many Red Indians. Neither did he possess that spirit of fanaticism which has carried many a better Mussulman than himself to the gates of Paradise. Then again the various Afridi clans are never of one mind. The spirit of national patriotism is utterly wanting in them. They do not understand it. They do not even understand that cohesion which is elsewhere born of ties of blood and family. A man's foes are more frequently those of his own household than not. Thus it was not surprising that counsels were divided amongst them. The Zakka Khel who were the most powerful clan, who blackmailed the rest by right of occupation of lands stretching from the farther mountains to the frontier of India; who lent no soldiers to the ranks of the British Army and had no pensions to lose—the traffickers in salt and (it is said) in slaves with Afghanistan, the wolves of the community, were all for war; and the rest finally joined in because they could not help it. It is impossible for an Afridi to see a fight and not join in—possibly because there is a future prospect of having to pay dearly for standing out.

Besides there was always that back door. At the worst they could shift across the hills into Afghanistan, and there was the prospect (so preached those pestilent mullahs) that something more than mere shelter would be accorded by the ruler of Kabul.

They therefore sent deputations to the Amir. The deputations did not cease from troubling even after we had walked through Tirah—but they got nothing more than excellent advice. Finally various local reasons for a combined rising on the part of all the clans were trumped up. There had been an increase in the salt-tax, and certain women, who had escaped over the border, had not been given up to have their throats cut. Of late years, too, nominations to the superior grades of rank in the Khaibar rifles had been taken from the Afridi headmen in whom they were originally vested, and had been appropriated by the commandant. I can easily imagine that such a change had been found advisable, but it gave deep offence.

The outbreak commenced by a fierce attack on the sarai and fort at Lundi Kotal in the Khaibar pass, which was garrisoned by the Afridi militia. Then was the spectacle witnessed of Afridi fighting against Afridi; and a right good fight they must have had! Many an old score was wiped out, and many a family feud squared in that Lundi Kotal battle. It would not be fair to say that the mere weight of the rupee kept the Khaibar rifles steady to their engagements. There is a quaint sense of honour amongst Pathans of all degrees which acts more or less strongly in keeping a man true to his salt. The Khaibar rifles did all that could be expected of them. They fought splendidly (one old Subahdar covering himself with glory) till they could fight no longer; and then they effected a retreat in good order to Peshawur. But, alas! whilst the Afridi fought for us, we failed to fight for ourselves; 9,500 troops about the Peshawur frontier looked on whilst 500 Afridis maintained British honour in the Khaibar. Over that little episode of the withdrawal of the British officer who should have headed the Khaibar defence, and the abandonment of the pass to its fate, it is best to draw a veil. There *can* be no excuse for it.

Thus the word went forth that we were afraid; and whatever may have been the spirit of tribal opposition in the wild country that lies between the Safed Koh and the Meranzai valley before that failure there was no mistake about it afterwards. The Orakzais had been looking on to see what the success of the Afridis might be. They had received a rough lesson or two from Sir William Lockhart previously which they had hardly time to forget. Now however they went forth on the war-path rejoicing, and set to work with a will. They too had a boundary grievance—but it was not that of the new boundary. It was an older one. Lockhart had put forts on the Samana range which shut them out from the cultivated plains of the Meranzai valley and stopped their recurrent raids in that direction, and this was their grievance.

The Orakzai geographical position differs from that of the Afridis in some essential particulars. They are Pathans like the Afridis, but of different origin. They have no real affinity or kinship with Afghans, and are probably more allied to the Pathans of the plains about Kohat than to those of the Afghan hills. It is through their country that the way to the heart of the Afridi mountains lies. They keep the front door to Maidán (which is near the Dargai pass across the Samana), whilst the back door is open to Afghanistan. But they possess no back door themselves, so that when once their valleys (Khanki and Mastura) are held, they are in the power of the enemy, and they must submit.

On the 23rd August the attack on the Khaibar positions took place. On the 25th the first demonstrations were made by the Orakzais on the Samana, and the first move against them was directed by General Yeatman Biggs from Kohat when the Ublan pass was stormed and captured. The moral effect of this advance was lost by our usual tactics of retiring from a position as soon as taken. The enemy reoccupied the pass and inflicted considerable damage on our retiring force. Then followed that series of engagements on the Samana under the August sun which are now historical, culminating in the brilliant defence of the badly constructed fort at Gulistan, and the magnificent, but unavailing, devotion of the little band of twenty heroes belonging to the 36th Sikh Regiment, who fought for the retention of another useless little fort at Saraghari, till the last of them perished in the flames that were lit by thousands of infuriated Orakzais and Afridis. The Afridis had joined the Orakzais by then. It was Sunday the 12th September when that heroic self-sacrifice was made. Rightly does one writer say, "There is nothing in romance, unless it is the siege of Torquilstone in *Ivanhoe*, which approaches in grandeur this defence of our Sikh sepoys against the rushes of fanatical hordes of Ghazis." There were many stirring episodes during the subsequent progress of the north-west frontier war; over and over again did our native troops show that the fighting qualities of Sikh and Gurkha are second to none in the whole world of soldiers; Gulistan, Chakdara, and Saraghari all told the same story, but we should be wrong to overlook the defence of Bhaluh Khel (a fort near Sada in the Kuram valley) which was conducted by Kuram levies, or that of the Lundi Kotal fort, which was held by Afridis against Afridis; for these two engagements taught us that we have other fighting men in our ranks besides Sikhs and Gurkhas. It would not be difficult to quote writers who brand our transfrontier neighbours—Swatis, Mohmands, Afridis, and Waziris alike—as cowards. They must know now that in calling them cowards they erred. It is perhaps one of the most useful lessons that we learnt from this boundary war—the lesson of respect for the people who fought well for their independence.

Meanwhile the settling of accounts with Mohmands and Mahmunds had progressed towards completion. On the 8th September the first move was made from Malakand, and by the first week in October a portion of the force that had been engaged in the operations immediately north of the Khaiber was in a position to join the Tirah field force which was concentrating at Kohat, under the command of Sir Willliam Lockhart, for the punishment of the Afridis.

CHAPTER XVI.

TIRAH

Tirah expeditionary force—Surveyors for the field—Transport and plan of campaign—Dargai—Sanpagha—Arhanga—Maidán—Afridi tactics by night and day—Surveying under fire—Bara valley and Shinkammar—Close of my Indian career.

SUCH, in brief outline, was the nature of the stirring succession of events which led up to the Tirah expedition, and which incidentally opened up opportunities for the completion of much that had been wanting in our frontier surveys from time immemorial. It is a curious fact that far beyond the rugged line of those frontier mountains in the deep recesses of which dwelt those tribes that loved to call themselves "independent," we were in the year 1896, better acquainted with geographical details than we were as regarded our own immediate border. Most of Afghanistan we knew by then, all of Baluchistan, and much of Persia; but the comparatively narrow width of border hills which we could scrutinise with our telescopes from the windows of Peshawur houses and the stations of the Derajat, was but a sketchy outline in our maps, an outline derived from such information as a few daring native explorers might bring, or from what we ourselves could gather when surveying on either side of it.

I hailed it therefore as a crowning piece of good luck, that in this, the very last year of my service in India, should occur an opportunity of filling in all the line of blank spaces—Tochi, Tirah, Mohmand, Swat, and Buner, that yet survived between the Gomul and the Indus.

But it was a severe strain on the staff of frontier surveyors (already well occupied with important work further south), and it was difficult to find workmen for the field. With Bythell,

Robertson, and Pirrie already well engaged in Mohmand, Swat, and Tochi districts (backed in each case by a staff of the best amongst our native surveyors), it was not easy to provide for Tirah. The qualities which make up a first-class frontier survey workman are not to be found in every technically well-educated surveyor. Enterprise, determination, strong physique for meeting the fatigue of incessant mountaineering, with great rapidity and precision in the manipulation of instrumental work have to be combined with that *suaviter in modo* which recommends a man to his superiors, and enables him to face with an equal mind the incessant worry (and occasional snubbing) that the constant demand for information and escorts must necessarily involve. A busy general cannot always be bothered with demands for assistance in pushing on scientific work which does not appear at first sight to offer any immediate or solid advantage. Indeed he often possesses excellent reasons for placing a temporary extinguisher on the military surveyor's efforts which he cannot divulge.

So it was with some anxiety that when the Tirah expedition (dealing with the darkest of all dark frontier districts) was organised, I looked round for help. Fortune favoured me, for my valued old friend and assistant, Colonel Wahab, returned from furlough ere the expedition had proceeded far, and I found in Lieutenant Leslie, R.E., and Lieutenant Holdich of the Cameronians, two young officers who with but scanty opportunities of practising the surveyor's art, yet proved to be most efficient volunteers. With them and Mr. Wainwright (a civil officer) as assistants, I accepted with confidence my appointment as Chief Survey Officer with the Tirah force; leaving the outlying districts to be negotiated by experienced officers who were already at the front.

Now the usual process of military surveying with a field force is much as follows. When the ground ahead is sufficiently secured, and the country fairly well cleared for the time being of large bodies of the enemy, the surveyor starts forth on his quest, having obtained such flying escort as may suit the circumstances of the case. Usually he has to commence by making out for himself a groundwork of triangulation (that is to say he has to fix the position of a large number of prominent points by means of theodolite observations and computations) for the assistants who follow with the plane table to base their mapping upon. This involves the climbing of the highest peaks that circumstances will admit of his climbing, and consequently, to support him in these excursions, he wants a body of capable mountaineers, well armed, but otherwise unhampered with weight. Then comes the slow toil of tugging up the precipitous rocks and slopes of the rough frontier peaks, thousands of feet up and thousands of feet down, with interval enough between, on a short winter's day ere the sun drops down into the sudden blackness of Indian night, to observe all that may be wanted for observation. Strange adventures frequently befall the military surveyor, and it is often a strange sight that greets him from the topmost pinnacle of the hills when he reaches them. On a "surveyor's" day the light grey haze of distance is marked in faint outline by the far-away ranges of frontier mountains—dim and mysterious (a hundred miles away may be) guarding the unknown gates of another world of exploration, but crumpled here and there into peaks and points such as may be searched out by the keen-eyed theodolite and grasped, and evermore fixed in order on the world's great map. Then comes the deeper tone of the nearer jagged backbones of minor ridges, standing up stiff (all length without breadth, like the pasteboard slips of a theatre), fainting into the background haze, or picked out now and then by depths of purple shadow as the fleeting clouds chase across the wide sky above. Nearer, and yet lower, are the deep rifts and valleys of the mountain on which he stands, divided by the dropping staircase of ridge and knoll, emphasised in their depths by the silver line of sinuous mountain stream pointing outwards to where a few black spots and dots indicate deserted village orchard trees—or the dark encampment of some blanket-covered nomads—he can hardly tell which. Only the theodolite can say. And about his feet are the yellow tufts of winter grass, scarce hiding the blocks of red laterite or the slippery slate needles on which he balances himself, a few ragged and weird junipers throwing out bare white arms in protest against the hardness of the times, a clear blue sky above and a sweeping lammergeir casting shadows from it; whilst the camp and the din of battle and the mixed language of Tommy are far away—forgotten for the time and unheeded.

Now this is all very well when once you have reached the top—but the getting up there, when repeated day after day, and extended to week after week, is apt to grow monotonous. Delightful as are the sensations of the triangulator as day by day the mystery of the mountain world unfolds itself before him, he experiences at times an excess of mountain climbing. But this climbing is essentially necessary to success. It is not to be avoided or shirked by any who hope for successful issue to scientific survey investigations, or a good final record.

Moreover it involves a certain risk of its own which is not altogether unattractive. Occasionally the rapid beat of the distant drum warns the man on the mountain that, whilst observing, he has been observed—and as the strumming on this instrument of war becomes more vigorous, it may be accepted as an intimation that somebody objects to his presence, and that an attempt to dislodge him is imminent. And if he still stays on, grasping with quick eye all the main features of the prospect before him —loth to leave ere he has got them all "down"—he may very well have to fight his way back to camp again. And this is the (not unredeemed) fault of some of the best of our native surveyors. They will *not* move. They become so absorbed in their work that not till a warning bullet imperils their mapping will they turn to go.

But, as I have already observed, this preliminary process of triangulation depends on the country being at least comparatively free from moving bodies of the enemy. During the progress of the Tirah expedition it is hardly necessary to remark that it never *was* free. It was impossible to get far enough, high enough, out of reach enough, to secure the certainty of a peaceful hour's work. From the very outset when we all sat down on the 15th October under the shadow of Dargai, to the final re-occupation of the Khaibar pass, no such excursions were possible. Well for us was it that we could do without them.

Afridiland is, as I have said, a narrow country, and we had been all round it (if we had not been into it) in previous years on previous quests. So we had to make as good use of the outliers and outriggers of those previous years of frontier surveying and triangulation as was possible—and on the whole they answered pretty well.

Now Dargai (or Chagru) was the pass over the Samána that led directly into the Orakzai valleys, and more remotely into Afridiland. This was the Afridi front door over which the Orakzais acted as gatekeepers. On the east it is overlooked by the peak of Samána Suk, under which a little further east lies the fort of Gulistan, which had recently made such a brilliant defence. On the west the peak and position of Dargai, overhanging a small village of that name, looked straight down on to the pass. Stretching away from the Dargai peak westward, was a line of mountain crest which curling slightly inward offered the chance of turning the Dargai position from the farther side of the range.

We all know the story. On the 18th October Dargai was captured almost without loss, with the assistance of a flank movement to the crest of the ridge. But this was only a reconnaissance, and the troops returned to camp. The Orakzais also returned to Dargai, and it is probable that they were joined there by Afridis. On the 20th the same position was retaken, without the assistance of the flank attack, and we lost heavily. When Highlanders, Sikhs, Gurkhas, and Englishmen finally reached the enemy's sungars, the enemy had disappeared down the hill on the far side. But the Orakzais had had almost enough fighting. There is no doubt they also lost heavily, in comparison with their numbers. Then followed the jolting, jerking, stumbling crowd of transport (animals and men) down the steep crumbling declivities of the hillside, over the stony flats below, and up the shelving sides of a three-cornered plateau, covered with a tangle of wild olive and acacia, into the Khanki valley of the Orakzai domain.

Much has been said in strong language, and much has been written, about that crowded transport which followed a great army of two divisions over the passes leading to Maidán. I hesitate to add my views. But I have seen transport in Abyssinia; dead mules and camels lying thick in piles round about the hyæna-haunted camps; I have seen it in Afghanistan;

camels lying in groups tearing each other's flesh, dying in the last agonies of hunger and cold; I have seen it also in the wild jungles of the eastern frontier—living men this time—rolling and vomiting in the last throes of a fever that was cholera, or a cholera that was fever; and considering the numbers, considering the difficulties, the narrowness of the ways, the exceeding toughness of those mountain slopes, and the fact that most of the transport was raised in a hurry and equipped with a rush, I feel inclined to congratulate the Government of India on the vast improvement that twenty-five years has effected. Room for improvement undoubtedly there still is, but I doubt if any army in the world of equal size would have squeezed itself into an equally tight place, with equal success, at so short a notice.

Our plan of campaign too appears to me to be beyond adverse criticism. It was the shortest, straightest, directest line by which to strike at the heart of the enemy. The very passes which formed the chief difficulty, formed also our best protection along the line of approach. We had finally only a mile or two of communications left subject to the sudden and fierce onslaught of the Afridi banditti. How would it have been had we passed by other long narrow nullah-bed ways, which would have given less climbing but twenty times the opportunity to our active foes? But as I am not a military critic, I apologise for the digression.

In the Khanki valley we had the Sanpagha pass facing us. The Sanpagha did not lead us into the land of the Afridis any more than did Dargai. It dropped us over into the Mastura valley of the Orakzais, and it was again an Orakzai position. The Khanki valley offers no special attractions in the matter of scenery. The flanking mountains are ragged and rough, and unbroken by the craggy peaks and fantastic outlines which generally give a weird sort of charm to frontier hills. The long slopes of the mountain spurs gradually shape themselves downwards into terraced flats, bounded by steep-sided ravines along which meander a few insignificant streams, and the whole scene, under the waning sun of late October, is a dreary expanse of misty dust colour, unrelieved by the brilliant patchwork which enlivens the landscape elsewhere. On a terraced slope between

TIRAH. THE ORAKZAI JIRGAH

the Khanki and Kandi-Mishti ravines, under the pass of Sanpagha, stands a mud-built village with an enclosure of trees called Gandaki; and it is through this village that the road to Sanpagha runs after crossing the Kandi-Mishti declivities, ere it winds its devious course up a long spur to the pass.

A mile or so above Gandaki, sloping steeply up from the river-bed there occurs a local eminence—a knoll—in the centre of which was found a convenient base for the first artillery position when the pass itself was captured, and this position afforded a fine view of the pass itself. Right in front are the long brown folds of the Sanpagha spurs, one long sinuous arm stretching directly down to the river as if to offer a convenient line of approach to the depression in the hills which marked the pass. On this spur another conspicuous knoll, which looked innocently unsuggestive, concealed the sungars from which a crowd of Orakzai defenders fled into the shadowed rifts of the mountains as the artillery shells dropped neatly into the midst of them; and on this knoll the artillery took up its second position after struggling up the steep hillsides in rear of the storming party. Here too after the advancing wave of attack had passed on, I found amongst the half-dried and crushed vegetation, sprinkled with fragments of shells and shreds of torn clothing, blossoms of Alpine gentian uplifting their deep blue bells to the deep blue sky. The conformation of the pass and its surroundings was almost a repetition of Dargai. A succession of steep hills in steps overhung its western flank, and afforded an excellent opportunity for a plunging fire on to the road beneath. These had to be carried in succession by direct front attack. The defence of this position was nearly the end of the Orakzai demonstration. Beyond the Sanpagha lay the elevated valley of Mastura (some 1,500 feet higher than the Khanki, itself 4,300 feet above sea-level) and 700 feet below the pass. The difference in elevation was at once apparent in the general appearance of the landscape.

Six thousand feet of altitude lifts Mastura above the dust-begrimed and heat-riddled atmosphere of Khanki or Meranzai, and gives it all the clear, soft beauty of an Alpine climate. Mastura is one of the prettiest valleys of the frontier. In spite of the lateness of the season apricots and mulberry trees had not yet parted with scarlet and yellow of the waning year. Each little hamlet clinging to the grey cliffs, or perched on the flat spaces of the bordering plateau below, was set in its own surrounding of autumn's gold-tinted jewellery; and in the blue haze born of the first breath of clear October frost, the crowded villages and the graceful watch-towers keeping ward over them were mistily visible across the breadth of the valleys, tier above tier on the far slopes of the mountains, till lost in the vagueness of the shadows of the hills.

It was with real regret that we turned away from the pretty Mastura scenery, and following a wide upland valley trending northwards, seamed and intersected with nullahs, found ourselves facing the Arhanga pass and the Afridis.

Not that we saw much of the Afridis at Arhanga, although this was the actual gateway of their Tirah. If they were there in any numbers they skilfully succeeded in concealing the fact. We had now passed through the Orakzai country and were beyond its people. Thenceforward their opposition was but intermittent, and half-hearted. They soon gave in altogether, and we had to deal with the Afridis alone. Passing down from the Arhanga pass we dropped straight into Maidán—that Afridi paradise—which is on nearly the same level as Mastura. It is the summer resort, the headquarters, of the Afridi people, and its praises had been sung by the bards of the border in the streets and bazaars of our frontier towns from time immemorial, till all men knew that Maidán was a place better suited for gods than men. Yet the first impression of it was disappointing.

Seen from the narrow defile of the Arhanga as one descended from the pass, there was but a vista of dust-coloured plain at the foot of dust-coloured hills. The beauty of Mastura was wanting, and it was not till one had climbed up to the general level of the Maidán platform, after crossing a river at the foot of the Arhanga, that one could distinguish the reason of it. Maidán, or the Afridi Tirah, lies close under the snowbound ridges of the Safed Koh. It is an oval plain about seven to eight miles long and three or four wide, including all cultivable slopes to the foot of the surrounding hills, and it slants inwards towards the centre of its northern side, where all the drainage gathered from the four corners of the plain is shot into a narrow corkscrew outlet leading to the Bara valley. Centuries of detritus accumulated in this basin have filled it up with rich alluvial soil—soil so deep that it is only where the mountain streams digging deep channels through it have forced their way to the common outlet, that it is possible to measure its depth. Deep and treacherous were these gorges for the unwary British soldier, who thinking that cover was to be found in them from Afridi bullets, discovered too late that they were but death-traps.

All these alluvial slopes are terraced, and revetted, and irrigated, till every yard is made productive, and here and there dotted about in clusters all over the plain are square-built two-storied mud and timber houses, standing in the shade of gigantic walnuts and mulberries. Up on the hillsides surrounding the Maidán basin, are wild olives in wide-grown clumps, almost amounting to forest, and occasional pomegranates. Higher still are the blue pines; but below on the shelving plains are nothing but fruit trees. There is everything here to make up a picture as attractive as that of Mastura; but strangely enough the colour and illusions of autumn had gone, and Maidán was a good fortnight nearer winter than Mastura. The soul of its beauty had fled. The soil of the alluvial clays was bitterly cold owing to rapid radiation, and from the Safed Koh ice-cold blasts seemed to whistle down now and then, just as a warning that the sooner we finished our business of burning villages and appropriating supplies the better for us.

The briars and hedgerows had already taken on a copper hue, and the leafless skeletons of trees were hardly to be traced in the monotonous dust-coloured haze. It was as if Maidán were prepared to settle down beneath its snow coverlet and sleep for the winter.

Not all at once did we grasp the true character of this frontier *cul-de-sac*, this back garden of the mountains, which scooped out of the Safed Koh and dominating nothing, possesses no village or town of any consequence (though full of houses), and through which no road runs between the highlands of the west and India. It is off the track of former India's conquerors, as it is off the track of modern military strategists.

From Dargai the surveyor and the plane table had come into action, and it was speedily found that the ordinary rules of survey procedure, where the surveyor waits for the country to be cleared, were no good in Tirah. It was a case of pushing on the plane table with the first advance, or of losing all opportunity whatsoever. There was no going back again over old ground; for the country, from first to last, never was cleared of the apparently ubiquitous Afridi. It has always appeared to me that in this short campaign the Afridi has received more credit than is strictly due to him. We know him well enough, and his measure has been taken over and over again. He has often been called a fool, but he is not such a fool as the Arab Dervish who masses himself in convenient form for annihilation by modern rifle fire. He plays his own game in his own hills admirably well; still there was nothing phenomenal either about his shooting or his tactics. Given that he possessed the best of long-range weapons, a perfect acquaintance with his own hills and the surroundings of his own villages, friends and advisers amongst our own troops, nearly two whole divisions crammed into a small space to shoot at, and above all a back door through which to betake himself in case of accidents, and the Afridi could hardly fail to score. Fortunately there were but few of them, as they worked together with skill and judgment, missing good opportunities no doubt now and then, but hardly ever failing to bring off a sudden determined rush upon an unsuspecting convoy without success. But such tactics are common to all hill tribes, and they were as successful in Abyssinia as in Maidán. We walked right through the Afridis country where we would. Not only Maidán, but all the contiguous valleys, Rajgul, Warán and the Bara—all learnt the lesson that no resistance, however plucky, could long defer inevitable judgment. Burning houses and the straight long columns of smoke going up to form a sombre black pall across the face of the sun, told their tale right through their country from end to end.

What made the Afridi defence of Tirah memorable was the effective use of our own weapons against us. Under the gathering darkness of an October night, one by one, with bent head and outstretched neck, sheepskin piled up on the shoulders, and long skinny legs protruding beneath, the Afridi could sometimes be seen in the distance stalking like an evil bird of prey under the shadow of the terraced hills—no two together—no word spoken—only a sudden disappearance with the first puff of a rifle, the first whistle of the bullet across his path. Creeping, crawling, hiding behind grey boulders and stones big enough to conceal an ordinary partridge, did they wriggle and turn themselves into the position where they would lie ere the night finally fell. Then would a dozen or so of the crack shots, men trained in our own ranks, carefully estimate the range of the camp, which, covering many a square acre of ground, was a big enough target in all conscience even for evening practice. Steady now! All together! And a volley of bullets comes spluttering, splashing, tearing, and smashing right into the middle of the camp, where tired men had perchance just sat down to a frugal dinner. Once more! The general's tent this time! We all know him—this for our evening salaam! and the sandbags artfully piled in front of the general's door are pitted with marks as of small-pox. By this time a few men and a few mules are stretched on the ground and the men are still guessing (if they have sense left in them) from what direction the bullets come. One officer has left the dinner-table with his arm smashed—another, still sitting at the camp mess-table, has quietly dropped his head on his plate, and his knife and fork gently slide out of fingers that will never grasp them again. And so it would go on till the black shadows of night shrouded the camp in darkness, unless maybe the orange star of a casual lamp again gave those hidden marksmen a target for night practice.

Once indeed these vultures of the night did a very plucky thing. They crawled inside the line of pickets, across the rough shingle of the nullah over which the camp was pitched, up the slopes of a steep island in the midst of the nullah-bed, which they hoped might give them a straight view into the headquarters camp. Then from a distance of about 100 to 150 yards suddenly burst the volley. But the shooting was not quite equal to the pluck of the venture. Some bark and branches were split from off a plane tree, and the walls of a house hard by resounded with the smack of a few bullets.

A few little spouts of dust were sent spinning about, and a syce was hit. That was all. The Gurkha scouts were out and they allowed no chance for a second volley.

Then was to be seen the strange sight of men burrowing! It was the only thing to be done. The *men* indeed made shelter trenches for themselves because they were ordered to do so, and they lay down in them. But there was no such order for officers, and the result was that an undue proportion of these evening casualties was theirs. It was however voted to be distinctly more cheerful to sit at the camp fire and mess-table in peace and contented security, when such a result could be attained with but little labour by digging. Some, indeed, slept below ground-level, but this generally involved a damp resting-place more distressful even than the chance of a casual bullet.

Afridi tactics by night were effective enough. They were almost more effective by day. Neither by night nor by day would they trust themselves to open resistance or solid attack, but by day they could watch from their nests above the valley the scattered threads of transport moving in lines for foraging purposes, the little band of scouts covering the survey party that was making its way slowly up the hillside, working its way comfortably to within their range; or they could hang about the cliffs and woods whilst an advance in force was in progress, ready to mass themselves with most surprising rapidity on any luckless party that might get involved in the spider-web of nullahs. There was not an army of them. I doubt whether on any occasion their numbers could be actually counted into thousands. Certainly no British officer ever counted them. But this small brigade of bandits owed quite as much of their extraordinary mobility to the fewness of their numbers, as to their loose organisation and mountaineering instincts. They simply played around the British force, and with the facilities that they possessed of attaining safe cover when too hard pressed, the hunting of them with an army of two divisions was not unlike hunting rabbits with a pack of foxhounds.

And yet it is difficult to see how a smaller force could have played havoc with their country, and kept open a line of communications. It was much the same to us whether there were

50,000 or 5,000. At all points was it necessary to be prepared for attack.

It was in face of an active, elastic, vigorous, guerilla form of warfare such as this that the surveyors had to carry on their work. Every movement of importance about the enemy's country was accompanied by a survey detachment, and it was often difficult to discover from day to day what the next day's opportunities might be. Leaving one detachment in Mastura valley with the first brigade I kept two others under Lieutenant Leslie and Lieutenant Holdich (it was pleasant to have this opportunity of making one's final exit from the Indian frontier campaigning the opportunity for introducing a son to active service) well at work in Maidán. A most successful experiment was made in the direction of training special bands of scouts (drawn from the 2nd and 5th Gurkhas) in hill warfare during this campaign. They were found to be most valuable auxiliaries to the force, and the surveyors owe them a deep debt of gratitude. To find an escort that was really trained to climbing was a novelty in this line of business. Many of the daily excursions up the hillsides were made under their protection. A good point once gained, the scouts scattered around and hid in anticipation of the inevitable gathering together of the Afridi vultures. A little round, white puff of smoke from behind a grey boulder or a rock, so far distant that seconds could be counted by fives as the sound of the shot fell on the ear, would be followed by the spat of a bullet somewhere near the plane-tabler. This was the first signal, and then the fun began. Gurkha and Afridi were occupied with the mutual joy of stalking each other. But the vultures rapidly multiplied, and a time would come when retirement down the hill by sections (each little party facing about in succession for the protection of the one left farthest to the rear during its rapid withdrawal) was necessary. Then the handicapped plane-table carrier was given a clear start, and the scouts followed at a fair interval of time. The instrument was but once or twice hit during this process, but the native surveyors (sepoys mostly) who invariably stood their ground to the very last second, all escaped.

More detrimental to our success than the activity of the

Afridi a great deal were the heavy grey snow mists that wreathed themselves about the peaks above the Bara valley when the march had begun to the Peshawur plains. Maidán had been mapped, the Chamkanni villages had been visited, Rajgul and Warán (where dwelt the great mullah Saiad Akbar) had given up their secrets, and Bara was nearly the last of the unknown corners of this unvisited land of Tirah. The headquarters of the force had broken up by then, and detachments were scattered. In Bara they had perhaps the worst and most difficult time of all, and the final exit from Afridiland terminated in the severe and unsatisfactory engagement at Shinkamar. It was hardly the royal progress of a victorious army.

Nevertheless everything had been done that could be done, short of collecting the enemy in a ring fence and giving him a sound thrashing. Every mile of the great unknown land had been visited; and every village of importance had paid its toll of burning houses. The veil had been lifted for ever from Tirah, and the Afridi acknowledged at last that he was beaten, although it took long to convince him. He had fought well, and he had fought with a singularly open mind. He apparently bore his enemy no ill-will; there was none of the ferocious animosity which distinguishes his own family feuds. Final terms were by no means arranged with the most obstinate of the Afridi clans before there was a rush for recruiting in the ranks of the British Army on the part of Afridis generally such as had never been previously known. Our wounded were respected and cared for, and there were many signs of a better understanding of the ethics of modern warfare amongst these wild hill people than has ever been recognisable hitherto.

With the mapping of the Afridi country the most important of our border blanks was filled in. But meanwhile Tochi, the Mohmand country, and Swat had all grown to connected mapping under the surveyor's hands. Buner alone remained; we had expected a stout resistance in Buner; and Buner shortly after was added to the geographical bag by Robertson; but it must be remembered that the occupation of that valley came at the end of this varied north-west frontier campaign, standing almost alone. We had retained much respect for the Bunerwals ever since the days of Ambeyla. But the admirable dispositions of General Blood's advance left no room for effective resistance. Buner was conquered (I believe) with the loss of one man!

And then, so far as I was concerned, the end came. The laws of the Indian Government (which are sometimes as the laws of the Medes and Persians) decreed that I should lose my appointment on my fifty-fifth birthday. This happened before the force broke up—but there could be no relaxation of the rule—so I handed over my charge on the field to my old friend Colonel Wahab, and returned to India a free man; thanking that Providence which had been good to me, in that during the last year of my Indian career, I had been able to put a round finish to the last of our frontier maps.

CHAPTER XVII.

CONCLUSION

Value of the northern Afghan boundary and of the "Durand" line respectively—Position on the frontier—Chitral—Khaibar and Kuram—Tochi—Gomul—Ultimate result of all forms of policy—Insecurity of Afghan national existence—The effect of its dissolution—Differences of race characteristics in north and south—An army for the Afghan frontier—Possibilities of future economic development.

JUST so far as long acquaintance with the heterogeneous agglomeration of peoples which constitutes the great body of "the tribes of the frontier," and an intimate knowledge of their surroundings derived from my experiences as a surveyor, justifies any general deductions as to the probable nature of our future political relations with them, I may perhaps be permitted to add a few words respecting such opinions as I have gradually formed.

We have contributed much to give a national entity to that nebulous community which we call Afghanistan (but which Afghans never call by that name) by drawing a boundary all round it and elevating it into the position of a buffer state between ourselves and Russia. All this has been done at great expense and with infinite pains; and we are now in a position to question the results of our labour and outlay. On the far north, that is to say, on the Russian side of Afghanistan, we have attained what is on the whole a very good and satisfactory boundary. It is not *all* good, but it is for the most part a boundary which a man cannot cross without well knowing that he is crossing it; and it sets a physical and definite limit to further intrigues by means of Russian exploration into Afghan territory. This seems to me to be a solid advantage. As Sir West Ridgeway has pointed out, the violation of that northern boundary is never likely to be cause for war, although war may lead to the disruption of the boundary. Whatever the cost of setting it up may have been, our trouble and expense have been justified. But on the near side of Afghanistan, between the independent tribes of our frontier and Afghanistan, what have we gained by demarcation? We know now the limit of our own administrative responsibilities. We know how far we can exercise control over the frontier tribespeople without interfering with Kabul prerogatives. We shall certainly respect our own boundary; and it will be well with us if, sooner or later, we do not find the necessity for maintaining this respect exceedingly inconvenient.

But whilst we have every reason to hope that Russia on her part will respect the boundary now placed in front of her, and will cease from troubling on the Afghan borderland, what surety have we that the Amir will do the same by the Indian frontier? Will he cease to receive deputations from his Afghan brotherhood who dwell on our side the line? Will he decline the asylum that his valleys and hills afford to tribespeople flying from our vengeance and keep open the doors for them so that they cannot be punished? Certainly he cannot cease to do either. The tenets of the Koran forbid him. And he has already explained at some length to his "dear friend" the late Viceroy, that he cannot prevent his soldiers swarming to the assistance of our tribal foes; nor stop the fanatical voice of the mullah; nor will he prevent the escape of political refugees from Kabul at critical junctures. All these things have happened recently, and the boundary will not prevent them happening again. Yet the Amir will not cease to draw his six lakhs subsidy a year for permitting that boundary to exist. He has steadily drawn that subsidy since the agreement of 1893 was signed in spite of his opposition to demarcation, and to withdraw it now would mean final rupture with the Afghan Court and acute frontier difficulties from the Helmund to Bajaor. We have indeed prevented his openly carrying war, or pushing his outposts into territory which is inconveniently close to us, although we cannot prevent him from keeping his army massed on our frontier. But seeing that the Amir has ever been far too acute to enter on war with England, it seems as if we might have effected the same result with less irritation to our frontier neighbours, and at a less cost to ourselves.

As for the independent tribes, they will finally accept the position; probably remove all unprotected pillars, and treat the boundary as if it did not exist. Where we are behind them—*i.e.* from Karachi to the Gomal, they have never troubled themselves about it. Where we are not behind them, and not in the position to safeguard its existence, the boundary will be treated as if it were not (when inconvenient), and as the symbol and sign of a binding engagement *on us* if tribal interests point that way.

The boundary may however be regarded as a visible expression of our present determination to set a limit to a "forward" policy; and as such it may be accepted with satisfaction by a very large number of politicians.

As regards our present position on the frontier, Chitral, that outermost manifestation of British suzerainty over Kashmir, was occupied as the result of a series of military manœuvres in the wild highlands south of the Hindu Kush, when we went to teach their barbarous inhabitants that English, and not Russian, interests were to be paramount in all regions from the flat plains of the Punjab to the hills and glaciers of the Pamirs. And who shall say that the lesson was not needed; or that the impression created on the mind of the rugged hillmen who, gathering from the glens and valleys of the far north, find in Chitral the outward and visible evidence of the "dominion of the Queen over palm and pine," is not salutary and even necessary? Otherwise the retention of Chitral may well be regarded as a doubtful advantage. A large garrison (*i.e.* a garrison large enough to be an effective factor in preserving the peace of Bajaor and Swat) cannot be spared for a part so far removed from all military centres. A small garrison, on the other hand, is but a temptation—a trailing of coat-tails; for there is not a position to be found in all these narrow valleys south of the Hindu Kush which could be made strong for permanent occupation except at an enormous outlay. Chitral has already proved its weakness. In Chitral were 400 Sikhs and many officers, shut up "as in a box" (as Ghulam Haidar expressed it), and being unable to use their guns, reduced to desperate straits for weeks together by a ragged, but apparently well-armed, foe collected from all corners of the frontier.

As an outpost to keep watch and ward for an advance from the north, Chitral is useless, for no serious menace is possible from the north. As a safeguard otherwise it is hard to say from what it will protect us. It is, in short, the outcome of political, not of military strategy. As a political centre it must be remembered that it possesses an outlook westwards over the hills and valleys through which the Amir's great commercial roads have been projected, as well as northward to the Hindu Kush passes. But it is at best an expensive and burdensome outpost (especially to the Kashmir state), and is, on the whole, the least satisfactory of all the forward positions that we have recently occupied.

The Khaibar and the Kuram entrances to Afghanistan speak for themselves. No need to enlarge on the obvious necessity for holding them strongly, and avoiding all appearance of weakness where they are concerned.

The Tochi occupation has given much scope for discussion that has not always been moderate or well-advised. The value of the Tochi valley route to Ghazni has remained so far an unsolved problem. We know however that it has been made use of in the past most effectively, and indications may yet be traced of a high-level road on the northern watershed of the valley, and of entrenchments in the open plains at its foot, which are all (or probably all) that remain to tell the tale of some of the fiercest, deadliest, and withal the most rapid, raids that have ever been fostered in Ghazni and spent themselves over the plains of the Punjab. Tochi moreover dominates much of the northern hills of that Switzerland of the frontier, Waziristan. We have not yet shut off Waziristan from Afghanistan, and the Waziris will be as ripe for mischief in the future as in the past. But Waziristan is now dovetailed in between the Gomul and the Tochi, and the influence of our military presence north and south, as well as east, cannot fail to make for peace and good order. The new policy of tribal levies (a policy of judicious "interference") which has proved so effective in Baluchistan, and which was so severely tried by our late experiences in the Khaibar, will go far towards inducing a more friendly intercourse between us and the Waziris. Our rupees will be taken readily enough; and although they may be spat upon, and reviled as the "dung of the donkey of antichrist,"* the ragged sons of Mahsud and Darwesh will think twice before they peril the loss of them.

If there is so much to be said for the occupation of the Tochi (a more or less isolated valley), surely there is yet more to be said for the occupation of the Gomul. The Tochi valley leads nowhere, so far as we are concerned at present. The Gomul leads to Ghazni, and is crowded with traffic at certain seasons of the year. The Gomul is the great highway of the Povindah, and the Povindah is of the best of the Ghilzai clans, the great trader of the frontier. Nasir and Suliman Khel—these are the chief tribes amongst the Ghilzai, and to them these traders chiefly belong. Thus we should have but little to say to the Ghilzais if they did not come to us—for we cannot go to them. They are not Afghans, although they are, next to the Durani, undoubtedly the strongest and most important of all tribal communities in Afghanistan. It is most important that we should be on good terms with such a people—a people of magnificent physique and great enterprise. And our occupation of the Gomul wins much good for the Ghilzai. No longer is he pestered and worried with the blackmailing of Waziri freebooters. He can make his annual passage of the pass in peace and security, and this alone might make it worth our while to hold the Gomul even if there were not the further advantage of sound strategy. From Wana we not only dominate the southern Waziri valleys, but we round off the line of frontier outposts which hold all the wild people of the Suliman mountains in check from Quetta to Waziristan. It secures the end of the chain, and can itself be supported and fed either from India by the Gomul pass, or from Quetta by the Zhob valley. Of all the new-found forward positions on the frontier, that of the Gomul seems to me to be most unimpeachable.

I hardly suppose, after all that has lately been written and

* An expression lately used by a border ruffian, who apologised to the Amir for accepting our rupees, but who held to his bargain with us all the same.

said, that there lives a man who imagines that we have reached finality either of position, or of policy, on the frontier. I have never quite been able to grasp the exact tenets of the various forms of political faith denoted by the "forward" policy; the policy of non-interference; the "new" policy. They all lead apparently to the same end. As surely as any politician arises who imitates the king in the nursery tale, who said "Thus far and no farther" to the incoming tide, or Clive, who announced in Council that nothing shall ever induce England to extend her interests beyond some long-forgotten limit in Lower Bengal, so surely do circumstances beyond his control arise to swamp his resolutions, and overflow his political landmarks. Policy does not seem quite equal to shaping the final ends of frontier evolution; though it may do much towards accelerating or retarding those inevitable processes which gradually produce order out of barbarism, and finally spread civilisation through uncivilised spaces.

What is there about Afghanistan, save and except the firm right hand of its present ruler, to guarantee its continued existence as a buffer state between England and Russia? No other country in the world is interested in its prolonged existence except these two. Afghanistan, as a national entity, can only exist by favour of military support of one or other of them. We need hardly inquire on which side the burden will always lie.

We must, as long as we can, maintain that country not only with our arms against all comers, but with financial support against her own inability (an inability which is hereditary, as you may see by the history at the end of this book) to hold together without it.

But something more even than assistance in arms and rupees is wanted to ensure a national existence to Afghanistan. That something she possesses at present in the strong government of the reigning Amir. But we cannot guarantee that it should last for ever, and then, what after him? We cannot tell; only we know this—that the nemesis of ignorance and superstition, and cruelty and barbarism will quickly arise if the hand of Abdur Rahman's successor is light and his government weak, and it will take more bolstering than all our political departments can together effect to keep life in Afghanistan if her heart at Kabul pulses feebly.

Doubtless the present position of Afghanistan as a buffer state between England and Russia is the outcome of the most careful and able political consideration; nor do I suppose that there is any authority in India (either military or civil) who does not admit both its wisdom and its convenience politically, and deprecate any attempt at its wilful destruction. But it is more than the wisest of our administrators dare hope that such a structure should last.

Disintegration may possibly commence by a Russian occupation of Herat; in which case we shall probably occupy Kandahar and Jalalabad; for some counter movement would certainly be necessary. After that Afghanistan will gradually fall to pieces. Of suggestions that I have lately heard for meeting the event of a Russian violation of the Afghan boundary, that which proposes that the army in India should stand gazing across the frontier wall, and leave the battle to be fought to an issue on some other field, seems to me the most foolish. For the inevitable result would be that we should have something like a mutiny on our hands as well as an active foe in the field.

Or possibly some popular explosion against the misgovernment of a weak ruler will of itself bring Afghanistan to partition. This is I know the expectation amongst some of the plain-spoken town-and-country politicians of Afghanistan.

And if partition should come, it is well to consider for a little what there is in Afghanistan which may be turned to our advantage. Everyone who has talked with Afghans knows that British administration at Kabul would be acceptable to a very large section of the Afghan people. Traders and merchants, and, as a rule, the Persian-speaking races of the Shiah sect, Kizzilbashes and Hazaras, would probably welcome British rule. And there are others whom it is not necessary to specify, who have frankly asked me when the British are coming, and who made it clear that the thought of their minds was "the sooner the better." Opposition would come from the nobles, the hangers-on of the Kabul Court, and from the fanatical section of the army and from the priests. But I doubt very much if the balance of popular opinion would not be in our favour.

But what would partition probably mean? For the sake of speculation let us consider Afghanistan as divided by the broad-backed water-divide of the Hindu Kush from its base in the elevated mountain regions south of the Tagdumbash Pamir till it loses itself in the hills of Bamian. This is the geographical division between Turkestan and the plains and valleys of the Kabul river. Continuing westwards, that trackless, wind-swept, uninhabited tangle of mountains that forms the backbone of the wild Hazara highlands, and gradually forks off westward to the Persian frontier, with its northern fingers pointing past Herat, and its southern shutting in the Herat valley from the broad wastes that reach to Kandahar, is the natural extension of this dividing line. The Herat valley forms an oasis balanced between the Turkestan plains of the Oxus on the north, and the basin of the Helmund on the south; and neither the ranges north of it, nor the broken ridges of the watershed south of it, present any great physical obstacle to approach. But eastwards from Herat the Hindu Kush and its western extensions constitute a great mountain barrier which is only passable at certain well-known points; and all this forms as definite a frontier as the Oxus river, and one far more difficult to step over.

Setting the Herat valley on one side, we have all the Turkman and Usbeg tribes on the north, and the Afghan and Ghilzai tribes on the south of this line, and we have also two distinct countries differing essentially in physical characteristics. Taking them as a whole (one must generalise sometimes), the northern races are not of the best material of which fighting men are made. Even the once-dreaded Turkmans, whose many tribal sections differ widely in their idiosyncrasies, do not seem to take so kindly to the military advantages offered them in Russian service as one might have expected. They are at least as good with the spade as with the spear. The Pathans of the south side of the Hindu Kush look on all Afghan Turkestan as the home of a "narm" (*i.e.* a "soft") race of people; and this is a verdict which my own observations would tend to confirm.

But south of that dividing band we have material for some of the very best fighting troops that Asia can produce. Because the Amir's army has melted away before us, and because the selling of a battle has become almost a matter of tradition amongst Afghan troops, it would be most erroneous to assume that they are always cowards and turncoats. Much has been said of the difficulty and the cost of raising an army for Afghanistan sufficient to guard our border, were that border conterminous with Russia. The army is there already; and it is an army which we practically maintain already. At least 40,000 of the Amir's troops are of first-class material (though I should not care to indicate exactly which are the best troops). What is it that is wanted, then, to turn good fighting material into a good fighting army?

We all know very well what it is. Nothing more nor less than the British captain, and the British subaltern. A large supply of those young men from whom we expect no more (as Lord Salisbury puts it) "than the ordinary attributes of an English gentleman" are what the Afghan army wants to become as formidable a force as any general need wish to command. Woe worth the day when England runs short of subalterns! They seem to be abundant at present, but quantity is not all that we must look to. Are our resources really unlimited of the right quality?—that quality which has made Sikhs and Gurkhas, Pathans, Ethiopians, Sudanese, and Egyptian fellaheen the most effective and most wonderful working military machinery that the world has ever seen.

Of the natural resources of Afghanistan it is not so easy to write hopefully. In spite of geological and climatic changes it is probable that much more might be made of the possibilities of increase in the cultivable area of the great Oxus basin than could be effected south of the Hindu Kush. Only those who have looked closely into the heart of Afghanistan can tell how small a proportion these smiling, verdant and fertile valleys of fruit and grain, with their little rivulets of well-trained water flow, their flower-bedecked banks and their acres of well-tilled vineyards and orchards, bear to the great mass of sterile country around. The Afghans have from time immemorial been great practical irrigation engineers. Every acre of rich soil is made to yield its abundance by means of every drop of water that can be extracted from overground or underground sources. The Hari Rud and the Kabul rivers are alike run dry by the processes of cultivation at certain seasons of the year. It would be rash to say that the cultivable area of Afghanistan could be *largely* increased, or much greater land revenues attained than are attained already.

But a revision of the whole system of trade duties and exactions would certainly lead to larger revenues, and in that direction the Amir might well bestow his talent for administrative reform at once.

Afghanistan has never stood alone, has never been self-supporting. With a just and firm government, freed for ever from the rapacity of Court officials and cleansed from Court corruption, it is possible that it might be made to pay its way, that it might at least defray the cost of its own defence. But it would not be safe to predict anything of such a country. It is enough at least for us to know that should force of circumstances ever impel us to undertake the administration of Afghan finance and place us alongside Russia with the Hindu Kush between us, there is no real need to regard such a situation as a national calamity, or to talk of it as an insupportable burden.

APPENDIX

A SHORT CHAPTER ON THE HISTORY OF AFGHANISTAN

AFGHANISTAN has but a small history, and that history is but a chapter of the greater one of England in India. How it first came to pass that England assumed the sponsorship of this conglomerate nationality, and that it has fallen to her to set the girdle of a boundary round about it; to sustain it by grants of arms and money; to adopt its ruler as an ally; and to maintain him as one the greatest Mahomedan potentates in the world—all these things belong to a phase of Anglo-Russian polity with which this book has nothing to do. But in order to understand the sequence of frontier history during the last twenty years, and to grasp a fairly correct idea of the underlying basis on which our present policy has been built up, and the reasons for defining the political boundary of Afghanistan, it is well to take at least a cursory glance at the complex problems involved in Afghan government as illustrated by its own short history, and its important geographical position.

The kingdom of Afghanistan includes amongst Afghans a vast population which is not Afghan; and the Afghan people on the other hand occupy a vast area of country which is no longer Afghanistan. Afghanistan has become a political designation applied to a conglomeration of people of many distinct nationalities, which have been formed into a kingdom without much assistance from us; but which, having been formed, is maintained by us, and in which the Afghan is the dominant race. How did Afghanistan first come into existence? and what is the nature of the claims which have been advanced on either side either for extension or contraction of Afghan territory? Perhaps its history may help to provide some sort of answer to these questions.

Little more than 150 years ago Afghanistan was an outlying

province of the great Moghul (or Turk) Empire of India, then fast falling into decay under the effete and corrupt rule of Mahomed Shah. Persia was in a similar position of approaching collapse under the Saffavi dynasty. The western Afghans under a Ghilzai leader had overrun the eastern provinces of Persia, had sacked Ispahan, and had made themselves hated of all men for their excesses and their barbarisms. Eastern Afghanistan had broken up into small independent states and chiefships, which defied the authority of the Moghul. The time was ripe for the appearance of one of those apostles of fire and sword who have ever, at periodic intervals, swept like destroying angels through the highlands of Asia, and carried all before them by virtue of ferocious energy and inborn military genius.

The nemesis of inefficient rule and gross excess in Persia arose in the person of a Turkman bandit named Nadir Shah. With his following of border robbers he swept the Afghans back from Persia on the east, turned the tide of Russian encroachment on the north; and finally ended by accepting (with well-expressed diffidence) the crown of Persia. Nadir Shah did not conquer Afghanistan. He did better. He bought the Afghans for service against India, and, with perhaps the best fighting material in the world at his back, he proceeded to the conquest and sack of Delhi; having been invited thereto by certain nobles who conceived that they had much to gain by a change of dynasty. Laden with a vast store of wealth, the result of this easy campaign, Nadir Shah was returning to his native country, when he was assassinated in his tent, and all his accumulation of treasure and loot fell into the hands of the Afghan contingent that was attached to his army.

It happened that an Afghan general of cavalry, one Ahmad Khan, of the Saddozai section of the Abdali clan, a Durani, was one of the first to learn the fate that had overtaken his chief. He lost no time in speeding away from the scene of the assassination to rejoin his own people, who formed the treasure guard, and who were slowly making their way towards Kandahar. All the treasure of Delhi fell into the hands of Ahmad Khan, and this treasure was the foundation of the Durani Empire. With it Ahmad Khan was able to satisfy the rapacity of the leading chiefs amongst his own countrymen, and to buy up the adherence of the Baluch chiefs as well. Without striking a blow, by the surprising rapidity and energy with which he turned to good account what must be regarded by the light of history as but a fortuitous accident (for he had nothing to do with his master's assassination), he attained the position of chief of the Duranis; and he was crowned king on a rocky eminence overlooking the site of the modern Kandahar, a city which first sprang into existence under his name—Ahmad Shahr.

Thus was founded the Durani Empire. Owing its birth to an accident, and nursed on the treasure amassed in India, it possessed from the very first no inherent stability, and never secured any respectable foothold amongst the empires of the world. The Durani Empire died a natural death ere it had existed for half a century; but because it was the foundation of the Afghan kingdom, and because visions of its magnitude pass before the eyes of every Amir who ascends the throne of Kabul, raising devout (if suppressed) aspirations for a possible reflex tide in the affairs of Islam, such as may once again give dominance to the creed of the prophet in Central Asia, and restore the ancient borders of that faded empire, it is well to note exactly of what it consisted, and where those borders really were.

We have seen that it started with a federation of such Afghan and Baluch chiefs as followed the fortunes of Nadir Shah, and these undoubtedly included all the predominant power and influence in western Afghanistan and Baluchistan. But not even the wealth of Delhi could avail for long to satisfy the rapacity of these noble barbarians. With the acquisition of wealth arose the insatiable demand for yet more wealth. What could be simpler under such circumstances than to renew their obligations (to India) and refill the exhausted coffers of the Imperial treasury by an appeal to the same source of supply that had periodically enriched High Asia for centuries previously? The appeal was made *more suo* by a series of well-organised expeditions into India, which not only replenished the Afghan treasury, but added vast areas to the dominion of the Durani. Not only was all Afghanistan, as we know it now (but with the exception of Kafirstan) under the Durani sway, but Baluchistan, and a large slice of the Persian Khorassan, including all Sistan (on both sides the Helmund), Sind, the Derajat, the Punjab as far as Lahore, Kashmir and the Yusafzai country were all Durani. Badakshan was tributary, and the Oxus, with a strip of the Turkman desert, formed the northern boundary, the north-eastern extremity of which was indicated by Kila Panja. Thus did the empire founded by Ahmad Shah extend far beyond the Indus into the heart of the Punjab. This Punjab concession was wrung from the Moghul emperor Mahomed Shah (together with a large subsidy, and the hand of the emperor's daughter) as the price at which another sack of Delhi was abandoned, or postponed.

The Durani Empire has long been dead, and the more compact kingdom of Afghanistan has been pieced together from its ruins. But none the less do visions of its departed greatness still dazzle the eyes of successive amirs of Kabul, and create that thirst for the reclamation of empire eastward which is not allayed even at the present day.

Ahmad Shah died in the retirement of his native valley (Maruf) after a twenty-six years' reign; and the disruption of the empire commenced at once. He was succeeded by his weak and dissolute son Timur, whose feeble administration and unlimited extravagance were not balanced by the soldierly qualities of his father. It was not long before the empire so loosely put together began to fall to pieces in his hands, and by the time that he died (in 1793) little remained of it but the natural limits of country occupied by the Afghan people. Kashmir was still Afghan; but the Punjab had mostly succumbed to the Sikhs; Sind had become consolidated under the Talpur dynasty, and Baluchistan under the Kambarani khans; whilst Persia had regained the eastern districts of Khorassan up to the Hari Rud, north of Sistan. Between the death of Timur in 1793 and the rise of the Barakzai dynasty in 1818 Afghanistan was the scene of a hideous family conflict between the many sons of Timur, which finally ended in the extinction of the Saddozai dynasty. Every provincial governor was a member of the ruling family, and every one of them set up an independent claim to the succession at Timur's death. Kashmir, Peshawur, the Derajat, Kandahar and Herat all proclaimed their independence, and became the nucleus of a fresh faction in the field. Zaman Shah, who governed from Peshawur as his father had done, was the first to secure the rights of succession, as he did actually reign for some years. But like all rulers of Afghanistan before his time and since, he speedily found it necessary to turn his attention to India as the never-failing bank on which to draw for the support of his rotten government. But Zaman Shah found a new and rapidly increasing difficulty to contend with—the difficulty created by interference with the rising British rule in India. Slowly but surely extending their influence towards the north-west, already throwing out long feelers towards the Punjab and Sind, the East India Company had now to be reckoned with in matters affecting the stability of the Moghul at Delhi; and the East India Company decided that the constant drain on the resources of Delhi for the support of a barbarous and ill-governed province, lying far beyond their sphere of political influence, was not to be tolerated further.

Then commenced the phase of political negotiation between the British in India and the Persian. Zaman Shah was deprived of his opportunity for a descent on India by the threat of invasion from Persia, and India was at last relieved of the ever-recurrent visitation of needy and rapacious highlanders from the barren and unproductive regions which lay beyond the Indus, regions which knew no form of government unsupported by an organised system of national robbery. This, and the ill-timed murder of his Barakzai wazir—Sardar Payanda Khan, completed the fall of Zaman Shah. He was deposed by his half-brother Mahmud (the Herat claimant) and had his eyes put out. Mahmud's success was but short-lived. He was speedily hunted out of Kabul and imprisoned by Shah Shuja (own brother to Zaman), the Kandahar claimant; and Shah Shuja, with Fateh Khan the son of the murdered wazir as his own prime minister, reigned in his stead. But Shah Shuja reckoned without his wazir Fateh Khan, who seized the first opportunity to avenge his father's death, after the manner of the Afghan people, by turning on Shah Shuja who was full brother to his father's murderer, and restoring Mahmud.

Thus was Shah Shuja forced to flee from Afghanistan and to seek refuge with the old Sikh Maharaja, Ranjit Singh, at Lahore. But Ranjit Singh did not receive him with cordiality. The internal troubles of Afghanistan had proved to be the opportunity of the Sikh. He had already possessed himself of all the Indian provinces of Afghanistan including the Derajat and Peshawur, and was little inclined to extend a cordial welcome to an unsuccessful Afghan refugee. He despoiled him of the most valuable possession left him (the Koh-i-Nur diamond) and then passed him on to the tender consideration of the East India Company's Government, which found him a temporary home at Ludinana. So passed for ever from the hands of the Afghan two of his most cherished possessions. Peshawur had been the favourite capital of Zaman Shah during his brief reign, as it had been that of Timur before him. Its delightful winter climate, in such strong contrast to the rigorous cold of Kabul, its great city full of the bustle and activity of frontier trade, its religious associations, and its magnificent surroundings, all seemed to render it unique amongst Afghan cities. There is no city on the plateau bounded by the hills west of the Indus that can compare with Peshawur either for wealth or beauty. Peshawur was to the rest of the cities of the Durani Empire what the Koh-i-Nur is still amongst diamonds. Small wonder then that each Amir of Kabul as he succeeds to the uneasy throne of Afghanistan, looks with unsatisfied yearnings towards Peshawur, and declines in his inmost heart to recognise the right of the infidel to retain that which is yet remembered as the crown and capital of Afghanistan. From the hands of the Sikh eventually both city and diamond passed to the crown of England, and both must ever remain inseparably connected with the memory of the ill-fated Shah Shuja.

It is at this period in the story of the dominion of Asia that the policy of England became actively concerned in the fate of Afghanistan. The same causes indeed, all more or less connected with the disruption of the Durani Empire, led to the same interest in the future status of the Afghan kingdom on either side her borders. There was the interest of Russia in those possibilities which might eventually favour general dismemberment, which interests were directed through the political channel of Persia; and the interest of England in maintaining the integrity of a solid barrier between herself in India and Russia in High Asia. But, still, England did nothing towards active participation in the building up of that barrier. She confined her attention strictly to the maintenance of that which was built up by the energy of those representatives of the new dynasty, the successors of the Barakzai wazir who had been murdered by Zaman Shah. It was not long before Mahmud and his son Kamran found themselves as much hampered by the superior ability and preponderating influence of the Prime Minister Fateh Khan, as Zaman Shah had been by Fateh Khan's father, and the usual Afghan measures were adopted by way of remedy. Fateh Khan was murdered with great barbarity in 1818, and at once the whole kingdom was convulsed with civil war and anarchy.

Out of the chaos arose the founder of the present Afghan kingdom in the person of Dost Mahomed Khan, brother of the murdered wazir Fateh Khan. Mahmud and his son Kamran retired to Herat which was maintained as an independent province, and the rest of Afghanistan was divided up between Dost Mahomed and his brothers. Afghanistan, as a kingdom, had already dwindled to something less than the narrow limits of those districts occupied by Afghan people. Kashmir and the Derajat (the trans-Indus plains south of Peshawur) had gone to the Sikhs, and Peshawur, the hill country north of Peshawur and Kohat, were only held by three brothers of Dost Mahomed as Sikh dependencies. Three other brothers occupied Kandahar, Kalat-i-Ghilzai and Girishk; and Dost Mahomed was left with Kabul, Jalalabad and Ghazni.

But from days that may be called prehistoric it has ever been the ruler of Kabul who has decided the destinies of the Afghan kingdom, and not infrequently those of India also. India has been invaded from the west—from Afghanistan and Baluchistan, times almost without number, although never, so far as historic records testify, from any point north-east of Kabul; yet for once that Kandahar, Makrán, or the Arabian Sea have opened a highway to her western portals, Kabul has figured as the base for invading forces at least a dozen times, from the days of Alexander to those of the founder of the "Moghul" dynasty in India. Dost Mahomed was not slow to make use of the strategic advantage which he possessed in holding the key of Afghanistan. Apparently without opposition he assumed the supreme control of the Kabul and Kandahar provinces under the title of Amir (or military commandant), and he was recognised as the *de facto* ruler of Afghanistan by the Indian Government when Barnes was first deputed in 1835 as political emissary to the Court of Kabul.

Bellew invites attention to the fact that this was the "prelude to a new phase in the history of Afghanistan and marks the era of a complete revolution in the political status of the country." . . . "The opening out of this close-shut region . . . was destined sooner or later to involve the two great European Powers, whose might and greatness were inseparably connected with their respective conquests and empire on the broad field of the Asiatic Continent, in a vigilant and jealous rivalry there for the maintenance of a just equilibrium. In the determination of this point of balance Russia and England were henceforth destined to work, and that not as a mere matter of choice or ambition, but as the imperious necessity of the birth and growth of their Asiatic empires—a necessity which must by the very nature of the situation yet impel them onwards each in his sphere till the natural boundary between the different nations and countries of the north and south is reached." . . . "Where this boundary line is, and when it will be acknowledged as the fixed line of separation between Russia and England are questions that are gradually answering themselves by the logic of facts and the onward roll of time."* Twenty years have passed since this was written, and twenty years ago Bellew had not heard of a "forward policy," or he might possibly have added that neither forward or backward or any other policy will eventually disturb that "logic of facts."

Barnes' mission to Kabul and the occupation of Peshawur by the Sikhs was enough to stimulate Russian Afghan policy into activity. Persia was invited to take Herat, and as Herat dominated Afghan

* *Afghanistan and the Afghans*, p. 44.

Turkestan south of the Oxus, and was even then reckoned as in some sort a key to India, the British Government intervened and set to work to restore the outlines of the Durani Empire. How far we succeeded is matter of comparatively recent history. The independence of Herat was maintained. Shah Shuja was restored to the throne of Kabul. The Barakzai Dost Mahomed was exiled, the Saddozai family representatives, Mahmud and Kamran, were recognised as independent rulers at Herat, and the house of Timur (which one would have thought had sufficiently proved its incapacity for government) again flourished in Afghanistan. But a government in which Saddozai incapacity was combined with British political interference soon came to an end. No need to recount the political disasters and the military blunders of the first Afghan campaign. The net result was that Shah Shuja was killed in the course of the disturbances in northern Afghanistan, and Dost Mahomed returned as ruler to Kabul. Thus again the position of the Afghan kingdom became much as Dost Mahomed had formed it before we interfered in its internal affairs.

But the Afghan Government still possessed no cohesion, and no inherent stability. All that had been gained was a ruler who was wiser by the extent of all he had seen and learnt of the strength of the British rule in India, and who thenceforth decided that come what might, he would adhere to his official friendship with England although he would not admit of the residence of a British official at Kabul. The British Government, on the other hand, had learnt that the Durani Empire was dead, past all efforts at resuscitation, and as it is on the lines of the Afghan kingdom as now pieced together from the bones of the dead Durani Empire by Dost Mahomed, that we have based our recent Afghan boundary policy, it is worth while to note carefully what was actually achieved by him before the next era of anarchy and civil war was introduced by his successors.

Firm as may have been the Amir's resolve to adhere to the friendship and alliance of the British, he nevertheless set to work at his own Court and in his own durbar to check any undesirable partiality on the part of his subjects towards the strong and just rule of the Farangi. There was then, and there has been ever since, a very strong yearning for the advantages of a firm and self-contained government on the part of a large section of the Afghan people who have everything to gain by the protection of trade, and the free intercourse between Afghanistan and India. For the trade of Afghanistan must ever lie Indiawards. The Central Asian states to the north send little to Afghanistan that Afghanistan itself cannot produce. Thus the bitter personal animosity evidenced by Dost Mahomed's support of the mullahs; his invectives against the unbeliever; his own outspoken hostility and the determined closure of all the gates of Afghanistan against Europeans, was founded on more than mere sentiment. It was the dread of the effects of too free an intercourse between his people and the English—the effects of too easy a comparison between the gross oppression (tempered indeed with a sort of haphazard justice, and occasional fits of leniency) which characterised the Kabul government, and the comparatively even-handed rule of Britain in India. Dost Mahomed's attitude towards the British Government in India is worth study, for it is the attitude of every Barakzai amir since his time. The blood of Dost Mahomed has flowed in the veins of all of them, and the foreign policy of Dost Mahomed has been with but small variation that of Sher Ali and Abdur Rahman.

Closely following on the Afghan war came our conquest of Sind and the Punjab, bringing us directly to that line of frontier which has been called "unscientific," but which, with certain considerable modifications on the lines of the most important routes connecting the interior of Afghanistan with India, *i.e.* the Khaibar, Kuram, Tochi, and Gomul, is still the frontier of the Punjab, not (*bien entendu*) the frontier of the Punjab as regards Afghanistan, but the division between the Punjab and those independent tribes which form the buffer between India and Afghanistan on the north-west, just as Afghanistan again forms the buffer between India and Russia.

In Baluchistan, south of the Punjab, the occupation of Quetta has introduced an entirely new distribution of political authority, and it would be more correct to say that the old Sind boundary has passed away for good, and that the frontier of India here marches with that of Afghanistan. But as regards the independent tribes of the north-west, some of them true Afghans of the Durani brotherhood, and all of them Pushtu-speaking people (Pathans) although a conglomeration of many nationalities, they must be regarded both from the side of the Punjab and from Afghanistan, as an unconquered people. The old Sikh dominion which we inherited by right of conquest ended practically at the foot of the hills to the north and west of the Punjab. It was probably adjusted on no settled system. It was the most convenient form of rounding off their possessions by a recognisable geographical feature. As far as they could collect revenue and taxes without disturbing the hornets' nest of barbarous tribespeople living in inaccessible valleys amidst the wilderness of rugged mountains which bounds India to the north-west, so far they claimed dominion of the soil and no further.

The difficulty of dealing with these independent clans is the difficulty of geographical position, not that of superior fighting propensities, for they own brotherhood with some millions of other Pathans who live in the plains of Peshawur, of Kohat and Bannu, who are no whit inferior to themselves in physique or fighting qualities, but who have submitted to us for fifty years. These Pathans of the plains we took over together with the country they occupied from the Sikhs. They claimed to be an unconquered people also, and it was long ere they learnt to submit tamely to British rule, and accept the authority of the Sahib and the Sirkar. But they soon learnt the lesson that untrained and undisciplined hordes, however brave, were no match for military organisation in the plains; and having learnt it they have long filled our ranks with many of the stoutest and truest-hearted sepoys that we possess. It is quite different with the tribesmen of the hills, who have ever proved, from the days of Alexander to those of Babar and the British, whether they be unarmed Kafirs of the most inaccessible of all Himalayan regions, or Pathans of Swat and Buner valleys, or Afridis, or Waziris, or any other border Pathan tribe, the most difficult of all people to subjugate, and the most impossible to control. And this is because of the rugged nature of their country, a country replete with the barren picturesqueness of rocky crag-crowned mountains dividing and dominating narrow valleys of exceeding fertility and great difficulty of approach. This belt of mountain country, which has figured, and is still figuring, so largely in the history of northern India, stretches westward from the Indus along the northern borders of the great Peshawur plain.

Here indeed it is something more than a belt, for it widens out into an unbroken mass of mountains extending to the great central backbone of the Hindu Kush. Circling round to the north-west of Peshawur it includes Bajaor and the Mohmand country, and thence runs southwards from Peshawur straight to the Arabian Sea, an unbroken band, forming a barrier between the plains of India and the plateau of Afghanistan. The Sulimani mountain system forms this barrier south of Waziristan, which thenceforward assumes the shape of a gigantic series of parallels and approaches (so regular is the continuity of the close-packed ridges, and so narrow are the intervening valleys) till it reaches the Arabian Sea and the Persian frontier. Not that it ends even there, but that is far enough for Indian geography.

South of the Gomul river our occupation of Quetta and of the valleys west of this belt has completely broken the resistance of the Pathan tribes. We hold as it were the back doors of their premises, and they are wise enough to be content with an independence which gives them full control of their own internal affairs, but does not admit of any interference with ours. It is to the north of the Gomul that we have at present to direct our attention. The tribes of Waziristan, of Tochi, of Kuram, Tirah, the Khaibar, the Mohmands, Swatis, etc., these are the people whose back doors are not in our hands. They open directly on to Afghanistan; they can be closed only by the Amir. Consequently the independence of these people is far more nearly absolute than that of any southern Baluch fraternity. On one side of them lies the old Sikh frontier of fifty years ago, which we have broadly accepted as the frontier of British India. On the other side there lay in Dost Mahomed's time no boundary at all; nor is there any doubt that, whatever may have been the views of the tribal authorities as to the degree of their own independence of Kabul authority, Dost Mahomed himself regarded them all as his subjects; and not only claimed sovereign rights up to the recognised Sikh frontier, but was much disturbed that the Peshawur valley with all the Pathan people of the plains were not recognised as his subjects as well. Yet these mountaineers were still an unsubdued and unconquered people. By all ties of religion, of tradition, and actual kinship, they were bound to the Amir and to Afghanistan; but the Amir then (as the Amir later) contented himself with the assertion of rights which he had never enforced by conquest, and which it was doubtful if he could maintain had he attempted to enforce them.

But however indefinite the eastern frontier of the Kabul province may have been when Dost Mahomed resumed his Amirship, he set about enlarging his borders to the north-west and west of Kabul with all the vigour of a great military leader, and with all that astuteness which has never been wanting in the Barakzai sirdars. He commenced with the conquest of the Balkh provinces, and revived the Oxus boundary of the Durani Empire on the north; he then (1854) shouldered his brother Ramdil Khan out of his possession of Kandahar, and established his authority in that direction.

This however led to an inevitable appeal to Persia for assistance on the part of Ramdil Khan, the ousted Governor; and ultimately to a friendly treaty between Dost Mahomed and the British Government in 1855, which was signed and sealed by his nominated heir Ghulam

Haidar and Sir John Lawrence on the parts of their respective governments at Peshawur.

The following year Yar Mahomed Khan, the successor of Shah Kamran, died at Herat, and the Persians immediately moved forward and occupied the city. True to our protestations of friendship with the Amir we declared war against Persia, forced them to resign Herat, and effected a treaty with the Amir which involved a definite alliance with Afghanistan entailing grants of arms and money, and involving a mission to Kandahar.

This treaty was signed at Peshawur by the Amir in person, and by Sir John Lawrence, in 1857.

Still Dost Mahomed adhered rigidly to his policy of preserving a close border on the north, declining to admit Europeans to Kabul, and only conceding a place in his Court to a native agent.

Hardly was the treaty signed when the Mutiny broke out, and at once the attitude of the Afghan Government towards the British Government in India during that momentous episode became of paramount importance. Now was an opportunity such as might never occur again for the Amir to assert his rights on his eastern frontier; to recover the lost Indus provinces of Afghanistan crowned by that city which was ever the desire of his heart—Peshawur; and to revive the ancient glories of the Durani Empire. And it is a matter of well-authenticated history that not only did the Amir (egged on thereto by the military advisers of his court) entertain that ambitious design, but that the chief authority of the Punjab was actually prepared to give back Peshawur once more to the Afghan as the price of his neutrality in the deadly struggle which then gripped India. Strange to say the hand of Dost Mahomed was stayed by the counsels of an Afghan, one of his sons, Azad Khan, who foresaw the final issue of the conflict and the advantages that might accrue from an adherence to the terms of the recent treaty. Thus he counselled discretion. Nor is it at all beyond conception that the dictates of an Afghan sense of obligation and honour served to restrain Dost Mahomed on this occasion, and to render Azad Khan's advice more acceptable. The treaty was absolutely fresh, the ink hardly dry, and the impressions of the Peshawur durbar could scarcely have been effaced in the mind of the Amir. Nothing had occurred on either side to invalidate the treaty or stir up enmity between the two governments. No boundary disputes had arisen—no unexpected advance had been made over debateable borderland—and on the other hand money was still flowing from India into the empty Afghan coffers. Under such circumstances even an Afghan sirdar will keep his engagements; and Dost Mahomed kept his.

Yet the struggle in his mind must have been a bitter one. Peshawur and the provinces which border the right bank of the Indus held millions of Pushtu-speaking people—many of them Afghans, bound by every tie of kindred and religion to the Kabul Government. Any movement on the part of the Amir would have been met half-way by the mixed Pushtu-speaking tribes of the Derajat; and, in such a crisis as the Mutiny, who can say what the result of such a movement might have been? England owed a debt of gratitude both to Dost Mahomed and his adviser Azad Khan—a debt which was but indifferently paid afterwards, when Azad Khan was in similar straits to those of India during the Mutiny.

In 1862 Ahmad Khan (whose political proclivities had always been in the direction of Russia and Persia in spite of the fact that the British Government had placed him in charge of Herat) died without a nominated successor, and the usual band of claimants immediately uprose, introducing the customary anarchy and confusion which attends such episodes in Afghan history. This was Dost Mahomed's opportunity. He advanced against Herat and captured that important frontier fortress in 1863, thus rounding off the borders of a kingdom which, if shorn of the fairest of the outlying provinces of the Durani Empire, was at least moulded to the geographical limits of the Afghan people, and could fairly claim precedence amongst the states of Central Asia.

With the completion of the conquest Dost Mahomed died. He died in his camp before the walls of the city which he had just captured, leaving behind him a kingdom to be fought for by his sons—a kingdom which, though again temporarily dismembered in the struggle for supreme dominion which supervened on his death, regained shape in the hands of his successor, Sher Ali, and is still, thanks to judicious bolstering on our part and the never-failing supply of that financial support without which the national existence of Afghanistan would long since have collapsed from natural causes, a geographical and political entity which may even claim to be the second great Mahomedan power of the world.

What, then, did Dost Mahomed leave as the boundaries of Afghanistan? On the north there was the Oxus from its then indefinite source to another indefinite point called Khwaja Sala. Dost Mahomed knew nothing about the source of the Oxus. The outlying province of Badakshan, and the remote districts of Darwaz and Wakhan, on the extreme north-east, were then unappropriated. Although they were nominally subsidiary still they were not recognised formally as any part of Afghanistan till the treaty of February, 1869, which was concluded between Sher Ali and Lord Mayo. Kafirstan was of course quite beyond the pale of practical politics, so that the northern limits of the Kabul province included little beyond the Kabul river valley to the plains of Peshawur. There was a small independent state with its capital at Kunar, and Bajaor was unsubdued; but the Mohmand population of the northern basin of the Kabul, (themselves Afghans) recognised the suzerainty of Kabul, and Dost Mahomed claimed (as every Amir has claimed since) his rights as sovereign up to the boundary that we inherited from the Sikhs. This brought Afghan territory to the foot of the Peshawur hills, and within a few miles of the city.

South of Peshawur, and cutting off that city from Kohat, there juts out a promontory of hills from the Afghan border which reaches nearly to the Indus. This promontory is occupied by Pushtu-speaking tribes that are not Afghan (*i.e.* Afridis, Orakzais, Jowakis, etc.) who have ever maintained their independence, though they have naturally recognised their affinity with the Pushtu-speaking Afghans on the west rather than with the Sikhs and Mahomedans of the Punjab. This promontory is the greatest blot in the scientific aptitude of the old Sikh frontier. It dominates Peshawur on the one side and Kohat on the other (flanking the main road from the Indus to the latter place), and through it there runs the only direct line of communication between Peshawur and the Derajat—a road which we have considerately left in the hands of the Afridis to be open or closed at their pleasure. Thus when most urgently required it is often apt to be closed. Over this outlying spit of independent territory Dost Mahomed held but shadowy authority. South of it the old Sikh frontier pursued an irregular and devious course, following the foot of the hills westward to Thal at the mouth of the Kuram river, then again deflecting eastwards round the base of a second, but smaller, promontory of Waziri hill territory (affording another geographical "ravelin" pointing into the plains of the Derajat), and beyond, winding with more or less irregularity along the foot of the hills, it reaches the borders of Sind. With the exception of the Kuram and Tochi valleys where Dost Mahomed had established his authority, these dominating hills south of Peshawur were held then (as now) by independent and self-governing communities of people speaking the Pushtu tongue possessing no kindred with the Afghans (being mostly of Indian origin), but yet allied by ties of faith and of a common language with Afghanistan rather than with India. Should outside arbitration or assistance in settling tribal quarrels be wanted, it was to the Amir that the appeal was made—certainly not to the Commissioner of those Indus provinces which are called the Derajat. Should a raid be organised for the purpose of raising their trans-border financial credit, it was the Hindoo bunniah of the plains who furnished the "objective." There was little to be gained on the Afghan side. Under no conceivable circumstances would these independent people be driven to take refuge in the plains of India. They might diverge amongst other kindred tribes, break up into sections and become gradually absorbed amongst kindred people, or they might migrate *en masse* to more remote and more congenial regions in the hills; but rather than be driven into the plains of India they would suffer extermination. Dost Mahomed was content to leave them alone. There was no necessity for reducing them by conquest. Little was to be gained in the matter of revenue, and great would be the difficulty of the tax-collector in districts consisting of barren and desolate hills teeming with quiet, out-of-the-way gullies and water-courses where the tax-collector might well be induced to cease from troubling. He held them in the hollow of his hand just as we now hold those other tribes of the Sind frontier who intervene between Baluchistan and the Indus plains. We hold them, not because we have conquered them, not because of those national characteristics which differentiate the Baluch from the Afghan (for both are equally attracted by the prospect of plunder and will make the most of such opportunities as Allah may set before them), but because they are now isolated. We are on both sides of them. The well-cultivated valleys of the Khaibar, Kuram, and Tochi, and the routes between India and Afghanistan to which these valleys gave access, were held by the Amir, but the wild hills of Waziristan and of the Suliman range were left to the wilder people who lived on them and loved them.

Between the Sind frontier and the frontier of Persia (the borderland of Afghanistan and Baluchistan) we need not follow the boundary of Dost Mahomed's time. It has little historical interest—but once Persia is touched at the southern edge of Sistan we come at once to historical ground again; for it was the Sistan boundary arbitration as much as anything that plunged us into our second war with Afghanistan. Sistan (Sewistan, or as it is sometimes called, Nimroz) has, under the more ancient name of Drangia, been ever celebrated in history for its wealth and productiveness. It was called the "granary of Asia." It borders both sides of the Helmund river where that river turns northward to empty itself finally in the great lagoons or "hamuns" which are called after its name. In the days of mediæval Arab occupation, Sistan was crowded with great cities, the centres of enormous trade, and we are but now re-discovering some of the once well-known trade routes which connected Sistan with the Arabian Sea coast or with India or with Mashad, Tehran, and the Caspian. Sistan on the left, or west, bank of the Helmund was watered by means of gigantic irrigation works which rivalled those of modern days in the Punjab or Godavery districts. Even now can the lines of these great engineering projects be traced over the face of those wide alluvial plains. Even now the skeletons of towns and cities dotting the Helmund valley at intervals along its lower reaches attest to the greatness and the riches of that Kaiani kingdom which was swept away by the ruthless hand of Nadir Shah about the middle of the last century. All this wealth might possibly again be called into existence; and both Afghan and Persian are well aware of it. Nor had the value of its geographical position with respect to Russia and Persia on the one side, and Baluchistan and India on the other, been overlooked. Russian explorers were over the ground in Dost Mahomed's time. Khanikoff was well received at Herat by our own nominee Ahmad Shah in the days when all Sistan was a recognised part of the Herat province; and doubtless when Dost Mahomed, at the close of his eventful reign, acquired the citadel of Herat by right of conquest he established thereby his right to rule Sistan undivided on both banks of the Helmund.

What is now Persian Sistan and Persian Baluchistan was only occupied by Persia some thirty-five years ago, during the troubles which supervened on the death of Dost Mahomed, and there are still living in Kirman and on that remote Baluch border, men who can recount the gradual progress of Persian encroachments, and tell good stories of the manner of it.

North of Sistan, beyond the Helmund lagoons there has never been a very definite boundary across the sparsely inhabited waste of wilderness and salt lakes that intervene between those lagoons and the bend of the Hari Rud river. As little or nothing is to be gained by encroachment here, little or no encroachment is recorded, and it is probable that the details of the boundary between Persia and Afghanistan known to Dost Mahomed's frontier officials were much the same as those known to these modern representatives. The Hari Rud from its bend northward carried the boundary to Sarrakhs, and from thence to the Oxus the western limits of Afghan Turkestan was that indefinite Turkman desert about which something has been said in the story of the Russo-Afghan Boundary Commission. Such was Dost Mahomed's kingdom as he left it, and such we have endeavoured to maintain it, without active military participation in the civil wars and troubles which have periodically beset it, but with the solid assistance of subsidies and arms bestowed on its successful sirdars and generals, without which (it cannot be too often repeated) Afghanistan would have no political existence whatsoever in the roll of Eastern kingdoms.

Recent Afghan history dating from Dost Mahomed's death and the succession of his son Sher Ali is within the memory of many of us.

Sher Ali began well. His administration was at first marked by conciliation of the commercial fraternity and careful cultivation of the priesthood; but he made no effort to prevent his people from sharing with the Hindustani fanatics the honour of the defence of the Ambeyla pass against us, and it was to the Afghan element then engaged that we principally owed (as we have since owed on other fields) the severity of our losses. But his conciliatory policy towards his subjects did not last, and opportunity was soon offered for his brothers Azim and Afzal (who proclaimed their rights of primogeniture) to take the field. Afzal was Governor of Balkh; and he was met on his own ground by Sher Ali. He was never actually defeated on any battle-field, but he was (*more Afghano*) enticed into a trap, and treacherously imprisoned. Sher Ali's attention had next to be turned to Abdur Rahman (Afzal's son and the present Amir) who was gradually driven out of Balkh. But this success was shortlived. The tables were completely turned by a coalition between Azim, who now appeared in the field again, after a vain appeal for British assistance, and his nephew Abdur Rahman. Afzal was released, Kabul captured, and Sher Ali driven to Kandahar; whilst Afzal was proclaimed Amir and recognised as such by us. Sher Ali's misfortunes did not end here. He was defeated at Kalát-i-Ghilzai in January, 1867, and again in Turkestan by Abdur Rahman, and finally lost Kandahar and retired on Herat.

Then again the tide of fortune turned. With the assistance of Persia and Russia (for it should be noted that whilst we have always refrained from active military interference in the civil wars of Afghanistan, Russia has never held her hand when there was a prospect of military success and subsequent influence in Kabul councils), and above all aided by the ability of his own son Yakub Khan, Sher Ali gradually regained all he had lost. Afzal meanwhile had died one of those natural deaths that occur so conveniently in certain crises of Afghan history, and again his brother reigned in his stead. Sher Ali, under cover of Yakub's advance, reached Ghazni, where Azim was induced to leave Kabul to come and fight him. Afghan treachery completed the rest. Ismail Khan (who was with Abdur Rahman in Balkh) had been bought over, and he descended on Kabul in Azim's absence and laid siege to the place. Azim saw that the game was up, and fled to Persia, where he died; and Sher Ali again resumed the throne.

Thus ended this war of succession, and the points about it chiefly worthy of note are, first, that Sher Ali owed his final position to Russia, and, secondly, that his son Yakub Khan had shown himself to be the best soldier in a family of soldiers, a capable leader and an astute politician.

In spite, however, of undoubted obligations to Russia, Sher Ali proved at once most anxious to cultivate friendly relations with the British. The fact was that the rapid advance of Russia (who during the civil war had acquired paramount influence in Samarkand and Bokhara, and was even then knocking at the gates that lead to the Oxus fords) frightened him and he heartily made overtures for a British alliance against Russia.

Then followed the memorable durbar of February 1869 when Sher Ali met Lord Mayo at Ambeyla. Never was there a more successful political function held on Indian soil. It is true that Sher Ali put forward demands that were extravagant, if not outrageous, and that he failed to secure a treaty which included an offensive and defensive alliance with the British Government; just as he also failed to secure the recognition of his son Abdulla Jan whom he nominated as his successor, instead of the more brilliant elder brother Yakub; but he returned to Kabul loaded with presents of money and arms, and he carried with him the expressed goodwill of the English Government. He thereby acquired an influence which strengthened his hands in the government of his country, and was recognised throughout Afghanistan as the guarantee for the security of the kingdom.

This desirable result must be largely credited to the personal influence of that prince amongst Indian viceroys, Lord Mayo. Gifted with a singular charm of manner, and that fine and commanding presence which is ever considered by orientals (at any rate by Afghans) as inseparable from the attributes of greatness, Lord Mayo produced an impression on Sher Ali the effect of which it is difficult to overestimate. At the close of the durbar Sher Ali offered his sword to the

Viceroy—the highest expression of esteem and personal regard that is known to the Afghan sirdar. The opinion has often been expressed by Indian politicians that had Lord Mayo lived, the war of 1878–9 would never have taken place.

For three or four years all went pretty well with our political relations with Afghanistan, but then the intrigues of Yakub and his flight to Herat and subsequent imprisonment, introduced a source of irritation which was not easily allayed. Sher Ali became more than ever anxious that Abdulla Jan should be formally recognised by our Government. His requests were not acceded to, and when in addition to this a boundary to western Afghanistan was set by the Sistan arbitration the whole spirit of friendly confidence between Kabul and Simla was at once swept away.

There is probably nothing that irritates the tender susceptibilities born of that overweening pride which is engendered in the mind of an oriental potentate by the daily and hourly adulation of a fulsome crowd of courtiers, than any apparent limit to his independence of action, or encroachment on his royal prerogatives. It at once reduces him to the common level of humanity, and fills the minds of his enemies with that secret rejoicing which is not unknown to the smaller units of a big public school when a notorious bully is arraigned by the headmaster. To Sher Ali who had entrusted us with this arbitration in full confidence, having had no reason to complain of the previous negotiations between England and Russia which had secured Badakshan and Wakhan to Afghanistan, the effect of the Sistan arbitration (which apportioned to Persia a large slice of territory on his western frontier which had hitherto been regarded as an integral part of the Durani Empire) was a matter of daily anathema in the Kabul durbar; where his condemnation and threats against the British Government were outspoken and plain. His honour as a Sunni Mussulman was dragged in the dust at the feet of the accursed Shiah, and moreover a strong strategic point on his border had been surrendered which might endanger the very existence of his kingdom. It was only after Khanikoff's mission to Sistan and the visit of Yakub (now in open rebellion) to Mashad, that Persia had ventured on a military occupation of this strip of territory west of the Helmund; and now it had been surrendered to them as owners by right of conquest.

Sher Ali's wrath was not to be appeased. It was indeed a case where successful interference on our part was an impossibility. For two years the Sistan negotiations had dragged themselves along, during which time our Commissioner (Sir F. Goldsmid) was subject to as much indignity on the part of Persia as of vituperation on the part of the Amir. When at length a special mission supplementing the original arbitration closed the proceedings, and the Persian representation with Major St. John's party returned to Tehran with the proposed agreement, it was thrown over by the reigning Shah, and the question remained unsettled till the year 1896 when the last Perso-Baluch Commission finally disposed of it.

Other untoward circumstances which occurred about this time tended to increase the flame thus lit by a boundary arbitration, and relations between Sher Ali and the British Government became so strained that ere long the spirit of friendly intercourse which had lately regulated the relations between the two governments was exchanged for one of active hostility on the one side, and of a generous but useless forbearance on the other. For several years nothing was known in India of the political proceedings of the Court at Kabul. It was at this juncture that an advance on the Sind frontier was made, and Quetta was occupied, and it was then that a new activity was introduced into the political relations between Afghanistan and Russia. A futile attempt was made from the side of India to bring the Amir to reason by the proposal of certain concessions with regard to the recognition of Abdulla Jan as his heir, and the negotiation of a treaty embodying an offensive and defensive alliance between the two governments; but it was too late.

Sher Ali declined to visit India in person or to be present at the Delhi assemblage when the Queen of England was proclaimed Empress of India. His representative who visited Peshawur on an unwilling embassy which it was hoped might lead to a better understanding between Kabul and Simla, repudiated the very basis on which any treaty of alliance could be framed, and flatly declined to admit the presence of British officers in Kabul. Finally Sher Ali occupied Ali Masjid and, buoyed up no doubt by Russian promises of assistance, assumed an offensive attitude towards India, whilst at the same time he received a Russian mission with all honour at his Court. What followed is matter of comparatively recent history—our attempt to force a mission upon him and the war with Afghanistan which was the necessary sequence of our failure.

The Treaty of Gandamak which closed the first phase of the Afghan war in June 1879 had considerable effect in contracting the position of Afghanistan at certain very important points of the Indian borderland, and in definitely advancing that boundary which we had hitherto held as a heritage from the Sikhs. On the Khaibar line of advance the boundary was shifted Afghanwards from the foot of the hills near Jamrud to Lundi Kotal, giving us the command of Ali Masjid and the Khaibar pass.

The Kuram valley was included within British jurisdiction, which carried our frontier to the Peiwar Kotal, the scene of one of our most successful victories; and on the southern border, our occupation of Quetta was recognised, and the Khojak mountains (which lie about sixty miles to the north-west of Quetta and approximately half-way between that station and Kandahar) brought within the British line; the boundary being drawn at the foot of the northern slopes of the range. But no actual demarcation of this part of the boundary was carried out as an immediate result of the treaty.

Such, briefly, is the chequered history of Afghanistan until it reaches the period at which our tale of the frontier begins. For fuller details of early Afghan history, the reader cannot do better than refer to Bellew's *Afghanistan and the Afghans.*

error in publication the Russian railway
to the Afghan frontier has been extended
nshidi settlement of Kushk. The Russian
of Kushk is on the boundary where the
made to cross it.

INDEX

A CATALOGUE OF BOOKS AND ANNOUNCEMENTS OF METHUEN AND COMPANY PUBLISHERS : LONDON 36 ESSEX STREET W.C.

CONTENTS

NOVEMBER 1900

NOVEMBER 1900

MESSRS. METHUEN'S ANNOUNCEMENTS

Travel, Adventure and Topography

THE INDIAN BORDERLAND: Being a Personal Record of Twenty Years. By Sir T. H. HOLDICH, K.C.I.E. Illustrated. *Demy 8vo.* 15*s. net.*

This book is a personal record of the author's connection with those military and political expeditions which, during the last twenty years, have led to the consolidation of our present position in the North-West frontier of India. It is a personal history of trans-frontier surveys and boundary demarcations, commencing with Penjdeh and ending with the Pamirs, Chitral, and Tirah.

MODERN ABYSSYNIA. By A. B. WYLDE. With a Map and a Portrait. *Demy 8vo.* 15*s. net.*

An important and comprehensive account of Abyssinia by a traveller who knows the country intimately, and has had the privilege of the friendship of King Menelik.

Revised by Commanding Officers.

THE HISTORY OF THE BOER WAR. By F. H. E. CUNLIFFE, Fellow of All Souls' College, Oxford. With many Illustrations, Plans, and Portraits. Vol. I. *Quarto.* 15*s.* Also in Fortnightly Parts. 1*s. each.*

The first volume of this important work is nearly ready. When complete, this book will give an elaborate and connected account of the military operations in South Africa from the declaration to the end of the present war. It must remain for some years the standard History of the War. Messrs. Methuen have been fortunate enough to secure the co-operation of many commanding officers in the revision of the various chapters.

The History is finely illustrated.

A PRISONER OF WAR. By COLONEL A. SCHIEL. *Crown 8vo.* 6*s.*

This remarkable book contains the experiences of a well-known foreign officer of the Boer Army—from 1896 to 1900—both as a Boer officer and as a prisoner in British hands. Colonel Schiel, who was captured at Elandslaagte, was a confidential military adviser of the Transvaal Government, and his story will cause a sensation.

DARTMOOR: A Descriptive and Historical Sketch. By S. BARING GOULD. With Plans and Numerous Illustrations. *Crown 8vo.* 6*s.*

This book attempts to give to the visitor a descriptive history of the antiquities and natural features of this district. It is profusely illustrated from paintings and from photographs. Plans are also given of the chief antiquities. The book is uniform with the author's well-known *Book of the West.*

THE SIEGE OF MAFEKING. By ANGUS HAMILTON. With many Illustrations. *Crown 8vo.* 6*s.*

This is a vivid, accurate, and humorous narrative of the great siege by the well-known Correspondent of the *Times.* Mr. Hamilton is not only an admirable writer, but an excellent fighter, and he took an active part in the defence of the town. His narrative of the siege is acknowledged to be far superior to any other account.

THE PEOPLE OF CHINA. By J. W. ROBERTSON-SCOTT. With a Map. *Crown 8vo.* 3s. 6d.

This book of 200 pages contains a complete account of the history, races, government, religion, social life, army, commerce, and attitude to foreigners of the Chinese.

THE RELIEF OF MAFEKING. By FILSON YOUNG. With Maps and Illustrations. *Crown 8vo.* 6s.

This book gives a spirited and vigorous account of the work accomplished by Mahon's flying column and its relief of Mafeking. It also relates the defeat of Colonel Villebois and his death. The book deals in the main with episodes in the war which have not yet been described in any work.

WITH THE BOER FORCES. By HOWARD C. HILLEGAS. With 16 Illustrations. *Crown 8vo.* 6s.

This highly interesting book is a narrative of the episodes of the Boer war by a correspondent with the Boer army. Mr. Hillegas was present at many of the most exciting and most dramatic episodes of the war. He was with the force which attempted to relieve Cronje at Paardeberg, was present during a considerable part of the siege of Ladysmith, at the battle of Colenso, at the surprise of Sanna's Post. His book, written with dramatic vigour, is a spirited description of the Boer methods, of their military strength, and contains vivid character sketches of most of the Boer leaders with whom Mr. Hillegas was on terms of fairly intimate friendship. This book, though written by one who sympathises with the Boers, is permeated by a spirit of chivalry, and it contains little that can offend the most sensitive of Englishmen. It throws a flood of light on many of the episodes which have been mysterious, and explains the secrets of the many successes which the Boers have won.

History and Biography

THE LETTERS OF ROBERT LOUIS STEVENSON TO HIS FAMILY AND FRIENDS. Edited with an Introduction and Notes by SIDNEY COLVIN. Fourth Edition. *Two volumes. Crown 8vo.* 12s.

This is a completely new edition of the famous Letters of Robert Louis Stevenson, published in 1899.

THE LIFE AND LETTERS OF SIR JOHN EVERETT MILLAIS, President of the Royal Academy. By his son J. G. MILLAIS. With over 300 Illustrations, of which 9 are in Photogravure. Cheaper Edition, Revised. *Two volumes. Royal 8vo.* 20s. *net.*

THE WALKERS OF SOUTHGATE: Being the Chronicles of a Cricketing Family. By W. A. BETTESWORTH. Illustrated. *Demy 8vo.* 15s.

A HISTORY OF EGYPT, FROM THE EARLIEST TIMES TO THE PRESENT DAY. Edited by W. M. FLINDERS PETRIE, D.C.L., LL.D., Professor of Egyptology at University College. Fully Illustrated. In Six Volumes. *Crown 8vo.* 6s. *each.*

Vol. VI. EGYPT UNDER THE SARACENS. By STANLEY LANE-POOLE.

Illustrated and Gift Books

THE LIVELY CITY OF LIGG. By GELETT BURGESS. With 53 Illustrations, 8 of which are coloured. *Small 4to.* 6s.

GOOP BABIES. By GELETT BURGESS. With numerous Illustrations. *Small 4to.* 6*s.*

THE EARLY POEMS OF ALFRED LORD TENNYSON. Edited, with Notes and an Introduction by J. CHURTON COLLINS, M.A. With 10 Illustrations in Photogravure by W. E. F. BRITTEN. *Demy 8vo.* 10*s.* 6*d.*

This beautiful edition contains ten charming sketches by Mr. Britten, reproduced in the highest style of Photogravure.

NURSERY RHYMES. With many Coloured Pictures by F. D. BEDFORD. *Super Royal 8vo.* 2*s.* 6*d.*

'An excellent selection of the best known rhymes, with beautifully coloured pictures exquisitely printed.'—*Pall Mall Gazette.*

Theology

THE PHILOSOPHY OF RELIGION IN ENGLAND. By ALFRED CALDECOTT, D.D. *Demy 8vo.* 10*s.* 6*d.*

[*Handbooks of Theology.*

A complete history and description of the various philosophies of religion which have been formulated during the last few centuries in England and America.

ST. PAUL'S SECOND AND THIRD EPISTLES TO THE CORINTHIANS. With Introduction, Dissertations, and Notes by JAMES HOUGHTON KENNEDY, D.D., Assistant Lecturer in Divinity in the University of Dublin. *Crown 8vo.* 6*s.*

THE SOUL OF A CHRISTIAN. By F. S. GRANGER, M.A., Litt.D. *Crown 8vo.* 6*s.*

Professor Granger abandons the conventional method of psychology by which the individual is taken alone, and instead, he regards him as sharing in and contributing to the catholic tradition. Hence the book deals not only with the average religious life, but also with the less familiar experiences of the mystic, the visionary, and the symbolist. These experiences furnish a clue to poetic creation in its various kinds, and further, to the miracles which occur during times of religious enthusiasm.

Oxford Commentaries.

THE ACTS OF THE APOSTLES. Edited, with an Introduction and Notes, by R. B. RACKHAM, M.A. *Demy 8vo.*

The Library of Devotion

Pott 8vo. Cloth 2s.; leather 2s. 6d. net.

NEW VOLUMES.

A GUIDE TO ETERNITY. By CARDINAL BONA. Edited with an Introduction and Notes by J. W. STANBRIDGE, B.D., late Fellow of St. John's College, Oxford.

THE PSALMS OF DAVID. With an Introduction and Notes by B. W. RANDOLPH, D.D., Principal of the Theological College, Ely.

A devotional and practical edition of the Prayer Book version of the Psalms.

LYRA APOSTOLICA. With an Introduction by Canon SCOTT HOLLAND, and Notes by H. C. BEECHING, M.A.

Belles Lettres

The Little Guides

Pott 8vo. Cloth, 3s.; leather, 3s. 6d. net.

NEW VOLUMES.

WESTMINSTER ABBEY. By G. E. TROUTBECK. Illustrated by F. D. BEDFORD.

SUSSEX. By F. G. BRABANT, M.A. Illustrated by E. H. NEW.

Little Biographies

Fcap. 8vo. Each Volume, cloth 3s. 6d.; leather, 4s. net.

Messrs. METHUEN will publish shortly the first two volumes of a new series bearing the above title. Each book will contain the biography of a character famous in war, art, literature or science, and will be written by an acknowledged expert. The books will be charmingly produced and will be well illustrated. They will make delightful gift books.

THE LIFE OF DANTE ALIGHIERI. By PAGET TOYNBEE. With 12 Illustrations.

THE LIFE OF SAVONAROLA. By E. L. HORSBURGH, M.A., With Portraits and Illustrations.

The Works of Shakespeare

New volumes uniform with Professor Dowden's *Hamlet*.

ROMEO AND JULIET. Edited by EDWARD DOWDEN, Litt.D. *Demy 8vo.* 3s. 6d.

KING LEAR. Edited by W. J. CRAIG. *Demy 8vo.* 3s. 6d.

Methuen's Standard Library

MEMOIRS OF MY LIFE AND WRITINGS. By EDWARD GIBBON. Edited, with an Introduction and Notes by G. BIRKBECK HILL, LL.D. *Crown 8vo. Gilt top.* 6s.

THE LETTERS OF LORD CHESTERFIELD TO HIS SON. Edited, with an Introduction and Notes by C. STRACHEY and A. CALTHROP. *Two volumes. Crown 8vo. Gilt top.* 6s. *each.*

The Novels of Charles Dickens

With Introductions by GEORGE GISSING, Notes by F. G. KITTON, and Illustrations.

Crown 8vo. Each Volume, cloth 3s. net, leather 4s. 6d. net.

The first volumes are:

THE PICKWICK PAPERS. With Illustrations by E. H. NEW. *Two Volumes.* [*Ready*

NICHOLAS NICKLEBY. With Illustrations by R. J. WILLIAMS. *Two Volumes.* [*Ready.*

BLEAK HOUSE. With Illustrations by BEATRICE ALCOCK. *Two Volumes.*

OLIVER TWIST. With Illustrations by E. H. NEW. *One Volume.*

The Little Library

With Introductions, Notes, and Photogravure Frontispieces.

Pott 8vo. Each Volume, cloth 1s. 6d. net.; leather 2s. 6d. net.

NEW VOLUMES.

THE EARLY POEMS OF ALFRED, LORD TENNYSON. Edited by J. C. COLLINS, M.A.

MAUD. By ALFRED, LORD TENNYSON. Edited by ELIZABETH WORDSWORTH.

A LITTLE BOOK OF ENGLISH LYRICS. With Notes.

PRIDE AND PREJUDICE. By JANE AUSTEN. Edited by E. V. LUCAS. *Two Volumes.*

PENDENNIS. By W. M. THACKERAY. Edited by S. GWYNN. *Three volumes.*

EOTHEN. By A. W. KINGLAKE. With an Introduction and Notes.

LAVENGRO. By GEORGE BORROW. Edited by F. HINDES GROOME. 2 Volumes.

CRANFORD. By Mrs. GASKELL. Edited by E. V. LUCAS.

THE INFERNO OF DANTE. Translated by H. F. CARY. Edited by PAGET TOYNBEE.

JOHN HALIFAX, GENTLEMAN. By Mrs. CRAIK. Edited by ANNIE MATHESON. *Two volumes.*

A LITTLE BOOK OF SCOTTISH VERSE. Arranged and Edited by T. F. HENDERSON.

A LITTLE BOOK OF ENGLISH PROSE. Arranged and Edited by Mrs. P. A. BARNETT.

Poetry

WRIT IN BARRACKS. By EDGAR WALLACE. *Cr. 8vo.* 3s. 6d.

Mr. Edgar Wallace, a member of the Royal Army Medical Corps, is a follower of Mr. Kipling, and his ballads of soldier life and sufferings are well-known in South Africa. They are spirited, pathetic, and true, and at the present time they should enjoy a considerable popularity.

THE RUBAIYAT OF OMAR KHAYYAM. Translated by EDWARD FITZGERALD, with a Commentary by H. M. BATSON, and a Biography of Omar by E. D. ROSS. 6s.

This edition of the famous book, the text of which is printed by permission of Messrs. Macmillan, is the most complete in existence. It contains FitzGerald's last text, and a very full commentary on each stanza. Professor Ross, who is an admirable Persian scholar, contributes a biography, containing many new, valuable, and interesting facts.

Scientific and Educational

THE CAPTIVI OF PLAUTUS. Edited, with an Introduction, Textual Notes, and a Commentary, by W. M. LINDSAY, Fellow of Jesus College, Oxford. *Demy 8vo.* 10s. 6d. *net.*

For this edition all the important MSS. have been re-collated. An appendix deals with the accentual element in early Latin verse. The Commentary is very full.

THE CONSTRUCTION OF LARGE INDUCTION COILS. By A. T. HARE, M.A. With numerous Diagrams. *Demy 8vo.* 6s.

THE SCIENCE OF HYGIENE. By W. C. C. PAKES, Guy's Hospital. With many illustrations. *Demy 8vo.* 15s.

THE PRINCIPLES OF MAGNETISM AND ELECTRICITY: AN ELEMENTARY TEXT-BOOK. By P. L. GRAY, B.Sc., formerly Lecturer on Physics in Mason University College, Birmingham. With numerous diagrams. *Crown 8vo.* 3s. 6d.

LACE-MAKING IN THE MIDLANDS, PAST AND PRESENT. By C. C. CHANNER and M. E. ROBERTS. With 16 full-page Illustrations. *Crown 8vo.* 2s. 6d.

AGRICULTURAL ZOOLOGY. By Dr. J. RITZEMA BOS. Translated by J. R. AINSWORTH DAVIS, M.A. With an Introduction by ELEANOR A. ORMEROD, F.E.S. With 155 Illustrations. *Crown 8vo.* 3s. 6d.

A SOUTH AFRICAN ARITHMETIC. By HENRY HILL, B.A., Assistant Master at Worcester School, Cape Colony. *Crown 8vo.* 3s. 6d.

This book has been specially written for use in South African schools.

A GERMAN COMMERCIAL READER. By S. BALLY, M.A. *Crown 8vo.* 2s. [*Methuen's Commercial Series.*

Fiction

THE MASTER CHRISTIAN. By MARIE CORELLI. *Crown 8vo.* 6*s.*

QUISANTE. By ANTHONY HOPE. *Crown 8vo.* 6*s.*

A MASTER OF CRAFT. By W. W. JACOBS, Author of 'Many Cargoes.' With 12 Illustrations by W. OWEN. *Crown 8vo.* 6*s.*

THE GATELESS BARRIER. By LUCAS MALET, Author 'The Wages of Sin.' *Crown 8vo.* 6*s.*

CUNNING MURRELL. By ARTHUR MORRISON, Author of 'A Child of the Jago,' etc. *Crown 8vo.* 6*s.*

FOR BRITAIN'S SOLDIERS: Stories for the War Fund. By RUDYARD KIPLING and Others. Edited by C. J. CUTCLIFFE HYNE. *Crown 8vo.* 6*s.*

A volume of stories, the proceeds of which will be given to the War Fund. Among the contributors are:—Rudyard Kipling, Sir W. Besant, S. R. Crockett, A. E. W. Mason, Max Pemberton, H. G. Wells, C. J. C. Hyne, Mrs. Croker.

THE FOOTSTEPS OF A THRONE. By MAX PEMBERTON. *Crown 8vo.* 6*s.*

SONS OF THE MORNING. By EDEN PHILLPOTTS, Author of 'The Children of the Mist.' With a frontispiece. *Crown 8vo.* 6*s.*

THE SOFT SIDE. By HENRY JAMES, Author of 'What Maisie Knew.' *Crown 8vo.* 6*s.*

TONGUES OF CONSCIENCE. By ROBERT HICHENS, Author of 'Flames.' *Crown 8vo.* 6*s.*

THE CONQUEST OF LONDON. By DOROTHEA GERARD, Author of 'Lady Baby.' *Crown 8vo.* 6*s.*

WOUNDS IN THE RAIN: A Collection of Stories relating to the Spanish-American War of 1898. By STEPHEN CRANE, Author of 'The Red Badge of Courage.' *Crown 8vo.* 6*s.*

WINEFRED. By S. BARING GOULD, Author of 'Mehalah.' With 8 Illustrations by EDGAR BUNDY. *Crown 8vo.* 6*s.*

THE STRONG ARM. By ROBERT BARR, Author of 'The Countess Tekla.' Illustrated. *Crown 8vo.* 6*s.*

THE SEEN AND THE UNSEEN. By RICHARD MARSH. Author of 'The Beetle,' 'Marvels and Mysteries,' etc. *Crown 8vo.* 6*s.*

SERVANTS OF SIN. By J. BLOUNDELLE BURTON, Author 'The Clash of Arms.' *Crown 8vo.* 6*s*.

PATH AND GOAL. By ADA CAMBRIDGE. *Crown 8vo.* 6*s*.

ELMSLIE'S DRAG-NET. By E. H. STRAIN. *Crown 8vo.* 6*s*.

A FOREST OFFICER. By MRS. PENNY. *Crown 8vo.* 6*s*.
A story of jungle life in India.

FITZJAMES. By LILIAN STREET. *Crown 8vo.* 3*s*. 6*d*.

The Novelist

A monthly series of novels by popular authors at Sixpence. Each Number is as long as the average Six Shilling Novel. Numbers I. to XII. are now ready:—

XIII. THE POMP OF THE LAVILETTES. GILBERT PARKER.

XIV. A MAN OF MARK. ANTHONY HOPE.

XV. THE CARISSIMA. LUCAS MALET.

XVI. THE LADY'S WALK. MRS. OLIPHANT.

XVII. DERRICK VAUGHAN. EDNA LYALL. [*November*.

Methuen's Sixpenny Library

A New Series of Copyright Books.

I. THE MATABELE CAMPAIGN. Maj.-General BADEN-POWELL.

II. THE DOWNFALL OF PREMPEH. Do.

III. MY DANISH SWEETHEART. W. CLARK RUSSELL.

IV. IN THE ROAR OF THE SEA. S. BARING GOULD.

V. PEGGY OF THE BARTONS. B. M. CROKER.

VI. BADEN-POWELL OF MAFEKING: a Biography. J. S. FLETCHER. [*November*.

VII. ROBERTS OF PRETORIA. J. S. FLETCHER. [*December*.

A CATALOGUE OF

MESSRS. METHUEN'S PUBLICATIONS

Poetry

Rudyard Kipling. BARRACK-ROOM BALLADS. By RUDYARD KIPLING. *68th Thousand. Crown 8vo.* 6s. *Leather*, 6s. *net.*

'Mr. Kipling's verse is strong, vivid, full of character. . . . Unmistakeable genius rings in every line.'—*Times.*

'The ballads teem with imagination, they palpitate with emotion. We read them with laughter and tears; the metres throb in our pulses, the cunningly ordered words tingle with life; and if this be not poetry, what is?'—*Pall Mall Gazette.*

Rudyard Kipling. THE SEVEN SEAS. By RUDYARD KIPLING. *57th Thousand. Cr. 8vo. Buckram, gilt top.* 6s. *Leather*, 6s. *net.*

'The Empire has found a singer; it is no depreciation of the songs to say that statesmen may have, one way or other, to take account of them.'—*Manchester Guardian.*

'Animated through and through with indubitable genius.'—*Daily Telegraph.*

"Q." POEMS AND BALLADS. By "Q." *Crown 8vo.* 3s. 6d.

"Q." GREEN BAYS: Verses and Parodies. By "Q." *Second Edition. Crown 8vo.* 3s. 6d.

E. Mackay. A SONG OF THE SEA. By ERIC MACKAY. *Second Edition. Fcap. 8vo.* 5s.

H. Ibsen. BRAND. A Drama by HENRIK IBSEN. Translated by WILLIAM WILSON. *Third Edition. Crown 8vo.* 3s. 6d.

A. D. Godley. LYRA FRIVOLA. By A. D. GODLEY, M.A., Fellow of Magdalen College, Oxford. *Third Edition. Pott 8vo.* 2s. 6d.

'Combines a pretty wit with remarkably neat versification. . . . Every one will wish there was more of it.'—*Times.*

A. D. Godley. VERSES TO ORDER. By A. D. GODLEY. *Crown 8vo.* 2s. 6d. *net.*

'A capital specimen of light academic poetry.'—*St. James's Gazette.*

J. G. Cordery. THE ODYSSEY OF HOMER. A Translation by J. G. CORDERY. *Crown 8vo.* 7s. 6d.

Belles Lettres, Anthologies, etc.

R. L. Stevenson. VAILIMA LETTERS. By ROBERT LOUIS STEVENSON. With an Etched Portrait by WILLIAM STRANG. *Second Edition. Crown 8vo. Buckram.* 6s.

'A fascinating book.'—*Standard.*
'Unique in Literature.'—*Daily Chronicle.*

G. Wyndham. THE POEMS OF WILLIAM SHAKESPEARE. Edited with an Introduction and Notes by GEORGE WYNDHAM, M.P. *Demy 8vo. Buckram, gilt top.* 10s. 6d.

This edition contains the 'Venus,' 'Lucrece,' and Sonnets, and is prefaced with an elaborate introduction of over 140 pp.
'We have no hesitation in describing Mr. George Wyndham's introduction as a masterly piece of criticism, and all who love our Elizabethan literature will find a very garden of delight in it.'—*Spectator.*

W. E. Henley. ENGLISH LYRICS. Selected and Edited by W. E. HENLEY. *Crown 8vo. Gilt top.* 3s. 6d.

'It is a body of choice and lovely poetry.'—*Birmingham Gazette.*

Henley and Whibley. A BOOK OF ENGLISH PROSE. Collected by W. E. HENLEY and CHARLES WHIBLEY. *Crown 8vo. Buckram, gilt top.* 6s.

H. C. Beeching. LYRA SACRA: An Anthology of Sacred Verse. Edited by H. C. BEECHING, M.A. *Crown 8vo. Buckram.* 6s.

'A charming selection, which maintains a lofty standard of excellence.'—*Times.*

"Q." THE GOLDEN POMP. A Procession of English Lyrics. Arranged by A. T. QUILLER COUCH. *Crown 8vo. Buckram.* 6s.

W. B. Yeats. AN ANTHOLOGY OF IRISH VERSE. Edited by W. B. YEATS. *Revised and Enlarged Edition. Crown 8vo.* 3s. 6d.

'An attractive and catholic selection.'—*Times.*

G. W. Steevens. MONOLOGUES OF THE DEAD. By G. W. STEEVENS. *Foolscap 8vo.* 3s. 6d.

W. M. Dixon. A PRIMER OF TENNYSON. By W. M. DIXON, M.A. *Cr. 8vo.* 2s. 6d.

'Much sound and well-expressed criticism. The bibliography is a boon.'—*Speaker.*

W. A. Craigie. A PRIMER OF BURNS. By W. A. CRAIGIE. *Crown 8vo.* 2s. 6d.

'A valuable addition to the literature of the poet.'—*Times.*

L. Magnus. A PRIMER OF WORDSWORTH. By LAURIE MAGNUS. *Crown 8vo.* 2s. 6d.

'A valuable contribution to Wordsworthian literature.'—*Literature.*

Sterne. THE LIFE AND OPINIONS OF TRISTRAM SHANDY. By LAWRENCE STERNE. With an Introduction by CHARLES WHIBLEY, and a Portrait. 2 *vols.* 7s.

Congreve. THE COMEDIES OF WILLIAM CONGREVE. With an Introduction by G. S. STREET, and a Portrait. 2 *vols.* 7s.

Morier. THE ADVENTURES OF HAJJI BABA OF ISPAHAN. By JAMES MORIER. With an Introduction by E. G. BROWNE, M.A. and a Portrait. 2 *vols.* 7s.

Walton. THE LIVES OF DONNE, WOTTON, HOOKER, HERBERT AND SANDERSON. By IZAAK WALTON. With an Introduction by VERNON BLACKBURN, and a Portrait. 3s. 6d.

Johnson. THE LIVES OF THE ENGLISH POETS. By SAMUEL JOHNSON, LL.D. With an Introduction by J. H. MILLAR, and a Portrait. 3 *vols.* 10s. 6d.

Burns. THE POEMS OF ROBERT BURNS. Edited by ANDREW LANG and W. A. CRAIGIE. With Portrait. *Second Edition. Demy 8vo, gilt top.* 6s.

'Among editions in one volume, this will take the place of authority.'—*Times.*

F. Langbridge. BALLADS OF THE BRAVE; Poems of Chivalry, Enterprise, Courage, and Constancy. Edited by Rev. F. LANGBRIDGE. *Second Edition. Cr. 8vo.* 3*s*. 6*d*. *School Edition.* 2*s*. 6*d*.

'The book is full of splendid things.'—*World.*

Methuen's Standard Library

Dante. LA COMMEDIA DI DANTE ALIGHIERI. The Italian Text edited by PAGET TOYNBEE, M.A. *Crown 8vo.* 6*s*.

'A carefully-revised text, printed with beautiful clearness.'—*Glasgow Herald.*

Gibbon. THE DECLINE AND FALL OF THE ROMAN EMPIRE. By EDWARD GIBBON. A New Edition, Edited with Notes, Appendices, and Maps, by J. B. BURY, LL.D., Fellow of Trinity College, Dublin. *In Seven Volumes. Demy 8vo. Gilt top.* 8*s*. 6*d*. *each. Also Cr. 8vo.* 6*s*. *each.*

'The time has certainly arrived for a new edition of Gibbon's great work. . . . Professor Bury is the right man to undertake this task. His learning is amazing, both in extent and accuracy. The book is issued in a handy form, and at a moderate price, and it is admirably printed.'—*Times.*

'At last there is an adequate modern edition of Gibbon. . . . The best edition the nineteenth century could produce.—*Manchester Guardian.*

'A great piece of editing.'—*Academy.*

'The greatest of English, perhaps of all, historians has never been presented to the public in a more convenient and attractive form. No higher praise can be bestowed upon Professor Bury than to say, as may be said with truth, that he is worthy of being ranked with Guizot and Milman.'—*Daily News.*

C. G. Crump. THE HISTORY OF THE LIFE OF THOMAS ELLWOOD. Edited by C. G. CRUMP, M.A. *Crown 8vo.* 6*s*.

This edition is the only one which contains the complete book as originally published. It contains a long Introduction and many Footnotes.

'"The History of Thomas Ellwood" holds a high place among the masterpieces of autobiography, and we know few books that better deserve reprinting. Moreover, Mr. C. G. Crump's new edition is accurate and convenient, and we commend it ungrudgingly to all those who love sound and vigorous English.' —*Daily Mail.*

Tennyson. THE EARLY POEMS OF ALFRED, LORD TENNYSON, Edited, with Notes and an Introduction by J. CHURTON COLLINS, M.A. *Crown 8vo.* 6*s*.

An elaborate edition of the celebrated volume which was published in its final and definitive form in 1853. This edition contains a long Introduction and copious Notes, textual and explanatory. It also contains in an Appendix all the Poems which Tennyson afterwards omitted.

'Mr. Collins is almost an ideal editor of Tennyson. His qualities as a critic are an exact and accurate scholarship, and a literary judgment, which has been trained and polished by the closest study of classics both ancient and modern. Mr. Collins' introduction is a thoroughly sound and sane appreciation of the merits and demerits of Tennyson.'—*Literature.*

The Works of Shakespeare

General Editor, EDWARD DOWDEN, Litt. D.

MESSRS. METHUEN have in preparation an Edition of Shakespeare in single Plays. Each play will be edited with a full Introduction, Textual Notes, and a Commentary at the foot of the page.

The first volume is:

HAMLET. Edited by EDWARD DOWDEN. *Demy 8vo.* 3*s*. 6*d*.

'An admirable edition. . . . A comely volume, admirably printed and produced, and containing all that a student of "Hamlet" need require.'—*Speaker.*

'Fully up to the level of recent scholarship, both English and German.—*Academy.*

The Novels of Charles Dickens

Crown 8vo. Each Volume, cloth 3s. net; leather 4s. 6d. net.

Messrs. METHUEN have in preparation an edition of those novels of Charles Dickens which have now passed out of copyright. Mr. George Gissing, whose critical study of Dickens is both sympathetic and acute, has written an Introduction to each of the books, and a very attractive feature of this edition will be the illustrations of the old houses, inns, and buildings, which Dickens described, and which have now in many instances disappeared under the touch of modern civilisation. Another valuable feature will be a series of topographical and general notes to each book by Mr. F. G. Kitton. The books will be produced with the greatest care as to printing, paper and binding.

The first volumes are:

THE PICKWICK PAPERS. With Illustrations by E. H. NEW. *Two Volumes.*

'As pleasant a copy as any one could desire. The notes add much to the value of the edition, and Mr. New's illustrations are also historical. The volumes promise well for the success of the edition.'—*Scotsman.*

The Little Library

'The volumes are compact in size, printed on thin but good paper in clear type, prettily and at the same time strongly bound, and altogether good to look upon and handle.'—*Outlook.*

Pott 8vo. Each Volume, cloth 1s. 6d. net, leather 2s. 6d. net.

Messrs. METHUEN intend to produce a series of small books under the above title, containing some of the famous books in English and other literatures, in the domains of fiction, poetry, and belles lettres. The series will also contain several volumes of selections in prose and verse.

The books will be edited with the most sympathetic and scholarly care. Each one will contain an Introduction which will give (1) a short biography of the author, (2) a critical estimate of the book. Where they are necessary, short notes will be added at the foot of the page.

Each book will have a portrait or frontispiece in photogravure, and the volumes will be produced with great care in a style uniform with that of 'The Library of Devotion.'

The first volumes are:

VANITY FAIR. By W. M. THACKERAY. With an Introduction by S. GWYNN. Illustrated by G. P. JACOMB HOOD. *Three Volumes.*

'Delightful little volumes.'—*Publishers' Circular.*

THE PRINCESS. By ALFRED, LORD TENNYSON. Edited by ELIZABETH WORDSWORTH. Illustrated by W. E. F. BRITTEN.

'Just what a pocket edition should be. Miss Wordsworth contributes an acceptable introduction, as well as notes which one is equally glad to get.'—*Guardian.*

IN MEMORIAM. By ALFRED, LORD TENNYSON. Edited, with an Introduction and Notes, by H. C. BEECHING, M.A.

'An exquisite little volume, which will be gladly welcomed.'—*Glasgow Herald.*

'The introduction, analysis, and notes by the Rev. H. C. Beeching are all of the sound literary quality that was to be expected.'—*Guardian.*

'The footnotes are scholarly, interesting, and not super-abundant.'—*Standard.*

'It is difficult to conceive a more attractive edition.'—*St. James's Gazette.*

The Little Guides

Pott 8vo, cloth 3s.; leather, 3s. 6d. net.

OXFORD AND ITS COLLEGES. By J. WELLS, M.A., Fellow and Tutor of Wadham College. Illustrated by E. H. NEW. *Third Edition.*

'An admirable and accurate little treatise, attractively illustrated.'—*World.*

'A luminous and tasteful little volume.'—*Daily Chronicle.*

CAMBRIDGE AND ITS COLLEGES. By A. HAMILTON THOMPSON. Illustrated by E. H. NEW.

'It is brightly written and learned, and is just such a book as a cultured visitor needs.'—*Scotsman.*

SHAKESPEARE'S COUNTRY. By B. C. WINDLE, F.R.S., M.A. Illustrated by E. H. NEW. *Second Edition.*

'Mr. Windle is thoroughly conversant with his subject, and the work is exceedingly well done. The drawings, by Mr. Edmund H. New, add much to the attractiveness of the volume.'—*Scotsman.*

'One of the most charming guide books. Both for the library and as a travelling companion the book is equally choice and serviceable.'—*Academy.*

'A guide book of the best kind, which takes rank as literature.'—*Guardian.*

Illustrated and Gift Books

Phil May. THE PHIL MAY ALBUM. *4to.* 6s.

'There is a laugh in each drawing.'—*Standard.*

A. H. Milne. ULYSSES; OR, DE ROUGEMONT OF TROY. Described and depicted by A. H. MILNE. *Small quarto.* 3s. 6d.

'Clever, droll, smart.'—*Guardian.*

Edmund Selous. TOMMY SMITH'S ANIMALS. By EDMUND SELOUS. Illustrated by G. W. ORD. *Fcap. 8vo.* 2s. 6d.

A little book designed to teach children respect and reverence for animals.

'A quaint, fascinating little book: a nursery classic.'—*Athenæum.*

S. Baring Gould. THE CROCK OF GOLD. Fairy Stories told by S. BARING GOULD. *Crown 8vo.* 6s.

'Twelve delightful fairy tales.'—*Punch.*

M. L. Gwynn. A BIRTHDAY BOOK. Arranged and Edited by M. L. GWYNN. *Demy 8vo.* 12s. 6d.

This is a birthday-book of exceptional dignity, and the extracts have been chosen with particular care.

John Bunyan. THE PILGRIM'S PROGRESS. By JOHN BUNYAN. Edited, with an Introduction, by C. H. FIRTH, M.A. With 39 Illustrations by R. ANNING BELL. *Crown 8vo.* 6s.

'The best "Pilgrim's Progress."'—*Educational Times.*

F. D. Bedford. NURSERY RHYMES. With many Coloured Pictures by F. D. BEDFORD. *Super Royal 8vo.* 5s.

S. Baring Gould. A BOOK OF FAIRY TALES retold by S. BARING GOULD. With numerous Illustrations and Initial Letters by ARTHUR J. GASKIN. *Second Edition. Cr. 8vo. Buckram.* 6s.

S. Baring Gould. OLD ENGLISH FAIRY TALES. Collected and edited by S. BARING GOULD. With Numerous Illustrations by F. D. BEDFORD. *Second Edition. Cr. 8vo. Buckram.* 6s.

'A charming volume.'—*Guardian.*

S. Baring Gould. A BOOK OF NURSERY SONGS AND RHYMES. Edited by S. BARING GOULD, and Illustrated by the Birmingham Art School. *Buckram, gilt top. Crown 8vo.* 6s.

H. C. Beeching. A BOOK OF CHRISTMAS VERSE. Edited by H. C. BEECHING, M.A., and Illustrated by WALTER CRANE. *Cr. 8vo, gilt top.* 3s. 6d.

History

Flinders Petrie. A HISTORY OF EGYPT, FROM THE EARLIEST TIMES TO THE PRESENT DAY. Edited by W. M. FLINDERS PETRIE, D.C.L., LL.D., Professor of Egyptology at University College. *Fully Illustrated. In Six Volumes. Cr. 8vo. 6s. each.*

VOL. I. PREHISTORIC TIMES TO XVITH DYNASTY. W. M. F. Petrie. *Fourth Edition.*

VOL. II. THE XVIITH AND XVIIITH DYNASTIES. W. M. F. Petrie. *Third Edition.*

VOL. IV. THE EGYPT OF THE PTOLEMIES. J. P. Mahaffy.

VOL. V. ROMAN EGYPT. J. G. Milne.

'A history written in the spirit of scientific precision so worthily represented by Dr. Petrie and his school cannot but promote sound and accurate study, and supply a vacant place in the English literature of Egyptology.'—*Times.*

Flinders Petrie. RELIGION AND CONSCIENCE IN ANCIENT EGYPT. By W. M. FLINDERS PETRIE, D.C.L., LL.D. Fully Illustrated. *Crown 8vo. 2s. 6d.*

'The lectures will afford a fund of valuable information for students of ancient ethics.'—*Manchester Guardian.*

Flinders Petrie. SYRIA AND EGYPT, FROM THE TELL EL AMARNA TABLETS. By W. M. FLINDERS PETRIE, D.C.L., LL.D. *Crown 8vo. 2s. 6d.*

'A marvellous record. The addition made to our knowledge is nothing short of amazing.'—*Times.*

Flinders Petrie. EGYPTIAN TALES. Edited by W. M. FLINDERS PETRIE. Illustrated by TRISTRAM ELLIS. *In Two Volumes. Cr. 8vo. 3s. 6d. each.*

'Invaluable as a picture of life in Palestine and Egypt.'—*Daily News.*

Flinders Petrie. EGYPTIAN DECORATIVE ART. By W. M. FLINDERS PETRIE. With 120 Illustrations. *Cr. 8vo. 3s. 6d.*

'In these lectures he displays rare skill in elucidating the development of decorative art in Egypt.'—*Times.*

C. W. Oman. A HISTORY OF THE ART OF WAR. Vol. II.: The Middle Ages, from the Fourth to the Fourteenth Century. By C. W. OMAN, M.A., Fellow of All Souls', Oxford. Illustrated. *Demy 8vo. 21s.*

'The whole art of war in its historic evolution has never been treated on such an ample and comprehensive scale, and we question if any recent contribution to the exact history of the world has possessed more enduring value.'—*Daily Chronicle.*

S. Baring Gould. THE TRAGEDY OF THE CÆSARS. With numerous Illustrations from Busts, Gems, Cameos, etc. By S. BARING GOULD. *Fourth Edition. Royal 8vo. 15s.*

'A most splendid and fascinating book on a subject of undying interest. The great feature of the book is the use the author has made of the existing portraits of the Caesars and the admirable critical subtlety he has exhibited in dealing with this line of research. It is brilliantly written, and the illustrations are supplied on a scale of profuse magnificence.'—*Daily Chronicle.*

F. W. Maitland. CANON LAW IN ENGLAND. By F. W. MAITLAND, LL.D., Downing Professor of the Laws of England in the University of Cambridge. *Royal 8vo. 7s. 6d.*

'Professor Maitland has put students of English law under a fresh debt. These essays are landmarks in the study of the history of Canon Law.'—*Times.*

H. de B. Gibbins. INDUSTRY IN ENGLAND: HISTORICAL OUTLINES. By H. DE B. GIBBINS, Litt.D., M.A. With 5 Maps. *Second Edition. Demy 8vo.* 10s. 6d.

H. E. Egerton. A HISTORY OF BRITISH COLONIAL POLICY. By H. E. EGERTON, M.A. *Demy 8vo.* 12s. 6d.

'It is a good book, distinguished by accuracy in detail, clear arrangement of facts, and a broad grasp of principles.'—*Manchester Guardian.*

Albert Sorel. THE EASTERN QUESTION IN THE EIGHTEENTH CENTURY. By ALBERT SOREL. Translated by F. C. BRAMWELL, M.A. *Cr. 8vo.* 3s. 6d.

C. H. Grinling. A HISTORY OF THE GREAT NORTHERN RAILWAY, 1845-95. By C. H. GRINLING. With Illustrations. *Demy 8vo.* 10s. 6d.

'Mr. Grinling has done for a Railway what Macaulay did for English History.'—*The Engineer.*

W. Sterry. ANNALS OF ETON COLLEGE. By W. STERRY, M.A. With numerous Illustrations. *Demy 8vo.* 7s. 6d.

'A treasury of quaint and interesting reading. Mr. Sterry has by his skill and vivacity given these records new life.'—*Academy.*

G. W. Fisher. ANNALS OF SHREWSBURY SCHOOL. By G. W. FISHER, M.A. With numerous Illustrations. *Demy 8vo.* 10s. 6d.

'This careful, erudite book.'—*Daily Chronicle.*

'A book of which Old Salopians are sure to be proud.'—*Globe.*

J. Sargeaunt. ANNALS OF WESTMINSTER SCHOOL. By J. SARGEAUNT, M.A. With numerous Illustrations. *Demy 8vo.* 7s. 6d.

A. Clark. THE COLLEGES OF OXFORD: Their History and their Traditions. Edited by A. CLARK, M.A., Fellow of Lincoln College. *8vo.* 12s. 6d.

'A work which will be appealed to for many years as the standard book.'—*Athenæum.*

T. M. Taylor. A CONSTITUTIONAL AND POLITICAL HISTORY OF ROME. By T. M. TAYLOR, M.A., Fellow of Gonville and Caius College, Cambridge. *Crown 8vo.* 7s. 6d.

'We fully recognise the value of this carefully written work, and admire especially the fairness and sobriety of his judgment and the human interest with which he has inspired a subject which in some hands becomes a mere series of cold abstractions. It is a work that will be stimulating to the student of Roman history.'—*Athenæum.*

J. Wells. A SHORT HISTORY OF ROME. By J. WELLS, M.A., Fellow and Tutor of Wadham Coll., Oxford. *Third Edition.* With 3 Maps. *Crown 8vo.* 3s. 6d.

This book is intended for the Middle and Upper Forms of Public Schools and for Pass Students at the Universities. It contains copious Tables, etc.

'An original work written on an original plan, and with uncommon freshness and vigour.'—*Speaker.*

O. Browning. A SHORT HISTORY OF MEDIÆVAL ITALY, A.D. 1250-1530. By OSCAR BROWNING, Fellow and Tutor of King's College, Cambridge. *In Two Volumes. Cr. 8vo.* 5s. *each.*

VOL. I. 1250-1409.—Guelphs and Ghibellines.

VOL. II. 1409-1530.—The Age of the Condottieri.

O'Grady. THE STORY OF IRELAND. By STANDISH O'GRADY, Author of 'Finn and his Companions.' *Crown 8vo.* 2s. 6d.

Byzantine Texts

Edited by J. B. BURY, M.A.

ZACHARIAH OF MITYLENE. Translated into English by F. J. HAMILTON, D.D., and E. W. BROOKS. *Demy 8vo.* 12*s.* 6*d.* *net.*

EVAGRIUS. Edited by Professor LÉON PARMENTIER and M. BIDEZ. *Demy 8vo.* 10*s.* 6*d.* *net.*

THE HISTORY OF PSELLUS. By C. SATHAS. *Demy 8vo.* 15*s.* *net.*

Biography

R. L. Stevenson. THE LETTERS OF ROBERT LOUIS STEVENSON TO HIS FAMILY AND FRIENDS. Selected and Edited, with Notes and Introductions, by SIDNEY COLVIN. *Third Edition. Demy 8vo, 2 vols.*, 25*s.* *net.*

'Irresistible in their raciness, their variety, their animation . . . of extraordinary fascination. A delightful inheritance, the truest record of a "richly compounded spirit" that the literature of our time has preserved.'—*Times.*

'There are few books so interesting, so moving, and so valuable as this collection of letters. One can only commend people to read and re-read the book. The volumes are beautiful, and Mr. Colvin's part of the work could not have been better done, his introduction is a masterpiece.'—*Spectator.*

'This splendid work.'—*World.*

'Of such absorbing interest is it, of such completeness in scope and beauty. Special tribute must be paid to the extraordinary completeness of the illustrations.'—*Graphic.*

J. G. Millais. THE LIFE AND LETTERS OF SIR JOHN EVERETT MILLAIS, President of the Royal Academy. By his Son, J. G. MILLAIS. With 319 Illustrations, of which 9 are in Photogravure. *Second Edition. 2 vols, Royal 8vo,* 32*s.* *net.*

'The illustrations make the book delightful to handle or to read. The eye lingers lovingly upon the beautiful pictures.'—*Standard.*

This charming book is a gold mine of good things.'—*Daily News.*

S. Baring Gould. THE LIFE OF NAPOLEON BONAPARTE. By S. BARING GOULD. With over 450 Illustrations in the Text and 12 Photogravure Plates. *Large quarto. Gilt top.* 36*s.*

'The main feature of this gorgeous volume is its great wealth of beautiful photogravures and finely-executed wood engravings, constituting a complete pictorial chronicle of Napoleon I.'s personal history from the days of his early childhood at Ajaccio to the date of his second interment.'—*Daily Telegraph.*

P. H. Colomb. MEMOIRS OF ADMIRAL SIR A. COOPER KEY. By Admiral P. H. COLOMB. With a Portrait. *Demy 8vo.* 16*s.*

Morris Fuller. THE LIFE AND WRITINGS OF JOHN DAVENANT, D.D. (1571-1641), Bishop of Salisbury. By MORRIS FULLER, B.D. *Demy 8vo.* 10*s.* 6*d.*

J. M. Rigg. ST. ANSELM OF CANTERBURY: A CHAPTER IN THE HISTORY OF RELIGION. By J. M. RIGG. *Demy 8vo.* 7*s.* 6*d.*

F. W. Joyce. THE LIFE OF SIR FREDERICK GORE OUSELEY. By F. W. JOYCE, M.A. *7s. 6d.*

W. G. Collingwood. THE LIFE OF JOHN RUSKIN. By W. G. COLLINGWOOD, M.A. With Portraits, and 13 Drawings by Mr. Ruskin. *Second Edition.* 2 *vols.* 8*vo.* 32*s.* *Cheap Edition. Crown* 8*vo.* 6*s.*

C. Waldstein. JOHN RUSKIN. By CHARLES WALDSTEIN, M.A. With a Photogravure Portrait, *Post* 8*vo.* 5*s.*

A. M. F. Darmesteter. THE LIFE OF ERNEST RENAN. By MADAME DARMESTETER. With Portrait. *Second Edition. Cr.* 8*vo.* 6*s.*

W. H. Hutton. THE LIFE OF SIR THOMAS MORE. By W. H. HUTTON, M.A. With Portraits. *Second Edition. Cr.* 8*vo.* 5*s.*

'The book lays good claim to high rank among our biographies. It is excellently, even lovingly, written.'—*Scotsman.*

S. Baring Gould. THE VICAR OF MORWENSTOW: A Biography. By S. BARING GOULD, M.A. A new and Revised Edition. With Portrait. *Crown* 8*vo.* 3*s.* 6*d.*

A completely new edition of the well known biography of R. S. Hawker.

Travel, Adventure and Topography

Sven Hedin. THROUGH ASIA. By SVEN HEDIN, Gold Medallist of the Royal Geographical Society. With 300 Illustrations from Sketches and Photographs by the Author, and Maps. 2 *vols. Royal* 8*vo.* 20*s. net.*

'One of the greatest books of the kind issued during the century. It is impossible to give an adequate idea of the richness of the contents of this book, nor of its abounding attractions as a story of travel unsurpassed in geographical and human interest. Much of it is a revelation. Altogether the work is one which in solidity, novelty, and interest must take a first rank among publications of its class.'—*Times.*

F. H. Skrine and E. D. Ross. THE HEART OF ASIA. By F. H. SKRINE and E. D. ROSS. With Maps and many Illustrations by VERESTCHAGIN. *Large Crown* 8*vo.* 10*s.* 6*d. net.*

'This volume will form a landmark in our knowledge of Central Asia. . . . Illuminating and convincing.'—*Times.*

R. E. Peary. NORTHWARD OVER THE GREAT ICE. By R. E. PEARY, Gold Medallist of the Royal Geographical Society. With over 800 Illustrations. 2 *vols. Royal* 8*vo.* 32*s. net.*

'His book will take its place among the permanent literature of Arctic exploration.'—*Times.*

E. A. FitzGerald. THE HIGHEST ANDES. By E. A. FITZGERALD. With 2 Maps, 51 Illustrations, 13 of which are in Photogravure, and a Panorama. *Royal* 8*vo*, 30*s. net.* Also a Small Edition on Hand-made Paper, limited to 50 Copies, 4*to*, £5, 5*s*.

'The record of the first ascent of the highest mountain yet conquered by mortal man. A volume which will continue to be the classic book of travel on this region of the Andes.'—*Daily Chronicle.*

F. W. Christian. THE CAROLINE ISLANDS. By F. W. CHRISTIAN. With many Illustrations and Maps. *Demy 8vo.* 12*s.* 6*d.* *net.*

'A real contribution to our knowledge of the peoples and islands of Micronesia, as well as fascinating as a narrative of travels and adventure.'—*Scotsman.*

H. H. Johnston. BRITISH CENTRAL AFRICA. By Sir H. H. JOHNSTON, K.C.B. With nearly Two Hundred Illustrations, and Six Maps. *Second Edition. Crown 4to.* 18*s. net.*

'A fascinating book, written with equal skill and charm—the work at once of a literary artist and of a man of action who is singularly wise, brave, and experienced. It abounds in admirable sketches.'—*Westminster Gazette.*

L. Decle. THREE YEARS IN SAVAGE AFRICA. By LIONEL DECLE. With 100 Illustrations and 5 Maps. *Second Edition. Demy 8vo.* 10*s.* 6*d. net.*

'Its bright pages give a better general survey of Africa from the Cape to the Equator than any single volume that has yet been published.'—*Times.*

A. Hulme Beaman. TWENTY YEARS IN THE NEAR EAST. By A. HULME BEAMAN. *Demy 8vo.* With Portrait. 10*s.* 6*d.*

Henri of Orleans. FROM TONKIN TO INDIA. By PRINCE HENRI OF ORLEANS. Translated by HAMLEY BENT, M.A. With 100 Illustrations and a Map. *Cr. 4to, gilt top.* 25s.

S. L. Hinde. THE FALL OF THE CONGO ARABS. By S. L. HINDE. With Plans, etc. *Demy 8vo.* 12*s.* 6*d.*

A. St. H. Gibbons. EXPLORATION AND HUNTING IN CENTRAL AFRICA. By Major A. ST. H. GIBBONS. With full-page Illustrations by C. WHYMPER, and Maps. *Demy 8vo.* 15*s.*

Fraser. ROUND THE WORLD ON A WHEEL. By JOHN FOSTER FRASER. With 100 Illustrations. *Crown 8vo.* 6*s.*

'A classic of cycling, graphic and witty.'—*Yorkshire Post.*

R. L. Jefferson. A NEW RIDE TO KHIVA. By R. L. JEFFERSON. Illustrated. *Crown 8vo,* 6*s.*

The account of an adventurous ride on a bicycle through Russia and the deserts of Asia to Khiva.

'An exceptionally fascinating book of travel.'—*Pall Mall Gazette.*

J. K. Trotter. THE NIGER SOURCES. By Colonel J. K. TROTTER, R.A. With a Map and Illustrations. *Crown 8vo.* 5*s.*

Michael Davitt. LIFE AND PROGRESS IN AUSTRALASIA. By MICHAEL DAVITT, M.P. 500 pp. With 2 Maps. *Crown 8vo.* 6*s.*

W. J. Galloway. ADVANCED AUSTRALIA. By WILLIAM J. GALLOWAY, M.P. *Crown 8vo.* 3*s.* 6*d.*

'This is an unusually thorough and informative little work.'—*Morning Post.*

W. Crooke. THE NORTH-WESTERN PROVINCES OF INDIA: THEIR ETHNOLOGY AND ADMINISTRATION. By W. CROOKE. With Maps and Illustrations. *Demy 8vo.* 10*s.* 6*d.*

A. Boisragon. THE BENIN MASSACRE. By CAPTAIN BOISRAGON. *Second Edition. Cr. 8vo.* 3*s.* 6*d.*

'If the story had been written four hundred years ago it would be read to-day as an English classic.'—*Scotsman.*

H. S. Cowper. THE HILL OF THE GRACES: OR, THE GREAT STONE TEMPLES OF TRIPOLI. By H. S. COWPER, F.S.A. With Maps, Plans, and 75 Illustrations. *Demy 8vo.* 10*s.* 6*d.*

W. B. Worsfold. SOUTH AFRICA. By W. B. WORSFOLD, M.A. *With a Map. Second Edition. Cr. 8vo.* 6s.

'A monumental work compressed into a very moderate compass.'—*World.*

Katherine and Gilbert Macquoid. IN PARIS. By KATHERINE and GILBERT MACQUOID. Illustrated by THOMAS R. MACQUOID, R.I. With 2 maps. *Crown 8vo.* 1s.

'A useful little guide, judiciously supplied with information.'—*Athenæum.*

A. H. Keane. THE BOER STATES: A History and Description of the Transvaal and the Orange Free State. By A. H. KEANE, M.A. With Map. *Crown 8vo.* 6s.

'A work of clear aims and thorough execution.'—*Academy.*

'A compact and very trustworthy account of the Boers and their surroundings.' —*Morning Post.*

Naval and Military

G. S. Robertson. CHITRAL: The Story of a Minor Siege. By Sir G. S. ROBERTSON, K.C.S.I. With numerous Illustrations, Map and Plans. *Second Edition. Demy 8vo.* 10s. 6d.

'It is difficult to imagine the kind of person who could read this brilliant book without emotion. The story remains immortal—a testimony imperishable. We are face to face with a great book.'—*Illustrated London News.*

'A book which the Elizabethans would have thought wonderful. More thrilling, more piquant, and more human than any novel.'—*Newcastle Chronicle.*

'As fascinating as Sir Walter Scott's best fiction.'—*Daily Telegraph.*

R. S. S. Baden-Powell. THE DOWNFALL OF PREMPEH. A Diary of Life in Ashanti, 1895. By Maj.-Gen. BADEN-POWELL. With 21 Illustrations and a Map. *Cheaper Edition. Large Crown 8vo.* 6s.

R. S. S. Baden-Powell. THE MATABELE CAMPAIGN, 1896. By Maj.-Gen. BADEN-POWELL. With nearly 100 Illustrations. *Cheaper Edition. Large Crown 8vo.* 6s.

J. B. Atkins. THE RELIEF OF LADYSMITH. By JOHN BLACK ATKINS. With 16 Plans and Illustrations. *Second Edition. Crown 8vo.* 6s.

This book contains a full narrative by an eye-witness of General Buller's attempts, and of his final success. The story is of absorbing interest, and is the only complete account which has appeared.

'The mantle of Archibald Forbes and G. W. Steevens has assuredly fallen upon Mr. Atkins, who unites a singularly graphic style to an equally rare faculty of vision. In his pages we realise the meaning of a modern campaign with the greatest sense of actuality. His pages are written with a sustained charm of diction and ease of manner that are no less remarkable than the sincerity and vigour of the matter which they set before us.'—*World.*

'Mr. Atkins has a genius for the painting of war which entitles him already to be ranked with Forbes and Steevens, and encourages us to hope that he may one day rise to the level of Napier and Kinglake.'—*Pall Mall Gazette.*

'It is the record told with insight and sympathy of a great conflict. It is as readable as a novel, and it bears the imprint of truth.'—*Morning Leader.*

H. W. Nevinson. LADYSMITH: The Diary of a Siege. By H. W. NEVINSON. With 16 Illustrations and a Plan. *Second Edition. Crown 8vo.* 6s.

This book contains a complete diary of the Siege of Ladysmith, and is a most vivid and picturesque narrative.

There is no exaggeration here, no straining after effect. But there is the truest realism, the impression of things as they are seen, set forth in well-chosen words and well-balanced phrases, with a measured self-restraint that marks the true artist. Mr. Nevinson is to be congratulated on the excellent work that he has done.'—*Daily Chronicle*.

'Of the many able and fascinating chroniclers of the sad and splendid story, Mr. Nevinson is among the ablest and most fascinating.'—*Pall Mall Gazette*.

E. H. Alderson. WITH THE MOUNTED INFANTRY AND THE MASHONALAND FIELD FORCE, 1896. By Lieut.-Colonel ALDERSON. With numerous Illustrations and Plans. *Demy 8vo.* 10*s.* 6*d.*

Seymour Vandeleur. CAMPAIGNING ON THE UPPER NILE AND NIGER. By Lieut. SEYMOUR VANDELEUR. With an Introduction by Sir G. GOLDIE, K.C.M.G. With 4 Maps, Illustrations, and Plans. *Large Crown 8vo.* 10*s.* 6*d.*

Lord Fincastle. A FRONTIER CAMPAIGN. By Viscount FINCASTLE, V.C., and Lieut. P. C. ELLIOTT-LOCKHART. With a Map and 16 Illustrations. *Second Edition. Crown 8vo.* 6*s.*

E. N. Bennett. THE DOWNFALL OF THE DERVISHES: A Sketch of the Sudan Campaign of 1898. By E. N. BENNETT, Fellow of Hertford College. With a Photogravure Portrait of Lord Kitchener. *Third Edition. Crown 8vo.* 3*s.* 6*d.*

W. Kinnaird Rose. WITH THE GREEKS IN THESSALY. By W. KINNAIRD ROSE. With Illustrations. *Crown 8vo.* 6*s.*

G. W. Steevens. NAVAL POLICY: By G. W. STEEVENS. *Demy 8vo.* 6*s.*

This book is a description of the British and other more important navies of the world, with a sketch of the lines on which our naval policy might possibly be developed.

D. Hannay. A SHORT HISTORY OF THE ROYAL NAVY, FROM EARLY TIMES TO THE PRESENT DAY. By DAVID HANNAY. Illustrated. 2 *Vols. Demy 8vo.* 7*s.* 6*d. each.* Vol. I., 1200-1688.

'We read it from cover to cover at a sitting, and those who go to it for a lively and brisk picture of the past, with all its faults and its grandeur, will not be disappointed. The historian is endowed with literary skill and style.'—*Standard*.

C. Cooper King. THE STORY OF THE BRITISH ARMY. By Colonel COOPER KING. Illustrated. *Demy 8vo.* 7*s.* 6*d.*

'An authoritative and accurate story of England's military progress.'—*Daily Mail*.

R. Southey. ENGLISH SEAMEN (Howard, Clifford, Hawkins, Drake, Cavendish). By ROBERT SOUTHEY. Edited, with an Introduction, by DAVID HANNAY. *Second Edition. Crown 8vo.* 6*s.*

'A brave, inspiriting book.'—*Black and White*.

W. Clark Russell. THE LIFE OF ADMIRAL LORD COLLINGWOOD. By W. CLARK RUSSELL. With Illustrations by F. BRANGWYN. *Third Edition. Crown 8vo.* 6*s.*

'A book which we should like to see in the hands of every boy in the country.'—*St. James's Gazette*.

E. L. S. Horsburgh. WATERLOO: A Narrative and Criticism. By E. L. S. HORSBURGH, B.A. With Plans. *Second Edition. Crown 8vo.* 5*s.*

'A brilliant essay—simple, sound, and thorough.'—*Daily Chronicle*.

H. B. George. BATTLES OF ENGLISH HISTORY. By H. B. GEORGE, M.A., Fellow of New College, Oxford. With numerous Plans. *Third Edition. Cr. 8vo.* 6*s.*

'Mr. George has undertaken a very useful task—that of making military affairs intelligible and instructive to non-military readers—and has executed it with a large measure of success.'—*Times*.

General Literature

S. Baring Gould. THE BOOK OF THE WEST. By S. BARING GOULD. With numerous Illustrations. *Two volumes.* Vol. I. Devon. Vol. II. Cornwall. *Crown* 8*vo.* 6*s. each.*

'They are very attractive little volumes, they have numerous very pretty and interesting pictures, the story is fresh and bracing as the air of Dartmoor, and the legend weird as twilight over Dozmare Pool, and they give us a very good idea of this enchanting and beautiful district.'—*Guardian.*

'A narrative full of picturesque incident, personal interest, and literary charm.'—*Leeds Mercury.*

S. Baring Gould. OLD COUNTRY LIFE. By S. BARING GOULD. With Sixty-seven Illustrations. *Large Cr.* 8*vo.* *Fifth Edition.* 6*s.*

'"Old Country Life," as healthy wholesome reading, full of breezy life and movement, full of quaint stories vigorously told, will not be excelled by any book to be published throughout the year. Sound, hearty, and English to the core.'—*World.*

S. Baring Gould. AN OLD ENGLISH HOME. By S. BARING GOULD. With numerous Plans and Illustrations. *Crown* 8*vo.* 6*s.*

'The chapters are delightfully fresh, very informing, and lightened by many a good story. A delightful fireside companion.'—*St. James's Gazette.*

S. Baring Gould. HISTORIC ODDITIES AND STRANGE EVENTS. By S. BARING GOULD. *Fourth Edition.* *Crown* 8*vo.* 6*s.*

S. Baring Gould. FREAKS OF FANATICISM. By S. BARING GOULD. *Third Edition.* *Cr.* 8*vo.* 6*s.*

S. Baring Gould. A GARLAND OF COUNTRY SONG: English Folk Songs with their Traditional Melodies. Collected and arranged by S. BARING GOULD and H. F. SHEPPARD. *Demy* 4*to.* 6*s.*

S. Baring Gould. SONGS OF THE WEST: Traditional Ballads and Songs of the West of England, with their Melodies. Collected by S. BARING GOULD, M.A., and H. F. SHEPPARD, M.A. In 4 Parts. *Parts I., II., III.,* 3*s. each.* *Part IV.,* 5*s.* *In one Vol., French morocco,* 15*s.*

'A rich collection of humour, pathos, grace, and poetic fancy.'—*Saturday Review.*

S. Baring Gould. YORKSHIRE ODDITIES AND STRANGE EVENTS. By S. BARING GOULD. *Fourth Edition.* *Crown* 8*vo.* 6*s.*

S. Baring Gould. STRANGE SURVIVALS AND SUPERSTITIONS. By S. BARING GOULD. *Cr.* 8*vo.* *Second Edition.* 6*s.*

S. Baring Gould. THE DESERTS OF SOUTHERN FRANCE. By S. BARING GOULD. 2 *vols.* *Demy* 8*vo.* 32*s.*

Cotton Minchin. OLD HARROW DAYS. By J. G. COTTON MINCHIN. *Cr.* 8*vo.* *Second Edition.* 5*s.*

W. E. Gladstone. THE SPEECHES OF THE RT. HON. W. E. GLADSTONE, M.P. Edited by A. W. HUTTON, M.A., and H. J. COHEN, M.A. With Portraits. *Demy* 8*vo.* *Vols IX and X.* 12*s.* 6*d. each.*

J. E. Marr. THE SCIENTIFIC STUDY OF SCENERY. By J. E. MARR, F.R.S., Fellow of St. John's College, Cambridge. Illustrated. *Crown* 8*vo.* 6*s.*

An elementary treatise on geomorphology—the study of the earth's outward forms. It is for the use of students of physical geography and geology, and will also be highly interesting to the general reader.

'A fascinating book, a real fairy tale.'—*Pall Mall Gazette.*

'Mr. Marr is distinctly to be congratulated on the general result of his work. He has produced a volume, moderate in size and readable in style, which will be acceptable alike to the student of geology and geography, and to the tourist.' —*Athenæum*.

'Can be read with pleasure alike by the expert and the general reader.' —*Manchester Guardian*.

M. N. Oxford. A HANDBOOK OF NURSING. By M. N. OXFORD, of Guy's Hospital. *Crown 8vo.* 3*s.* 6*d.*

This is a complete guide to the science and art of nursing, containing copious instruction both general and particular.

'The most useful work of the kind that we have seen. A most valuable and practical manual.'—*Manchester Guardian*.

E. V. Zenker. ANARCHISM. By E. V. ZENKER. *Demy 8vo.* 7*s.* 6*d.*

'Herr Zenker has succeeded in producing a careful and critical history of the growth of Anarchist theory.

A. Silva White. THE EXPANSION OF EGYPT: A Political and Historical Survey. By A. SILVA WHITE. With four Special Maps. *Demy 8vo.* 15*s. net.*

'This is emphatically the best account of Egypt as it is under English control that has been published for many years.'—*Spectator*.

Peter Beckford. THOUGHTS ON HUNTING. By PETER BECKFORD. Edited by J. OTHO PAGET, and Illustrated by G. H. JALLAND. *Demy 8vo.* 10*s.* 6*d.*

'Beckford's "Thoughts on Hunting" has long been a classic with sportsmen, and the present edition will go far to make it a favourite with lovers of literature.'—*Speaker*.

E. B. Michell. THE ART AND PRACTICE OF HAWKING. By E. B. MICHELL. With 3 Photogravures by G. E. LODGE, and other Illustrations. *Demy 8vo.* 10*s.* 6*d.*

A complete description of the Hawks, Falcons, and Eagles used in ancient and modern times, with directions for their training and treatment. It is not only a historical account, but a complete practical guide.

'A book that will help and delight the expert.'—*Scotsman*.

'Just after the hearts of all enthusiasts.'—*Daily Telegraph*.

'No book is more full and authorative than this handsome treatise.' —*Morning Leader*.

H. G. Hutchinson. THE GOLFING PILGRIM. By HORACE G. HUTCHINSON. *Crown 8vo.* 6*s.*

'Without this book the golfer's library will be incomplete.'—*Pall Mall Gazette*.

J. Wells. OXFORD AND OXFORD LIFE. By Members of the University. Edited by J. WELLS, M.A., Fellow and Tutor of Wadham College. *Third Edition. Cr. 8vo.* 3*s.* 6*d.*

'We congratulate Mr. Wells on the production of a readable and intelligent account of Oxford as it is at the present time, written by persons who are possessed of a close acquaintance with the system and life of the University.'—*Athenæum*.

C. G. Robertson. VOCES ACADEMICÆ. By C. GRANT ROBERTSON, M.A., Fellow of All Souls', Oxford. *With a Frontispiece. Pott 8vo.* 3*s.* 6*d.*

'Decidedly clever and amusing.'—*Athenæum*.

Rosemary Cotes. DANTE'S GARDEN. By ROSEMARY COTES. With a Frontispiece. *Second Edition. Fcp. 8vo.* 2*s.* 6*d. Leather*, 3*s.* 6*d. net.*

'A charming collection of legends of the flowers mentioned by Dante.'—*Academy*.

Clifford Harrison. READING AND READERS. By CLIFFORD HARRISON. *Fcp. 8vo.* 2*s.* 6*d.*

'An extremely sensible little book.'—*Manchester Guardian*.

L. Whibley. GREEK OLIGARCHIES: THEIR ORGANISATION AND CHARACTER. By L. WHIBLEY, M.A., Fellow of Pembroke College, Cambridge. *Crown 8vo.* 6*s.*

L. L. Price. ECONOMIC SCIENCE AND PRACTICE. By L. L. PRICE, M.A., Fellow of Oriel College, Oxford. *Crown 8vo.* 6*s.*

J. S. Shedlock. THE PIANOFORTE SONATA: Its Origin and Development. By J. S. SHEDLOCK. *Crown 8vo.* 5*s.*

'This work should be in the possession of every musician and amateur. A concise and lucid history and a very valuable work for reference.'—*Athenæum.*

A. Hulme Beaman. PONS ASINORUM; OR, A GUIDE TO BRIDGE. By A. HULME BEAMAN. *Fcap 8vo.* 2*s.*

A practical guide, with many specimen games, to the new game of Bridge.

E. M. Bowden. THE EXAMPLE OF BUDDHA: Being Quotations from Buddhist Literature for each Day in the Year. Compiled by E. M. BOWDEN. *Third Edition.* 16*mo.* 2*s.* 6*d.*

F. Ware. EDUCATIONAL REFORM. By FABIAN WARE, M.A. *Crown 8vo.* 2*s.* 6*d.*

An attempt by an expert to forecast the action and influence of the New Secondary Education Act, with suggestions for useful developments.

'Mr. Ware's book may be warmly commended to all who have at heart the desire for the intellectual prosperity of the British race.'—*Morning Post.*

'Any one who really wants to know how education stands to-day should read it.'—*Literature.*

Philosophy

L. T. Hobhouse. THE THEORY OF KNOWLEDGE. By L. T. HOBHOUSE, Fellow of C.C.C., Oxford. *Demy 8vo.* 21*s.*

'The most important contribution to English philosophy since the publication of Mr. Bradley's "Appearance and Reality."'—*Glasgow Herald.*

W. H. Fairbrother. THE PHILOSOPHY OF T. H. GREEN. By W. H. FAIRBROTHER, M.A. *Second Edition. Cr. 8vo.* 3*s.* 6*d.*

'In every way an admirable book.'—*Glasgow Herald.*

F. W. Bussell. THE SCHOOL OF PLATO. By F. W. BUSSELL, D.D., Fellow of Brasenose College, Oxford. *Demy 8vo.* 10*s.* 6*d.*

F. S. Granger. THE WORSHIP OF THE ROMANS. By F. S. GRANGER, M.A., Litt.D. *Crown 8vo.* 6*s.*

Theology

W. R. Inge. CHRISTIAN MYSTICISM. The Bampton Lectures for 1899. By W. R. INGE, M.A., Fellow and Tutor of Hertford College, Oxford. *Demy 8vo.* 12*s.* 6*d. net.*

A complete survey of the subject from St. John and St. Paul to modern times, covering the Christian Platonists, Augustine, the Devotional Mystics, the Mediæval Mystics, and the Nature Mystics and Symbolists, including Böhme and Wordsworth.

'It is fully worthy of the best traditions connected with the Bampton Lectureship.'—*Record.*

S. R. Driver. SERMONS ON SUBJECTS CONNECTED WITH THE OLD TESTAMENT. By S. R. DRIVER, D.D., Canon of Christ Church, Regius Professor of Hebrew in the University of Oxford. *Cr. 8vo.* 6*s.*

'A welcome companion to the author's famous "Introduction."'—*Guardian.*

T. K. Cheyne. FOUNDERS OF OLD TESTAMENT CRITICISM. By T. K. CHEYNE, D.D., Oriel Professor at Oxford. *Large Crown 8vo.* 7*s.* 6*d.*

A historical sketch of O. T. Criticism.

Walter Lock. ST. PAUL, THE MASTER-BUILDER. By WALTER LOCK, D.D., Warden of Keble College. *Crown 8vo.* 3*s.* 6*d.*

'The essence of the Pauline teaching is condensed into little more than a hundred pages, yet no point of importance is overlooked. We gladly recommend the lectures to all who wish to read with understanding.'—*Guardian.*

H. Rashdall. DOCTRINE AND DEVELOPMENT. By HASTINGS RASHDALL, M.A., Fellow and Tutor of New College, Oxford. *Cr. 8vo.* 6*s.*

'A very interesting attempt to restate some of the principal doctrines of Christianity, in which Mr. Rashdall appears to us to have achieved a high measure of success. He is often learned, almost always sympathetic, and always singularly lucid.'—*Manchester Guardian.*

H. H. Henson. APOSTOLIC CHRISTIANITY: As Illustrated by the Epistles of St. Paul to the Corinthians. By H. H. HENSON, M.A., Fellow of All Souls', Oxford. *Cr. 8vo.* 6*s.*

H. H. Henson. DISCIPLINE AND LAW. By H. HENSLEY HENSON, B.D., Fellow of All Souls', Oxford. *Fcap. 8vo.* 2*s.* 6*d.*

H. H. Henson. LIGHT AND LEAVEN: HISTORICAL AND SOCIAL SERMONS. By H. H. HENSON, M.A. *Crown 8vo.* 6*s.*

Bennett and Adeney. A BIBLICAL INTRODUCTION. By W. H. BENNETT, M.A., and W. F. ADENEY, M.A. *Crown 8vo.* 7*s.* 6*d.*

'It makes available to the ordinary reader the best scholarship of the day in the field of Biblical introduction. We know of no book which comes into competition with it.'—*Manchester Guardian.*

W. H. Bennett. A PRIMER OF THE BIBLE. By W. H. BENNETT. *Second Edition. Cr. 8vo.* 2s. 6*d.*

'The work of an honest, fearless, and sound critic, and an excellent guide in a small compass to the books of the Bible.'—*Manchester Guardian.*

C. F. G. Masterman. TENNYSON AS A RELIGIOUS TEACHER. By C. F. G. MASTERMAN. *Crown 8vo.* 6*s.*

'A thoughtful and penetrating appreciation, full of interest and suggestion.'—*World.*

William Harrison. CLOVELLY SERMONS. By WILLIAM HARRISON, M.A., late Rector of Clovelly. With a Preface by 'LUCAS MALET.' *Cr. 8vo.* 3*s.* 6*d.*

Cecilia Robinson. THE MINISTRY OF DEACONESSES. By Deaconness CECILIA ROBINSON. With an Introduction by the Lord Bishop of Winchester. *Cr. 8vo.* 3*s.* 6*d.*

'A learned and interesting book.'—*Scotsman.*

E. B. Layard. RELIGION IN BOYHOOD. Notes on the Religious Training of Boys. By E. B. LAYARD, M.A. 18*mo.* 1*s.*

T. Herbert Bindley. THE OECUMENICAL DOCUMENTS OF THE FAITH. Edited with Introductions and Notes by T. HERBERT BINDLEY, B.D., Merton College, Oxford. *Crown 8vo.* 6*s.*

A historical account of the Creeds.

'Mr. Bindley has done his work in a fashion which calls for our warmest gratitude. The introductions, though brief, are always direct and to the point; the notes are learned and full, and serve admirably to elucidate the many difficulties of the text.'—*Guardian.*

H. M. Barron. TEXTS FOR SERMONS ON VARIOUS OCCASIONS AND SUBJECTS. Compiled and Arranged by H. M. BARRON, B.A., of Wadham College, Oxford, with a Preface by Canon SCOTT HOLLAND. *Crown 8vo.* 3*s.* 6*d.*

W. Yorke Fausset. THE *DE CATECHIZANDIS RUDIBUS* OF ST. AUGUSTINE. Edited, with Introduction, Notes, etc., by W. YORKE FAUSSET, M.A. *Cr. 8vo.* 3*s.* 6*d.*

F. Weston. THE HOLY SACRIFICE. By F. WESTON, M.A., Curate of St. Matthew's, Westminster. *Pott 8vo.* 6*d. net.*

À Kempis. THE IMITATION OF CHRIST. By THOMAS À KEMPIS. With an Introduction by DEAN FARRAR. Illustrated by C. M. GERE. *Second Edition. Fcap. 8vo.* 3*s.* 6*d.* *Padded morocco,* 5*s.*

'Amongst all the innumerable English

editions of the "Imitation," there can have been few which were prettier than this one, printed in strong and handsome type, with all the glory of red initials.'—*Glasgow Herald.*

J. Keble. THE CHRISTIAN YEAR. By JOHN KEBLE. With an Introduction and Notes by W. LOCK, D.D., Warden of Keble College. Illustrated by R. ANNING BELL. *Second Edition. Fcap. 8vo.* 3s. 6d. *Padded morocco.* 5s.

'The present edition is annotated with all the care and insight to be expected from Mr. Lock.'—*Guardian.*

Oxford Commentaries

General Editor, WALTER LOCK, D.D., Warden of Keble College, Dean Ireland's Professor of Exegesis in the University of Oxford.

THE BOOK OF JOB. Edited, with Introduction and Notes, by E. C. S. GIBSON, D.D., Vicar of Leeds. *Demy 8vo.* 6s.

'The publishers are to be congratulated on the start the series has made.'—*Times.*

'It is in his patient, lucid, interest-sustaining explanations that Dr. Gibson is at his best.'—*Literature.*

'We can hardly imagine a more useful book to place in the hands of an intelligent layman, or cleric, who desires to elucidate some of the difficulties presented in the Book of Job.'—*Church Times.*

'The work is marked by clearness, lightness of touch, strong common sense, and thorough critical fairness.

'Dr. Gibson's work is worthy of a high degree of appreciation. To the busy worker and the intelligent student the commentary will be a real boon; and it will, if we are not mistaken, be much in demand. The Introduction is almost a model of concise, straightforward, prefatory remarks on the subject treated.'—*Athenæum.*

Handbooks of Theology

General Editor, A. ROBERTSON, D.D., Principal of King's College, London.

THE XXXIX. ARTICLES OF THE CHURCH OF ENGLAND. Edited with an Introduction by E. C. S. GIBSON, D.D., Vicar of Leeds, late Principal of Wells Theological College. *Second and Cheaper Edition in One Volume. Demy 8vo.* 12s. 6d.

'We welcome with the utmost satisfaction a new, cheaper, and more convenient edition of Dr. Gibson's book. It was greatly wanted. Dr. Gibson has given theological students just what they want, and we should like to think that it was in the hands of every candidate for orders.'—*Guardian.*

AN INTRODUCTION TO THE HISTORY OF RELIGION. By F. B. JEVONS, M.A., Litt.D., Principal of Bishop Hatfield's Hall. *Demy 8vo.* 10s. 6d.

'The merit of this book lies in the penetration, the singular acuteness and force of the author's judgment. He is at once critical and luminous, at once just and suggestive. A comprehensive and thorough book.'—*Birmingham Post.*

THE DOCTRINE OF THE INCARNATION. By R. L. OTTLEY, M.A., late fellow of Magdalen College, Oxon., and Principal of Pusey House. *In Two Volumes. Demy 8vo.* 15s.

'A clear and remarkably full account of the main currents of speculation. Scholarly precision . . . genuine tolerance . . . intense interest in his subject—are Mr. Ottley's merits.'—*Guardian.*

AN INTRODUCTION TO THE HISTORY OF THE CREEDS. By A. E. BURN, B.D., Examining Chaplain to the Bishop of Lichfield. *Demy 8vo.* 10s. 6d.

'This book may be expected to hold its place as an authority on its subject.—*Spectator.*

The Churchman's Library

General Editor, J. H. BURN, B.D., Examining Chaplain to the Bishop of Aberdeen.

THE BEGINNINGS OF ENGLISH CHRISTIANITY. By W. E. COLLINS, M.A. With Map. *Cr. 8vo.* 3*s.* 6*d.*

'An excellent example of thorough and fresh historical work.'—*Guardian.*

SOME NEW TESTAMENT PROBLEMS. By ARTHUR WRIGHT, M.A., Fellow of Queen's College, Cambridge. *Crown 8vo.* 6*s.*

THE KINGDOM OF HEAVEN HERE AND HEREAFTER. By CANON WINTERBOTHAM, M.A., B.Sc., LL.B. *Cr. 8vo.* 3*s.* 6*d.*

'A most able book, at once exceedingly thoughtful and richly suggestive.'—*Glasgow Herald.*

THE WORKMANSHIP OF THE PRAYER BOOK: Its Literary and Liturgical Aspects. By J. DOWDEN, D.D., Lord Bishop of Edinburgh. *Crown 8vo.* 3*s.* 6*d.*

'Scholarly and interesting.'—*Manchester Guardian.*

EVOLUTION. By F. B. JEVONS, Litt.D., Principal of Hatfield Hall, Durham. *Crown 8vo.* 3*s.* 6*d.*

'A well-written book, full of sound thinking happily expressed.'—*Manchester Guardian.*

'A singularly fresh and stimulating book.'—*Speaker.*

'We have no hesitation in saying that this is much the best general account of the philosophical consequences of the theory of Evolution that has yet appeared.'—*Guardian.*

The Churchman's Bible

General Editor, J. H. BURN, B.D.

Messrs. METHUEN are issuing a series of expositions upon most of the books of the Bible. The volumes will be practical and devotional, and the text of the authorised version is explained in sections, which will correspond as far as possible with the Church Lectionary.

THE EPISTLE OF ST. PAUL TO THE GALATIANS. Explained by A. W. ROBINSON, Vicar of All Hallows, Barking. *Fcap. 8vo.* 1*s.* 6*d.* *net.*

'The most attractive, sensible, and instructive manual for people at large, which we have ever seen.'—*Church Gazette.*

ECCLESIASTES. Explained by A. W. STREANE, D.D. *Fcap. 8vo.* 1*s.* 6*d.* *net.*

'Scholarly, suggestive, and particularly interesting.'—*Bookman.*

THE EPISTLE OF PAUL THE APOSTLE TO THE PHILIPPIANS. Explained by C. R. D. BIGGS, B.D. *Fcap. 8vo.* 1*s.* 6*d.* *net.*

'Mr. Biggs' work is very thorough, and he has managed to compress a good deal of information into a limited space.'—*Guardian.*

The Library of Devotion

Pott 8vo, cloth, 2s.; leather, 2s. 6d. net.

'This series is excellent.'—THE BISHOP OF LONDON.
'Very delightful.'—THE BISHOP OF BATH AND WELLS.
'Well worth the attention of the Clergy.'—THE BISHOP OF LICHFIELD.
'The new "Library of Devotion" is excellent.'—THE BISHOP OF PETERBOROUGH.
'Charming.'—*Record.* 'Delightful.'—*Church Bells.*

THE CONFESSIONS OF ST. AUGUSTINE. Newly Translanted, with an Introduction and Notes, by C. BIGG, D.D., late Student of Christ Church. *Third Edition.*

'The translation is an excellent piece of English, and the introduction is a masterly exposition. We augur well of a series which begins so satisfactorily.'—*Times.*

THE CHRISTIAN YEAR. By JOHN KEBLE. With Introduction and Notes by WALTER LOCK, D.D., Warden of Keble College, Ireland Professor at Oxford.

'The volume is very prettily bound and printed, and may fairly claim to be an advance on any previous editions.'—*Guardian.*

THE IMITATION OF CHRIST. A Revised Translation, with an Introduction, by C. BIGG, D.D., late Student of Christ Church. *Second Edition.*

A practically new translation of this book, which the reader has, almost for the first time, exactly in the shape in which it left the hands of the author.

'A nearer approach to the original than has yet existed in English.'—*Academy.*

A BOOK OF DEVOTIONS. By J. W. STANBRIDGE, B.D., Rector of Bainton, Canon of York, and sometime Fellow of St. John's College, Oxford.

'It is probably the best book of its kind. It deserves high commendation.'—*Church Gazette.*

LYRA INNOCENTIUM. By JOHN KEBLE. Edited, with Introduction and Notes, by WALTER LOCK, D.D., Warden of Keble College, Oxford. *Pott 8vo.* 2*s.*; *leather*, 2*s.* 6*d. net.*

'This sweet and fragrant book has never been published more attractively.'—*Academy.*

'The work is given in as dainty a form as any it has yet taken.'—*Scotsman.*

'The analysis and notes are discriminating, scholarly, and helpful.'—*Church Review.*

A SERIOUS CALL TO A DEVOUT AND HOLY LIFE. By WILLIAM LAW. Edited, with an Introduction, by C. BIGG, D.D., late Student of Christ Church.

This is a reprint, word for word and line for line, of the *Editio Princeps.*

THE TEMPLE. By GEORGE HERBERT. Edited, with an Introduction and Notes, by E. C. S. GIBSON, D.D., Vicar of Leeds.

This edition contains Walton's Life of Herbert, and the text is that of the first edition.

'As neat and desirable an edition of the work as can be found.'—*Scotsman.*

Leaders of Religion

Edited by H. C. BEECHING, M.A. *With Portraits, Crown 8vo.* 3*s.* 6*d.*

A series of short biographies of the most prominent leaders of religious life and thought of all ages and countries.

The following are ready—

CARDINAL NEWMAN. By R. H. HUTTON.

JOHN WESLEY. By J. H. OVERTON, M.A.

BISHOP WILBERFORCE. By G. W. DANIELL, M.A.

CARDINAL MANNING. By A. W. HUTTON, M.A.

CHARLES SIMEON. By H. C. G. MOULE, D.D.

JOHN KEBLE. By WALTER LOCK, D.D.

THOMAS CHALMERS. By Mrs. OLIPHANT.

LANCELOT ANDREWES. By R. L. OTTLEY, M.A.

AUGUSTINE OF CANTERBURY. By E. L. CUTTS, D.D.

WILLIAM LAUD. By W. H. HUTTON, B.D.

JOHN KNOX. By F. MACCUNN.

JOHN HOWE. By R. F. HORTON, D.D.

BISHOP KEN. By F. A. CLARKE, M.A.

GEORGE FOX, THE QUAKER. By T. HODGKIN, D.C.L.

JOHN DONNE. By AUGUSTUS JESSOPP, D.D.

THOMAS CRANMER. By. A. J. MASON.

BISHOP LATIMER. By R. M. CARLYLE and A. J. CARLYLE, M.A.

Other volumes will be announced in due course.

Fiction

SIX SHILLING NOVELS

Marie Corelli's Novels

Crown 8vo. 6s. each.

A ROMANCE OF TWO WORLDS. *Twenty-first Edition.*

VENDETTA. *Sixteenth Edition.*

THELMA. *Twenty-third Edition.*

ARDATH: THE STORY OF A DEAD SELF. *Twelfth Edition.*

THE SOUL OF LILITH. *Ninth Edition.*

WORMWOOD. *Tenth Edition.*

BARABBAS: A DREAM OF THE WORLD'S TRAGEDY. *Thirty-fifth Edition.*

'The tender reverence of the treatment and the imaginative beauty of the writing have reconciled us to the daring of the conception, and the conviction is forced on us that even so exalted a subject cannot be made too familiar to us, provided it be presented in the true spirit of Christian faith. The amplifications of the Scripture narrative are often conceived with high poetic insight, and this "Dream of the World's Tragedy" is a lofty and not inadequate paraphrase of the supreme climax of the inspired narrative.'—*Dublin Review.*

THE SORROWS OF SATAN. *Forty-second Edition.*

'A very powerful piece of work. . . . The conception is magnificent, and is likely to win an abiding place within the memory of man. . . . The author has immense command of language, and a limitless audacity. . . . This interesting and remarkable romance will live long after much of the ephemeral literature of the day is forgotten. . . . A literary phenomenon . . . novel, and even sublime.'—W. T. STEAD in the *Review of Reviews.*

Anthony Hope's Novels

Crown 8vo. 6s. each.

THE GOD IN THE CAR. *Ninth Edition.*

'A very remarkable book, deserving of critical analysis impossible within our limit; brilliant, but not superficial; well considered, but not elaborated; constructed with the proverbial art that conceals, but yet allows itself to be enjoyed by readers to whom fine literary method is a keen pleasure.'—*The World.*

A CHANGE OF AIR. *Fifth Edition.*

'A graceful, vivacious comedy, true to human nature. The characters are traced with a masterly hand.'—*Times.*

A MAN OF MARK. *Fifth Edition.*

'Of all Mr. Hope's books, "A Man of Mark" is the one which best compares with "The Prisoner of Zenda."'—*National Observer.*

THE CHRONICLES OF COUNT ANTONIO. *Fourth Edition.*

'It is a perfectly enchanting story of love and chivalry, and pure romance. The Count is the most constant, desperate, and modest and tender of lovers, a peerless gentleman, an intrepid fighter, a faithful friend, and a magnanimous foe.'—*Guardian.*

PHROSO. Illustrated by H. R. MILLAR. *Fourth Edition.*

'The tale is thoroughly fresh, quick with vitality, stirring the blood.'—*St. James's Gazette.*

'From cover to cover "Phroso" not only engages the attention, but carries the reader in little whirls of delight from adventure to adventure.'—*Academy.*

SIMON DALE. Illustrated. *Fifth Edition.*

'There is searching analysis of human nature, with a most ingeniously constructed plot. Mr. Hope has drawn the contrasts of his women with marvellous subtlety and delicacy.'—*Times.*

THE KING'S MIRROR. *Third Edition.*

'In elegance, delicacy, and tact it ranks with the best of his novels, while in the wide range of its portraiture and the subtilty of its analysis it surpasses all his earlier ventures.'—*Spectator.*

'"The King's Mirror" is a strong book, charged with close analysis and exquisite irony; a book full of pathos and moral fibre—in short, a book to be read.'—*Daily Chronicle.*

Gilbert Parker's Novels

Crown 8vo. 6s. each.

PIERRE AND HIS PEOPLE. *Fifth Edition.*

'Stories happily conceived and finely executed. There is strength and genius in Mr. Parker's style.'—*Daily Telegraph.*

MRS. FALCHION. *Fourth Edition.*

'A splendid study of character.'—*Athenæum.*

THE TRANSLATION OF A SAVAGE.

'The plot is original and one difficult to work out; but Mr. Parker has done it with great skill and delicacy.'—*Daily Chronicle.*

THE TRAIL OF THE SWORD. Illustrated. *Seventh Edition.*

'A rousing and dramatic tale. A book like this, in which swords flash, great surprises are undertaken, and daring deeds done, in which men and women live and love in the old passionate way, is a joy inexpressible.'—*Daily Chronicle.*

WHEN VALMOND CAME TO PONTIAC: The Story of a Lost Napoleon. *Fourth Edition.*

'Here we find romance—real, breathing, living romance. The character of Valmond is drawn unerringly.'—*Pall Mall Gazette.*

AN ADVENTURER OF THE NORTH: The Last Adventures of 'Pretty Pierre.' *Second Edition.*

'The present book is full of fine and moving stories of the great North, and will add to Mr. Parker's already high reputation.'—*Glasgow Herald.*

THE SEATS OF THE MIGHTY. Illustrated. *Tenth Edition.*

'Mr. Parker has produced a really fine historical novel.'—*Athenæum.*

'A great book.'—*Black and White.*

THE POMP OF THE LAVILETTES. *Second Edition. 3s. 6d.*

'Living, breathing romance, unforced pathos, and a deeper knowledge of human nature than Mr. Parker has ever displayed before.'—*Pall Mall Gazette.*

THE BATTLE OF THE STRONG: a Romance of Two Kingdoms. Illustrated. *Fourth Edition.*

'Nothing more vigorous or more human has come from Mr. Gilbert Parker than this novel. It has all the graphic power of his last book, with truer feeling for the romance, both of human life and wild nature.'—*Literature.*

S. Baring Gould's Novels

Crown 8vo. 6s. each.

'To say that a book is by the author of "Mehalah" is to imply that it contains a story cast on strong lines, containing dramatic possibilities, vivid and sympathetic descriptions of Nature, and a wealth of ingenious imagery.'—*Speaker.*

'That whatever Mr. Baring Gould writes is well worth reading, is a conclusion that may be very generally accepted. His views of life are fresh and vigorous, his language pointed and characteristic, the incidents of which he makes use are striking and original, his characters are life-like, and though somewhat exceptional people, are drawn and coloured with artistic force. Add to this that his descriptions of scenes and scenery are painted with the loving eyes and skilled hands of a master of his art, that he is always fresh and never dull, and it is no wonder that readers have gained confidence in his power of amusing and satisfying them, and that year by year his popularity widens.'—*Court Circular.*

ARMINELL. *Fifth Edition.*
URITH. *Fifth Edition.*
IN THE ROAR OF THE SEA. *Seventh Edition.*
MRS. CURGENVEN OF CURGENVEN. *Fourth Edition.*
CHEAP JACK ZITA. *Fourth Edition.*
THE QUEEN OF LOVE. *Fifth Edition.*
MARGERY OF QUETHER. *Third Edition.*
JACQUETTA. *Third Edition.*
KITTY ALONE. *Fifth Edition.*
NOÉMI. Illustrated. *Fourth Edition.*
THE BROOM-SQUIRE. Illustrated. *Fourth Edition.*
THE PENNYCOMEQUICKS. *Third Edition.*
DARTMOOR IDYLLS.
GUAVAS THE TINNER. Illustrated. *Second Edition.*
BLADYS. Illustrated. *Second Edition.*
DOMITIA. Illustrated. *Second Edition.*
PABO THE PRIEST.

Conan Doyle. ROUND THE RED LAMP. By A. CONAN DOYLE. *Seventh Edition. Crown 8vo. 6s.*

'The book is far and away the best view that has been vouchsafed us behind the scenes of the consulting-room.'—*Illustrated London News.*

Stanley Weyman. UNDER THE RED ROBE. By STANLEY WEYMAN, Author of 'A Gentleman of France.' With Illustrations by R. C. WOODVILLE. *Fifteenth Edition. Crown 8vo. 6s.*

'Every one who reads books at all must read this thrilling romance, from the first page of which to the last the breathless reader is haled along. An inspiration of manliness and courage.'—*Daily Chronicle.*

Lucas Malet. THE WAGES OF SIN. By LUCAS MALET. *Thirteenth Edition. Crown 8vo. 6s.*

Lucas Malet. THE CARISSIMA. By LUCAS MALET, Author of 'The Wages of Sin,' etc. *Third Edition. Crown 8vo. 6s.*

George Gissing. THE TOWN TRAVELLER. By GEORGE GISSING, Author of 'Demos,' 'In the Year of Jubilee,' etc. *Second Edition. Cr. 8vo. 6s.*

'It is a bright and witty book above all things. Polly Sparkes is a splendid bit of work.'—*Pall Mall Gazette.*

'The spirit of Dickens is in it.'—*Bookman.*

George Gissing. THE CROWN OF LIFE. By GEORGE GISSING, Author of 'Demos,' 'The Town Traveller,' etc. *Crown 8vo. 6s.*

'Mr. Gissing is at his best.'—*Academy.*

'A fine novel.'—*Outlook.*

S. R. Crockett. LOCHINVAR. By S. R. CROCKETT, Author of 'The Raiders,' etc. Illustrated. *Second Edition. Crown 8vo. 6s.*

'Full of gallantry and pathos, of the clash

of arms, and brightened by episodes of humour and love. . . .'—*Westminster Gazette*.

S. R. Crockett. THE STANDARD BEARER. By S. R. CROCKETT. *Crown 8vo.* 6*s*.

'A delightful tale.'—*Speaker*.

'Mr. Crockett at his best.'—*Literature*.

Arthur Morrison. TALES OF MEAN STREETS. By ARTHUR MORRISON. *Fifth Edition. Cr. 8vo.* 6*s*.

'Told with consummate art and extraordinary detail. In the true humanity of the book lies its justification, the permanence of its interest, and its indubitable triumph.'—*Athenæum*.

'A great book. The author's method is amazingly effective, and produces a thrilling sense of reality. The writer lays upon us a master hand. The book is simply appalling and irresistible in its interest. It is humorous also; without humour it would not make the mark it is certain to make.'—*World*.

Arthur Morrison. A CHILD OF THE JAGO. By ARTHUR MORRISON. *Third Edition. Cr. 8vo.* 6*s*.

'The book is a masterpiece.'—*Pall Mall Gazette*.

'Told with great vigour and powerful simplicity.'—*Athenæum*.

Arthur Morrison. TO LONDON TOWN. By ARTHUR MORRISON, Author of 'Tales of Mean Streets,' etc. *Second Edition. Crown 8vo.* 6*s*.

'We have idyllic pictures, woodland scenes full of tenderness and grace. . . . This is the new Mr. Arthur Morrison gracious and tender, sympathetic and human.'—*Daily Telegraph*.

'The easy swing of detail proclaims the master of his subject and the artist in rendering.'—*Pall Mall Gazette*.

M. Sutherland. ONE HOUR AND THE NEXT. By THE DUCHESS OF SUTHERLAND. *Third Edition. Crown 8vo.* 6*s*.

'Passionate, vivid, dramatic.'—*Literature*.

'It possesses marked qualities, descriptive, and imaginative.'—*Morning Post*.

Mrs. Clifford. A FLASH OF SUMMER. By Mrs. W. K. CLIFFORD, Author of 'Aunt Anne,' etc. *Second Edition. Crown 8vo.* 6*s*.

'The story is a very beautiful one, exquisitely told.'—*Speaker*.

Emily Lawless. HURRISH. By the Honble. EMILY LAWLESS, Author of 'Maelcho,' etc. *Fifth Edition. Cr. 8vo.* 6*s*.

Emily Lawless. MAELCHO: a Sixteenth Century Romance. By the Honble. EMILY LAWLESS. *Second Edition. Crown 8vo.* 6*s*.

'A really great book.'—*Spectator*.

'One of the most remarkable literary achievements of this generation.'—*Manchester Guardian*.

Emily Lawless. TRAITS AND CONFIDENCES. By the Honble. EMILY LAWLESS. *Crown 8vo.* 6*s*.

Eden Phillpotts. THE HUMAN BOY. By EDEN PHILLPOTTS, Author of 'Children of the Mist.' With a Frontispiece. *Fourth Edition. Crown 8vo.* 6*s*.

'Mr. Phillpotts knows exactly what schoolboys do, and can lay bare their inmost thoughts; likewise he shows an all-pervading sense of humour.'—*Academy*.

E. W. Hornung. THE AMATEUR CRACKSMAN. By E. W. HORNUNG. *Crown 8vo.* 6*s*.

'An audaciously entertaining volume.'—*Spectator*.

Jane Barlow. A CREEL OF IRISH STORIES. By JANE BARLOW, Author of 'Irish Idylls.' *Second Edition. Crown 8vo.* 6*s*.

'Vivid and singularly real.'—*Scotsman*.

Jane Barlow. FROM THE EAST UNTO THE WEST. By JANE BARLOW. *Crown 8vo.* 6*s*.

Mrs. Caffyn. ANNE MAULEVERER. By Mrs. CAFFYN (Iota), Author of 'The Yellow Aster.' *Second Edition. Crown 8vo.* 6*s*.

Benjamin Swift. SIREN CITY. By BENJAMIN SWIFT, Author of 'Nancy Noon.' *Crown 8vo.* 6*s*.

'"Siren City" is certainly his best book, and it is the work of a strong man. It has sobriety, not only of manner, but of spirit.'—*Academy*.

J. H. Findlater. THE GREEN GRAVES OF BALGOWRIE. By JANE H. FINDLATER. *Fourth Edition. Crown 8vo.* 6*s*.

'A powerful and vivid story.'—*Standard*.

'A beautiful story, sad and strange as truth itself.'—*Vanity Fair*.

'A very charming and pathetic tale.'—*Pall Mall Gazette*.

'A singularly original, clever, and beautiful story.'—*Guardian*.

'Reveals to us a new writer of undoubted faculty and reserve force.'—*Spectator*.

'An exquisite idyll, delicate, affecting, and beautiful.'—*Black and White*.

J. H. Findlater. A DAUGHTER OF STRIFE. By JANE HELEN FINDLATER. *Crown 8vo.* 6*s*.

J. H. Findlater. RACHEL. By JANE H. FINDLATER. *Second Edition. Crown 8vo.* 6*s*.

'A not unworthy successor to "The Green Graves of Balgowrie."'—*Critic*.

Mary Findlater. OVER THE HILLS. By MARY FINDLATER. *Second Edition. Cr. 8vo.* 6*s*.

'A strong and wise book of deep insight and unflinching truth.'—*Birmingham Post*.

Mary Findlater. BETTY MUSGRAVE. By MARY FINDLATER. *Second Edition. Crown 8vo.* 6*s*.

'Handled with dignity and delicacy. . . . A most touching story.'—*Spectator*.

Alfred Ollivant. OWD BOB, THE GREY DOG OF KENMUIR. By ALFRED OLLIVANT. *Third Edition. Cr. 8vo.* 6*s*.

'Weird, thrilling, strikingly graphic.'—*Punch*.

'We admire this book. . . . It is one to read with admiration and to praise with enthusiasm.'—*Bookman*.

'It is a fine, open-air, blood-stirring book, to be enjoyed by every man and woman to whom a dog is dear.'—*Literature*.

B. M. Croker. PEGGY OF THE BARTONS. By B. M. CROKER, Author of 'Diana Barrington.' *Fourth Edition. Crown 8vo.* 6*s*.

Mrs. Croker excels in the admirably simple, easy, and direct flow of her narrative, the briskness of her dialogue, and the geniality of her portraiture.'—*Spectator*.

Mary L. Pendered. AN ENGLISHMAN. By MARY L. PENDERED. *Crown 8vo.* 6*s*.

'Her book is most healthy in tone, and leaves a pleasant taste in the mouth.'—*Pall Mall Gazette*.

'A very noble book. It is filled with wisdom and sympathy.'—*Literary World*.

'At once sound and diverting.'—*Academy*.

Morley Roberts. THE PLUNDERERS. By MORLEY ROBERTS, Author of 'The Colossus,' etc. *Crown 8vo.* 6*s*.

'The author secures and maintains the reader's lively interest in his clever absurdities.'—*Pall Mall Gazette*.

'The whole atmosphere is one of high spirits and high comedy.'—*Globe*.

'Mr. Roberts writes of real people who do things and know things.'—*Black and White*.

Norma Lorimer. MIRRY-ANN. By NORMA LORIMER, Author of 'Josiah's Wife.' *Crown 8vo.* 6*s*.

'The heroine is rare and striking, but thorough woman and altogether lovable, and the plot is brisk and well sustained.'—*Pall Mall Gazette*.

'It is a Manx story, and a right able story. The atmosphere is excellent, the descriptive passages fine, and the story is one which will repay perusal.'—*Glasgow Herald*.

'A Manx novel which is at once sincere, poetical, and in the best sense true.'—*Academy*.

Helen Shipton. THE STRONG GOD CIRCUMSTANCE. By HELEN SHIPTON. *Crown 8vo.* 6*s*.

'A story of high merit and many attractions.'—*Scotsman*.

'An up-to-date story—and a very beautiful one—of self-sacrifice.'—*Daily Telegraph*.

'A most effective story, written with both insight and imagination.'—*Leeds Mercury*.

Violet Hunt. THE HUMAN INTEREST. By VIOLET HUNT, Author of 'A Hard Woman,' etc. *Crown 8vo.* 6*s.*

'Clever observation and unfailing wit.'—*Academy.*

'The insight is keen, the irony is delicate.'—*World.*

H. G. Wells. THE STOLEN BACILLUS, and other Stories. By H. G. WELLS. *Second Edition. Crown 8vo.* 6*s.*

'The impressions of a very striking imagination.'—*Saturday Review.*

H. G. Wells. THE PLATTNER STORY AND OTHERS. By H. G. WELLS. *Second Edition. Cr. 8vo.* 6*s.*

'Weird and mysterious, they seem to hold the reader as by a magic spell.'—*Scotsman.*

Richard Marsh. MARVELS AND MYSTERIES. By RICHARD MARSH, Author of 'The Beetle.' *Crown 8vo.* 6*s.*

'While under their immediate influence the reader is conscious of nothing but thrilling excitement and curiosity.'—*Glasgow Herald.*

'Ingeniously constructed and well told.'—*Morning Leader.*

'Admirably selected and of the very best.'—*Christian World.*

Esmé Stuart. CHRISTALLA. By ESMÉ STUART. *Crown 8vo.* 6*s.*

'The story is happily conceived, and entertaining throughout.'—*Scotsman.*

'An excellent story, pathetic, and full of humour.'—*Athenæum.*

'We wish that we came across more books like this clever and charming story.—*Leeds Mercury.*

Sara Jeannette Duncan. A VOYAGE OF CONSOLATION. By SARA JEANNETTE DUNCAN, Author of 'An American Girl in London.' Illustrated. *Third Edition. Cr. 8vo.* 6*s.*

'A most delightfully bright book.'—*Daily Telegraph.*

'The dialogue is full of wit.—*Globe.*

Sara Jeannette Duncan. THE PATH OF A STAR. By SARA JEANNETTE DUNCAN, Author of 'A Voyage of Consolation.' Illustrated. *Second Edition. Crown 8vo.* 6*s.*

'Richness and fullness of local colouring, brilliancy of style, smiting phrases, and the display of very pretty humour are graces which are here in profusion. The interest never flags.'—*Pall Mall Gazette.*

C. F. Keary. THE JOURNALIST. By C. F. KEARY. *Cr. 8vo.* 6*s.*

'It is rare indeed to find such poetical sympathy with Nature joined to close study of character and singularly truthful dialogue: but then "The Journalist" is altogether a rare book.'—*Athenæum.*

W. E. Norris. MATTHEW AUSTIN. By W. E. NORRIS, Author of 'Mademoiselle de Mersac,' etc. *Fourth Edition. Crown 8vo.* 6*s.*

'An intellectually satisfactory and morally bracing novel.'—*Daily Telegraph.*

W. E. Norris. HIS GRACE. By W. E. NORRIS. *Third Edition. Cr. 8vo.* 6*s.*

W. E. Norris. THE DESPOTIC LADY AND OTHERS. By W. E. NORRIS. *Crown 8vo.* 6*s.*

W. E. Norris. CLARISSA FURIOSA. By W. E. NORRIS. *Cr. 8vo.* 6*s.*

'As a story it is admirable, as a *jeu d'esprit* it is capital, as a lay sermon studded with gems of wit and wisdom it is a model.'—*The World.*

W. E. Norris. GILES INGILBY. By W. E. NORRIS. *Illustrated. Second Edition. Crown 8vo.* 6*s.*

'Interesting, wholesome, and charmingly written.'—*Glasgow Herald.*

W. E. Norris. AN OCTAVE. By W. E. NORRIS. *Second Edition. Crown 8vo.* 6*s.*

'A very perfect exposition of the self-restraint, the perfect knowledge of society and its ways, the delicate sense of humour, which are the main characteristics of this very accomplished author.'—*Country Life.*

Ernest Glanville. THE DESPATCH RIDER. By ERNEST GLANVILLE, Author of 'The Kloof Bride.' *Crown 8vo.* 6*s.*

A highly interesting story of the present Boer War by an author who knows the country well, and has had experience of Boer campaigning.

W. Clark Russell. MY DANISH SWEETHEART. By W. CLARK RUSSELL. *Illustrated. Fourth Edition. Crown 8vo.* 6s.

Robert Barr. IN THE MIDST OF ALARMS. By ROBERT BARR. *Third Edition. Cr. 8vo.* 6s.

'A book which has abundantly satisfied us by its capital humour.'—*Daily Chronicle.*

'Mr. Barr has achieved a triumph.'—*Pall Mall Gazette.*

Robert Barr. THE MUTABLE MANY. By ROBERT BARR. *Second Edition. Crown 8vo.* 6s.

'Very much the best novel that Mr. Barr has yet given us. There is much insight in it, and much excellent humour.'—*Daily Chronicle.*

Robert Barr. THE COUNTESS TEKLA. By ROBERT BARR. *Third Edition. Crown 8vo.* 6s.

'Of these mediæval romances, which are now gaining ground, "The Countess Tekla" is the very best we have seen. The story is written in clear English, and a picturesque, moving style.'—*Pall Mall Gazette.*

Andrew Balfour. BY STROKE OF SWORD. By A. BALFOUR. Illustrated. *Fourth Edition. Cr. 8vo.* 6s.

A banquet of good things.'—*Academy.*

'A recital of thrilling interest, told with unflagging vigour.'—*Globe.*

'An unusually excellent example of a semi-historic romance.'—*World.*

Andrew Balfour. TO ARMS! By ANDREW BALFOUR. Illustrated. *Second Edition. Crown 8vo.* 6s.

'The marvellous perils through which Allan passes are told in powerful and lively fashion.'—*Pall Mall Gazette.*

Andrew Balfour. VENGEANCE IS MINE. By ANDREW BALFOUR, Author of 'By Stroke of Sword.' *Illustrated. Crown 8vo.* 6s.

A vigorous piece of work, well written, and abounding in stirring incidents.'—*Glasgow Herald.*

J. Maclaren Cobban. THE KING OF ANDAMAN: A Saviour of Society. By J. MACLAREN COBBAN. *Crown 8vo.* 6s.

'An unquestionably interesting book. It contains one character, at least, who has in him the root of immortality.'—*Pall Mall Gazette.*

J. Maclaren Cobban. THE ANGEL OF THE COVENANT. By J. MACLAREN COBBAN. *Cr. 8vo.* 6s.

R. N. Stephens. AN ENEMY TO THE KING. By R. N. STEPHENS. *Second Edition. Cr. 8vo.* 6s.

'It is full of movement, and the movement is always buoyant.'—*Scotsman.*

'A stirring story with plenty of movement.'—*Black and White.*

R. N. Stephens. A GENTLEMAN PLAYER. By R. N. STEPHENS, Author of 'An Enemy to the King.' *Crown 8vo.* 6s.

'A bright and spirited romance of adventure, full of movement and changing action.'—*Scotsman.*

R. Hichens. BYEWAYS. By ROBERT HICHENS. Author of 'Flames, etc.' *Second Edition. Cr. 8vo.* 6s.

'The work is undeniably that of a man of striking imagination.'—*Daily News.*

J. S. Fletcher. THE PATHS OF THE PRUDENT. By J. S. FLETCHER. *Crown 8vo.* 6s.

J. B. Burton. IN THE DAY OF ADVERSITY. By J. BLOUNDELLE-BURTON. *Second Edition. Cr. 8vo.* 6s.

'Unusually interesting and full of highly dramatic situations.'—*Guardian.*

J. B. Burton. DENOUNCED. By J. BLOUNDELLE-BURTON. *Second Edition. Crown 8vo.* 6s.

'A fine, manly, spirited piece of work.'—*World.*

J. B. Burton. THE CLASH OF ARMS. By J. BLOUNDELLE-BURTON. *Second Edition. Cr. 8vo.* 6s.

'A brave story—brave in deed, brave in word, brave in thought.'—*St. James's Gazette.*

J. B. Burton. ACROSS THE SALT SEAS. By J. BLOUNDELLE-BURTON. *Second Edition. Crown 8vo.* 6s.

'The very essence of the true romantic spirit.'—*Truth.*

W. C. Scully. THE WHITE HECATOMB. By W. C. SCULLY, Author of 'Kafir Stories.' *Cr. 8vo.* 6*s*.

'Reveals a marvellously intimate understanding of the Kaffir mind.'—*African Critic.*

W. C. Scully. BETWEEN SUN AND SAND. By W. C. SCULLY, Author of 'The White Hecatomb.' *Cr. 8vo.* 6*s*.

'The reader passes at once into the very atmosphere of the African desert: the inexpressible space and stillness swallow him up, and there is no world for him but that immeasurable waste.'—*Athenæum.*

OTHER SIX-SHILLING NOVELS

Crown 8vo.

DANIEL WHYTE. By A. J. DAWSON.

THE CAPSINA. By E. F. BENSON.

DODO: A DETAIL OF THE DAY. By E. F. BENSON.

THE VINTAGE. By E. F. BENSON. Illustrated by G. P. JACOMB-HOOD.

ROSE À CHARLITTE. By MARSHALL SAUNDERS.

WILLOWBRAKE. By R. MURRAY GILCHRIST.

THINGS THAT HAVE HAPPENED. By DOROTHEA GERARD.

SIR ROBERT'S FORTUNE. By Mrs. OLIPHANT.

THE TWO MARYS. By Mrs. OLIPHANT.

THE LADY'S WALK. By Mrs. OLIPHANT.

LONE PINE: A ROMANCE OF MEXICAN LIFE. By R. B. TOWNSHEND.

WILT THOU HAVE THIS WOMAN? By J. MACLAREN COBBAN.

A PASSIONATE PILGRIM. By PERCY WHITE.

SECRETARY TO BAYNE, M.P. By W. PETT RIDGE.

ADRIAN ROME. By E. DAWSON and A. MOORE.

THE BUILDERS. By J. S. FLETCHER.

GALLIA. By MÉNIE MURIEL DOWIE.

THE CROOK OF THE BOUGH. By MÉNIE MURIEL DOWIE.

A BUSINESS IN GREAT WATERS. By JULIAN CORBETT.

MISS ERIN. By M. E. FRANCIS.

ANANIAS. By the Hon. Mrs. ALAN BRODRICK.

CORRAGEEN IN '98. By Mrs. ORPEN.

THE PLUNDER PIT. By J. KEIGHLEY SNOWDEN.

CROSS TRAILS. By VICTOR WAITE.

SUCCESSORS TO THE TITLE. By Mrs. WALFORD.

KIRKHAM'S FIND. By MARY GAUNT.

DEADMAN'S. By MARY GAUNT.

CAPTAIN JACOBUS: A ROMANCE OF THE ROAD. By L. COPE CORNFORD.

SONS OF ADVERSITY. By L. COPE CORNFORD.

THE KING OF ALBERIA. By LAURA DAINTREY.

THE DAUGHTER OF ALOUETTE. By MARY A. OWEN.

CHILDREN OF THIS WORLD. By ELLEN F. PINSENT.

AN ELECTRIC SPARK. By G. MANVILLE FENN.

UNDER SHADOW OF THE MISSION. By L. S. McCHESNEY.

THE SPECULATORS. By J. F. BREWER.

THE SPIRIT OF STORM. By RONALD ROSS.

THE QUEENSBERRY CUP. By CLIVE P. WOLLEY.

A HOME IN INVERESK. By T. L. PATON.

MISS ARMSTRONG'S AND OTHER CIRCUMSTANCES. By JOHN DAVIDSON.

DR. CONGALTON'S LEGACY. By HENRY JOHNSTON.

TIME AND THE WOMAN. By RICHARD PRYCE.

THIS MAN'S DOMINION. By the Author of 'A High Little World.'

DIOGENES OF LONDON. By H. B. MARRIOTT WATSON.

THE STONE DRAGON. By MURRAY GILCHRIST.

A VICAR'S WIFE. By EVELYN DICKINSON.

ELSA. By E. M'QUEEN GRAY.

THE SINGER OF MARLY. By I. HOOPER.

THE FALL OF THE SPARROW. By M. C. BALFOUR.

A SERIOUS COMEDY. By HERBERT MORRAH.

THE FAITHFUL CITY. By HERBERT MORRAH.

IN THE GREAT DEEP. By J. A. BARRY.

BIJLI, THE DANCER. By JAMES BLYTHE PATTON.

JOSIAH'S WIFE. By NORMA LORIMER.

THE PHILANTHROPIST. By LUCY MAYNARD.

VAUSSORE. By FRANCIS BRUNE.

THREE-AND-SIXPENNY NOVELS

Crown 8vo.

DERRICK VAUGHAN, NOVELIST. *42nd thousand.* By EDNA LYALL.

A SON OF THE STATE. By W. PETT RIDGE.

CEASE FIRE! By J. MACLAREN COBBAN. *Crown 8vo.* 3s. 6d.

A stirring Story of the Boer War of 1881, including the Siege of Potchefstrom and the Defeat of Majuba.

'Brightly told and drawn with a strong and sure hand.'—*St. James's Gazette.*

'A capital novel.'—*Scotsman.*

'Fact and fiction are so deeply woven together that the book reads like a fascinating chapter of history.'—*Pall Mall Gazette.*

THE KLOOF BRIDE. By ERNEST GLANVILLE.

A VENDETTA OF THE DESERT. By W. C. SCULLY.

SUBJECT TO VANITY. By MARGARET BENSON.

THE SIGN OF THE SPIDER. *Fifth Edition.* By BERTRAM MITFORD.

THE MOVING FINGER. By MARY GAUNT.

JACO TRELOAR. By J. H. PEARCE.

THE DANCE OF THE HOURS. By 'VERA.'

A WOMAN OF FORTY. By ESMÉ STUART.

A CUMBERER OF THE GROUND. By CONSTANCE SMITH.

THE SIN OF ANGELS. By EVELYN DICKINSON.

AUT DIABOLUS AUT NIHIL. By X. L.

THE COMING OF CUCULAIN. By STANDISH O'GRADY.

THE GODS GIVE MY DONKEY WINGS. By ANGUS EVAN ABBOTT.

THE STAR GAZERS. By G. MANVILLE FENN.

THE POISON OF ASPS. By R. ORTON PROWSE.

THE QUIET MRS. FLEMING. By R. PRYCE.

DISENCHANTMENT. By F. MABEL ROBINSON.

THE SQUIRE OF WANDALES. By A. SHIELD.

A REVEREND GENTLEMAN. By J. M. COBBAN.

A DEPLORABLE AFFAIR. By W. E. NORRIS.

A CAVALIER'S LADYE. By Mrs. DICKER.

THE PRODIGALS. By Mrs. OLIPHANT.

THE SUPPLANTER. By P. NEUMANN.

A MAN WITH BLACK EYELASHES. By H. A. KENNEDY.

A HANDFUL OF EXOTICS. By S. GORDON.

AN ODD EXPERIMENT. By HANNAH LYNCH.

TALES OF NORTHUMBRIA. By HOWARD PEASE.

HALF-CROWN NOVELS

Crown 8vo.

HOVENDEN, V.C. By F. MABEL ROBINSON.

THE PLAN OF CAMPAIGN. By F. MABEL ROBINSON.

MR. BUTLER'S WARD. By F. MABEL ROBINSON.

ELI'S CHILDREN. By G. MANVILLE FENN.

A DOUBLE KNOT. By G. MANVILLE FENN.

DISARMED. By M. BETHAM EDWARDS.

IN TENT AND BUNGALOW. By the Author of 'Indian Idylls.'

MY STEWARDSHIP. By E. M'QUEEN GRAY.

JACK'S FATHER. By W. E. NORRIS.

A LOST ILLUSION. By LESLIE KEITH.

THE TRUE HISTORY OF JOSHUA DAVIDSON, Christian and Communist. By E. LYNN LYNTON. *Eleventh Edition. Post 8vo.* 1s.

The Novelist

MESSRS. METHUEN are making an interesting experiment which constitutes a fresh departure in publishing. They are issuing under the above general title a Monthly Series of Novels by popular authors at the price of Sixpence. Many of these Novels have never been published before. Each Number is as long as the average Six Shilling Novel. The first numbers of 'THE NOVELIST' are as follows:—

I. DEAD MEN TELL NO TALES. E. W. HORNUNG.

II. JENNIE BAXTER, JOURNALIST. ROBERT BARR.

III. THE INCA'S TREASURE. ERNEST GLANVILLE.

IV. A SON OF THE STATE. W. PETT RIDGE.

V. FURZE BLOOM. S. BARING GOULD.

VI. BUNTER'S CRUISE. C. GLEIG.

VII. THE GAY DECEIVERS. ARTHUR MOORE.

VIII. PRISONERS OF WAR. A. BOYSON WEEKES.

IX. THE ADVENTURE OF PRINCESS SYLVIA. Mrs. C. F. WILLIAMSON.

X. VELDT AND LAAGER: Tales of the Transvaal. E. S. VALENTINE.

XI. THE NIGGER KNIGHTS. F. NORREYS CONNELL.

XII. A MARRIAGE AT SEA. W. CLARK RUSSELL.

Books for Boys and Girls

A Series of Books by well-known Authors, well illustrated.

THREE-AND-SIXPENCE EACH

THE ICELANDER'S SWORD. By S. BARING GOULD.

TWO LITTLE CHILDREN AND CHING. By EDITH E. CUTHELL.

TODDLEBEN'S HERO. By M. M. BLAKE.

ONLY A GUARD-ROOM DOG. By EDITH E. CUTHELL.

THE DOCTOR OF THE JULIET. By HARRY COLLINGWOOD.

MASTER ROCKAFELLAR'S VOYAGE. By W. CLARK RUSSELL.

SYD BELTON: Or, The Boy who would not go to Sea. By G. MANVILLE FENN.

THE WALLYPUG IN LONDON. By G. E. FARROW.

ADVENTURES IN WALLYPUG LAND. By G. E. FARROW. 5*s*.

The Peacock Library

A Series of Books for Girls by well-known Authors, handsomely bound, and well illustrated.

THREE-AND-SIXPENCE EACH

THE RED GRANGE. By Mrs. MOLESWORTH.

THE SECRET OF MADAME DE MONLUC. By the Author of 'Mdle. Mori.'

OUT OF THE FASHION. By L. T. MEADE.

DUMPS. By Mrs. PARR.

A GIRL OF THE PEOPLE. By L. T. MEADE.

HEPSY GIPSY. By L. T. MEADE. 2*s*. 6*d*.

THE HONOURABLE MISS. By L. T. MEADE.

University Extension Series

A series of books on historical, literary, and scientific subjects, suitable for extension students and home-reading circles. Each volume is complete in itself, and the subjects are treated by competent writers in a broad and philosophic spirit.

Edited by J. E. SYMES, M.A.,
Principal of University College, Nottingham.
Crown 8vo. Price (with some exceptions) 2*s*. 6*d*.

The following volumes are ready:—

THE INDUSTRIAL HISTORY OF ENGLAND. By H. DE B. GIBBINS, Litt.D., M.A., late Scholar of Wadham College, Oxon., Cobden Prizeman. *Seventh Edition, Revised. With Maps and Plans.* 3*s*.

A HISTORY OF ENGLISH POLITICAL ECONOMY. By L. L. PRICE, M.A., Fellow of Oriel College, Oxon. *Third Edition.*

PROBLEMS OF POVERTY: An Inquiry into the Industrial Conditions of the Poor. By J. A. HOBSON, M.A. *Fourth Edition.*

VICTORIAN POETS. By A. SHARP.

THE FRENCH REVOLUTION. By J. E. SYMES, M.A.

PSYCHOLOGY. By F. S. GRANGER, M.A. *Second Edition.*

THE EVOLUTION OF PLANT LIFE: Lower Forms. By G. MASSEE. *With Illustrations.*

AIR AND WATER. By V. B. LEWES, M.A. *Illustrated.*

THE CHEMISTRY OF LIFE AND HEALTH. By C. W. KIMMINS, M.A. *Illustrated.*

THE MECHANICS OF DAILY LIFE. By V. P. SELLS, M.A. *Illustrated.*

ENGLISH SOCIAL REFORMERS. By H. DE B. GIBBINS, Litt. D., M.A.

ENGLISH TRADE AND FINANCE IN THE SEVENTEENTH CENTURY. By W. A. S. HEWINS, B.A.

THE CHEMISTRY OF FIRE. The Elementary Principles of Chemistry. By M. M. PATTISON MUIR, M.A. *Illustrated.*

A TEXT-BOOK OF AGRICULTURAL BOTANY. By M. C. POTTER, M.A., F.L.S. *Illustrated.* 3s. 6d.

THE VAULT OF HEAVEN. A Popular Introduction to Astronomy. By R. A. GREGORY. *With numerous Illustrations.*

METEOROLOGY. The Elements of Weather and Climate. By H. N. DICKSON, F.R.S.E., F.R. Met. Soc. *Illustrated.*

A MANUAL OF ELECTRICAL SCIENCE. By GEORGE J. BURCH, M.A., F.R.S. *With numerous Illustrations.* 3s.

THE EARTH. An Introduction to Physiography. By EVAN SMALL, M.A. *Illustrated.*

INSECT LIFE. By F. W. THEOBALD, M.A. *Illustrated.*

ENGLISH POETRY FROM BLAKE TO BROWNING. By W. M. DIXON, M.A.

ENGLISH LOCAL GOVERNMENT. By E. JENKS, M.A., Professor of Law at University College, Liverpool.

THE GREEK VIEW OF LIFE. By G. L. DICKINSON, Fellow of King's College, Cambridge. *Second Edition*

Social Questions of To-day

Edited by H. DE B. GIBBINS, Litt. D., M.A.

Crown 8vo. 2s. 6d.

A series of volumes upon those topics of social, economic, and industrial interest that are at the present moment foremost in the public mind. Each volume of the series is written by an author who is an acknowledged authority upon the subject with which he deals.

The following Volumes of the Series are ready :—

TRADE UNIONISM—NEW AND OLD. By G. HOWELL. *Second Edition.*

THE CO-OPERATIVE MOVEMENT TO-DAY. By G. J. HOLYOAKE. *Second Edition.*

MUTUAL THRIFT. By Rev. J. FROME WILKINSON, M.A.

PROBLEMS OF POVERTY. By J. A. HOBSON, M.A. *Fourth Edition.*

THE COMMERCE OF NATIONS. By C. F. BASTABLE, M.A., Professor of Economics at Trinity College, Dublin. *Second Edition.*

THE ALIEN INVASION. By W. H. WILKINS, B.A.

THE RURAL EXODUS. By P. ANDERSON GRAHAM.

LAND NATIONALIZATION. By HAROLD COX, B.A.

A SHORTER WORKING DAY. By H. DE B. GIBBINS, D.Litt., M.A., and R. A. HADFIELD, of the Hecla Works, Sheffield.

BACK TO THE LAND: An Inquiry into the Cure for Rural Depopulation. By H. E. MOORE.

TRUSTS, POOLS AND CORNERS. By J. STEPHEN JEANS.

THE FACTORY SYSTEM. By R. W. COOKE-TAYLOR.

THE STATE AND ITS CHILDREN. By GERTRUDE TUCKWELL.

WOMEN'S WORK. By LADY DILKE, Miss BULLEY, and Miss WHITLEY.

SOCIALISM AND MODERN THOUGHT. By M. KAUFMANN.

THE HOUSING OF THE WORKING CLASSES. By E. BOWMAKER.

MODERN CIVILIZATION IN SOME OF ITS ECONOMIC ASPECTS. By W. CUNNINGHAM, D.D., Fellow of Trinity College, Cambridge.

THE PROBLEM OF THE UNEMPLOYED. By J. A. HOBSON, B.A.

LIFE IN WEST LONDON. By ARTHUR SHERWELL, M.A. *Second Edition.*

RAILWAY NATIONALIZATION. By CLEMENT EDWARDS.

WORKHOUSES AND PAUPERISM. By LOUISA TWINING.

UNIVERSITY AND SOCIAL SETTLEMENTS. By W. REASON, M.A.

Classical Translations

Edited by H. F. FOX, M.A., Fellow and Tutor of Brasenose College, Oxford.

ÆSCHYLUS — Agamemnon, Chöephoroe, Eumenides. Translated by LEWIS CAMPBELL, LL.D., late Professor of Greek at St. Andrews. 5*s.*

CICERO—De Oratore I. Translated by E. N. P. MOOR, M.A. 3*s.* 6*d.*

CICERO—Select Orations (Pro Milone, Pro Murena, Philippic II., In Catilinam). Translated by H. E. D. BLAKISTON, M.A., Fellow and Tutor of Trinity College, Oxford. 5*s.*

CICERO—De Natura Deorum. Translated by F. BROOKS, M.A., late Scholar of Balliol College, Oxford. 3*s.* 6*d.*

CICERO DE OFFICIIS. Translated by G. B. GARDINER, M.A. *Crown 8vo.* 2*s.* 6*d.*

HORACE: THE ODES AND EPODES. Translated by A. GODLEY, M.A., Fellow of Magdalen College, Oxford. 2*s.*

LUCIAN—Six Dialogues (Nigrinus, Icaro - Menippus, The Cock, The Ship, The Parasite, The Lover of Falsehood). Translated by S. T. IRWIN, M.A., Assistant Master at Clifton; late Scholar of Exeter College, Oxford. 3*s.* 6*d.*

SOPHOCLES — Electra and Ajax. Translated by E. D. A. MORSHEAD, M.A., Assistant Master at Winchester. 2*s.* 6*d.*

TACITUS—Agricola and Germania. Translated by R. B. TOWNSHEND, late Scholar of Trinity College, Cambridge. 2*s.* 6*d.*

Oxford Classical Texts.

Messrs. METHUEN are about to publish in conjunction with the Clarendon Press a series of classical texts edited by competent scholars from the best MSS.

THUCYDIDIS HISTORIAE, LIBRI I.-IV. By H. STUART JONES. *Paper Covers*, 3s. *Limp Cloth*, 3s. 6d.

PLATONIS OPERA, TOM. I. (TETRALOGIAE I.-II.) By J. BURNET. *Paper Covers*, 5s. *Limp Cloth*, 6s.

LVCRETI CARI DE RERVM NATVRA. By C. BAILEY. *Paper Covers*, 2s. 6d. *Limp Cloth*, 3s.

CORNELII TACITI OPERA MINORA. By H. FURNEAUX. *Paper Covers*, 1s. 6d. *Limp Cloth*, 2s.

AESCHYLI TRAGOEDIAE CUM FRAGMENTIS. By A. SIDGWICK. *Paper Covers*, 3s. *Limp Cloth*, 3s. 6d.

APOLLONII RHODII ARGONAUTICA. By R. C. SEATON. *Paper Covers*, 2s. 6d. *Limp Cloth*, 3s.

ARISTOPHANIS COMOEDIAE. TOM. I. By F. W. HALL and W. M. GELDART. *Paper Covers*, 3s. *Limp Cloth*, 3s. 6d.

XENOPHONTIS OPERA. TOM. I. (Historia Graeca). By E. C. MARCHANT. *Paper Covers*, 2s. 6d. *Limp Cloth*, 3s.

Educational Books

CLASSICAL

THE NICOMACHEAN ETHICS OF ARISTOTLE. Edited with an Introduction and Notes by JOHN BURNET, M.A., Professor of Greek at St. Andrews. *Demy 8vo.* 15s. *net.*

This edition contains parallel passages from the Eudemian Ethics, printed under the text, and there is a full commentary, the main object of which is to interpret difficulties in the light of Aristotle's own rules.

'An edition which reflects every credit upon its author's learning and critical acumen, and which cannot but prove heartily welcome to all classes of Greek scholars.'—*Scotsman.*

'It forms a valuable addition to the existing literature on the subject.'—*Glasgow Herald.*

'We must content ourselves with saying, in conclusion, that we have seldom, if ever, seen an edition of any classical author in which what is held in common with other commentators is so clearly and shortly put, and what is original is (with equal brevity) of such value and interest.'—*Pilot.*

PLAUTI BACCHIDES. Edited with Introduction, Commentary, and Critical Notes by J. M'COSH, M.A. *Fcap. 4to.* 12s. 6d.

A GREEK ANTHOLOGY. Selected by E. C. MARCHANT, M.A., Fellow of Peterhouse, Cambridge, and Assistant Master at St. Paul's School. *Crown 8vo.* 3s. 6d.

PASSAGES FOR UNSEEN TRANSLATION. By E. C. MARCHANT, M.A., Fellow of Peterhouse, Cambridge; and A. M. COOK, M.A., late Scholar of Wadham College, Oxford; Assistant Masters at St. Paul's School. *Crown 8vo.* 3s. 6d.

'We know no book of this class better fitted for use in the higher forms of schools.'—*Guardian.*

TACITI AGRICOLA. With Introduction, Notes, Map, etc. By R. F. DAVIS, M.A., Assistant Master at Weymouth College. *Crown 8vo.* 2s.

TACITI GERMANIA. By the same Editor. *Crown 8vo.* 2*s.*

HERODOTUS: EASY SELECTIONS. With Vocabulary. By A. C. LIDDELL, M.A. *Fcap. 8vo.* 1*s.* 6*d.*

SELECTIONS FROM THE ODYSSEY. By E. D. STONE, M.A., late Assistant Master at Eton. *Fcap. 8vo.* 1*s.* 6*d.*

PLAUTUS: THE CAPTIVI. Adapted for Lower Forms by J. H. FREESE, M.A., late Fellow of St. John's, Cambridge. 1*s.* 6*d.*

DEMOSTHENES AGAINST CONON AND CALLICLES. Edited with Notes and Vocabulary, by F. DARWIN SWIFT, M.A. *Fcap. 8vo.* 2*s.*

EXERCISES IN LATIN ACCIDENCE. By S. E. WINBOLT, Assistant Master in Christ's Hospital. *Crown 8vo.* 1*s.* 6*d.*

An elementary book adapted for Lower Forms to accompany the shorter Latin primer.

NOTES ON GREEK AND LATIN SYNTAX. By G. BUCKLAND GREEN, M.A., Assistant Master at Edinburgh Academy, late Fellow of St. John's College, Oxon. *Crown 8vo.* 3*s.* 6*d.*

Notes and explanations on the chief difficulties of Greek and Latin Syntax, with numerous passages for exercise.

NEW TESTAMENT GREEK. A Course for Beginners. By G. RODWELL, B.A. With a Preface by WALTER LOCK, D.D., Warden of Keble College. *Fcap. 8vo.* 3*s.* 6*d.*

THE FROGS OF ARISTOPHANES. Translated by E. W. HUNTINGFORD, M.A., Professor of Classics in Trinity College, Toronto. *Cr. 8vo.* 2*s.* 6*d.*

GERMAN

A COMPANION GERMAN GRAMMAR. By H. DE B. GIBBINS, D.Litt., M.A., Headmaster at Kidderminster Grammar School. *Crown 8vo.* 1*s.* 6*d.*

GERMAN PASSAGES FOR UNSEEN TRANSLATION. By E. M'QUEEN GRAY. *Crown 8vo.* 2*s.* 6*d.*

SCIENCE

DAIRY BACTERIOLOGY. A Short Manual for the Use of Students. By Dr. ED. VON FREUDENREICH, Translated by J. R. AINSWORTH DAVIS, M.A. *Second Edition, Revised. Crown 8vo.* 2*s.* 6*d.*

OUTLINES OF BIOLOGY. By P. CHALMERS MITCHELL, M.A. *Illustrated. Cr. 8vo.* 6*s.*

A text-book designed to cover the new Schedule issued by the Royal College of Physicians and Surgeons.

A MONOGRAPH OF THE MYXOGASTRES. By GEORGE MASSEE. With 12 Coloured Plates. *Royal 8vo.* 18*s. net.*

'A work much in advance of any book in the language treating of this group of organisms. Indispensable to every student of the Myxogastres.'—*Nature.*

ORNAMENTAL DESIGN FOR WOVEN FABRICS. By C. STEPHENSON, of The Technical College, Bradford, and F. SUDDARDS, of The Yorkshire College, Leeds. With 65 full-page plates. *Demy 8vo. Second Edition.* 7*s.* 6*d.*

'The book is very ably done, displaying an intimate knowledge of principles, good taste, and the faculty of clear exposition.'—*Yorkshire Post.*

GENERAL ELEMENTARY SCIENCE. By J. T. DUNN, D.Sc., and V. A. MUNDELLA. With many Illustrations. *Crown 8vo.* 3*s.* 6*d.*

[*Methuen's Science Primers.*

THE WORLD OF SCIENCE. Including Chemistry, Heat, Light, Sound, Magnetism, Electricity, Botany, Zoology, Physiology, Astronomy, and Geology. By R. ELLIOTT STEEL, M.A., F.C.S. 147 Illustrations. *Second Edition. Cr. 8vo.* 2*s.* 6*d.*

ELEMENTARY LIGHT. By R. E. STEEL. With numerous Illustrations. *Crown 8vo.* 4*s.* 6*d.*

VOLUMETRIC ANALYSIS. By J. B. RUSSELL, B.Sc., Science Master at Burnley Grammar School. *Cr. 8vo.* 1*s.*

'A collection of useful, well-arranged notes.' —*School Guardian.*

Textbooks of Technology

Edited by PROFESSORS GARNETT and WERTHEIMER.

HOW TO MAKE A DRESS. By J. A. E. WOOD. *Illustrated. Cr. 8vo. Second Edition.* 1*s.* 6*d.*

'Though primarily intended for students, Miss Wood's dainty little manual may be consulted with advantage by any girls who want to make their own frocks. The directions are simple and clear, and the diagrams very helpful.'—*Literature.*

CARPENTRY AND JOINERY. By F. C. WEBBER. With many Illustrations. *Cr. 8vo.* 3*s.* 6*d.*

'An admirable elementary text-book on the subject.'—*Builder.*

PRACTICAL MECHANICS. By SIDNEY H. WELLS. With 75 Illustrations and Diagrams. *Cr. 8vo.* 3*s.* 6*d.*

PRACTICAL PHYSICS. By H. STROUD, D.Sc., M.A., Professor of Physics in the Durham College of Science, Newcastle-on-Tyne. Fully illustrated. *Crown 8vo.* 3*s.* 6*d.*

MILLINERY, THEORETICAL, AND PRACTICAL. By Miss HILL, Registered Teacher to the City and Guilds of London Institute. With numerous Diagrams. *Crown 8vo.* 2*s.*

PRACTICAL CHEMISTRY. By W. FRENCH, M.A. Part I. With numerous diagrams. *Crown 8vo.* 1*s.* 6*d.*

'An excellent and eminently practical little book.'—*Schoolmaster.*

ENGLISH

ENGLISH RECORDS. A Companion to the History of England. By H. E. MALDEN, M.A. *Crown 8vo.* 3*s.* 6*d.*

THE ENGLISH CITIZEN: HIS RIGHTS AND DUTIES. By H. E. MALDEN, M.A. 1*s.* 6*d.*

A DIGEST OF DEDUCTIVE LOGIC. By JOHNSON BARKER, B.A. *Crown 8vo.* 2s. 6d.

A CLASS-BOOK OF DICTATION PASSAGES. By W. WILLIAMSON, M.A. *Third Edition, Cr. 8vo.* 1s. 6d.

A SHORT STORY OF ENGLISH LITERATURE. By EMMA S. MELLOWS. *Crown 8vo.* 3s. 6d.

The history of English literature told in a simple style for young students. It is particularly rich in biographical detail, and contains a considerable number of illustrative extracts.

'A lucid and well-arranged account of the growth of English literature.'—*Pall Mall Gazette.*

TEST CARDS IN EUCLID AND ALGEBRA. By D. S. CALDERWOOD, Headmaster of the Normal School, Edinburgh. In three packets of 40, with Answers. 1s. Or in three Books, price 2d., 2d., and 3d.

THE METRIC SYSTEM. By LEON DELBOS. *Crown 8vo.* 2s.

A theoretical and practical guide, for use in elementary schools and by the general reader.

METHUEN'S COMMERCIAL SERIES

Edited by H. DE B. GIBBINS, Litt.D., M.A.

BRITISH COMMERCE AND COLONIES FROM ELIZABETH TO VICTORIA. By H. DE B. GIBBINS, Litt.D., M.A. *Third Edition.* 2s.

COMMERCIAL EXAMINATION PAPERS. By H. DE B. GIBBINS, Litt.D., M.A. 1s. 6d.

THE ECONOMICS OF COMMERCE. By H. DE B. GIBBINS, Litt.D., M.A. 1s. 6d.

FRENCH COMMERCIAL CORRESPONDENCE. By S. E. BALLY, Master at the Manchester Grammar School. *Second Edition.* 2s.

GERMAN COMMERCIAL CORRESPONDENCE. By S. E. BALLY. 2s. 6d.

A FRENCH COMMERCIAL READER. By S. E. BALLY. *Second Edition.* 2s.

COMMERCIAL GEOGRAPHY, with special reference to the British Empire. By L. W. LYDE, M.A. *Second Edition.* 2s.

A PRIMER OF BUSINESS. By S. JACKSON, M.A. *Third Ed.* 1s. 6d.

COMMERCIAL ARITHMETIC. By F. G. TAYLOR, M.A. *Third Edition.* 1s. 6d.

PRÉCIS WRITING AND OFFICE CORRESPONDENCE. By E. E. WHITFIELD, M.A. 2s.

A GUIDE TO PROFESSIONS AND BUSINESS. By H. JONES. 1s. 6d.

THE PRINCIPLES OF BOOK-KEEPING BY DOUBLE ENTRY. By J. E. B. M'ALLEN, M.A. *Cr. 8vo.* 2s.

COMMERCIAL LAW. By W. DOUGLAS EDWARDS. 2s.

WORKS BY A. M. M. STEDMAN, M.A.

INITIA LATINA: Easy Lessons on Elementary Accidence. *Fourth Edition. Fcap. 8vo.* 1s.

FIRST LATIN LESSONS. *Sixth Edition. Crown 8vo.* 2s.

FIRST LATIN READER. With Notes adapted to the Shorter Latin Primer and Vocabulary. *Fifth Edition revised.* 18*mo.* 1*s.* 6*d.*

EASY SELECTIONS FROM CÆSAR. Part I. The Helvetian War. *Second Edition.* 18*mo.* 1*s.*

EASY SELECTIONS FROM LIVY. Part I. The Kings of Rome. 18*mo.* *Second Edition.* 1*s.* 6*d.*

EASY LATIN PASSAGES FOR UNSEEN TRANSLATION. *Seventh Edition.* *Fcap.* 8*vo.* 1*s.* 6*d.*

EXEMPLA LATINA. First Lessons in Latin Accidence. With Vocabulary. *Crown* 8*vo.* 1*s.*

EASY LATIN EXERCISES ON THE SYNTAX OF THE SHORTER AND REVISED LATIN PRIMER. With Vocabulary. *Eighth and cheaper Edition, re-written.* *Crown* 8*vo.* 1*s.* 6*d.* Issued with the consent of Dr. Kennedy. KEY 3*s.* *net.*

THE LATIN COMPOUND SENTENCE: Rules and Exercises. *Second Edition.* *Cr.* 8*vo.* 1*s.* 6*d.* With Vocabulary. 2*s.*

NOTANDA QUAEDAM: Miscellaneous Latin Exercises on Common Rules and Idioms. *Fourth Edition.* *Fcap.* 8*vo.* 1*s.* 6*d.* With Vocabulary. 2*s.*

LATIN VOCABULARIES FOR REPETITION: Arranged according to Subjects. *Ninth Edition.* *Fcap.* 8*vo.* 1*s.* 6*d.*

A VOCABULARY OF LATIN IDIOMS. 18*mo.* *Second Edition.* 1*s.*

STEPS TO GREEK. *Second Edition, Revised.* 18*mo.* 1*s.*

A SHORTER GREEK PRIMER. *Crown* 8*vo.* 1*s.* 6*d.*

EASY GREEK PASSAGES FOR UNSEEN TRANSLATION. *Third Edition Revised.* *Fcap.* 8*vo.* 1*s.* 6*d.*

GREEK VOCABULARIES FOR REPETITION. Arranged according to Subjects. *Second Edition.* *Fcap.* 8*vo.* 1*s.* 6*d.*

GREEK TESTAMENT SELECTIONS. For the use of Schools. *Third Edition.* With Introduction, Notes, and Vocabulary. *Fcap.* 8*vo.* 2*s.* 6*d.*

STEPS TO FRENCH. *Fifth Edition.* 18*mo.* 8*d.*

FIRST FRENCH LESSONS. *Fourth Edition Revised.* *Crown* 8*vo.* 1*s.*

EASY FRENCH PASSAGES FOR UNSEEN TRANSLATION. *Fourth Edition revised.* *Fcap.* 8*vo.* 1*s.* 6*d.*

EASY FRENCH EXERCISES ON ELEMENTARY SYNTAX. With Vocabulary. *Second Edition.* *Crown* 8*vo.* 2*s.* 6*d.* KEY 3*s.* *net.*

FRENCH VOCABULARIES FOR REPETITION: Arranged according to Subjects. *Ninth Edition.* *Fcap.* 8*vo.* 1*s.*

SCHOOL EXAMINATION SERIES

EDITED BY A. M. M. STEDMAN, M.A. *Crown* 8*vo.* 2*s.* 6*d.*

FRENCH EXAMINATION PAPERS IN MISCELLANEOUS GRAMMAR AND IDIOMS. By A. M. M. STEDMAN, M.A. *Eleventh Edition.*

A KEY, issued to Tutors and Private Students only, to be had on application to the Publishers. *Fourth Edition.* *Crown* 8*vo.* 6*s.* *net.*

LATIN EXAMINATION PAPERS IN MISCELLANEOUS GRAMMAR AND IDIOMS. By A. M. M. STEDMAN, M.A. *Tenth Edition.*

KEY (*Fourth Edition*) issued as above. 6*s.* *net.*

GREEK EXAMINATION PAPERS IN MISCELLANEOUS GRAMMAR AND IDIOMS. By A. M. M. STEDMAN, M.A. *Sixth Edition.*

KEY (*Second Edition*) issued as above. 6*s.* *net.*

GERMAN EXAMINATION. PAPERS IN MISCELLANEOUS GRAMMAR AND IDIOMS. By R. J. MORICH, Clifton College. *Fifth Edition.*

KEY (*Second Edition*) issued as above. 6*s.* *net.*

HISTORY AND GEOGRAPHY EXAMINATION PAPERS. By C. H. SPENCE, M.A., Clifton College. *Second Edition.*

SCIENCE EXAMINATION PAPERS. By R. E. STEEL, M.A., F.C.S. *In two vols.*

Part I. Chemistry ; Part II. Physics.

GENERAL KNOWLEDGE EXAMINATION PAPERS. By A. M. M. STEDMAN, M.A. *Third Edition.*

KEY (*Second Edition*) issued as above. 7*s.* *net.*

EXAMINATION PAPERS IN ENGLISH HISTORY. By J. TAIT WARDLAW, B.A., King's College, Cambridge. *Crown 8vo.* 2*s.* 6*d.*